AFFECTIVE LEARNING TOGETHER

e L`

In the twenty-first century, being able to collaborate effectively is important at all ages, in everyday life, education and work, within and across diverse cultural settings. People are increasingly linked by networks that are not only means for working and learning together, but are also ways of maintaining social and emotional support. Collaborating with others requires both elaborating on new ideas together and being able to manage interpersonal relations. In order to design and facilitate effective collaborative situations, the challenge is therefore to understand the interrelations between social, affective and cognitive dimensions of interactions in groups.

Affective Learning Together contains in-depth theoretical reviews and case studies of group learning in a variety of educational situations and taught disciplines, from small groups working in the secondary school classroom, to teams of medical students and more informal working groups at university level. Contributors provide detailed analyses of the dynamics of interpersonal relations and affects, in relation to processes of meaning and knowledge elaboration, including discussion of:

- the variety of social learning situations and experiences;
- social identities in group learning;
- emotion, motivation and knowledge elaboration;
- conflict, arguments and interpersonal tensions in group learning.

Bringing together a broad range of contributions from internationally recognized researchers who are seeking to broaden, deepen and integrate the field of research on collaborative learning, this book is essential reading for all serious students of contemporary educational research and practice.

Michael Baker is a CNRS (Centre National de la Recherche Scientifique) Research Director, working in the Economic and Social Sciences Department of Télécom ParisTech Graduate Engineering School in Paris, France.

Jerry Andriessen is a former Associate Professor at Utrecht University, the Netherlands, and now works as an independent researcher (http://www.wisenmunro.org).

Sanna Järvelä is a Professor in the field of learning and educational technology in the Department of Educational Sciences, University of Oulu, Finland.

New perspectives on learning and instruction

Editor in Chief – Mien Segers
(Leiden University and Maastricht University – The Netherlands)
Assistant Editor – Isabel Raemdonck *(Leiden University – The Netherlands)*

New Perspectives on Learning and Instruction is published by Routledge in conjunction with EARLI (European Association for Research on Learning and Instruction). This series publishes cutting edge international research focusing on all aspects of learning and instruction in both traditional and non-traditional educational settings. Titles published within the series take a broad and innovative approach to topical areas of research, are written by leading international researchers and are aimed at a research and post-graduate student audience.

Also available:

AFFECTIVE LEARNING TOGETHER

Social and emotional dimensions of collaborative learning

Edited by Michael Baker, Jerry Andriessen and Sanna Järvelä

Routledge
Taylor & Francis Group

LONDON AND NEW YORK

First published 2013
by Routledge
2 Park Square, Milton Park, Abingdon, Oxon OX14 4RN

Simultaneously published in the USA and Canada
by Routledge
711 Third Avenue, New York, NY 10017

Routledge is an imprint of the Taylor & Francis Group, an informa business

British Library Cataloguing in Publication Data
A catalogue record for this book is available from the British Library

Library of Congress Cataloging in Publication Data
Affective learning together : social and emotional dimensions of collaborative
learning/edited by Michael Baker, Jerry Andriessen and Sanna Järvelä.
   p. cm.
   1. Affective education. 2. Educational psychology. 3. Learning—Social
aspects. 4. Emotions. 5. Group work in education. 6. Team learning
approach in education. I. Baker, Michael, 1960- II. Andriessen,
Jerry. III. Järvelä, Sanna.
   LB1072A45 2013
   371.14'8—dc23   2012030806

ISBN: 978-0-415-69687-6 (hbk)
ISBN: 978-0-415-69688-3 (pbk)
ISBN: 978-0-203-06968-4 (ebk)

Typeset in Bembo
by Cenveo Publisher Services

MIX
Paper from
responsible sources
FSC
www.fsc.org   FSC® C004839

Printed and bound by CPI Group (UK) Ltd, Croydon, CR0 4YY

CONTENTS

CONTRIBUTORS

Jerry Andriessen Wise & Munro Learning Research, The Hague

Christa S. C. Asterhan School of Education, The Hebrew University, Jerusalem

Michael Baker Centre National de la Recherche Scientifique, Télécom ParisTech

Béatrice Cahour Centre National de la Recherche Scientifique, Télécom ParisTech

Charles Crook Learning Sciences Research Institute, University of Nottingham

Crina Damşa InterMedia, University of Oslo

Anne Deiglmayr Institute of Behavioral Sciences, ETH Zurich

Tsafrir Goldberg Faculty of Education, The University of Haifa

Sanna Järvelä Department of Educational Sciences and Teacher Education, Learning and Educational Technology Research Unit (LET), Oulu

Hanna Järvenoja Department of Educational Sciences and Teacher Education, Learning and Educational Technology Research Unit (LET), Oulu

Richard Joiner Department of Psychology, University of Bath

Klas Karlgren Department of Learning, Informatics, Management and Ethics Karolinska Institute, Stockholm

Jay Lemke Department of Communication, University of California, San Diego

Karen Littleton Faculty of Education and Language Studies, The Open University, Milton Keynes

Sten Ludvigsen InterMedia, University of Oslo

Nathalie Muller Mirza Institute of Psychology, Faculty of Political and Social Sciences, University of Lausanne

Dejana Mullins Human Capital Advisory Services, Deloitte Consulting GmbH

Mirjam Pardijs Wise & Munro Learning Research, The Hague

Baruch B. Schwarz School of Education, The Hebrew University, Jerusalem

Patrick Sins School of Education, Saxion University of Applied Sciences and ICLON, Leiden University Graduate School of Teaching

Hans Spada Institute of Psychology, University of Freiburg

1

INTRODUCTION

Visions of learning together

Michael Baker, Jerry Andriessen and Sanna Järvelä

Prelude

The following is an extract from a discussion between two sixteen-year-old pupils who were working together on solving a problem in a secondary school classroom.

[1] *John*: Ok, there, there's the … /

[2] *Susan*: / … transformer. Do the transfer arrow.

[3] *John*: There are several to be done. One there. Should we put another one there?

[4] *Susan*: Pprrrttt!

[5] *John*: You see, it leaves from a reservoir and it comes back to a reservoir

[6] *Susan*: Is that right!?

[7] *John*: A reservoir to start with and a reservoir to end with

[8] *Susan*: Have we got two batteries, John?

[9] *John*: No!

[10] *Susan*: Have we got two batteries??

[11] *John*: No

[12] *Susan*: Then why do you say such rubbish?!

[13] *John*: What did we forget, then?

[14] *Susan*: But no. I. … You know there, it's obvious that it's like that. That's what I thought. Look, there's the wire. Wait … Me, I thought it was like that! That the two wires … you see, the energy goes out from there. It goes whooosshh across the two wires and arrives there. You understand? So that the two wires went like that and arrived there. Do you understand what I'm trying to say? I mean that it goes from there, like that: from the reservoir, there's a wire that goes from the reservoir and it takes it to the bulb, you agree? And that's the way it is. There's the other wire, I'd have put it like that

[15] *John*: Yeah but that's not right! Look at what they say: "an energy chain …" /

[16] *Susan*: / I don't give a damn

[17] *John*: What?

[18] *Susan*: I'm telling you I don't give a damn. For me, that's the way it is.

As we shall explain, this extract is intended to illustrate what this book is about. The way that students try to solve problems together, and what they learn by so doing, depends on the relationships between three dimensions of their collective activity: the task they are trying to achieve and what is to be learned (the cognitive dimension), how they relate to each other (the socio-relational dimension) and what they feel about that (the affective dimension).

What is happening in this discussion? We shall say more shortly about the problem the students are trying to solve, about the school and the students' background. But we have deliberately chosen to delay giving such information because we believe that it is possible to understand what was going on here on another level, even on the basis of such a rudimentary transcription (for example, it does not give information about non-verbal communication, tone of voice, and so on, apart from conventional symbols of written language such as "!" and "?".).

When we try to understand what was going on in a discussion between other people, we draw on the fact that we too are human beings: trying to understand other people is not the same as trying to understand physical processes, such as the weather or the malfunctioning of a car. It is not the same because we are also human beings, and can "put ourselves in the place of", or empathise with the people we are studying, trying to feel and think what we would feel and think if we were in their place. We can not (usually) do this with meteorology and car motors. Moreover, with respect to this example, we assume that the majority of readers of this book were once also girls or boys at school, and so can put themselves to some extent in the place of Susan and John. Such empathetic understanding does not, however, obviate the necessity for finding theoretically founded, systematic and commonly agreed indicators in the dialogue that support our interpretations: we are simply pointing out that it is nevertheless a foundation of our understanding. Our narrative of interpretation of the discussion between the two students, attempting to "put ourselves in their shoes", is as follows.[2]

At first, John tries to put forward an idea about the solution to the problem (line 1), but Susan interrupts him, completing his sentence for him, telling him what he should do to solve the problem (line 2). She has lost patience with him by now; he is just too slow, and not very good at these types of problems. John complies, in an apparently neutral way, despite the fact he has been interrupted, pointing out that there is more to be done; but, sensing Susan's irritation, he is not sure now, and so asks her, in a conciliatory way, if she agrees and what the answer should be (line 3). Susan really finds him stupid; she can't resist ridiculing his idea ("Pprrrttt!"). John tries to defend himself; but Susan attacks his defence in a particularly humiliating way: instead of simply stating why he is wrong, she leads him to admit something obvious and undeniable (that there is of course only one battery on the table, not two) which shows that what he says must be "rubbish!". At this point, John is upset and confused about what to say: he has been interrupted, told what to do, then told and led to admit that what he says is basically stupid. However, he controls his emotions, maintains his initial degree of politeness, and asks what Susan thinks. Susan explains her view at some length (line 14), her ideas are gradually becoming clearer to her. During this time, John is still upset; he is aware that Susan's extended explanation is probably superior to his own; he can hardly listen because of the turmoil inside him, and so unsurprisingly, he rejects what she says out of hand, and sticks to his ground (his previous defence). Susan is now more sure that she is right and that John is wrong; she has no more patience, and does not "give a damn" about what he says. As everyone knows, being told that one is talking rubbish and that the person who one is speaking with does not give a damn about what one says is an aggressive way of being spoken to that is likely to arouse emotions such as anger and sadness.

In one sense, in accordance with our narrative, our question: "what is happening in this discussion?" could be answered quite simply: John proposed an idea, Susan repeatedly rejected what he said, out of hand, in a way that made John feel hurt and ridiculous; so when she presented her own idea, even though he knew he was wrong and she was right, he was not able to listen, only to try to defend himself and hit back. In other words, what is happening here is quite simply the enactment, the manifestation, of a social, interpersonal relationship between two adolescent students in the classroom, with all the emotions that that involves, "around" the solving of a school problem.

We have deliberately chosen to present this type of socio-relational and affective interpretation first, before giving necessary information about the problem-solving task and the educational context, in order to make a point: very often, in collaborative learning research, cognitive aspects have been considered to be primary, and the aspects that we referred to, to be secondary. But what is going on from the students' points of view? Are students primarily trying to solve a problem, which requires them, secondarily, to get on with each other? Or is it the other way round? Is the knowledge students are supposed to acquire and elaborate in school, as it were, "incidentally" wrapped in a social guise, as presented by the teacher, the textbook authors, the other students? Or is that knowledge inseparable from, situated in, the particular social situation?

That is what this book is about: *the study of the relations between, cognitive, social and affective dimensions of interactions produced in collaborative learning situations.* It is about redressing the balance, about attempting to consider these dimensions on an equal footing, as aspects of the unified phenomenon of people, human beings, eminently social, in flesh and blood, trying to interact with and understand each other, in order to come to grips with knowledge, as it is presented in societally and historically situated institutions called schools.

In order to add substance to our narrative on the extract, couched initially on socio-relational and affective planes, we now turn to its cognitive and social dimensions. In analytical terms, the distinctions between these dimensions are, we would claim, quite clear in the above extract. For example, in lines 8 to 12 above, Susan engages in an argumentative strategy called *reductio ad absurdum*: along the *cognitive dimension*, she uses an interpersonal reasoning strategy that requires John to admit an obvious perceptual fact (that there are not two batteries on the table), then requires him to invalidate his own proposal, as a consequence. But it also seems clear that describing Susan's statement in line 12 in purely cognitive terms, as a statement concerning invalidation of a proposition, is highly reductive: it is also clear that constraining someone to verbalise the inadequacy of their own views (rather than straightforwardly informing them of this) can be humiliating (cold rationality itself can, in a sense, be personally violent), and that accusing someone of talking rubbish amounts to saying that they are stupid, which says something about the interpersonal relation between them and which also (as can be seen from what ensues) arouses negative emotions and expression of negative affects on the part of John. We propose that all of these dimensions need to be taken into account in understanding what takes place in the dialogue and thus what the students could potentially learn.

Here is some information about the problem-solving task. The students are sitting at the back of a secondary school classroom in the city of Lyon (France), in a class that provides additional but not essential training in science for students who are following a "literary" stream. Each group of two students in the classroom has a simple electrical circuit on the table in front of them, consisting of a battery linked, by two wires (from its positive and negative terminals), to a bulb. They link up the circuit and observe that the bulb lights up. They have been asked to draw a diagram that represents (or models) the circuit in terms of reservoirs, transfers and transformers of energy. The answer that the teacher would like them to discover (see Tiberghien & Megalakaki, 1995) is that the battery is a reservoir of electrical energy, which is transferred via the wires to the bulb, which in turn transforms this energy into light and heat that are transferred to a type of "reservoir" which does not correspond to a tangible object (like the battery), called "the environment". What is at stake here is the principle of conservation of energy (energy cannot go "nowhere" from the bulb), and the fact that energy can have different manifestations (heat, light, electrical work, etc.). In a sense, therefore, the whole didactical point of this educational task is to lead the students to understand the scientific concept of energy, and to be able to distinguish this from, in this case, electricity. Students often confuse energy and electricity as it circulates in a circuit. In this extract, John proposes that the energy goes out from the battery and back to the bulb, in a circle, which satisfies the requirement that the energy must go somewhere from the bulb. But, as Susan points out, that implies the absurd conclusion that there must be a second battery for the energy of the bulb to go to (there is manifestly only one battery!) and that thus the bulb would never go out(!). Susan is right and John has got it wrong. John has confused energy transfer with circulation of electrical current. Susan grapples with the distinction between energy and electrical circuits; she does realise that although current flows round in a circuit, energy must go "whoosh" in the same direction across the wires from the battery to the bulb.

How does this task-related information relate to or inform the interpretation along the socio-relational and affective dimensions? Assuming that the students did in fact understand the relevant reasoning, this information could enable us to understand why each student rejected the other's solution, and the extent to which each should or should not have done so, from a normative perspective. But it cannot explain everything about the way in which the dialogue actually unfolded: John could have tried to listen to Susan's ideas, and to understand her criticisms of his own, in which case the dialogue would have gone differently. But we attribute the fact that he did not do so to the *way* in which Susan rejected his ideas, to the fact that he was not only defending his ideas but also defending *himself*, as a person, from an aggressive personal attack on his sense of self-worth, in relation to all the negative emotions that that must have aroused. What students learn from working together will partly be a function of the way that they interacted, the extent to which each was able to understand and address the ideas of others, and to reflect on their own. And the way that they interact will be a function of the inextricable "interactions" between cognitive, socio-relational and situational aspects of that interaction. It follows that in order to understand how learning emerges from collaboration between students, we have to try to understand how cognitive, socio-relational and affective dimensions interrelate. The problem is compounded by the fact that there exist quite different theories of each of these dimensions. Therefore, our aim here is not to produce a single integrative theory, but rather to find more limited and localised bridges between ways of seeing each dimension.

How do interpersonal relations, the circulation of emotions, collaborative problem-solving and learning interrelate? Do emotions always "get in the way" of task performance? Might not, on the other hand, a particularly bland, emotionally "flat" interaction also be uninteresting for learning? Can there not be too much emotion or too little? Might not what counts as too much or too little depend on the nature of the prior interpersonal relationship? Perhaps good friends can disagree and call each other names whilst preserving their friendship (playful insults might be part of friendship), whilst people who have a more fragile, or nascent interpersonal relationship (not to speak of enemies) might not be able to take the risk of (im)polite disagreement?

This book is oriented towards addressing these, and other, questions.

In the rest of this chapter, before introducing the chapters of the book, we try to situate the emergence of the topic of this book within the evolutions of recent paradigms of collaborative learning research, beginning, successively, with views from the cognitive, the social and the affective.

Views from the cognitive

Over the last thirty years, there has been a general shift of focus in educational psychology research, from the study of the individual learner to the study of how individuals learn from working together in small groups (see Dillenbourg, Baker, Blaye & O'Malley, 1996, for a synthesis). Up to the 1980s, the two dominant cognitivist theories — that of human problem-solving as information processing (Newell & Simon, 1972) and that of the development and transformation of cognitive "schemes" in response to feedback on actions from the environment (Piaget, 1964) — were centred on processes at work in the individual learner. In a sense, it seems "natural" to focus on the individual: after all, are not individual students the ones who learn and are who given diplomas? But, on one hand, a focus on the individual does not justify a purely cognitive vision of social beings; and on another, we should not conflate societal needs for evaluating individual educational attainment with the identification of an object of scientific study. Furthermore, as we shall discuss, it is also possible to take the group or even the institution as an object for the study of learning (or, relatively stable transformation). What is at stake here is the question as to whether or not, in moving from the individual to the group and the collective, qualitatively different phenomena arise that require different research approaches.

Each of the theoretical approaches mentioned above has given rise to attempts to extend them, in order to take into account the learner working with others. These developments had different motivations — internal and external to the paradigm — in each case. In the case of so-called "classical cognitivism", this change was associated with the critique of the theory of situated cognition and learning (Lave, 1988; Lave & Wenger, 1990) that seemed to require the broadening of the field of study beyond the individual in the experimental laboratory to the (again "so-called") "real world" of educational practice, the supermarket and the workplace, where collective activity is the norm. In effect, should the burden of proof be on group activity, to show that it is more effective than learning alone, or should it be the other way around? Increasing awareness of the importance of distributed teamwork, across continents and cultures, within globalised economies, with Internet-based technologies as primary vectors of societal change, were no doubt associated with this recognition that the group, the collective, rather than a secondary conjunction of individuals, was perhaps primary. In terms that were internal to the paradigm, the conjecture according to which detailed symbolic models of individual learners trying to solve limited problems could and would, in principle, scale up to real-world problems was slow in being demonstrated.

Notwithstanding, at least in its initial phase, the attempt to change the object of study from the individual to the group (or the individual within the group) took place whilst attempting to retain the same theory, and its associated methods. In these terms, a group of students is a set of individual problem-solvers, who communicate to each other their problem-solving processes. The words "communicate to each other" are crucial here: what exactly does such communication consist in? Although models of communication and dialogue were rarely made explicit in such frameworks, the underlying idea was often that of transmission and reception of information, which is in fact coherent with the information-processing paradigm. We could easily add encoding and decoding of information, and "noise" in the communication channel to such a model. In other terms, this paradigm was searching for a genuine model of communicative interaction, to be put into relation with the cognitive processing model.

One promising and influential approach to integrating cognition and dialogue has stemmed from the work of Roschelle and Teasley (1995), who extended the notion of the individual problem-solving space to that of the "joint problem-space": collaborating problem-solvers are working on creating a shared representation of the problem to be solved. And indeed, collaboration itself has been defined as the joint attempt to create such a shared space (Dillenbourg, 1999). From this it is a logical step to see the interactive processes of collaboration as *grounding*, according to the theory of H. Clark (1996), and the joint problem-space as the "common ground" of mutual beliefs about shared meanings of discursive objects (cf. Baker, Hansen, Joiner & Traum, 1999). This is a coherent vision of "inter-cognition", rather than of socio-cognition.

In methodological terms, the inter-cognitive approach gave rise at first to the search for categories of communication in interaction whose frequencies could be correlated with learning effects (see also on this point the subsequent discussion of socio-cognitive conflict). For example, it might be that learners who engage in attempts to explain and understand the task they are engaged in, to a greater extent than those who do not do so, would learn more (Ploetzner, Dillenbourg, Preier & Traum, 1999). This approach depends on coding the interaction and counting the codes. The problem is that an interaction is a process, not a succession of discrete elements to be coded and counted. It is difficult to identify discrete utterances in dialogues between students that definitely are or are not explanations: explanation often seems to be an "undercurrent" to extended sequences of interaction. A similar, yet more profound, problem arises with the attempt to divide interaction into parts that are "social" and others that are "cognitive". A "social" part is supposed to be not concerned with the problem-solving task. It would involve having fun, name-calling, saying hello and goodbye, and so on. A "cognitive" part of the interaction would be everything that the social part is not: it is concerned with the task, planning and understanding it. But of course this hard-and-fast distinction between the cognitive and the social breaks down; because every utterance made in a social interaction that has a cognitive content (such as a proposed problem solution) also has "social" (socio-relational) implications (see the discussion of the dialogue extract above). If the stated solution contradicts the solution proposed by another student, then that student may well feel worried, embarrassed, stupid, or threatened.

In sum, classical cognitivism, the theory of human thinking as information processing, in order to be extended from the individual to the group, requires deep integration with a theory of communicative interaction. Otherwise, the categories of interactions that are analysed, although stemming from cognitive theories of problem-solving and learning, will be essentially *ad hoc*. This approach does recognise the importance of "the social", as a factor to be added to the cognitive. For example, a common practice is to study "friendship pairs" (Jones & Issroff, 2005), or to create groups of learners based on their affinities, otherwise the students expend an amount of effort on getting to know each other that detracts from trying to solving the problem. This practice is in concordance with early work in social psychology which showed that groups will tend to disaggregate if their members are required to put more effort into maintaining the group than into solving the problem with respect to which the group was convened (Lewin, 1959). But simply "adding on" the social dimension to an unchanged theory of cognition seems to be an inadequate degree of theoretical integration.

Let us now turn to the Piagetian variety of cognitivism and its socio-cognitive extensions. Piaget's theory of human cognitive development essentially concerned changes in the individual's schemas, in relation to biological maturation and interaction with the *milieu* (the relevant environment, or life space). Although that *milieu* can involve interventions by other human beings, and despite attempts to reconstruct, from Piaget's sparse remarks on the subject of what his theory of the influence on the social environment would have been, the least that can be said is that this aspect was not his main preoccupation. Furthermore, it has been pointed out (Perret-Clermont, Perret & Bell, 1991, p. 42) that by subsuming intrapersonal mental operations and interpersonal cooperation under the notion of logical operations, Piaget in fact obviated reflection on the relations between the two.

Piaget had already stated that, when confronted with negative feedback, or conflict, from the milieu with respect to an action, the subject could try to ignore it (*refoulement*), and thus that this would not necessarily lead to reorganisation of cognitive schemas invariant across this type of action. A group of Piaget's successors (e.g. the authors of Doise, Mugny & Perret-Clermont, 1975), working on the social psychology of cognitive development, hypothesised that when the negative feedback had a social origin, originating from and in the presence of other people, it would be socially marked and thus more difficult to avoid. This is the theory of socio-cognitive conflict (Doise & Mugny, 1981), of the conflict between cognitive representations (schema) of a problem, at a particular developmental stage, of different children who were asked by the experimenter to try to solve that problem together. The processes by which the incidence of such socio-cognitive conflicts should lead to cognitive progress were as follows (Doise & Mugny, 1981). In social situations, once children become aware of different responses, this leads them to doubt them, resulting in an inter-individual disequilibrium. Social factors oblige the learners to find a solution to this interpersonal conflict. This leads to intra-individual disequilibrium, associated with emotional activation, awakening of "epistemic curiosity" and desire to resolve the cognitive dissonance. The search for overcoming the interpersonal disequilibrium leads to overcoming the intrapersonal disequilibrium and thus to cognitive progress.

During the 1990s, several negative results were obtained (e.g. Blaye, 1990) concerning the correlation between the frequencies of socio-cognitive conflicts and enhanced learning effects. But this may have been due to the fact that the types of problems (puzzles) children were given to solve may not leave room for extended discussion. More generally, it has been recognised (see e.g. Mevarech & Light, 1992, as well as the more recent work of Andriessen & Coirier, 1999; Muller Mirza & Perret-Clermont, 2009) that what is important is to understand the processes by which learners try to resolve socio-cognitive conflicts in argumentative interactions in a cooperative way.

For our purposes here, we remark that the neo-Piagetian theory of socio-cognitive conflict was aimed at close integration between cognitive, social and affective factors in learning, even though it is only quite recently that the processes of how they interrelate, in argumentative interaction, are beginning to be elucidated. But how, exactly, are the social and the cognitive articulated, within this theory? As Perret-Clermont and colleagues (Perret-Clermont et al., 1991) have discussed, in a first generation of this research, specific factors of social interactions were considered as causal factors, eliciting cognitive transformations within individuals. In the second generation of this research, social interactions were studied not as "causes" of cognitive change, but as mediators of the co-construction of meaning in context. In a series of experimental studies, these authors highlighted the subjects' attempts not only to solve the problem set by the experimenter, but also to construct a meaning for the situation in which they found themselves. The child enters into a sort of guessing game to try to decode the experimenter's expectations and, as a consequence, "it is no longer possible to decide a priori if a competence is purely cognitive or also involves the social competence of displaying that behavior. Intelligence, then, can be considered as intrinsically a sociability" (ibid., p. 55). We could encapsulate this point in the lapidary statement "cognition is social". But what is meant in this case is that in any situation where an individual is in contact with others, it is empirically impossible to disentangle the individual's cognitive processes from adaptation to context and the interlocutor. The influencing factors are not physical or "objective", but socio-cognitively (co-)constructed, (inter-)subjective meanings of those physical factors. We shall pursue this point below, from another theoretical perspective.

Views from the social

For L.S. Vygotsky, we could also reiterate that "cognition is social"; but here, cognition (consciousness, psychological, psychical processes) and "the social" need to be understood in different senses from the theories discussed above, and in multiple senses. In *Consciousness as a problem of the psychology of behaviour* (1925/2003), within the context of a profound discussion of the reflexology of the day, Vygotsky was concerned to establish that the proper object of study of psychology should be behaviour, not animal-like reflexes, and to argue that consciousness emerges from a chain of stimuli and responses, where responses become new stimuli for oneself. A stimulus originating in another person is not considered to be like any other physical stimulus: "consciousness is in a certain sense a type of social contact with oneself" (ibid., p. 91). In receiving social stimuli from other people, individuals in some way incorporate the social into the chains of stimuli and responses that constitute their own consciousnesses. The individual is a social being. A "social stimulus" is different from a physical one to the extent that human beings, contrary to other animals, can gain knowledge from the experience from other human beings of experiences that they have not had directly (to take up Vygotsky's own examples, of Mars or of the Sahara). In this sense, the social relates to the cognitive to the extent that behaviour, being at the root of consciousness, has a "social component": we learn not just from so-called "direct experience" with Nature, but also from the experience of others, who, like ourselves, have acquired knowledge as the result of the experience of previous generations ("historical experience"), that is not transmitted by heredity. It is "in speech that can be found the source of social behaviour and of consciousness": "the mechanism of social behaviour and the mechanism of consciousness are thus one and the same things" (Vygotsky, 1925/2003, p. 89). Five years later, Vygotsky (1930/1978) made the role of speech (of language, considered as a system of signs) as a bridge or unifying medium between the cognitive and the social more explicit: "[t]he internalization of cultural forms of behavior involves the reconstruction of psychological activity on the basis of sign operations" (Vygotsky, 1930/1978, p. 57). As is well known, concerning Vygotsky's theory, "in consciousness, the social element has primacy in fact and in time. The individual element constructs itself as derivative from and secondary, on the basis of the social" (Vygotsky, 1925/2003, p. 90).

For our purposes here, what we shall retain from Vygotsky's work is that understanding the relations between the cognitive and the social requires not only finding a conception of cognition that can "fit" with the social, but also considering the social on different "levels"[3] or timescales (see, e.g., Cole & Engeström, 1993). Although our primary concern here is with the *hic et nunc* of learning that can occur in interactions between students engaged in cooperative problem-solving, such an enterprise requires a broader vision that relates the study of such *microgenesis* with the levels of *ontogenesis* (the social elaboration of knowledge) and of *sociogenesis*, when the social, institutionalised and artefactually mediated organisation of knowledge elaboration is in focus: "human cognition is a multi-layered phenomenon" (Ludvigsen, 2009, p. 303). It is important to note that this phenomenon is unitary, with respect to which the "levels" just mentioned are theoretical and methodological visions: "[c]ognitive and social activities are interwoven, and can only be separated analytically" (Ludvigsen, 2009, p. 303).

One way of extending this multilevel approach to socio-cognition is to take into account socio-institutional rules, practices, and the division of labour (Cole & Engeström,1993). Another way of opening out the specific concrete situation of interaction between students to other levels of analysis is via a conception of language in terms of socially situated discourse genres (Bakhtine, 1929/1977; see also Wertsch's, 1991, attempt to recreate the Vygotsky/Bakhtine intellectual encounter that never historically took place). Language, discourse, is a cultural-historical product; the way that it is used is or should be adapted to specific socio-institutional situations; it constitutes the bridge between the self and others, between the individual, society and culture; it is the transformational motor of human development. In some sense, the words we use are not our own, they belong to a linguistic culture, we borrow and reuse them rather than inventing them to express our individual thoughts. Specific collaborative learning situations in schools can thus be seen as "arenas" that have "windows" open to the circulation of different discourse genres, from school, everyday life, the home. One aspect of learning in school concerns the elaboration of a new "inter-genre"(Baker, 2009) that is relevant and acceptable to the school situation and to the students' youth culture (Pasquier, 2005), or to be able to articulate genres and varied scientific discourses, within conditions of accountability (Mäkitalo, Jakobsson & Säljö, 2009). Discourse genres can be defined in different ways, according to the knowledge domain (physics, literature, cattle breeding) and socio-institutional situations (family, school, with friends, at table tennis club, …) with which they are associated, as well as in terms of the principal discursive processes that they involve (e.g. argumentation, negotiation, deliberation, inquiry: see Walton, 1989, p. 10).

Across the intersection of these dimensions, discourses have different "ground rules" in the contextual background. For example, in traditional educational discourse (e.g. Mercer, 2000) it is a shared background assumption that the teacher who asks a question of the student wants to check the latter's understanding, not to acquire information; the teacher evaluates the students' utterances, not the other way round. Many such ground rules that bear on educational situations have national and cultural, rather than purely institutional, origins: for example, in France, a discourse of incitation to racism and negationism is forbidden by law in any public arena, and therefore also at school (Golder, 1996).

Understanding the articulation of the social and the cognitive in collaborative learning situations requires going beyond a purely internalist microanalysis, to situate (non-)verbal collective activity along its socio-linguistic and socio-cultural (historical) dimensions: the students' multiple voices and visions are not invented by them on the fly, they "come from" somewhere outside and in the background of the interactive situation. These discourses embody alternative conceptualisations, whose confrontation needs to be understood.

The social and cultural dimensions of collaborative learning can also be understood on micro and macro levels and timescales in terms of two intellectual traditions that have very different origins to the cultural-historical approach discussed above, namely, the socio-anthropological theory of *situated learning* (see above) and the micro-sociological approach of *conversation analysis* (e.g. Schegloff & Sacks, 1973). It is not our aim to provide an extensive review of these approaches here; we shall limit ourselves to a few remarks in relation to the purposes of this book.

Within the theory of situated learning — whilst eschewing theoretical eclecticism — we remark that the notion of a "community of practice" is a useful concept for understanding the relations between the social and the cognitive, to the extent that it stands as an intermediary unit of analysis, between the cultural-historical level and the ontogenetic level (within an individual's lifespan). And yet, the processes of progressive integration into such communities, beginning from peripheral legitimate participation, work on a long timescale and are difficult to pinpoint on the microgenetic level of "negotiating with the situation". There have been several attempts to use such a theory for understanding what is happening in students' interactions (e.g. Edwards, 1993). In such an approach, "what children really think" (to paraphrase the title of Edwards' 1993 paper) is seen as locally determined, situated in the interaction. In some sense, this is surely the case: the theory according to which interactions between students reflect simple expressions of their pre-existing cognitive states is largely discredited. But although cognition might be locally determined and situated in the interaction, it does come from "somewhere": the students have a history, a culture and a future. What did they "bring to" the interaction, where did it come from, and what do they "take away" with them? There must be some way of interrelating the levels of analysis here too.

Conversation analysis has been seen by some (but by no means all) researchers as a means of describing the local enactment of cognition. In psychology, this is the basis of discursive psychology (Edwards, 1997). For example, Koschmann (2002) has introduced the richly suggestive notion of understanding "interactive meaning-making" as part of the research agenda in Computer-Supported Collaborative Learning research. More generally, conversation analysis sees the interactive encounter, giving rise to a conversation, as an enactment of social rituals: encounters must be opened and closed in certain ways, they must unfold by allowing participants to take turns in an orderly fashion, in order for them to preserve their self-images and to negotiate the images of ourselves that others communicate, apparent transgressions of the rituals must be repaired. People must find make sense together in their exchange, whilst preserving, respecting, themselves and others. It is clear that this is interactive work to be done in any social encounter, and the extent that this work requires effort and attention will interact with effort and attention concerning the cognitive dimension of the problem to be solved for which the interaction is convened in the first place. In other terms, we need to understand how the unfolding of the social ritual of conversation, described by conversation analysis, relates to the interactive elaboration of knowledge. The point we are making is rather banal, and yet it has received little attention in the collaborative learning research literature: if some students in the group do not respect the others, their ideas, interrupting them without consideration, talk too much, and so on, this will create interpersonal problems to be solved, and this will detract from solving other types of problems.

Since Levinson's (1983) clear definition, CA (Conversation Analysis) approaches have been distinguished from DA (Discourse Analysis) approaches, the latter deriving mainly from varieties of speech act theory (Austin, 1962). For our aims here, it is necessary to go beyond a dichotomy according to which CA is preoccupied solely with the social, and DA solely with the cognitive dimensions of communicative interaction (i.e., in this latter case, cognitive attitudes, such as belief, towards propositions). As we have discussed, it is possible to approach (situated) cognition from a CA perspective (that has been applied to many task-oriented dialogues as well as to everyday conversation); and, we would argue (with Trognon, 1999), the speech act, as a unit of analysis, encapsulates both the cognitive and socio-institutional dimensions. This is clearly apparent in so-called performative utterances, which realise changes in the world by their very utterance. For example,

"I name this ship the Baltic Queen" requires the speaker to have a certain social position, in a particular social context, for the ship to become effectively named in that way. But more everyday speech acts such as assertions and questions also have conditions of relevance that point outwards to interpersonal obligations and social contexts. When we assert something to someone, we commit ourselves to being ready to give a justification; we also say something about what we think they do not know or accept. Questions, in classrooms, lawcourts and the street, have quite different meanings when produced by teachers, students, judges, defendants, friends and enemies.

We have so far discussed several different levels, and units of analysis, according to which social-cognitive relations can be apprehended: history, culture, institution, community of practice, the rituals of any social interaction …, as well as the role of the collective institution of language in mediating collective activity, traversing the socio-cognitive boundary. It is important to note that the attendant processes of transformation of systems, depending on the unit of analysis across these different levels, work on different timescales (cf. Cole & Engeström, 1993). Thus, there is a need, in collaborative learning research, to go beyond the study of specific interactive encounters to understand development of the nature of collaboration over successive interactions (Mercer, 2008).

A further "meso-" level of analysis to be taken into account is that of the specific and dynamic *interpersonal relationships* between students (and their teachers). It seems clear that more work needs to be done on this in collaborative learning research, to go further than friend/enemy, like/dislike dichotomies. In any case, interpersonal relationships are also sensitive to tasks and contexts: one could have a good working relationship with someone at work or school, on specific tasks, yet a different relationship (if one has one at all) outside those situations. It is not because two students are friends that they will have a good working relationship in school (Andriessen, Baker & van der Puil, 2010). More generally, collaborative learning research has mostly been entered into from the background of cognitive psychology, whereas the long-since well-developed social psychology of group dynamics has hardly been taken into account. Another area of social psychology that is relevant to collaborative learning on a cultural level is *social identity theory* (Moscovici, 1976); clearly, students interact with each other, and learn, partly as a function of their cultural identities "as a boy", "a girl", a "good student" or a "bad student".

Having discussed different theoretical approaches to understanding the relations between the cognitive and the social in collective learning situations, on different levels, with different units of analysis, we now turn, finally, to views of collaborative learning interactions from the affective.

Views from the affective

Most modern authors would agree (e.g. Cosnier, Dols & Fernandez, 1986; Picard et al., 2004; Jones & Issroff, 2005; Boehner, DePaula, Dourish & Sengers, 2007) that there has been a bias towards the cognitive in learning research, at the expense of the affective. Traditionally, rational and objective thinking was given precedence, and was supposed to be radically different from "irrational" emotions. Certainly, it is common knowledge that "too much" emotion can prevent clear thinking; but too little emotion can be associated with low engagement. In a review of recent research on this question, Picard and colleagues (2004) argue for emotions as being associated with different "modes of thinking". Although a positive mood is not best for all types of thinking, it has been shown to be associated with greater creativity and flexibility in problem-solving, as well as better decision-making. However, "[t]o date there is no comprehensive, empirically validated, theory of emotion that addresses learning" (Picard et al., 2004).

Moreover, it is now being recognised that emotions should not be considered as a separate "realm" of human activity unto themselves; and that what is required is a perspective that integrates them with cognitive and social aspects of learning and development. Already in 1932, Vygotsky, in reviewing the work of his illustrious predecessors such as Darwin, Freud, James and Claparède, had concluded that the emotions are not "a country[4] within a country", some primitive vestige of evolution that would and should disappear with human progress, but that "emotions can only be understood within all of the dynamics of human life" (Vygotsky 1932/2003, p. 142).

Everyone knows what emotions are, such as fear, anger, sorrow, joy; and yet, curiously, emotions are notoriously difficult to define. In general, emotions are usually analysed in terms of three main components (Cosnier, Dols & Fernandez, 1986): (1) a subjective sensation; (2) physiological manifestations, and (3) observable behavioural manifestations (see Cahour, this volume). For example, in the case of anger, the subjective sensation might be simply the awareness that one is angry; physiological manifestations might be increased heart rate, respiration, blushing; and behavioural manifestations might include shouting, insulting and making violent gesticulations. Vygotsky's (1932/2003) early critical discussion of experimental work on emotions also showed that there is no simple one-to-one relation between subjectively felt emotions, physiological manifestations and emotional expression. For example, when the physiological states commonly associated with an emotion such as joy are biochemically or neurosurgically created, subjects do not necessarily report feeling such emotions (or they may say that they feel them "despite themselves", that they experience a "forced grimace"). Such a claim is in accordance with Vygotsky's (ibid.) argument according to which the unit of analysis of psychology must be a dialectical relation between the psychical and the physiological.

What emotions are there to be analysed? Here again, taxonomies abound, often turning on the distinction between so-called "basic" and "complex" emotions, where the latter are compositions of the former. On the basis of a meta-analysis of influential emotion research, Cosnier (1994) stated that authors agreed on selecting joy, surprise, fear, anger and sadness as basic emotions,[5] and thereafter diverged (for example, with respect to shame, guilt, distress, love). A very basic point of agreement is with respect to situating emotions along, at least, the two axes of intensity and valency (positive or negative).

If there is little agreement on defining emotion(s), neither is there agreement in the literature on distinctions between terms such as emotion, affect and sentiment.

But it could be said that to use the term "emotion" is generally to use an everyday notion, and/or to foreground physiological manifestations; and that to use the term "affect" is to foreground psychological awareness and understanding of emotions, as well as their communicable modes of expression. Since our aim here is to understand how emotions (in general) relate to the unfolding of socio-cognition in collaborative learning interactions, we are concerned primarily with *affect*, and shall use this term from now on.

This current state of polyphony in emotions research raises at the very least a challenge for elaborating a vision of collaborative learning interactions from the point of view of affects. We shall not attempt an extensive review of this research here; rather, we shall make some exploratory remarks about how the affective dimension could be taken into account along the different levels of analysis of collaborative learning interactions which we discussed, above, in terms of the relations between the cognitive and the social dimensions, namely cultural, institutional, community of practice, discourse genre and social *milieu*, and microgenetic levels.

Affect is not the simple expression of a biological reaction to a situation; it is intimately bound up with culturally mediated conceptions of social action and its conditions of appropriateness. Our affects in given situations depend on how we represent those situations. In a collaborative learning situation, a student's representations of the task (its interestingness, its degree of difficulty) and of other students (a "theory of mind"), as more or less friendly, cooperative and competent, will relate to the emotions felt and expressed, to their regulation, which in turn will interact with cooperation on solving the problem itself.

Vygotsky gives the following example of cultural mediation of affect:

> our affects manifest themselves in a complex system of concepts, and who does not know that the jealousy experienced by a man via Islamic concepts of faithfulness is different from the jealousy of another who disposes of a different system of representations, has understood nothing about the fact that this sentiment is historical, that it transforms itself fundamentally as a function of the ideological and psychological milieu, even though a certain biological foundation is maintained that forms the basis of the sentiment.
>
> *Clot, 2003, p. 32, citing Vygotsky[6]*

Understanding this dimension of affect in collaborative learning is important with respect to examining the generalisability of results, but it may also be important in multicultural educational settings, as well as in understanding the role of other social representations such as gender.

But a cultural vision goes further than this, in arguing that affects should not be seen primarily as "internal, individual and delineable" phenonomena (Boehner et al., 2007, p. 275), but rather as situated in social and cultural contexts that give them meaning (ibid.), to be experienced through our interactions with others. In the context of human–computer interaction research, these authors argue that we should shift emphasis away from trying to develop systems that aim to identify the "right" emotion, as a means of user-adaptation, on the basis of a supposedly universal catalogue of facial expressions, prosodic contours, and so on, and focus on supporting users in co-interpreting emotions.

> Just as verbal interaction is more than the transmission of information through a conduit, but is rather a form of social action, [...] so too is affect a form of social action, both in the ways in which it achieves social ends collectively, and in the ways in which collective meaning shapes individual experience.
>
> *Boehner et al., 2007, p. 280*

Different cultures each comprise a variety of more or less dominant educational subcultures that, at a particular point in history, may be organised in structures of authority, and with respect to the status of knowledge, that provoke and legitimise the expression of affect in different ways. Early research in social psychology (Lewin, 1948) on the influence of styles of leadership on interactive dynamics in youth groups showed notable differences between groups with three different "social climates": "autocratic", "democratic" and "laissez-faire". In autocratically managed groups, the adolescents alternated between passive obedience and violent revolt. In the democratic group, aggressivity was at the lowest level, and was discharged little by little: this way of managing turned out to be the most productive for achieving the group's task. Perhaps surprisingly, the highest level of aggressivity was observed in the laissez-faire group, where the adolescents expressed frustration that they could not achieve the task without the monitor's help. There are implications here, for how to give guidance to groups on the level of affective management, that remain to be explored.

The near-equivalent of these social "climates" can be found in different *educational scenarios* (Andriessen & Sandberg, 1999), characterised by different rules and norms of an educational situation, and in which there are appropriate tasks and learning goals for students, and corresponding roles and epistemological status for the teacher. In a traditional transmission-reception based educational scenario, the teacher is seen as the authority, and knowledge is seen as travelling from teacher to students (cf. the remarks made above, on the model of communication inherent in classical cognitivism). Learners have to understand what teachers mean, and students' misunderstandings are seen as misconceptions to be repaired. This view of a teacher as authority and students as empty vessels, on knowledge as being correct or wrong, creates a specific social climate. Research has shown that most first-year college students believe that multiple points of view may exist, but generally attribute this to shortcomings in authority (Perry, 1970). Students in the social climate associated with knowledge transmission scenarios who are requested to work on an open-ended design project may be disturbed or shocked that neither the client nor the professor has a definite answer to the problem at hand (Jonassen, Marra & Palmer, 2004). Of course, in an educational scenario where responsibilities are distributed differently (such as the *negotiation scenario*: Andriessen & Sandberg, 1999), we find students' emotions about learning to be less fixated on teachers, since there will be more room for curiosity and student initiative, as well as a more demo-cratic attitude towards collaboration and the results of collaboration in educational contexts.

The general conclusion from the social psychology studies discussed above was that frustration in groups leads to aggression. In collaborative learning situations, frustration, or its opposite, positive motivation, can concern other members of the group (for example, in "production blocking", when a participant is not allowed to intervene) and the task itself, where success may produce pleasure, and inability to solve a problem can be frustrating and demotivating.

As Jones and Issroff (2005) have argued, in some on-line learning communities, the expression of emotions is not solely a "factor" that "interferes with" learning; to the contrary, giving emotional support, motivating each other to continue with studies and generally creating a sense of belonging to a community can be the very *raison d'être* of these groups.

On the level of specific interactions between students, research shows that affect needs to be regulated just as much as any other aspect (e.g. problem-solving, action coordination), and that speech plays an important role in this (Cosnier et al., 1986). On an intrapersonal level, since Freud's research (1899/1925) it is clear that the verbal expression of emotions can transform the way that they are experienced in the individual (the "talking cure"). Cosnier and Huyghues-Despointes (2000) argue that affective regulation operates via two pathways: that of interactional and cognitive regulation, and a second pathway of sharing affect that is more physiolog-ical and non-verbal, i.e. the phenomenon of *emotional contagion* or *empathy* (when the other smiles or laughs, we tend to smile or laugh too). We can of course exer-cise a degree of control of the expression of our emotions, within constraints of what is represented as interpersonally and socially acceptable. When students per-ceive collaborative situations as becoming too emotional, they may have to expend more effort on emotional self-control, the blocking of empathy, and thus expend less on the task.

The precise analysis of affects in interactions can proceed on local and general levels, viewing them either as discrete phenomena or else as ubiquitous dimensions of interactions. Although, classically, speech act theory (Searle,) identifies "expressives" as a particular category of speech acts, the equally classical work of Jakobson (1963) proposes a theory within which the "expressive function" of language in communi-cation, involving the speaker's degree of emotional engagement, is to be considered alongside others (conative, phatic, metalinguistic, referential and poetic). In other terms, whilst there might rarely be speech acts that have a purely expressive and emo-tive function, this function can also, contextually, be realised by any speech act.

On the level of more extended interactive exchanges, the classic work of Bales (1950) on interaction process analysis aimed to understand relations between the "socio-emotional" and "task area" dynamics of groups. His method included explicit categories for interventions that increase and release tension in groups. For example, tension is released by showing solidarity, laughing, joking and generally agreeing; it is increased by asking for help, showing antagonism and generally disagreeing.

A major dimension of tension/relaxation therefore concerns the agreement/disagreement axis (see sections 4 and 5 of this volume). The work of Muntigl and Turnbull (1998) studied how the way that disagreements are managed in interactions relates to "facework" (Brown & Levinson, 1987), the interactive management of the images of ourselves and of others that we project. They found that the degree of aggressiveness, or degree of damage to "face", of different ways of disagreeing with a claim determined the argumentative strategy that would be used. For example, a very aggressive way of disagreeing is to state that the initial claim is irrelevant; a less aggressive way is to make an alternative claim. They found that the greater the degree of aggressiveness of the disagreement, the more it was likely that the person who had made the claim would defend it (and thereby defend him- or herself). The management of "face", of interpersonal consideration and self-other-images, relates deeply to argumentation and reasoning in interaction. In largely exploratory work, Andriessen, Baker and van der Puil (2011) have attempted to identify indicators of affective tension and relaxation in interactions, from a synthesis of the literature (for example, interrupting creates tension), and to plot out a tension/relaxation curve for collaborative learning interactions. This curve was compared with the argumentative structure of students' debates, and it was found that tension release seemed to lag behind the logical structure of conflict resolution. Thus, although a particular cognitive conflict might be resolved in logical terms, the next such conflict could be influenced by remanance of socio-affective tension from a previous conflict.

If one way to study the socio-affective dimension of interactions is to study its fluctuation throughout interactions, in relation to its cognitive dimension, another is to experimentally introduce emotion-provoking events into an interaction, and to study their influence on the ensuing unfolding of the interaction structure. Bertrand and colleagues (2000) described a study in which small groups of subjects were instructed that they would be asked to taste and evaluate the quality of chocolates, within market research for a well-known manufacturer. During the experimental sessions, two simulated emotion-provoking events were introduced, without the subjects' knowledge: the experimenter was called to the telephone, being told that his son had been taken to hospital; another experimenter stepped into the group; when the first experimenter returned, she remarked (falsely) that her bag has been stolen from the experimentation room. Analysis of the interaction corpus revealed the cyclical operation of a variety of discursive activities: prostration in silence (being lost for words), verbalisation and evaluation of the reasonableness of the emotions, minimisation of their importance (e.g. forced laughter). It was clear that the management of emotional events (cf. for example, how students would manage a quarrel, with insults to a member of the group) requires real interactive work. Major emotions cannot be dealt with in a few turns or sequences, and have a major impact on the whole interaction.

In general, therefore, affects in interactions need to be seen as fluctuating phenomena that may be more or less thematised and worked on throughout those interactions. Their control and mutual regulation must go hand in hand with task-level, intersubjective and interactional regulation. Research needs to be carried out on the interrelations of these regulations, with respect to task and group characteristics.

A third method, complementary to the naturalistic and experimental study of affect in interactions, is to carry out interviews with subjects concerning their subjectively felt emotions, just after the interaction has taken place, with special (phenomenologically inspired) techniques that seek to avoid post-hoc rationalisation (Cahour, 2006; Cahour, this volume). A challenge for research would be to articulate these research methods and findings.

In conclusion to this gallop through some aspects of research on affect, interaction and cognition, it emerges that affects are intimately bound up with culturally and socially mediated representations of situations; they are not add-ons to cognition and relationships, they are aspects of ways of thinking and working in relation to others and to problems. They need to be regulated just as much as any other part of human life. Different ways of organising educational situations will favour different modes of intrapersonal and interpersonal regulation, along multiple dimensions, and different modes of collaborative learning. Research should aim to study the relations between these modes of regulation on cultural, institutional and interpersonal levels.

Groundwork

Our aim in this introduction and in this book is neither to propose nor to advocate the development of a *Grand Theory of Everything*, for what must be one of the most complex and human of human activities, that of trying to work with others on solving problems as a means to learning, understanding oneself, others, the problem and the situation. Our more modest aims are threefold. Firstly, as stated above, although we realise that any specific research must foreground some dimension rather than another, we want to argue for *redressing the balance* between cognitive, social and affective dimensions of group learning, given that research to date has mostly foregrounded the cognitive dimension. Secondly, we want to argue for the usefulness of an *integrated vision* of collaborative learning situations, along the dimensions we have described, at different levels of analysis. Thirdly, in critically reviewing the diversity of theoretical approaches, on different levels (cultural-historical, social practice, institutional, interpersonal and microgenetic), we want to *highlight interdisciplinary gaps*, or pinpoint areas of research from other disciplines on topics that have been little studied in collaborative learning (such as interpersonal relationships, social representations and, of course, emotions themselves). In other words, we want to extend the field and research agenda of collaborative learning research. Without advocating theoretical eclecticism, we believe it is not impossible that elements of new localised theories and models could be elaborated that span some theoretical bridges in new and interesting ways (for example, how exactly does social representation theory relate to conversation analysis and theories of collaborative problem-solving?). We conjecture that adopting such an integrated theoretical vision would make a concrete difference to research methods and to the actual data that are collected, as well as to their analysis. It would also make a difference to how we propose to design and organise educational situations for collaborative learning.

To return briefly to the example interaction extract quoted at the beginning, the corpus from which it was drawn was collected fifteen years ago (in 1994). At that time, collaborative learning was a very little used educational practice in France; neither the students nor the teacher were used to doing it. Having a better understanding of the organisation of the school, of the classroom (the style of authority), the motivation of students in this stream to actually learn physics, the social backgrounds and affinities of the students, could all have led to proposing a different way of organising the teaching and the groups, as an extension of existing practices. With greater understanding of how affects and motivation can best be regulated in groups, in relation to problem-solving, we could have given better training to students and teachers as to how to collaborate effectively.

Collaborative learning research seems to have attained a state of maturity whereby the problems addressed in this book can at least be posed, defined and pursued.

This book

Affective Learning Together emerged from the work of an exploratory research workshop entitled "Social, cognitive and affective dimensions of collaborative learning interactions: towards an integrated analysis", financed by the European Science Foundation, that took place in Paris in May 2009. The workshop brought together established and promising younger researchers working on the social and emotional aspects of group learning, across Europe. Authors have significantly extended their initial work, in coordination with each other, to cover a broad ground of theories, methods and case studies on the social and affective dimensions of group learning. Other distinguished scholars from the USA and Israel were invited to contribute to the book.

We chose to use the term *affective* [learning] in the title of the book, partly as a word-play on, and contrast with, the term *effective* [learning]. It has seemed to go without saying that educational researchers should try to respond to the crucial societal need to make teaching–learning situations more effective, in the sense of their enabling more students to attain greater mastery in a shorter time. Since knowledge acquisition and elaboration is the goal, it has also gone without saying that the study of cognitive processes are emphasised. Major intellectual developments in cognitive science over the last forty years have gradually displaced the very nature of "the cognitive" towards "the social" (see Crook, this volume). Whilst the attendant debates are addressed in this book, they cannot be resolved here. We nevertheless claim that in order to understand the conditions and processes of *effective* educational situations involving group interaction, the *affective* dimension of interpersonal relations also needs to be taken into account.

Secondly, the choice of the term *group*, rather than *collaborative* learning in the title of this book, is also of import. The beginnings of collaborative learning research in fact focused on the most restricted "group"[7] possible: the dyad, two students in a face-to-face *tête-à-tête*. There would be much to be said about the practical, methodological and theoretical reasons behind this choice, and its limitations. For our purposes here, we simply remark that one of the aims of this book is to broaden the range of group or social learning situations under consideration, to the various more or less tightly coupled or institutionally organised ways that students can "be together" and learn (see Crook, this volume).

The aim of this book is thus to broaden the focus of collaborative learning research, to include a wider variety of social learning situations, beyond face-to-face interaction in the classroom, whilst laying the ground for the emergence of diverse research approaches that take into account the relations between cognition, social relations and emotions. It explores how necessarily *affective* interpersonal relations between students relate to what is most *effective* for learning in collaboration. When students try to solve a problem together, they can gain advantages from this, by sharing ideas; but working with others can sometimes also be a new problem in itself. Relating to others involves managing and protecting one's own and others' personal identities, friendships and animosities, as well as trying to listen to, understand, and generally get on with each other, with all the emotions and their relations to motivation that are involved.

In analogy with the "linguistic turn" in Western twentieth-century philosophy (a term coined by Richard Rorty), and in the aftermath of the cognitive revolution" beginning in the 1950s and extending over almost thirty years, there have recently been two main related developments in cognitive, human and social sciences, specifically in relation to learning: the "social turn" (see Crook, this volume) and the "emotional turn" (see, e.g., Picard et al., 2004; Cahour, this volume). The social turn is reflected, in this context, by the ascendance of theories of situated learning and communities of practice, as well as the growing influence of post-Vygotskian cultural-historical activity theory. The emotional turn has been associated with the recognition of the need to go beyond the conception of the cold isolated abstract thinker, to embrace a broader range of human experience, "hot cognition", and even the social and cultural dimensions of emotions in relation to cognition. The social and the affective thus need to be dealt with together, in relation to cognition, and in this case collaborative or social learning, as they are in this book.

This book is divided into five sections. Since we assume that the cognitive dimension of collaborative learning has received the most attention in research, the "foundations" discussed in the three chapters of the first section of the book concern primarily social and affective dimensions of learning together.

Crook (Chapter 2) describes the recent turn towards emphasising social interaction and social practice, in human sciences (including educational sciences), as well as in the world of work, where employers seek better social and coordination skills in their employees. Across a diversity of social learning situations, the chapter discusses what it means for students to be learning in more or less loosely coupled ways "together". These situations extend beyond small group work (either face to face or at a distance), to include various kinds of one (teacher) to many (student) engagements (such as tutorials, lectures, student feedback), and informal gatherings of students working in the same place, in spaces provided for them. It is argued here that, beyond social input from others, and intersubjectivity, human beings have a strong drive to seek and engage in the specific experience of engaging in shared activities, including in educational situations. We need to understand the specific nature of this experience, what motivates it, and how it is played out, in order to provide appropriate contexts and meditational means.

The second chapter of this section (Chapter 3), by Cahour, discusses the foundations of research on emotions, in relation to learning in social interaction. Emotions are complex phenomena with masking, co-occurrence, and ambivalence processes. Their different dimensions and their emergence through appraisal of the situation are described and previous studies indicate how emotions orient action and decision, influence creativity and reasoning, as well as judgements and recall. The circulation of affects in interactions implies phenomena such as face management, empathy and emotional contagion. An extract of two students' collaborative learning is analysed to show possible interpretations of their feelings during the interaction, and the necessity to have access to non-verbal expressions and subjective descriptions of masked emotions and their motivation.

The third chapter of this section (Chapter 4), written by Lemke, argues that an integrated conceptualisation of meaning-making and feeling is needed in order to understand their joint role in learning together. Feelings are reconceived as more active, interactive, distributed, situated, culture- and event-specific, and functioning on and across multiple timescales. A unified theoretical model of meaning-and-feeling is outlined, in research settings where unpredictable learning is always occurring, and is subordinate to play and playfulness. The minute-to-minute and month-to-month integration of socio-affective feelings and semiotic meaning-making cumulates into learning for the individual and for the group.

The second section of the book deals with social relations and identities in group learning, and comprises two chapters. The first chapter (Chapter 5), written by Damsa, Ludvigsen and Andriessen, analyses co-construction of knowledge and how shared understanding is achieved between participants in a learning activity. It uses a social-cultural approach and asserts that differences in experiences and knowledge in relation to the knowledge domain often account for gaps at epistemic, social or relational level. The study shows that becoming aware of these gaps and closing them is a fundamentally interactional process that requires participants' effort to relate to each other, and deal with each other's knowledge, goals and motives. However, institutional demands appear to play an important role in this multi-layered process and influence the way participants interact in their efforts to create shared conceptualisations and to deal with disagreements at relational level. Sharing tasks and committing to meet the institutional aims and demands appear to be insufficient to reach shared understanding and co-construct new conceptualisations.

The second chapter of section two (Chapter 6), written by Joiner and Littleton, discusses the role of gender differences in collaborative learning situations, relating to different types of tasks that students are asked to carry out in school. The way that we interact with other people depends to a significant extent on the way that we represent ourselves and others, in terms of social roles and representations. We can see ourselves and others, for example, as more or less competent or caring, and with institutionalised statuses of doctor, mother, father, teacher or male or female. Social representations such as *gender* are important parts of a child's everyday life, and have important influences on their conversational interactions and, therefore, in collaborative learning settings, on the nature of their learning. The first part of the chapter provides an in-depth review of what is known about the influence of gender in whole-class interactions, guided by the teacher, and in small group interactions involving different combinations of same- or different gender participants. The second discusses alternative theories of the way that gender influences joint activity, with respect to different meditational means. On the basis of a summary of several convergent recent research findings, it is argued that the use of computers in education emphasises gender differences in a way that needs to be taken into account in pedagogical design. A study is reported where children aged between 13 and 14 years old (24 boys and 24 girls) were placed into either same-gender or mixed gender pairs and worked on a computer version and a paper version of the same task. There was no difference in the language used by girls and boys when they worked in mixed gender pairs on the paper version of the task; however, as expected, boys made more assertive and controlling utterances than girls and girls made more supportive utterances than boys when they worked in mixed gender pairs on the computer version of the task.

The third section of the book deals with integration of research on emotions and on collaborative learning, with special emphasis on how students' fluctuating emotions in their interactions relate to their motivations to learn, and to learn together. Mullins, Deiglmayr and Spada (Chapter 7) provide an in-depth critical review of the complex relations between cognitive, motivational and emotional processes at work in collaborative learning situations. Here, motivation is defined as an interaction between the subjective values that people attach to achieving learning goals (how much do they want to achieve them, and why?) and their subjective expectations of being able to achieve them (to what extent do they see themselves and their group as able to achieve?). The factors influencing values and expectancies in collaborative interactions are reviewed, and their influences on emotions and collaborative problem-solving are discussed. The chapter concludes with four illustrations from the authors' research projects that highlight the interplay of motivational and emotional factors during students' knowledge co-construction. For example, the positive or negative effects on motivation and learning are shown with respect to "scripting" the students' collaboration, and emotional and motivational reactions to educational feedback are discussed.

Written by two experts on the role of motivation in learning, Järvenoja and Järvelä, Chapter 8 of the book establishes a bridge between research on collaborative learning and research on motivation and emotional engagement. Since motivation is "the fuel that mobilises students to use the potential of their cognitive capacity and skills", this is closely related to emotion. Initially motivated students can become demotivated in collaborative learning, by affective and relational problems that arise; they could also increase their motivation by the positive emotions they experience by interacting with others and benefiting from their collaboration. It is therefore argued that effective collaborative learning requires appropriate individual and mutual regulation of motivation and emotions. This claim is supported by an illustrative analysis of the work of a group of four students who, when faced with a socio-emotionally challenging situation, managed to restore emotional balance and thus assure a solid ground for collaboration by regulating the situation together. In conclusion, the authors discuss pedagogical approaches to scaffolding motivational and emotional self-awareness in groups.

Changes on different levels of social and group organisation can create "tensions"on relational and affective planes. The processes by which people seek to resolve such tensions are the subjects of the two chapters comprising the fourth part of the book.

Sins and Karlgren (Chapter 9) discuss how developing professionalism resides in the potential for practitioners to learn from and with one another in ways that support transformations of their knowledge practices. However, negotiation between multiple perspectives, interests, practices may lead to tension. While tension can disable learning, it is argued that identifying these tensions should be viewed as a significant source for development. The chapter presents two cases which show similar patterns of how tensions drive practice transformation: one in the field of medical simulation training and the other in pedagogical design in the context of a school–university partnership.

Andriessen, Paradis and Baker (Chapter 10) describe how the need to maintain a mutually satisfactory collaborative working relationship conditions how groups of students regulate their activity in order to deal with the tensions that arise from relations between them and progression (or perceived lack of it) with respect to the task. The authors adopt a developmental perspective, providing rich interpretations, or "thick descriptions", of a series of six working sessions, during which a group of three students designed a student area for a town. The students' interpersonal relationship was revealed to be sufficiently resilient to be able to absorb or dissipate various tensions arising from the task, each other, and group–external aspects (such as the teacher's monitoring). It is argued that development in such cases can be not only a matter of change, but also of actively remaining the same — in this case, as a group — in the face of an evolving situation.

The English noun "argument" can refer to either an emotionally heated or angry dispute, or else simply to the dispassionate giving of reasons for a statement that is not mutually accepted. An argument is a verbal conflict, of all or any of wills, views, personalities, identities or persons. The growing research literature on the role of argumentation in collaborative learning (e.g. Muller Mirza & Perret-Clermont, 2009) has moved towards addressing the role of interpersonal and affective dimensions. This tendency is represented and deepened in the final section (5) of this book, in the form of three chapters.

Muller Mirza (Chapter 11) explores relations between the two main meanings of "argument" mentioned above — an emotionally heated dispute, or else a reasoned debate — from a psychosocial and socio-cultural perspective. She argues that in order to understand meaning-making practices operating within the interactive encounter, it is necessary to situate them within a broader social framework, the interpersonal plane and the "thinking space" that it engenders. Following an in-depth review of the socio-cultural perspective on argumentation, a case study is analysed in which students played roles of protagonists in important controversies throughout the history of psychology, using a computer tool for creating shared argument diagrams. It was found that provided the debate was given an appropriate social setting in which the students felt "safe" to express divergent views, without threatening their interpersonal relationships, adopting roles led them to find even stronger arguments, to change their perspectives and, furthermore, to modify their epistemological positions towards accepting multiple perspectives on the topic. In conclusion, Vygotsky's notion of "drama", played out in a fictional and electronic setting, is discussed in terms of its potentiality for creating a thinking space that neutralises too emotionally intense interpersonal encounters and thus favours personal development.

On the basis of an extensive review of the literature on the role of argumentation in collaborative learning, Asterhan (Chapter 12) argues that groups of students that show the largest learning gains are characterised by a particular way of preserving a delicate balance between critically examining each other's ideas, whilst maintaining a collaborative, friendly atmosphere that avoids excessive face threats. Three different types of socio-cognitive conflict regulation are discussed, along these lines: consensual dialogue, adversarial argumentation and co-constructive dialectical argumentation. Together with illustrative examples from a situation where groups of students discussed evolutionary theory, the first two types are shown to be less productive with respect to learning. Co-constructive dialectical argumentation displays the greatest potential for learning, to the extent that it involves a general willingness to consider and critically examine arguments, collaboration and mutual respect, and the ability to perceive the interaction as a competition between ideas rather than between individuals. What is essential for collaborative learning from argumentation is that motivated students should be able to temporarily put their egos aside, whilst having enough self-confidence to voice ideas that could be proven wrong. As well as this interplay between self-confidence, motivation, social relations and the cognitive dimension of argument, it is argued that relevant factors are gender, existing dominant discourse patterns, and previous experience in collaborative argument.

In the final chapter of the book (Chapter 13), Schwarz and Goldberg discuss personal and group identities relating to cultural origins (cf. Joiner and Littleton, chapter 6 of this volume, on gender identities), with their associated emotions, as resources for historical peer reasoning. Reluctance in designing learning situations that mobilise emotions has been grounded on the belief that they can override rational thinking, especially in social interactions between students, where the need to protect group esteem is important. This chapter provides a counter-example of the negative role of emotions in learning, in a discipline where social and emotional influences are prominent, that of group discussions in history, on relatively recent issues relating to students' differing family ethnic origins and identities. The focus here is on the interplay between historical reasoning, collective memory, identity formation and the regulation of emotions in argumentative discussions between students, in relation to the "melting pot" integration policy of the new state of Israel. On the basis of a detailed analysis of a case study discussion between a student of Ashkenazi origin, and another of Mizrahi origin, the authors of this chapter show that, although emotions heated up with the surfacing of identity loyalties and collective memories, thus to some extent biasing thinking (use of evidence and evaluation of its reliability), this also enhanced reasoning in two main ways. First, it served as a motive for the students to find new arguments to protect their images and identities; second, it made them more conscious of the contextual motivations of in-group historical figures. In this way, the authors of this chapter argue that, although dealing with historical issues where group identities and thus strong emotions are at stake can be seen as an irrational confirmation of those identity commitments, it can also be a process that leads students to better-argued personal viewpoints, which take others' views into account within a generally more universalistic standpoint.

We hope that this book establishes the ground for future research on the dynamic relations between knowledge elaboration, interpersonal relations and the interactive circulation of affects, in social or group learning situations. Given its exploratory nature, it criss-crosses a broad contemporary landscape of theoretical and methodological approaches, research problems, issues and educational situations. Here and there on that landscape there are clashes between persons, their identities, discourses, motivations and feelings, as well as tensions inherent in the development of the societies and cultures in which they participate. We hope that readers of this book will come to feel the tensions at play in this emerging avenue of research, and be inspired to participate in their resolutions.

Acknowledgements

We would like to thank the European Science Foundation for funding the exploratory research workshop out of which this book emerged. Many thanks to Marie Baquero and to Corinne Chevalier for organisational support, and to Télécom ParisTech for additional finance. The corpus from which an extract is reproduced in this chapter was collected and constituted with Andrée Tiberghien and Jean Gréa.

Notes

1   Full details concerning this extract, together with a detailed analysis, can be found in Baker (1999). The students' names have, of course, been changed, whilst preserving their gender. The transcription is reproduced in a minimal form here. The extract is translated from the original French. "Pprrrttt" is an attempt to transcribe what was manifestly a mocking or

ironical exclamation, a guffaw. "/" on at the end of an utterance by one speaker, followed by the same sign on the subsequent utterance, signifies an interruption of speech.

2　We are not claiming that this is the only valid interpretation (it can be compared with those of the readers), only that it is a possible one. For illustrative purposes here, we deliberately suspend the methodological principle of not allowing interpretation to go beyond what can be explicitly substantiated from the data.

3　We put the term "level" in scare-quotes in order to indicate that we do not consider such levels in an hierarchical way, nor do we subscribe to reductionism.

4　A more literal translation might be "state", rather than country; but we wanted to avoid here the possible association with mental states.

5　As Cosnier (1994) points out, this list is not far from that proposed by Descartes (1664/1964) for "primitive passions", i.e. admiration, love, hatred, desire, joy and sadness.

6　Clot quotes from a translation of Vygotsky's work into German: Vygotski, L. (1985). Die psychischen Systeme. In *Ausgewählte Schriften*. Cologne: Pahl-Rugeinstein.

7　In fact, the dyad is not really a group. The latter might be said to begin from four participants and on to an upper limit of around eight members, depending on the interactive circumstances. The trilogue is also a special case, since it often leads to two faced with one. Beyond eight participants, the group will tend towards the creation of sub-groups in interaction.

References

Andriessen, J. & Coirier, P. (Eds.) (1999) *Foundations of Argumentative Text Processing*. Amsterdam: University of Amsterdam Press.

Andriessen, J. & Sandberg, J. (1999) Where is education heading and how about AI? *International Journal of Artificial Intelligence in Education*, 10, 130–50.

Andriessen, J., Baker, M. & van der Puil, C. (2011) Socio-cognitive tension in collaborative working relations. In Ludvigsen, S., Lund, A., Rasmussen, I. & Saljo, R. (Eds.), *Learning across Sites: New Tools, Infrastructures and Practices*. Routledge, Abingdon.

Austin, J.L. (1962) *How to Do Things with Words*. Cambridge: Cambridge University Press.

Baker, M. (2009) Intersubjective and intrasubjective rationalities in pedagogical debates: Realizing what one thinks. In B. Schwarz, T. Dreyfus & R. Hershkowitz (Eds.), *Transformation of Knowledge Through Classroom Interaction*, pp. 145–58. London: Routledge.

Baker, M.J. (1999) Argumentation and constructive interaction. In J. Andriessen & P. Coirier (Eds.), *Studies in Writing: Vol. 5. Foundations of Argumentative Text Processing*, 179–202. Amsterdam: University of Amsterdam Press.

Baker, M.J., Hansen, T., Joiner, R. & Traum, D. (1999) The role of grounding in collaborative learning tasks. In P. Dillenbourg (Ed.), *Collaborative Learning: Cognitive and Computational Approaches*, pp. 31–63. Amsterdam: Pergamon/Elsevier Science.

Bakhtine, M. [Volochinov, V.N.] (1929/1977) *Le Marxisme et la philosophie du langage*. [Marxism and philosophy of language]. Paris: Minuit. (1st edn: Voloshinov, Leningrad 1929).

Bales, R. (1950) *Interaction Process Analysis*. Cambridge, M.A.: Addison-Wesley.

Bertrand, R., Matsangos, A., Périchon, B. & Vion, R. (2000) L'observation et l'analyse des affects dans l'interaction [The observation and analysis of affects in interactions]. In C. Plantin, M. Doury & V. Traverso (Eds.), *Les emotions dans les interactions* [Emotions in Interactions], pp. 169–81. Lyon: Presses Universitaires de Lyon.

Blaye, A. (1990) Peer interaction in solving a binary matrix problem: possible mechanisms causing individual progress. In H. Mandl, E. De Corte, N. Bennett & H.F. Friedrich (Eds.), *Learning and Instruction*, Vol. 2(1) pp. 45–56. Pergamon Press Oxford.

Boehner, K., DePaula, R., Dourish, P. & Sengers, P. (2007) How emotion is made and measured. *Journal of Human-Computer Studies*, 65, 275–91.

Brown, P. & Levinson, S. (1987) *Politeness: Some Universals in Language Usage.* Cambridge: Cambridge University Press.

Cahour, B. (2006) Les affects en situation d'interaction cooperative: proposition méthodologique [Affects in cooperative interaction situations: a methodological proposal]. *Travail Humain*, tome 69, no. 4, 379–400.

Clark, H.H. (1996) *Using Language.* Cambridge: Cambridge University Press.

Clot, Y. (2003) Vygotski: la conscience comme liaison [Vygotsky: consciousness as connexion]. In F. Sève & G. Fernandez (trans.), *Conscience, inconscient, emotions* [Consciousness, the unconscious, emotions], pp. 7–59. Paris: La Dispute.

Cole, M. & Engeström, Y. (1993) A cultural-historical approach to distributed cognition. In G. Salomon (Ed.), *Distributed Cognitions: Psychological and Educational Considerations*, pp. 1–46. Cambridge: Cambridge University Press.

Cosnier, J. (1994). *Psychologie des émotions et des sentiments.* [The psychology of emotions and sentiments]. Paris: Retz.

Cosnier, J. & Huyghues-Despointes, S. (2000) Les mimiques du créateur, ou l'auto-référence des representations affectives [The mimics of the creator, or the self-reference of affective representations]. In C. Plantin, M. Doury & V. Traverso (Eds.), *Les emotions dans les interactions* [Emotions in Interactions], pp. 157–68. Lyon: Presses Universitaires de Lyon.

Cosnier, J., Dols, J.M.F. & Fernandez, A.J. (1986) The verbalisation of emotional experiences. In K. Scherer, H.C. Wallbott & A.B. Summerfield (Eds.), *Experiencing Emotion: A Crosscultural Study*, pp. 117–28. Cambridge: Cambridge University Press.

Descartes, R. (1664/1964) *Les passions de l'âme* [The passions of the soul]. Paris: Vrin.

Dillenbourg, P. (1999) What do you mean by "collaborative learning"? In P. Dillenbourg (Ed.), *Collaboration Learning: Cognitive and Computational Approaches*, pp. 1–19. Amsterdam: Pergamon.

Dillenbourg, P., Baker, M.J., Blaye, A. & O'Malley, C. (1996) The evolution of research on collaborative learning. In P. Reimann & H. Spada (Eds.), *Learning in Humans and Machines: Towards an Interdisciplinary Learning Science*, pp. 189–211. Oxford: Pergamon.

Doise, W. & Mugny, G. (1981) *Le développement social de l'intelligence* [The social development of intelligence]. Paris: InterÉditions.

Doise, W., Mugny, G. & Perret-Clermont, A.N. (1975) Social interaction and the development of cognitive operations. *European Journal of Social Psychology*, 5(3), 367–83.

Edwards, D. (1993) But what do children really think?: Discourse analysis and conceptual content in children's talk. *Cognition and Instruction*, 11 (3 & 4), 207–25.

Edwards, D. (1997) *Discourse and Cognition.* London: Sage Publications.

Freud, S. (1899/1925) Le rêve et son interprétation. [The dream and its interpretation]. Paris: Gallimard. French translation of Über den Traum.

Golder, C. (1996) *Le développement des discours argumentatifs.* [The development of argumentative discourses]. Lausanne: Delachaux & Niestlé.

Jakobson, R. (1963) *Essais de linguistique générale* [Essays on general linguistics]. Paris: Les éditions de minuit.

Jonassen, D., Marra, R. & Palmer, B. (2004) Epistemological development: An implicit entailment of constructivist learning environments. In N.M. Steel & S. Dijkstra (Eds.), *Curriculum, Plans, and Processes in Instructional Design*, pp. 75–88. Mahwah, N.J.: Lawrence Erlbaum Associates.

Jones, A. & Issroff, K. (2005) Learning technologies: Affective and social issues in computer-supported collaborative learning. *Computers and Education*, 44, 395–408.

Koschmann, T. (2002) Dewey's contribution to the foundations of CSCL research. *CSCL 2002 Proceedings*, pp. 17–23. Hillsdale, N.J.: Lawrence Erlbaum Associates.

Lave, J. (1988) *Cognition in Practice.* Cambridge: Cambridge University Press.

Lave, J. & Wenger, E. (1990) *Situated Learning: Legitimate Peripheral Participation*. Cambridge: Cambridge University Press.

Leinonen, P. & Järvelä, S. (2006) A visualization tool as a catalyst for interpersonal evaluation of knowledge. In G. Clarebout & J. Elen (Eds.), *Avoiding Simplicity, Confronting Complexity: Advances in Studying and Designing (Computer-Based) Powerful Learning Environments*. Rotterdam: Sense Publishers.

Levinson, S.C. (1983) *Pragmatics*. Cambridge: Cambridge University Press.

Lewin, K. (1948) *Resolving Social Conflicts*. New York: Harper and Brothers.

Lewin, K. (1959) *Psychologie dynamique*. [Dynamic psychology]. Paris: Presses Universitaires de France.

Ludvigsen, S. (2009) Sociogenesis and cognition: The struggle between social and cognitive activities. In B. Schwarz, T. Dreyfus & R. Hershkowitz (Eds.), *Transformation of Knowledge through Classroom Interaction*, pp. 302–18. London: Pergamon.

Mäkitalo, Å., Jakobsson, A. & Säljö, R. (2009) Learning to reason in the context of sociosci-entific problems. In K. Kumpulainen, C.E. Hmelo-Silver and M. César (Eds.), *Investigating Classroom Interaction: Methodologies in Action*, pp. 7–26. Rotterdam: Sense Publishers.

Mercer, N. (2000) *Words and Minds: How We Use Language to Think Together*. London: Routledge.

Mercer, N. (2008) The seeds of time: Why classroom dialogue needs a temporal analysis. *The Journal of the Learning Sciences*, 17(1), 33–59.

Mevarech, Z.R. & Light, P.H. (1992) Peer-based interaction at the computer: Looking backward, looking forward. *Learning and Instruction*, 2, 275–80.

Moscovici, S. (1976) *La psychanalyse, son image et son public* [Psychoanalysis, its image and its readership]. Paris: Presses Universitaires de France.

Muller Mirza, N. & Perret-Clermont, A.-N. (Eds.) (2009) *Argumentation and Education*. Dordrecht: Springer Verlag.

Muntigl, P. & Turnbull, W. (1998) Conversational structure and facework in arguing. *Journal of Pragmatics*, 29, 225–56.

Newell, A., & Simon, H.A. (1972) *Human Problem Solving*. Englewood Cliffs, N.J.: Prentice-Hall.

Pasquier, D. (2005) *Cultures lycéennes. La tyrannie de la majorité*. [High-school student cultures: the tyranny of the majority]. Paris: Autrement.

Perret-Clermont, A.-N., Perret, J.-F. & Bell, N. (1991) The social construction of meaning and cognitive activity in elementary school children. In L.B. Resnick, J.M. Levine & S.D. Teasley (Eds.), *Perspectives on Socially Shared Cognition*, pp. 41–62. Washington, D.C.: American Psychological Association.

Perry, W.G. (1970) *Intellectual and Ethical Development in the College Years: A Scheme*. New York: Holt, Rinehart and Winston.

Piaget, J. (1964) *Six études de psychologie*. [Six studies in psychology]. Paris: Denoël.

Picard, R.W., Papert, S., Bender, W., Blumberg, B., Breazel, C., Cavallo, D., Machover, T., Resnick, M., Roy, D. & Strohecker, C. (2004) Affective learning — a manifesto. *BT Technology Journal*, 22(4), 253–69.

Ploetzner, R., Dillenbourg, P., Preier, M. & Traum, D. (1999) Learning by explaining to oneself and to others. In Pierre Dillenbourg (Ed.), *Collaborative Learning: Cognitive and Computational Approaches*. Dordrecht: Elsevier Science Publishers B.V., pp. 103–21.

Roschelle, J. & Teasley, S.D. (1995) The construction of shared knowledge in collaborative problem solving. In C. O'Malley (Ed.), *Computer Supported Collaborative Learning*. NATO ASI Series, pp. 69–7. Berlin: Springer-Verlag.

Schegloff, E.A. & Sacks, H. (1973) Opening up closings. *Semiotica*, 8 (4), 289–327.

Tiberghien, A. & Megalakaki, O. (1995) Contribution to a characterisation of a modelling activity case of a first qualitative approach of energy concept. *European Journal of Psychology of Education*, X, No.4, 369–83.

Trognon, A. (1999) Elements d'analyse interlocutoire. [Elements of Interlocutionary Analysis]. In M. Gilly, J.P. Roux & A. Trognon (Eds.), *Apprendre dans l'interaction* [Learning in Interaction], pp. 69–94. Nancy: Presses Universitaires de Nancy.

Vygotski, L. (1925/2003) La consciences comme problème de la psychologie du comportement [*Consciousness as a problem of the psychology of behaviour*]. In *Conscient, inconscient, emotions* [Consciousness, the unconscious and emotions], translated from the original Russian edition of Vygotsky's works by F. Sève and G. Fernandez, pp. 61–94. Text of a conference given at the Moscow Psychological Institute in 1924. Paris: La Dispute.

Vygotsky, L.S. (1930/1978) *Mind in Society: The Development of Higher Psychological Processes.* Cambridge, MA: Harvard University Press.

Vygotski, L.S. (1932/2003) Les emotions et leur développement chez l'enfant [Emotions and their development in the child]. In *Conscient, inconscient, emotions* [Consciousness, the unconscious and emotions], trans. F. Sève and G. Fernandez, pp. 123–53. Text of a lecture on psychology pronounced at the Leningrad Superior Pedagogical Institute in 1932. Paris: La Dispute.

Walton, D.N. (1989) *Informal Logic: A Handbook for Critical Argumentation.* Cambridge: Cambridge University Press.

Wertsch, J.V. (1991) *Voices of the Mind: A Sociocultural Approach to Mediated Action.* London: Harvester Wheatsheaf.

SECTION 1

Foundations: social and affective dimensions

2

VARIETIES OF "TOGETHERNESS" IN LEARNING – AND THEIR MEDIATION

Charles Crook

Introduction

In recent years, a wide range of intellectual traditions concerned with human action have adopted a "social turn". That is to say, theorists have turned away from perspectives centred upon individual minds and turned towards perspectives that highlight social interaction and social practice. Of course, such perspectives had already flourished in certain sectors of scholarship. Yet even in social psychology and sociology, familiar issues of identity, relationships, and authority have now come to be understood in terms of the detailed dynamic of interacting with others (Schiffrin, 1994). More surprisingly, the mainstream of cognitive psychology increasingly theorises human thinking "outside of the box": that is, as human activity distributed over social and cultural resources (Clark, 1997). Indeed, it is the sheer reach of this social turn that is perhaps most striking. So, it is evident within postmodern theories of knowledge (Berger and Luckman, 1966), particularly within the domain of science and technology studies (Latour and Woolgar, 1991). It is evident within linguistics (Lakoff, 1987), within cultural theory (D'Andrade and Strauss, 1992), and within the study of organisations (Brown and Duguid, 2000).

Because this trend might be seen as in conflict with political traditions of individualism, it is interesting – as Gee (1999) has pointed out – that the social turn has been embraced in the heartlands of capitalist economic activity. Thus it is now commonplace for employers to regret the limited capability of graduates for coordinating with others (CBI, 2009). Peoples' role in the modern workplace is more likely to be understood in terms of participation in "communities of practice" (Wenger, McDermott, and Snyder, 2002) than in terms of individual actors located within processes of production (Brown and Duguid, 2000). So the social turn is not simply some abstract, academic conceptualisation of human nature; increasingly, it has become a practical imperative for the coordination of human action – in the workplace, for example.

Accordingly, technical tools and environmental designs have emerged for the purposes of supporting such coordination. In particular, digital media are now rich in services for social networking and various forms of socially participative knowledge building. Such services are well illustrated in what has become known as "web 2.0". Evangelists for this technology are fond of reinforcing their own involvement in the social turn by invoking a favoured central claim about human nature: "Human beings are social creatures – not occasionally or by accident but always" (Shirky, 2009, p. 14).

In sum, our intrinsically social nature is highlighted by theory, cultivated by employers, and resourced by new technology. So, it should surely loom large in current thinking about *education*. There are certainly trends in educational attitude and policy that echo the social turn as outlined above. This is apparent in ambitions to flatten the otherwise hierarchical traditions of instruction: that is, ambitions that foreground learners and learning – rather than teachers and teaching. That perspective is evident in Alison King's popular alliteration, re-assigning the teacher to a "guide on the side" (King, 1995). In policy terms, a similar flattening of authority is apparent in the educational slogans of government, such as "voice and choice" (Miliband, 2006). Finally, in relation to learning technology, the thrust of recent innovation has been in terms of "*social* software"(Grant, Owen, Sayers, and Facer, 2006) or resources that cultivate in young learners a willingness to collaborate, participate, and publish (Crook, 2008).

To psychologists with a special interest in learning, there is a challenge to map this evolving landscape of practice: how should we define (and achieve) a vision of learning that is richly infused with this social quality? The pervasive social turn identified above ensures that there are many theories of learning that foreground social processes (for example, Bandura, 1977; Lave and Wenger, 1990; Rogoff, 2003). However, scrutiny of perspectives reflecting this "turn" reveals that their social analyses are conducted at a wide range of granularities. The social turn is manifest in macro-level analyses (what might be termed "societal-social" – invoking institutional structures and cultural narratives, for example) but also expressed as more micro-level analyses (what might be termed "interpersonal-social"– conversation analysis and tutorial scaffolding, for example). In what follows, a consideration of the social experience of learning will be developed at a fairly micro-level. Perhaps this could be termed the more "psychological" level. It will highlight the forms of *interpersonal exchange* that are prominent and commonplace within routine educational practices. However, a special interest here concerns the *mediation* of such learning exchanges. To adopt a meditational perspective on any human action is to foreground the tools that govern such action: to identify the symbolic and material resources that we adopt to "mediate" our actions upon the world. Although a special interest here is in *re*-mediation: that is, an interest in understanding the consequences of newly emerging technologies entering into familiar practices – with implications for how those practices are re-configured through such new meditational means. There are two reasons for this orientation to mediation. One is that when established patterns of social exchange are re-mediated, the experiences or outcomes of those exchanges are often found to be disturbed. Through such disturbance, the dynamic that previously sustained the activity is more clearly exposed. For instance, in their reaction to changing mediation of their practice, participants themselves may identify a sense of something lost (or something gained). Meanwhile we as research observers – noticing such de-stabilising impacts – may come to recognise the processes that must previously have been sustaining the structure of that practice. A second reason is purely practical: observation of re-mediation should help us design learning encounters that are more productive – both affectively and cognitively.

In sum, the aim of this essay is to broaden and deepen our understanding of the social turn in learning – through theorising, illustrating, and adopting the notion of "togetherness" as a state that can be cultivated in learning contexts. It is suggested that when this state is active it contributes to the affective dimension of learning that is the central concern of the present volume. However, special attention is directed here to the impact of adopting new (digital) technologies of communication (new meditational means) as resources for the structuring of communication within learning. If a sense of togetherness is important to the motivation and the affect of learning (as suggested here), then the impact of such re-mediations deserves to be noticed and understood.

In sum, the remainder of this chapter is organised as follows. First, a distinctive sense of the social will be defined and theorised around the term "togetherness". The experience of such sociality in learning will then be considered in relation to three circumstances of educational communication: conversation, exposition, and community. We shall dwell on the manner in which the mediation of interactions within each of these circumstances configures the depth and extent of emergent "togetherness" – reflecting on how it may be optimised as a productive force within learning.

Defining "togetherness" in learning

Some theories of learning (behaviourism and connectionism, for instance) do not provide frameworks that particularly distinguish *social* input from input arising within other forms of environmental interaction. Yet some other learning theories are more attentive to the need to do this (various forms of social constructivism, for instance). Such theories will focus on the dynamic of how people interact with each other, as they engage within social contexts of learning. Their analyses are often anchored to a seminal paper by Premack and Woodruff (1978) in which the distinctive capacity of human beings to *teach* is identified as a clue to understanding their *learning*. Premack and Woodruff locate that capacity for teaching in a uniquely human feature of social interaction: namely, the mutuality now widely researched as "theory of mind" (Baron-Cohen, Leslie, and Frith, 1985).

Through this phrase, we are led to something deeper than what is to be found in simple declarations such as: "Human beings are social creatures…" (Shirky, 2009). These do not offer much of an imperative for analysis or design. After all, ants are "social creatures". If there is a claim here for giving special attention to the sociality of human learning, it must refer to something more than learning from stimuli that happen to arise in the behaviour of others, because mere exposure learning (especially imitation) is widespread among animals living in close social proximities. So, we need a more nuanced conception of the social, at least when pursuing something inherently human. Perhaps, as Hobson (1993) puts it, we need to understand how: "adult human beings are social by virtue of their status as persons who conceive themselves and others to be persons with special properties and special value". In one line of current theorising, the process whereby this special person understanding is worked out in social interaction has been termed "intersubjectivity" (Rommetveit, 1974).

If "subjectivity" describes the various states of self-knowing that humans enjoy, then "*inter* subjectivity" involves bringing such states into coordination with those of another person. The ability to do so assumes that one human being can "mindread" (Byrne and Whiten, 1991) another. This is possible, it is argued, because we humans entertain an implicit "theory of mind": we suppose that the actions of other people are governed by their (hidden) mental processes. As Bruner (1996) has put it: "We are the intersubjective species par excellence" (p. 20). Yet, while learning that genuinely builds upon mindreading greatly enriches what can be achieved, mindreading alone does not quite capture something that is profoundly social about much human learning. That missing quality is one that supports the richest form of such learning: namely, the form that is of concern in this chapter and which should be identified next.

It might be natural to suppose that a distinctively human form of social learning depended only on this ability to read (and integrate with) other peoples' minds: their desires, beliefs, intentions, perceptions, and so on (Tomasello, Kruger, and Ratner, 1993). When mutuality was exercised, this would not only empower the sensitive adjustments we associate with effective teaching, but it would also animate more *collaborative* occasions of learning. Certainly, such mutuality of cognitive engagement is a firm basis for managing learning in social encounters. For example, it resources the sustained effort of "grounding" learning conversations: an investment whereby participants can mutually work to declare, develop and update the corpus of their shared knowledge (Baker, Hansen, Joiner, and Traum, 1999). Moreover, it has long been supposed that such intersubjectivity of cognition was distinctive to human beings, albeit not apparent within us until the early years of childhood. However, more recent reviews of evidence (e.g., Carpenter, 2010) indicate that not only does such intersubjectivity occur much earlier during human infancy than was supposed, but also it may not be uniquely human – because it can also be observed in other primate species. However, what is not observed in other primates (but which is still found early in human development) is a certain disposition that may usefully be associated with a "togetherness" of learning – a notion that is under consideration here. That disposition is one for a *sharing* of activity. So, whereas it was natural to assume that intersubjectivity was the "main thing" in human teaching and collaboration, it is this "intersubjectivity plus" that really identifies something powerful and distinctively human within social learning.

The ability to understand the psychological states of others is one thing (see above), but the motivation to strive for a *sharing* of those states within interactions is another (Tomasello, Carpenter, Call, Behne, and Moll, 2005). Studies of social inter-action during early infancy suggest a deep human motive for engaging in shared activity. For example, infants will persist in declaratively pointing at an object if their adult partner [researcher] avoids incorporating the identified object into their engagement. This seems an active invitation to shared attention: the infants being satisfied only when this (sharing) was achieved (Liszkowski, Carpenter, Henning, Striano, and Tomasello, 2004). Similar conclusions emerge from studies comparing human infants with other primates (chimpanzees reared by human keepers) in terms of their interaction with researchers during problem-solving activities. Children did not particularly differ in terms of adopted cognitive strategy. Yet they did differ in terms of their enthusiasm for participating in a social game without material reward, and in their appetite for resetting and repeating the game after its problem had clearly been solved. The researchers comment: "In our opinion, [chil-drens'] attempts to return the object [i.e., repeat the game] are indicative of their interest in continuing a cooperative activity, which to them is rewarding in itself" (Liszowski et al., 2004, p. 653). Finally, Gräfenhain, Behne, Carpenter, and Tomasello (2009) demonstrate how children of 2–3 years can display *commitment* to shared activity. Suppose a game was started as a sharing experience. Although it could be completed individually, if the adult partner artificially interrupted it, children reacted to indicate that they expected continued participation.

Therefore, a substantial developmental literature of this sort (cf., Carpenter, 2010) now points towards a profound observation. Namely, that human beings have a unique motive to seek and engage in shared experiences. Of course, this claim does not promise that they will do so at every opportunity. Moreover, any given opportunity that is taken may be more or less successful, more or less gratify-ing of this underlying motive. A practical challenge then is to understand some of the conditions in which the underlying motive to share is most productively engaged – say in relation to situations of learning.

It can be assumed that such a motive gets satisfied when an awareness of sharing is registered. There will be certain characteristics of interactions that signal this "sharing" is in progress. The satisfaction of this motive is associated with a positive affect that arises within shared experience (Crook, 1998, 2000; Jones and Issroff, 2005). The extent of such affect – the extent of an awareness of sharing – has been linked to participants' monitoring their successful accumulation of common knowl-edge (Buchs, Butera, and Mugny, 2004). This in turn may reflect a sense of cognitive intimacy associated with that achievement, or perhaps the degree of inter-actional synchrony that it affords (Argyle, 1991). The origins of such motives for sharing are beyond the scope of the present discussion. But they may have a role in furnishing the dialogues that sustain language development (Pickering and Garrod, 2004). Other researchers make links from this distinctively human feature to the evolution of specialised neural structures (Grossmann and Johnson, 2007; Saxe, 2006).

At this point, it may help to summarise what has been said so far about social learning. This will allow extracting a notion of "togetherness" that will guide the remainder of the discussion. First, there is the social cognition that is based upon mutual mindreading. That is to say, human beings – perhaps not uniquely – are adept at reading the psychological states of others. They naturally use this ability to explain the actions of others. But they also use it to coordinate their thinking and perhaps achieve goals that are in their joint interest and distinct from what they might have achieved alone. Second, there is what Carpenter (2010) calls "the social cognition of social cognition". That is, human beings monitor the sociality of their own social engagement. They are drawn towards coordinating with others, in part, because of a general motive – uniquely human – to enter into shared states of experience. Third, the affect generated in satisfying this motive for sharing serves to stimulate and sustain joint activity. Given these three observations, what becomes intriguing is how and when particular occasions of the first state of affairs (humans simply coordinating through mutual mindreading) gives rise to an instance of the second state of affairs (an affectively charged orientation towards shared experience). So we can usefully explore what dictates that any given occasion of cognitive coordination will give rise to a special sort of social awareness: namely one in which the recognition that "we are sharing an experience" becomes a matter of participants' active concern. For convenience of reference, we can say that when social actors become aware of this state of affairs, what they are doing is orienting to the "togetherness" of their situation.

Note a couple of important points about this conceptualisation of joint activity. First, there is no implication that the *outcomes* of such motivated coordination will always be richer than what individuals might have achieved alone. Sometimes the outcomes will be superior but they need not be (West, Brodbeck, and Richter, 2004; Weldon, 2000). Second, invoking unique human motives (such as sharing) should not imply an imperative that they are to be exercised whenever some opportunity for social thinking arises. However potent the motive to share might be for cultural learning (Tomasello, Kruger, and Ratner, 1993), that motive will become shaped (perhaps attenuated) in individuals according to the circumstances of their personal history. Yet, against a background of such individual variation, it is still reasonable to expect some predictability: some structure in the conditions of social action that create the conditions for that sense of togetherness to "kick in".

General formats for togetherness in learning

In this section, attention is given to the origins of any such structure in social action that tends to see feelings of togetherness in this way. The form it might take during learning is derived here from broad considerations of human psychological development. This means asking how the routine social experiences of growing up might shape the forms of shared meaning that we actively seek when in situations of organised learning. The distinctions made here will then form the basis of a more focused review of those various learning situations identified – and the mediational means active within them.

It is supposed here that the interactions of (formal) learning are naturally derived from more familiar interactions: namely, those that are inevitably encountered within our earliest social exchanges with others. Of course, the profile and intensity of interactions within formal learning may eventually come to differ from this everyday grounding. However, it remains likely that social exchanges specific to any particular cultural domain (such as education in this case) are at first appropriated from simpler competencies: from those communication formats that human beings become familiar with in their natural or domestic circumstances.

Many psychologists of development have illustrated how our earliest engagements with the world are dominated by dynamic interactions with others (Schaffer, 1977; Trevarthen, 1992). Within those "proto-conversations" (Stern, 1985) we experience contingency (between what we do and what is done to us in return by others) and we thereby cultivate a confidence with intersubjective communication (Trevarthen, 1998). However, such exchanges also involve exposure to monologue, or more narrative verbal inputs, as people (caregiving adults in particular) guide our actions, verbally entertain us, tell us bedtime stories, and so forth. Finally, during development we become immersed in various kinds of corporate activity, whereby the sense of sharing is more loosely constructed through simple membership in groups of other people. This suggests three broad forms of shared activity: conversational togetherness, expository togetherness, and group togetherness. Only the first, conversational, format is based on a clear mutuality of interaction: that is, where the exchange involves participants in comparable species of action that interleave to influence each other in comparable ways. These three forms of being together-in-learning will be explored in the sections that follow.

Research should attend to how the "social cognition of social cognition" (Carpenter, 2010) takes place within these broad contexts of social exchange. Or to put matters less obliquely: research should consider how an individual's reflective awareness of the shared nature of experience is aroused during their activity with others. This is a matter of how the exchanges within that joint activity are *mediated*. That will take place through three general mediational routes. (1) Language: there will be modes of discourse that are more or less self/other referential. They draw attention more or less firmly to a mutuality within what is being done. (2) Other tools of communication: an exchange may be mediated by technologies that vary in how vividly they convey the state of shared experience. (3) Ecological designs: the environment of action may vary in how directly in conveys an active state of shared experience.

In the remainder of this chapter the distinctions raised above will be used to identify various key contexts of educational practice that support a sense of togetherness in learning. Of special interest is the shifting mediation of these contexts – as this arises from participants adopting new patterns of discourse, new technologies, and new environmental designs. There is a temptation to assimilate the term "togetherness" into the everyday sense of physical co-presence. Yet the notion demands that communication occurs within that co-presence. However, experience with new technologies alerts us to the fact that this sense of being together with someone can be achieved under a wider variety of communication conditions. We can feel together in a computer conference, we can feel together through hand-written correspondence. The theoretical interest here is one of understanding the dynamic of psychological states associated with social learning: while the practical interest is one of optimising the deployment of mediational resources that support social learning.

(1) Conversational togetherness in learning: one-to-one engagements

This section, as in the ones that follow, considers how togetherness-in-learning might be constructed in relation to the finer-grained events of interpersonal interaction. Consideration is not given to the management of more overarching educational structures, such as the design of a convivial environment for learning or the design of resources that foster relationships between, say, teacher and students. So, features of educational practice such as the creation of "rapport" (Tickle-Degnen and Rosenthal, 1990) are not considered even though it is acknowledged that such higher-order social practices can influence students' general *receptivity* to shared understanding (Argyle, 1990; Gillies and Ashman, 1998). What is considered below is: (i) one-to-one engagements that involve student and tutor and (ii) one-to-one engagements that involve students working with peers.

(i) Teacher–student shared meaning: tutoring interactions

What is termed here "tutoring" concerns the closest of interpersonal interactions that might be arranged to involve teacher and student. The term defines occasions when teacher and student are engaged in a sustained and relatively circumscribed dialogue. At present, the most widely discussed theorisation of such interactions is based on the metaphor of scaffolding (Wood, Bruner and Ross, 1976). This in turn is derived from Vygotsky's (1934/1978) formulation of a zone of proximal development, whereby a novice learner is moved towards understanding through a constructive interaction with a more experienced partner.

A key notion in describing how a scaffolding tutorial relationship might be optimised has been "contingency" (Wood, 2001). The important function that the management of contingency is supposed to serve is the need for a tutoring interaction to be adaptive: that is, the tutoring partner should be fully sensitive and sympathetic to the evolving nature of the learner's understanding – as revealed in their action and talk. However, it is increasingly emphasised that this sensitive interactional "matching" applies not only to the *cognitive* moves that a learner might make in some tutored activity, but also to the changing *affective* state of the learner (Salonen, Vauras, and Efklides, 2005). As Salonen and colleagues observe: "An additional set of possible scaffolding mismatches relates more directly to the domains of motivational and emotional regulation. Motivational regulatory mis-matches include, for instance, the teacher's verbalized negative expectations, deprecatory attributions, and failure to modulate the learner's negative verbalized expectations and attributions" (Salonen et al., 2005, p. 201). These authors illustrate the risk of this matching being "theory based" (on teachers' generalised beliefs about a student) rather than "evidence based" (on direct observation of student action). As yet, there has been relatively little empirical exploration of the structure of effective scaffolding dialogue that best guides the process.

However, Stone's (1993) critique of the scaffolding metaphor illustrates how a more semiotic approach to tutoring discourse can be helpful in suggesting how togetherness is crafted in such exchanges. A hint at what might be entailed in the semiosis of tutoring is contained in Lepper and Chabay's (1988) records of classroom teachers at work. They note how much of what teachers say avoids the directness of "telling" and cultivates an indirectness – more like "hinting". Of course, much routine talk will always be elliptical – it will have an incompleteness that requires interpretation on the part of the listener. However, a more demanding form of incompleteness than ellipsis is *prolepsis* (Rommetveit, 1974) and this seems to be a natural style adopted in talk-for-teaching (Stone, 1994). In this case the talk is anticipatory: it makes forward references that are oblique; they are left suspended or incomplete. The conversational flow can be regained only if the listener does some work on constructing what their partner might be meaning. Indeed, it is the deliberate demand for negotiating a joint understanding around the incompleteness that distinguishes prolepsis from simple ellipsis.

The tutorial value of such devices lies in the cognitive construction work that proleptic talk demands of the learner. However, we may suppose that a by-product of this particular kind of interactive exchange is a heightening of the participants' sense of shared experience. It is signalled by a partner's conscious effort to manage and sustain a shared focus of interest and attention. Indeed similar effects may arise from the deployment of analepsis, whereby the incompleteness of talk depends upon an assumption of shared knowledge about the *past* (rather than implicit predictions about the future). Such interactional devices will enrich the sense of a private togetherness in an exchange.

Re-mediation of tutoring: the case of intelligent systems

The highly skilled nature of the mindreading that underpins such cognitive coordination is something that presents a challenge to the construction of an artificial "intelligent tutoring system". Moreover, the combination of needing to design both mutual mindreading and a sense of shared experience serves to amplify the challenge of any such automation. Some researchers are recognising the significance of the affective and sharing dimension of tutorial encounters and are attempting to meet this challenge (Cooper, Brna, and Martins, 2000; Bhatt, Evens, and Argamon, 2004; Hevelen, Nijholt, and Akker, 2005). However, projecting agency (such as intersubjectivity) into a machine's interaction is a pretence that can undermine the plausibility of such exchanges (du Boulay, Luckin, and del Soldato, 1999).

The relatively slow progress in building systems that furnish a convincing tutorial exchange is an indication of the significance of those interpersonal resources that construct a sense of shared experience. These depend on that quality of intersubjectivity that arises within a human developmental history of social interaction and which is not to be programmed in computational systems.

Re-mediation of tutoring: the case of feedback on assessment

One important form of teacher–student conversation is the exchange that is organised around feedback on student assignments. Interest in the present context must be in an affective response within the cultivation of shared understanding around a piece of work offered up by the learner.

Although such interaction is retrospective (looking back at work submitted) rather than the more forward-facing knowledge construction of conventional tutorial exchanges, it may well support the same variety of dialogue and that, in turn, may create the same quality of shared experience. However, this is an arena in which re-mediation could disturb normal elements of tutorial togetherness. The provision of such feedback can readily migrate from practices that include a significant live or face-to-face structure towards processes that are managed more online. Crook, Gross, and Dymott (2006) report on this migration in relation to one academic discipline in UK higher education. Their observations indicated widespread adoption of procedures that managed the flow of student work in a more centralised way. These included the provision of written feedback according to standard *pro forma*. The net effect has been that student and teacher (author and reader) have become decoupled from any direct or conversational encounter. Such circumstances risk contributing to a general drawing apart of staff and students in higher education (Cotten and Wilson, 2006).

In focus group conversation, it was found that student reaction to this proceduralization was not favourable. Comments often dwelt upon the apparently impersonal nature of the process. For example: "So most of the time it's not that personalised so maybe they are just doing it because it's something they have to do" and "you feel as if someone's marking your work…they don't know who you are. They don't care who you are, they just want to get it done as quickly as possible so they can move onto whatever it is they have to do next". The loss of this personal contact was sometimes contrasted unfavourably with what students had enjoyed at school where feedback had a more dialogic quality (cf., Pryor and Torrance, 1998). Elsewhere such trends have been taken to illustrate an increasingly commodified discourse of higher education (e.g., Parker, 2003).

Professional guidance on the management of feedback illustrates the emergence of practices that are unlikely to stimulate a sense of togetherness in this particular context. For instance: "using our word processors to compose 'statement banks', from which we can draw often-needed feedback explanations from a collection of frequently used comments which apply to the work of many students, and stitch these comments together to make a composite feedback message to individual students" (Race and Brown, 2001).

(ii) Student–student shared meaning: collaborative interactions

Unlike tutoring, peer-based conversational togetherness involves more symmetrical relationships in terms of what partners know and, therefore, a more improvised and less guided structure to the interaction. Such joint activity can nevertheless be convened in different ways. If participants split up a task and work on different elements towards a common goal, then this has been termed "cooperation". In contrast, "collaborations" are encounters in which the task remains integrated and participants work closely on it together. Both arrangements involve the construction of shared understandings. Cooperation achieves this through fostering participants' orientation to a shared goal (albeit reached through different routes). Collaborators also have such a goal, of course, but their experience of shared activity is potentially more intense. The source of the togetherness in this form of learning lies not just in that awareness of common purpose, but also in the extended social experience of working towards it.

Indeed, research on collaboration has dwelt upon the structure of the discourse that participants deploy to approach their shared problem goal (Barron, 2000). From the point of view of capturing the process in research, one of the interesting ironies of effective collaboration is that the more successful the collaborators are at sharing, the less they need to engage in explicit communication. Thus the index of "intensity" is the *absence* of certain communication – a "silence" made possible through tacit understanding. A further important point about this kind of interaction is that it can depend heavily on the availability of shared referential resources (Crook, 1995). Just as the study of individual cognition stresses the extent to which thinking is *externalised* into cultural tools and designs (Clark, 1997), so cognition that is collaborative makes use of such external resources – but shared resources for shared cognition. Thus it is likely that the intensity of togetherness rests partly on the ease with which collaborators can make use of such resources.

Togetherness in student–student learning interactions is not, of course, a necessary outcome of simply convening these interactions. Not all students welcome such group work (Cantwell and Andrews, 2002; Underwood, 2003). Moreover, once within it, not all students choose to engage (Barron, 2000; Kreijns, Kirschner, and Jochems, 2003). Thus, the motive to seek shared experience – and the affect that arises therein – is moderated by such factors as assessment regimes, personality tensions, and perception of competitive pressures. Of course, it is also moderated by the mediational means chosen to sustain it. Examples of the consequences of adjusting these mediational means (through new technologies) are considered next.

Re-mediation of collaborative interactions: networked conversations

The growth and reach of the internet has encouraged the re-mediation of traditional student–student engagements through new digital tools. A particular promise of such networked communication is that it removes barriers associated with participants being co-present: that is, learning together in the same place and at the same time. In many respects such tools have had a very useful impact. They have opened up educational opportunities in the form of distance education initiatives. But they are also increasingly visible within traditional educational contexts as a supplement to conventional face-to-face interaction: an ingredient of "blended learning". It is perhaps here that it becomes important to judge whether implementing such re-mediational replacement risks disturbing something previously taken from the face-to-face format.

There are two broad features of online communication practices that, when adopted for learning conversations, are likely to re-configure feelings of togetherness. One is the reduced range of communicative cues that are available in synchronous or asynchronous online communications. The other is the way in which the design of virtual contexts affords a fragmentation of communication.

It is widely appreciated that online communication is limited by restrictions in visual, paralinguistic, and behavioural cues to participants' intended meaning (and its shared construction). Kreijns et al. (2003) have reviewed some of these constraints and concluded that instructors and designers overlook the need to resource the more social channels of communication. Attention has been more on the support of cognitive channels – thereby failing to realise the significance of students enjoying informal social exchange. Because it is exchanges with this quality that help ground a sense of togetherness within this form of conversational learning. Designers sensitive to this issue are increasingly addressing the need to plan for it (e.g., Van der Pol, Admiraal, and Simons, 2006).

It is less clear what follows from student–student engagements becoming more diffusely and intermittently spread over the range of internet-based communication services (social networking sites, microblogs, cloud computing servers, and so on). On the one hand, these resources potentially draw more participants into collaborative exchanges. On the other hand, the form that these exchanges take may be felt more as "coordination" than collaboration: that is, the fragmented nature of networked communication may deny collaborators the depth of shared experience that arises in more singular but sustained media. Understanding the extent of togetherness as experienced in these new contexts is a pressing research challenge.

(2) Expository togetherness in learning: one-to-many engagements

As the relative length of these three chapter sections must suggest, it is the first format for togetherness-in-learning (conversational interaction) that is the most iconic and the richest in form. It is the one about which there is most to be said. Shared meaning is surely most vigorously constructed in arenas of mutual conversation. However, in the remaining two sections that explore the notion of togetherness, the case is made for acknowledging learning exchanges in which learners are in a more subtle form of mutuality. In these two cases, communication is apparently only one way (one-*to*-many, this section) or explicit communication is lacking altogether (one-*in*-many, next section).

Teacher–class shared meaning: exposition

Exposition (in particular the pervasive case of the lecture) has suffered a great deal of criticism as a learning format. Indeed, in everyday talk the verb "lecture" has taken on negative connotations ("I asked for a advice: he gave me a lecture"), while in educational debate it is dismissed in the critical slogan "sage on the stage" (King, 1995). It may therefore seem strange to be linking it here with modes of togetherness. Yet it is useful to approach occasions of exposition in terms of their potential for creating an experience of shared activity: a sense of togetherness in learning.

A one-to-many format like the lecture is not included in social frameworks of learning because of its typically monologic quality. However, Bakhtin (1981) suggests that human listeners (and readers) will naturally find dialogue within monologue. In the context of the lecture, this means we regard the audience as (potentially) engaged in an implicit dialogue with the presenter. Potentially, the exposition can invite this kind of hidden exchange. On this conception, students are "active": they are drawn to attend, interpret, elaborate, predict, and so forth. DeWinstanley and Bjork (2002) outline some of the ways in which a lecture may be structured to precipitate this active engagement. However, their analysis does not invoke the experience of sharing that might be achieved by such structure. Yet the strategic use of communication within exposition may make this happen: so understanding the lecture in terms of togetherness is a neglected challenge.

Davis (2007) provides a theatrical analysis of lecturing that distinguishes monologue, dialogue, and soliloquy. Although the potential for stimulating an implicitly social dialogue is not addressed in detail, the particular identification of soliloquy as a mode of exposition raises interesting issues around the cultivation of shared experience. In exposition of this kind, the speaker is reflective and personal in a way that distances them from audience. Yet this exposure of a "private" reflection creates a basis for an audience to acquire a sense of intimacy or shared knowledge. In a sustained session or across a course of sessions, such management of intersubjectivity may be cultivated despite the apparently monologic quality of the genre.

Re-mediating the lecture: visual and virtual supports

If strategic use of voice may function to create togetherness during one-to-many educational practices, other mediational means may do so less readily. There are two technologies that dominate the support of lecturing and that can be considered in these terms: namely, PowerPoint and the learning platform (or virtual learning environment).

The sheer scale of adopting PowerPoint suggests its benefit to teachers. On the other hand, there is a critical literature that questions the rhetorical constraints of the tool (Tufte, 2003). Such critique is often expressed in terms of the cognitive load associated with multimodal processing or the "production line" feel that presentation templates can bring. But, in addition, visual presentations may deflect engagement away from a speaker and towards an (impersonal) text-and-image representational format. Potentially, this decoupling of a speaker from their audience could impair the sense of togetherness that has been identified above as a significant dimension of productive exposition.

The same kind of decoupling might be a consequence of one-to-many educational practices making careless use of learning platforms. One recent survey of how lecturing staff create materials relevant to their courses suggests that they rarely adopt a personal style of communication with students (Crook and Cluley, 2009). This may be a re-mediational loss associated with VLE-based support of the expository process. The rather distant tone that is typical of such authoring may be failing to resource a useful sense of togetherness that students participating in one-to-many educational contexts might be striving to find.

(3) Corporate togetherness in learning: one-in-many engagements

One consequence for education of the "social turn" is fresh interest in the design of spaces where students learn – in particular, reconfiguring them to be more "sociable". So, there is great interest in how a social experience of learning can be built into the ecology of private study spaces (Goodyear, 2008; Oblinger, 2006). Ambitious programmes such as the UK's "Building Schools for the Future" project indicate how renewal of design in learning spaces has become a major interest (Woolner, Hall, Wall, Higgins, and McCaughey, 2007). However, the most visible developments lie in the re-design of university libraries: configuring them to include more open and casual spaces for study (Bennett, 2003) – an initiative that is not universally welcomed within the librarianship community (Gayton, 2008).

That uncertainty should encourage researching these new designs to consider how they are used and understood by students. Gemma Mitchell and I (Crook and Mitchell, in press) have recently conducted such a study. One particular observation arising from it will be highlighted here. This will allow an expansion of the distinctions made above in regard to social learning. Doing so will allow very loose coupling of interpersonal relations to count as togetherness, even though explicit communication is minimal.

The study considered a university library learning space that encouraged conversation, offered flexible and convivial furniture, gave access to shared digital tools, and was integrated with all other library building resources. Students using the space were observed and interviewed; some were asked to keep an audio diary that allowed them to place their use of this space in the context of their wider practices of private study. Collaborative exchanges of the classic kind were rather rare in this space. That is, the use of it was not dominated by small groups of students discussing their work – although quite a lot of general informal discussion did take place. However, many students reported that the possibility for organised collaboration was not what made the space attractive. It was attractive because the presence of others studying in a relaxed atmosphere furnished a motive for their own individual study: a motive perhaps arising from a sense of reassurance from the co-presence of peers with common predicaments and goals. This was so even though it was acknowledged that the noise of periodic informal conversation and playfulness could be a distraction.

This corporate togetherness might be termed a kind of "ambient social learning". It does seem appropriate to categorise it as another form of togetherness in learning. Its potency may be understood in terms of individuals recognising a shared purpose in their activity – as structured by the designs and resources of the learning space. That sense of togetherness through sharing echoes what Benedict Anderson (2006) has termed "imagined communities", whereby the sense of corporate togetherness is inferred from shared modes of communicating and acting that serve to signal a common goal and purpose.

Carpenter (2010) has noted that all social animals act to be *with* others but has suggested that only humans may act to be *like* others. It is probably not appropriate to associate a student's decision to congregate in shared study space with such a motive of imitation. But it does seem to indicate a related kind of motive: one that generates a positive affect from the sense of shared experience – without intentional communication of that sharing but as something inferred from the relationship of others to corporate activity.

Concluding remarks

That learning should be "social" is an idea whose time has truly come. Yet it is an idea that deserves further theorising if policy, practice, and design are to be guided by it. In particular, it will be important to establish whether celebrating the social in human learning can mean something deeper than simply responding to "social stimuli" – responding in a way that fails to distinguish them from other forms of input to learning. It has been argued here that there is indeed an element of human social learning that is distinctive and powerful. It arises from a motive to achieve shared experiences. The realisation of that motive has been termed here "togetherness". A sense of togetherness is made possible by the human capacity for intersubjectivity and the distinctively human motive for seeking and fostering shared experiences. As it may be cultivated in contexts of learning this sense of "thinking together" requires understanding of the various social practices that can stimulate it. Its presence is an important source of affect that commonly arises in situations of teaching and learning. In terms of this book's central concern with emotions in learning, conditions for togetherness can be said to generate experiences of mutual action that have strong affective tone. We may suppose that such experiences create greater strength of emotion the more fully articulated they are through participant histories of joint action. This in turn creates within (social) learning a platform of conditions for productive forms of knowledge building.

The review above has highlighted how such experiences of togetherness-in-learning can be traced to a wide range of educational contexts. It was suggested that young people enter formal education with experience in three formats of social communication – broadly, these are conversation, exposition, and community.

Educational practice appropriates our familiarity with these formats. Each of them offers the possibility of learning together but with different routes towards creating shared experience.

The present review has also been at pains to stress how such togetherness is inevitably mediated. That may be through ways of talking but also through the use of particular communication tools, or the engagement with particular ecological designs. It is easy to assume that the quality of togetherness is given by the general format of communication alone. However, several examples remind us how that quality might be disturbed by re-mediation. For example: new tools for managing feedback conversation, new tools for supporting expository talk, new spaces in which students may gather for study. With proper attention to the working of such mediation, it should be possible to create educational experiences that take advantage of a human appetite for shared experience.

References

Anderson, B. (2006) *Imagined Communities*. New York: Verso.

Argyle, M. (1990) The nature of rapport. *Psychological Inquiry*, 1(4), pp. 297–300.

Argyle, M. (1991) *Cooperation*. London: Routledge.

Bakhtin, M. (1981) *The Dialogic Imagination*. Austin: University of Texas.

Baker, M., Hansen, T., Joiner, R., and Traum, D. (1999) The role of grounding in collaborative learning tasks. In Dillenbourg, P. (ed.), *Collaborative Learning: Cognitive and Computational Approaches*. Oxford: Pergamon. 31–63.

Bandura, A. (1977) *Social Learning Theory*. New York: General Learning Press.

Barron, B. (2000) Achieving coordination in collaborative problem-solving groups. *Journal of the Learning Science*, 9(4), pp. 403–36.

Baron-Cohen, S., Leslie, A.M., and Frith, U. (1985) Does the autistic child have a "theory of mind"? *Cognition*, 21(1), pp. 37–46.

Bennett, S. (2003) *Libraries Designed for Learning*. Washington DC.

Berger, P.L. and Luckman, T. (1966) *The Social Construction of Reality: A Treatise on the Sociology of Knowledge*. Garden City, NY: Doubleday.

Bhatt, K., Evens, M., and Argamon, S. (2004) Hedged responses and expressions of affect in human/human and human/computer tutorial interactions. In: *Proceedings of Cognitive Science (CogSci)*, Chicago, USA, pp. 114–19.

Buchs, C., Butera, F., and Mugny, G. (2004) Resource interdependence, student interactions and performance in cooperative learning. *Educational Psychology*, 24(3), pp. 291–314.

Brown, J.S. and Duguid P. (2000) *The Social Life of Information*. Boston, MA: Harvard Business School.

Bruner, J. (1996) *The Culture of Education*. Cambridge, MA: Harvard University Press.

Byrne, R. and Whiten, A. (1991) Computation and mindreading in primate tactical deception. In A. Whiten (ed.), *Natural Theories of Mind*. Oxford: Basil Blackwell.

Cantwell, R. and Andrews, B. (2002) Cognitive and psychological factors underlying secondary school students' feelings towards group work. *Educational psychology*, 22(1), pp. 75–90.

Carpenter, M. (2010) Social cognition and social motivations in infancy. In Goswami, U. (ed.), *The Wiley-Blackwell Handbook of Childhood Cognitive Development*, 2nd edn. Oxford: Wiley-Blackwell.

Clark, A. (1997) *Being There: Putting Brain, Body, and World Together Again*. Cambridge MA: MIT Press.

Cooper, B., Brna, P., and Martins, A. (2000) "Effective affective in intelligent systems – Building on evidence of empathy in teaching and learning. In Paiva, A. (ed.), *Affect in Interactions: Towards a New Generation of Computer Interfaces*. Berlin: Springer, pp. 21–34.

Cotten, S.R. and Wilson, B. (2006) Student-faculty interactions: Dynamics and determinants. *Higher education*, 51(4), pp. 487–519.

Crook, C.K. (1995) On resourcing a concern for collaboration within peer interactions. *Cognition and Instruction*, 13(4), pp. 541–7.

Crook, C. (1998) Children as computer users: The case of collaborative learning. *Computers & Education*, 30(3–4), pp. 237–47.

Crook, C. (2000) "Motivation and the ecology of collaborative learning". In R. Joiner, K. Littleton, D. Faulkner, and D. Miell (eds.), *Rethinking Collaborative Learning*. London: Free Association Press, pp. 161–78.

Crook, C. (2008) Web 2.0 Technologies for Learning: The current landscape – opportunities, challenges and tensions. Coventry: Becta. Retrieved 3 March 2010 from http://research.becta.org.uk/upload-dir/downloads/page_documents/research/web2_technologies_learning.pdf.

Crook, C.K. and Cluley, R. (2009) The teaching voice on the learning platform: seeking classroom climates within a virtual learning environment. *Learning, Media and Technology*, 34(3), pp. 199–213.

Crook, C.K. and Mitchell, G. (in press). Ambience in social learning: student engagement with new designs for learning spaces. *Cambridge Journal of Education*.

Crook, C.K., Gross, H., and Dymott, R. (2006) Assessment relationships in higher education: the tension of process and practice. *British Educational Research Journal*, 32(1), pp. 95–114.

Confederation of British Industry (CBI) (2009) *Future Fit: Preparing Graduates for the World of Work*. London: Confederation of British Industry Higher Education Task Force.

D'Andrade, R. and Strauss, C. (1992) *Human Motives and Cultural Models*. Cambridge: Cambridge University Press.

Davis, J. (2007) Dialogue, monologue and soliloquy in the large lecture class. *International Journal of Teaching and Learning in Higher Education*, 19(2), pp. 178–82.

DeWinstanley, P.A. and Bjork, R.A. (2002) "Successful lecturing": Presenting information in ways that engage effective processing. In D. Halpern and M. Hakel (eds.), *Applying the Science of Learning to University Teaching and Beyond*. San Francisco, CA: Jossey-Bass, pp. 19–31.

du Boulay, B., Luckin, R., and del Soldato, T. (1999) The plausibility problem: Human teaching tactics in the "hand" of a machine. In Lajoie, S. and Vivet, M. (eds.), *Artificial Intelligence in Education: Open Learning Environments: New Computational Technologies to Support Learning, Exploration and Collaboration*. Le Mans, France, pp. 225–32.

Gayton, J.T. (2008) Academic libraries: "Social" or "communal"? The nature and future of academic libraries. *The Journal of Academic Librarianship*, 34(1), pp. 60–6.

Goodyear, P. (2008) Flexible learning and the architecture of learning places. In Spector, M., Merrill, D., van Merrienboer, J., and Driscoll, M. (eds.), *Handbook of Research on Educational Communications and Technology*. New York: Routledge, pp. 251–7.

Gee, J. (1999) *The New Literacy Studies and the "Social Turn"*. Retrieved on 15 May 2010 from http://www.schools.ash.org.au/litweb/page300.html.

Gillies, R. and Ashman, A. (1998) Behavior and interactions of children in cooperative groups in lower and middle elementary grades. *Journal of Educational Psychology*, 90(4), pp. 746–57.

Grant, L., Owen, M., Sayers, S., and Facer, K. (2006) *Social Software and Learning*. Opening Education Reports. Bristol: Futurelab. Retrieved 15 May 2010 from http://www.futurelab.org.uk/resources/documents/opening_education/Social_Software_report.pdf.

Gräfenhain, M., Behne, T., Carpenter, M., and Tomasello, M. (2009) Young children's understanding of joint commitments. *Developmental Psychology*, 45(5), pp. 1430–43.

Grossmann, T. and Johnson, M. (2007) The development of the social brain in human infancy. *European Journal of Neuroscience*, 25(4), pp. 909–19.

Hevelen, D., Nijholt, A., and Akker, R. (2005) Affect in tutoring dialogues. *Applied Artificial Intelligence*, 19(3-4), pp. 287–311.

Hobson, P.R. (1993) The emotional origins of social understanding. *Philosophical Psychology*, 6(3), pp. 227–49.

Jones, A. and Issroff, K. (2005) Learning technologies: Affective and social issues in computer-supported collaborative learning. *Computers & Education*, 44(4), pp. 395–408.

King, A. (1995) From sage on the stage to guide on the side. *College Teaching*, 41(1), pp. 30–5.

Kreijns, K., Kirschner, P. A., and Jochems, W. (2003) Identifying the pitfalls for social interaction in computer-supported collaborative learning environments: a review of the research. *Computers in Human Behavior*, 19(3), pp. 335–53.

Lakoff, G. (1987) *Women, Fire, and Dangerous Things*. Chicago: University of Chicago Press.

Latour, B. and Woolgar, S. (1991) *Laboratory Life: The Construction of Scientific Facts*. Princeton, NJ: Princeton University Press.

Lave, J. and Wenger, E. (1990) *Situated Learning: Legitimate Peripheral Participation*. Cambridge, UK: Cambridge University Press.

Lepper, M.R. and Chabay, R.W. (1988) Socializing the intelligent tutor: bringing empathy to computer tutors. In Mandl, H. and Lesgold, A. (eds.), *Learning Issues for Intelligent Tutoring Systems*. New York: Springer-Verlag.

Liszkowski, U., Carpenter, M., Henning, A., Striano, T., and Tomasello, M. (2004) Twelve-month-olds point to share attention and interest. *Developmental Science*, 7(3), pp. 297–307.

Miliband, D. (2006) Choice and voice in personalised learning. In: *OECD Schooling for Tomorrow: Personalising Education*. Paris: Organisation for Economic Co-operation and Development Publications, pp. 21–30.

Oblinger, D. (ed.) (2006) *Learning Spaces*. Boulder, CO: Educause.

Parker, J. (2003) Reconceptualising the curriculum: From commodification to transformation. *Teaching in Higher Education*, 8(4), pp. 529–43.

Pickering, M.J. and Garrod, S. (2004) Toward a mechanistic psychology of dialogue. *Behavioral and Brain Sciences*, 27(2), pp. 169–226.

Premack, D. and Woodruff, G. (1978) Does the chimpanzee have a theory of mind? *Behavioral and Brain Sciences*, 1(4), pp. 515–26.

Pryor, J. and Torrance, H. (1998) The interaction of teachers and pupils in formative assessment: Where psychological theory meets social practice. *Social Psychology of Education*, 2, pp. 151–76.

Race, P. and Brown, S. (2001) *The ILTA Guide*. York: ILTHE (Also available and last accessed 21 May 2010 at http://education.guardian.co.uk/Print/0,3858,4321650,00.html).

Rogoff, B. (2003) *The Cultural Nature of Human Development*. New York: Oxford University Press.

Rommetveit, R. (1974) *On Message Structure: A Framework for the Study of Language and Communication*. New York: Wiley.

Salonen, P., Vauras, M., and Efklides, A. (2005) Social interaction: What can it tell us about metacognition and co-regulation in learning? *European Psychologist*, 10(3), pp. 199–205.

Saxe, R. (2006) Uniquely human social cognition. *Current Opinion in Neurobiology*, 16(2), pp. 235–9.

Schaffer, H.R. (1977) *Studies in Mother Infant Interaction*. New York: Norton.

Schiffrin, D. (1994) *Approaches to Discourse*. Chicago: University of Chicago Press.

Shirky, C. (2009) *Here Comes Everybody: How Change Happens When People Come Together.* London: Penguin Books.

Stern, D.N. (1985) *The Interpersonal World of the Infant: A View from Psychoanalysis and Developmental Psychology.* New York: Basic Books.

Stone, C.A. (1993) What's missing in the metaphor of scaffolding? In E. Forman, N. Minick, and C.A. Stone (eds.), *Contexts for Learning: Sociocultural Dynamics in Children's Development.* New York: Oxford University Press, pp. 169–83.

Tickle-Degnen, L. and Rosenthal, R. (1990) The nature of rapport and its nonverbal correlates. *Psychological Inquiry*, 1(4), pp. 285–93.

Tomasello, M., Carpenter, M., Call, J., Behne, T., and Moll, H. (2005) Understanding and sharing intentions: The origins of cultural cognition. *Behavioral and Brain Sciences*, 28(5), pp. 675–735.

Tomasello, M., Kruger, A., and Ratner, H. (1993) Cultural learning. *Behavioral and Brain Sciences*, 16(3), pp. 495–552.

Trevarthen, C. (1992) An infant's motive for speaking and thinking. In A. Heen Wold (ed.), *The Dialogical Alternative: Towards a Theory of Language and Mind.* Oslo: Scandinavian University Press.

Trevarthen, C. (1998) The concept and foundations of infant intersubjectivity. In S. Bråten (ed.), *Intersubjective Communication and Emotion in Early Ontogeny.* Paris: Cambridge University Press, pp. 15–46.

Tufte, E.R. (2003) *The Cognitive Style of PowerPoint.* Cheshire Connecticut: Graphics Press.

Underwood, J.D.M. (2003) Student attitudes towards socially acceptable and unacceptable group working practices. *British Journal of Psychology*, 94(3), pp. 319–37.

Van der Pol, J., Admiraal, W., and Simons, P. (2006) Context enhancement for co-intentionality and co-reference in asynchronous CMC, *Artificial Intelligence and Society*, 20(3), pp. 301–13.

Vygotsky, L.S. (1934/1978) *Mind in Society.* Cambridge, MA: Harvard University Press.

Weldon, M.S. (2000) Remembering as a social process. *The Psychology of Learning and Motivation*, 40, pp. 67–120.

Wenger, E., McDermott, R., and Snyder, W. (2002) *Cultivating Communities of Practice: A Guide to Managing Knowledge.* Cambridge, MA: Harvard Business School Press.

West, M.A., Brodbeck, F.C., and Richter, A.W. (2004) Does the "romance of teams" exist? The effectiveness of teams in experimental and field settings. *Journal of Occupational and Organizational Psychology* 77, (4), pp. 467–74.

Wood, D. (2001) Scaffolding, contingent tutoring, and computer-supported learning. *International Journal of Artificial Intelligence in Education*, 12(3), pp. 280–92.

Wood, D., Bruner, J.S., and Ross, G. (1976) The role of tutoring in problem solving. *Journal of Child Psychology and Psychiatry*, 17(2), pp. 89–100.

Woolner, P., Hall, E., Wall, K., Higgins, S., and McCaughey, C. (2007) A Sound Foundation? What we know about the impact of environments on learning and the implications for Building Schools for the Future. *Oxford Review of Education*, 33(1), pp. 47–70.

3

EMOTIONS

Characteristics, emergence and circulation in interactional learning

Béatrice Cahour

Introduction

The taking into account of emotions in different processes relating to human action and interaction has amplified over the last twenty years; and it has led to individuals being considered as beings who not only think, act and interact but who also, in so doing, feel, desire and are animated by affective movements that motivate and orient them.

A purely cognitive vision of relatively isolated individuals who act according to their knowledge, beliefs and reasoning has been replaced by a vision of more social and situated individuals, who are in interaction and relation with their peers, impregnated by the culture that surrounds them, and who react as a function of a social and technological context in which they find themselves. Yet they remain often as individuals who think and interact with minds that appear cold, without much consideration of the sentiments that can preoccupy them.

Vygotsky (1997) had already emphasised that

> "the separation of the intellectual aspect of our consciousness from its affective and volitional aspect is one of the major and fundamental shortcomings of all traditional psychology. Thinking is thereby inevitably transformed into an autonomous current of ideas that think themselves; it is cut off from all the fullness of real life, impulses, interests, and real tendencies of Man who thinks".
>
> *p. 61 [our translation]*

For the last twenty years, despite the development of research on emotions, there have been difficulties in integrating such considerations into the study of many areas of human activity. One of the aims of the present book is to address this problem in the field of learning in social interactions between peers. In this chapter we therefore aim to present the key notions in the domain of emotions research (limiting ourselves to the human and social sciences), and to explore their relevance for processes of collaborative learning.

Bodily and cognitive aspects of emotions

In the first instance, there is no agreed definition of emotion. But a generally agreed characterisation of emotions — and we mean emotion in a broad sense, including all types of affective movements — is that they have a bodily component, inscribed in physical sensations, and a cognitive component in terms of mental activities. Psychoanalysts speak of "soma" and "psyche" (Green, 1973), others of body and mind; but all agree that both are active when people feel something on an emotional level. This much being said, the question of the primacy of the bodily or the cognitive has given rise to — and still does — different or else conflicting standpoints. This was already the case with the famous James-Cannon controversy, opposing the priority of the bodily response that would determine the emotion, to the priority of the cognitive interpretation of the situation and the subjective feeling, as determining the emotion before the bodily reaction.[1] This is still the case, to the extent that certain approaches are more centred on cognitive processes linked to emotions, whereas others are focused on physiological reactions, even though these viewpoints today seem more complementary or consensual.

In effect, to varying degrees, emotions at the least comprise:

— *a subjective feeling* that participants can verbalise, more or less easily, which corresponds to the consciousness that they have of what they feel. The methods of investigation used in this case are principally verbalisations, either from questionnaires with pre-defined items (lists of categories of emotions in which the participants choose the appropriate emotion), or else from more free verbalisations, and interview methods. The latter aim to put participants back into the situation using videos of their previous interactions or with specific methods of posing questions (Vermersch, 1994) that help them to remember, whilst limiting rationalisation and transformation of what happened for them at the moment studied (by limited recall and by social desirability). This type of method, that takes care to help participants to be in a state of evocation of specific situations, in a position of embodied speech rather than analytic and generalising speech, seems appropriate for reliability of information obtained, if one wishes to understand how emotions emerge during collective situations.
— *bodily reactions*, which lead to, for example, an acceleration of heartbeat, perspiration, heating of the skin and differentiated brain activation. These physiological reactions are certainly measurable from bodily states, but they remain generally difficult to interpret; they indicate that an activation (arousal) has occurred, but its nature (positive/negative? emotion or load?) is difficult to identify, and they do not enable determination of the precise emotions involved (anger, fear, surprise …?).
— *expressive behaviours*, such as facial expressions, prosody, bodily posture and discourse that will differ according to the experienced emotion or sentiment.

These behaviours have the advantage of being observable, but they are often ambiguous; notably, it is difficult to differentiate facial expressions of fear, surprise and doubt from each other, whereas these sentiments are rather different. In addition, sentiments can be voluntarily camouflaged for social reasons, notably for preserving face; displeasure is thus often hidden, and a more neutral and less socially risky emotion can be simulated in its place. Discourse that is produced in social situations of interaction, more than non-verbal behaviours, is controllable and can often not correspond to the emotions experienced by the person.

It can be seen that these three aspects of emotions, together with their attendant methodological approaches, can be complementary, notably because bodily reactions make manifest what is not controllable. In other words, internal bodily movements, expressive behaviours reveal what is made visible socially and shared in interaction, and verbalisations indicate subjective lived experience that can be recalled to consciousness.

These three basic components of emotion[2] are more or less intense depending on the situation. A feeling of trust, for example, will have bodily manifestations that are less clear than an emotion such as intense anger. It should also be emphasised again that such bodily manifestations do not necessarily coincide with subjective feelings or expressive behaviours; someone who is angry might allow only neutral expressions to be made manifest, or could say that he or she is calm with respect to one aspect of an activity yet show frustration with another aspect of it (Cahour et al., 2007).

Complexity of emotions: masking, co-occurrence, ambivalence

Emotions are often complex in the sense that they can be mixed; some of the emotions can be camouflaged in order to control relations to others; they can be multiple and blended at a given instant (I can, at the same time, or almost, be amused by what someone says to me and be irritated by the noise made by another), or ambivalent (I can simultaneously be attracted to and feel repulsion for a given person or situation). For instance, Scherer (1998) showed how several emotions of anger, sadness and worry were blended when people lost their luggage in an airport. According to Frijda (1987) the question as to whether each complex emotion can be mapped onto a particular more basic one, or if the blending generates a different very specific whole, is a matter of dispute and empirical investigation. We might think that when several emotions co-exist, they have an impact on each other; but this phenomenon is very difficult to validate empirically.

In the case of *masking*, or social camouflage (Rimé, 2005; Cahour, 2006), where the person more or less deliberately hides an emotion that seems to him to be shameful or inappropriate to the circumstances (like a teacher feeling lost in his classroom), there co-exist an "authentic" emotion and a more "simulated" emotion (even though this can be so to different degrees). Masking can be quite opaque for participants themselves. For example, one can observe participants who recount a dramatic event that happened to them whilst at the same time laughing, without doing so voluntarily. Masking can have a function of establishing distance from events, for participants who do not want to relive the associated painful affects, and which thus minimises the dramatic aspect of the narrative.

A different behavioural aspect can "translate" each of the emotions. Martin et al. (2006) describe a television extract from a drama that speaks of the participant's father who is in prison: anger is perceptible on the basis of facial expressions and gestures; yet despair is perceptible on the level of prosody. In this case one might think that nervousness and anger camouflage (to the hearer or even for the participant) a sentiment of despair that is much deeper. Often, anger is a sign that a "zone of sensitivity" of the person — that potentially generates depression or confusion — has been touched upon: the reaction that enables such a state of depression to not be felt so much is the expression of anger.

In general, it seems that once several emotions are perceptible, that do not seem to be compatible, it is often necessary to consider that the most authentic affect is the one that is socially the least valued in the context, since affects that are considered to be negative for one's self-image are frequently camouflaged, consciously or unconsciously. This is often the case with negative valencies (anger, sadness, annoyance, …) rather than with positive valencies, except in situations where a negative valency is socially expected, for example following bad news.

In the same way, non-verbal expressions (facial expressions, gestures, postures) and para-verbal aspects of speech (e.g. prosody), when they are clear and definitive (and not neutral), often reveal authentic emotions, whilst at the same time the attendant discourse presents other emotions. In a study of the relation of trust between clients and insurance agents, we observed, for example, that a woman explained that she was very annoyed by the agent, who had insinuated that her financial situation was not very promising, whilst at the same time sighing deeply, which indicated that she had also experienced worry and weariness (Cahour, 2006). One could similarly also think of people who firmly state that they are very confident, such as a student before an exam or a teacher faced with a particularly difficult class, whilst also having a voice that trembles, betraying a problem that is denied in their discourse. In actual fact, non-verbal expressions (and even sometimes the voices of professional actors and singers) are less controllable than verbal expression in discourse.

With respect to complex emotions that are blended at a given moment, it seems interesting to differentiate them according to whether they relate to the same object or to different objects. We can thus distinguish:

— **co-occurring affects**, for example, being at the same time embarrassed by an aspect of a collaborative activity and satisfied by another aspect of this activity. Co-occurring affects can emerge within different aspects of a collaborative activity with a given group of people, and often relate to different aspects of this same activity. For example, a student in a working group who feels positively excited by the fact that the group is working constructively but at the same time feels a bit sad that his previous proposal had been rejected by the group.

Co-occurring affects can also relate to more clearly differentiated objects that have few links between them, such as a teacher being satisfied because his son has just succeeded in an exam whilst at the same time being annoyed by a group of agitated students. Even if there is no link between these two events, other than that they affect the same person, they can nevertheless compensate for each other, the positive attenuating the violence of the negative, and the negative attenuating the joy of the good news (Cahour et al., 2007).

— **ambivalent affects**, involving opposed affects with respect to the same object. Ambivalence is a concept originating in the domain of psychiatry, but which is also relevant to normal psychical functioning. They involve sentiments or contradictory tendencies towards a given object or person. In psychoanalysis, ambivalence is described as the presence within a person of an opposed pair of impulsions of the same intensity, as a conflict where the positive and negative components of an affective attitude are simultaneously present (typically, the love–hate conflict described by Freud, 1910, towards a given person). There can also be attraction and fear *vis-à-vis* someone or a situation, and these two affects will lead to contradictory actions, of coming closer and moving away. Another example could be pleasure and guilt with respect to an activity: chatting with a good friend when one knows that he would need to work instead, for example.

It can be seen that, for complex emotions perhaps more than for simple emotions, whether it is a case of co-occurrence with respect to two objects or else ambivalence with respect to a given object, the delicate question arises as to the extent to which emotions can be brought into consciousness. Why might this be more difficult than in the case of so-called basic emotions? When one experiences an emotion to a high degree (e.g. I am joyful, or sad), it is difficult to not be conscious of it; whereas when one experiences mixed emotions, it is a more delicate matter to unravel them and to bring such complexity into consciousness. When one studies real situations, that allow space for the emergence of such quite natural complexity, one is often confronted with co-occurring emotions. Several cases need to be identified:

— emotions that are conscious, and thus easily verbalised;
— emotions that are clearly identifiable from non-verbal expressive behaviour;
— emotions that are not conscious and verbalised in the first instance, but which can be verbalised during interviews that allow participants to re-enter situations and become reflexively conscious of what was pre-reflexive;
— emotions that are repressed into the domain of the unconscious, yet which could potentially be brought to light during therapy.

The emotions that are classically listed as "basic" and universal are: fear, joy, anger, sadness, disgust and surprise (Ekman, Friesen & Ellsworth, 1972). There are sometimes additions to the list, according to the researchers concerned, and numerous categorisations exist, where there is an attempt to group emotions of the same type together (e.g. anger, irritation, agitation can be grouped together). Such typological approaches are, for example, used to design questionnaires on the emotions that are experienced in different situations. Of course, the number of emotions that are worth studying in natural settings is infinitely larger.

Emotions can also be analysed in terms of various different dimensions, the most classical and important of which are:

— *valency*, which corresponds to a more or less positive or negative tonality of the experienced sentiment, partly related to the pleasure/displeasure, agreeable/disagreeable, oppositions;
— degree of *arousal*, which represents the level of intensity of the emotion, from, for example, a mild irritation to full-blown rage;
— the degree of *control* that persons consider to have over their emotional states is also a frequently cited dimension.

We also propose to characterise affective states on the basis of the following dimensions:

— the fact that a *triggering event* of the affect (or its object) is more or less identifiable; this is often the case for brief and intense emotions (termed "basic") such as anger, fear, joy, surprise, disgust. It is less the case, for example, with a general state of moroseness, which can occur without persons being very able to identify what started it off, or for a sentiment of confidence, that can arise progressively from diverse elements.
— the level of *bodily reaction* (physiological and/or expressive): basic emotions are often more bodily marked than sentiments such as confidence or dissatisfaction. Someone could, nevertheless, have a vivid sentiment of distrust that might be associated with withdrawal and characteristic behavioural expressions. Sentiments that are sometimes termed "existential" (Ratcliffe, 2005), as with sentiments of power, control, presence, connection, also have quite subtle bodily manifestations.
— the fact that the affect is in the background (or even not conscious) or that it attracts the attention of the subject to a greater degree and is in the field of *consciousness*: for example, an underlying affective state of joy, of which the person is not very aware, in comparison with intense joy that overwhelms the subject who is conscious of it.
— the *duration* of the affect: a brief emotion of joy can last only a few minutes, whereas a joyful humour can last several days or weeks. The temporal evolution of the affective state can also be taken into account with, for example, affects that die out progressively or will transform into a stable mood.

It seems to us more important to characterise affective states along these dimensions than to "label" this or that affect as an emotion (basic or complex), sentiment or mood. Thus, sadness can be considered to be an emotion if it is linked to a specific event and is of short duration, or else as a mood if it lasts and is in the background. The same is the case for joy, which could be a short and intense emotion, or else a latent mood.

The emergence of emotions

After this discussion on the nature of emotions, the question as to how they emerge arises. How is it that, in a given situation, an emotion appears and evolves? Here we refer to distinguishable emotions that stand out from the general affective "tonality" in which the individual is plunged. For we are constantly in the process of feeling something, in a more or less intense way, and being-in-the-world in a certain affective rapport whose fluctuations are frequent and subtle. It is thus from this constant flux that particular affective states emerge or become salient.

The emergence of an emotion is an eminently singular and subjective phenomenon, which depends on individual characteristics, in interaction with the specific situation and the meaning that it has for the person.

Many researchers working on the psychology of emotions (e.g. Arnold, 1960; Frijda, 1986; Lazarus, 1991; Scherer, Schorr & Johnstone, 2001) postulate that affective states are essentially generated by a process of *appraisal* of the situation by the persons, as a function of the meaning that they attribute to it, as well as their interests and goals (Rimé, 2005), or, more broadly speaking, their motivational dispositions or "concerns" (Frijda, 1986), including beliefs, values, and aspects of previous experience that are mobilised in the situation. The axiom of this theory is that individuals are constantly evaluating their relations to their environments in terms of their implications for their well-being. For example, students who are working in groups in school may "appraise" such a situation as meaning "having fun together", "doing something new", "wasting time", "passing time (un)pleasantly", and so on. The meaning they attribute to such a situation will influence their emotions, which, when perceived by others, will influence the overall affective "climate" of the group, its problem-solving and learning, which, in turn will transform appraisals and emotions. We are thus faced with a complex system of multidirectional influences between contextual meaning, emotion, collaboration and learning.

Lazarus (1991), along with Arnold (1960), pioneers of this research orientation, distinguish primary and secondary appraisal: primary appraisal has to do with whether or not what is happening is relevant to one's values, goal commitments, beliefs about one's self and the world, and situational intentions; and, "if so, in what way" (Lazarus, 2001, p. 42). "Secondary appraisal focuses on what can be done about a troubled person-environment relationship, that is the coping options, the social and intrapsychic constraints against acting them out, and expectations about the outcomes of that relationship (…) do I need to act? What can be done? Is it feasible? Which option is the best? Am I capable of carrying it out?" (ibid., p. 43).

To take a simple example, a school examination situation can be frightening for those for whom it is absolutely essential to succeed, but much less so for those for whom less is at stake. The notion of subjective evaluation, or appraisal, of the situation seems perhaps to orient too much emotion towards a product of elaborated reflexion (even if researchers concerned underline the fact that this evaluation is more or less conscious). But one must consider the fact that it may be a question here of a highly personal appreciation of what is (un)desirable, relating to what is important for the individual (Averill, 1980). Such appraisals are often carried out in a way that can only be verbalised partially, or even very little symbolised and not conscious, and can take place on the level of "thought-sensation", of the type "I like/don't like it", "it suits me/doesn't suit me", "I feel it but don't know why". And such notions are interesting, since they do not reduce to a reasoned evaluation. Authors working within the framework of the theory of appraisal tend to emphasise the roles of symbolic processes in the emergence of emotions, and, in certain situations, there can effectively be the beginnings of reasoning prior to the expression of emotions.

We must also mention, even if they may be less relevant to the study of cooperative learning, others' research approaches that insist on the intuitive nature and the immediacy of emotion that is hardly brought into consciousness. This is notably the case with Jouvent (2009), who described a person who only just avoided being knocked down by a bus, together with the "emotional time" that was corporeal and brief, where "my fear was there to save my life", but where "I did not have the time to think". The neurophysiologist Damasio (1994), on the basis of his theory of "bodily markers", which have been inscribed from experience and then give rise to processes of immediate recognition of a type of situation that has had positive or negative consequences for the person, participates in a direction of research that is more centred on the immediacy of emotional reactions, anchored in bodily (literally, in-corporated) learning.

Psychoanalysis is perhaps the orientation that reconciles to the greatest extent these two dimensions of affect, i.e. the bodily and the psychological, and which, of course, also develops the mechanisms by which the unconscious is made manifest via affects. This also seemed to be essential to Vygotsky (2003), who insisted on the fact that there is a fight between elements for "entering into the field of consciousness, with the suppression of certain elements by others", but these elements "continue to exist just below the threshold of consciousness as desires for representation" (p. 222). According to Green (1973, p. 20), affect is "trapped between the body and the mind" ("*le corps et l'esprit*"), and psychoanalysis centres on the concept of impulse, comprising (1) affects, that in turn comprise a source of energy for feeling, (2) representations of things, that are relatively unconscious and make a bridge between sensibility and the intellect, and (3) representations of words, the symbolic and intellectual aspect. Affects represent the most archaic aspect of human beings, original affects being linked to the body of the mother; they are considered by Green to be simultaneously subjective experiences and forces. "Affect" is "a categorical term grouping together all the qualitative aspects of emotional life, in the broadest sense ... a mass of states that belong to the scale pleasure-displeasure" (1973, p. 12). "Emotion" is generally used in a more narrow sense and does not include moods, for instance, which last longer (that is why we often specify "emotions in a broad sense").

Today, it is quite clear that affective states (or "emotions in the broad sense") orient thought processes and relations to others. But, as we shall discuss below, research has unfortunately often been carried out in experimental situations, although this work has at least the merit of having brought several interesting phenomena to light.

Orientation of action and orientation of decision

In the first instance, researchers generally agree on the fact that emotions prepare for action, that they have a function of impulsion for action, that they orient or re-orient what the person is ready to put into effect. For some researchers, emotions are major motivational states that translate tendencies towards action (Tomkins, 1995; Izard, 1977; Arnold, 1960). For example, fear engenders distance and avoidance, whereas anger arouses attack, and curiosity leads to coming closer. According to Oatley & Johnson-Laird (1995), when there is a necessity to redirect action and to revise plans, it is emotion that orients action during this interim period.

> Emotions are generally viewed as provisions for dealing with adaptive dilemmas presented by interactions with the environment; states of action readiness are defined as modes of readiness for establishing, changing or abandoning relationships with the environment ... Modes of action readiness are motivational states ... defined by their relational aims (e.g. self protection, hostility, rejection, interaction enhancement) ... action readiness is at the functional level of what emotions are for in the first place.
>
> *Frijda & Zeelenberg, 2001, p. 143*

From the standpoint of an approach that emphasises the corporeal aspects of emotions, Damasio (1994) observed that the lowering in the capacity to feel emotions in patients with cerebral lesions was associated with difficulties in making choices in personal and social domains. He concluded that emotions orient decision-making, and hypothesised the existence of "somatic markers". Such markers would function as automatic alarm signals, which indicate that it is dangerous to choose the option that leads to a given result: "somatic markers represent a particular case of the perception of secondary emotions, in the framework of which they have been linked by learning to predictable consequences of certain scenarios" (p. 225), and will thus have an influence on decision-making. Damasio thinks that this mechanism, when it operates without conscious awareness, can be the source of what we call intuition, "this mysterious means by which we arrive at the solution of a problem *without* submitting it to reasoning" (p. 242). In this theory, the body is central (as for James, 1892; or Prinz, 2005), since the emotion associated with a situation is inscribed bodily, and short-circuits evaluation processes of a symbolic nature. In this case, emotion corresponds more to a reflexive association.[3] It is nevertheless surprising to observe that, without having recourse to emotions because they are brain-injured, when these persons are confronted with the problem of choosing, they may continue to analyse advantages and disadvantages of each option, without being able to make a final decision.

Other researchers also emphasise the fact that emotions establish priorities amongst goals, and help in the management of unexpected situations (Oatley, 1992;

Tomkins, 1995). Finally, Isen (1993) showed that when they are in a positive affective state (induced, for example, by the announcement of their success in a prior task), medical students make more rapid diagnoses on the basis of case descriptions of patients who could possibly have cancer.

Influence of affective states on creativity and reasoning

Isen (1993) and his team have shown that positive affective states improve creativity in that participants in which a positive state has been induced (for example, by announcing to them that they have succeeded in a test, by making them read amusing stories, or by offering them a present) generate more associations between ideas, more unusual verbal associations, and produce a more rich context for thinking. They succeed better at creativity tests (practical, semantic, scientific). Such participants also have more flexible cognitive organisation for categorisation and identification of similarities and differences. They are more able to understand how to categorise atypical members, especially for natural categories, recipes or persons. Amabile et al. (2005) confirmed the link between positive affects and creativity in natural work settings in seven companies; positive affects are an antecedent to creativity, a consequence of, or concomitant to creativity; and these authors also insist on the cognitive flexibility that positive affects bring.

By contrast, persons who are in such a positive state avoid disagreements and risk (Isen, 1993). They thus remain efficient if the task suits them and if it is sufficiently agreeable, interesting or important, since they seek to protect themselves from the loss of the positive state. It also appears that the positive state induces heuristic reasoning, which raises the question as to whether this is or is not to the detriment of systematic processing of information. Although Isen (ibid.) suggests that a positive emotional state induces more efficient and deep resolution of problems, Schwartz (2002) has shown that negative affective states are preferable for analytical tasks and causal reasoning; such negative states would lead to more focused and deep processing according to this research. However, these results must be viewed with caution; effects are not yet very clear, and were obtained in experimental settings rather than ecological situations.

Congruency between emotional states and different cognitive processes

The emotions associated with a situation can generate, amplify and transform beliefs (Frijda, Manstead & Bem, 2000), and a change in belief can produce a change in emotional reactions.

Judgements and evaluations also seem to depend quite closely on general emotional states, or moods: a positive mood leads to more positive evaluations, whether it is a matter of simulations of job interviews (Baron, 1987), films to be judged as happy/sad/agressive, or satisfaction/unsatisfaction with respect to current politics (Forgas Moylan, 1987). It seems that there is a certain congruency between emotional states and judgements: people who are in positive emotional states will more positively evaluate someone to be employed, a film they have just seen, or their political satisfaction, whereas their evaluations will tend to be more negative when they are in a negative mood.

In general, memorised autobiographical elements that have an emotional intensity are recalled better (Oatley & Jenkins, 1996), as has been shown in several longitudinal studies (Linton, 1982; Wagenaar, 1986), and memory recall also seems to be congruent with mood: Bower (1981) has thus shown that a happy or sad mood, induced by hypnosis, leads to recall of either, respectively, happy or sad events from childhood; and Isen (1993) emphasises the fact that a positive mood renders positive memorised elements more accessible.

The circulation of affects in interactions

As shown by Carnevale and Isen (1986), a positive state facilitates negotiation in a bargaining task: people are less likely to abandon the negotiation, more likely to come to an optimal agreement, and engage less in aggressive tactics. In this case, people also have a better representation of the other's view, and change perspective more easily. In general, people in such positive states are also more ready to help others, and have a more altruistic social behaviour, except when such an action could depress them (Isen, 1993; 1987), in which case one finds the will to maintain the positive state.

Such a desire to maintain a positive emotional state is also found in interactions in small groups, where participants attempt to manage the emotional situation not only for themselves, but also for the group and for the other partners of the collaboration (Cahour & Pemberton, 2001). If the group is not too competitive and conflictual, then it functions minimally by negotiation, empathy and the search for mutual grounding and mutual respect, so that the global equilibrium of the group is not disturbed and avoids an aggressive escalation. The psychological literature on emotions is often subject-centred and not much group-oriented, dealing mostly with individuals' ways of evaluating the critical situation and of coping for their own sakes. Goffman's theory of face management (Goffman, 1967) is highly relevant here, because it takes into account the reciprocal objective of "maintaining faces" of oneself (face is an image of self with a social value claimed by the person) and of the other participants, by avoiding threatening faces and by maintaining social order. Goffman's "face work" corresponds to the actions taken to be consistent with face; and losing face results in a loss of the internal emotional support that protects oneself in social situations. There are rituals around face management (thanks, agreement, repair …) and other tact strategies.

In some cases interlocutors try to manage the emotional situation not only for themselves, but also for group equilibrium and for the other participants. In Goffman's terms (ibid.), face protection and face management are active, for example, when a participant in collaboration calms down his internal anger after having received an insult, and uses an alliance with a third participant to avoid a direct conflict; he then protects his own face by simulating indifference by shrugging his shoulders, whereas he has felt vexed. His first internal reaction was aggressive and he was willing to go to fight, but he calmed down this immediate impulse, which would have increased the conflict and the aggressive escalation.

The classroom is, of course, a place where trying to keep an equilibrium in such a way that conflicts do not become violent for the participants is a principle that both teachers and students need to respect.

Empathy is also an affective phenomenon that is important in interactional settings, be it the classroom, the workplace or the private sphere. According to Hoffman (2000) it is "the spark of human concern for others, the glue that makes social life possible" (p.3) and it is generally defined as an affective response or a process by which emotions are shared without losing sight of whose feeling belongs to whom, and by which one knows or feels what another person feels (Brunel and Martiny, 2004; Decety & Meyen, 2008). This ability to be in contact with others' emotions is a primary source of intersubjectivity; it has a role in moral development, motivates pro-social behaviour and inhibits aggression towards others (Hoffman 2000). Rogers (1975), who largely used this concept in his therapeutic approach, defines it as a process for entering into the perceptive world of others that allows becoming sensitive to all the affective movements produced in them. Empathy may be more or less voluntary or passive, and its passive side is like affective contagion which can exist in groups of persons, becoming, for instance, tense when some of the participants become aggressive, or in a happy and joking mood when some of them begin joking.

The role of unconscious bodily synchronisation and of imitation is very important in such processes of empathy and contagion; and Merleau-Ponty (1945) insisted on the importance of the participation of the body in mutual understanding ("*intercorporalité*") and for "feeling the other inside" and not only outside, by this intersection of bodily sensations.

In educational settings, empathy and emotional contagion between the participants permits this understanding mediated by the body, allows guessing of the internal state of the other, feeling if (s)he is tense, doubting, attentive, disagreeing, etc., and allows the interaction to be regulated accordingly.

Of course, affective experience will differ for participants of an interaction, they can be reactive and totally different for the different participants, some feeling relaxed because the situation suits them, whereas others will be upset or nervous because the same situation does not please them at all.

The literature on group emotions considers the notion of "emotional climate" in terms of shared or convergent emotions (or moods) in a group, and differentiates it from the sum of individual emotions (Scherer & Tran, 2001). However, in empirical studies, individual emotions are generally considered to inform the researchers about the group's emotions. Emotional contagion in groups fulfils the need for being better integrated or socialised into the group (Kelly & Barsade, 2001); and social identification of individuals allows workgroup cohesion and information sharing (Garcia-Prieto, Mackie, Tran & Smith, 2007). Positive emotional contagion that group members experience also improves cooperation, increases perceived task performance and decreases conflict, according to a study by Barsade (2002) in the domain of managerial decision-making in groups. The context which has an impact on experienced feelings includes the emotional norms and rules of the group and its history, but also the physical setting (e.g. noise, architecture), the other groups around, the organisational system of the company (in terms, for instance, of valorisation), and the leader of the group (Kelly & Barsade, 2001; Brief & Weiss, 2002). The role of the leaders is considered to be important for group emotions, even if the followers also determine the leadership style and behaviour. Barsade and Gibson (2007) showed that leaders must express positive moods and suppress expression of anxiety or sadness that demotivates followers. "Transformational" leaders, who are empathetic, optimistic, and cause positive changes in their followers and the system (in contrast to the transactional leaders who are in a logic of give and take), are shown to be influential on the emotions and performance of healthcare workers (Bono, Jackson-Foldes, Vinson & Muros, 2007). These studies provide some interesting results about the group emotions, the factors which influence them and their impact on group dynamics, even though the overall vision is somewhat global, and does not explore the on-going emergence of emotions during cooperative interactions.

The example of John and Susan's collaborative problem-solving

We now discuss the application of some of the concepts discussed above to collaborative learning, with respect to the interaction extract proposed in Chapter 1 of this book (Baker, Andriessen & Järvelä) that we reproduce below, for ease of reading:

[1] *John*: Ok, there, there's the … /

[2] *Susan*: / … transformer. Do the transfer arrow.

[3] *John*: There are several to be done. One there. Should we put another one there?

[4] *Susan*: Pprrrttt!

[5] *John*: You see, it leaves from a reservoir and it comes back to a reservoir

[6] *Susan*: Is that right!?

[7] *John*: A reservoir to start with and a reservoir to end with

[8] *Susan*: Have we got two batteries, John?

[9] *John*: No!

[10] *Susan*: Have we got two batteries??

[11] *John*: No

[12] *Susan*: Then why do you say such rubbish?!

[13] *John*: What did we forget, then?

[14] *Susan*: But no. I ….You know there, it's obvious that it's like that. That's what I thought. Look, there's the wire. Wait … Me, I thought it was like that! That the two wires … you see, the energy goes out from there. It goes whooosshh across the two wires and arrives there.

You understand? So that the two wires went like that and arrived there. Do you understand what I'm trying to say? I mean that it goes from there, like that: from the reservoir, there's a wire that goes from the reservoir and it takes it to the bulb, you agree? And that's the way it is. There's the other wire, I'd have put it like that

[15] *John*: Yeah but that's not right! Look at what they say: "an energy chain …" /

[16] *Susan*: / I don't give a damn

[17] *John*: What?

[18] *Susan*: I'm telling you I don't give a damn. For me, that's the way it is.

Let us first consider the global structure of this short extract of a longer interaction between these two students who are trying to solve a physics problem together in the classroom.

John proposes a solution in (3) that Susan, after a question of clarification, rejects rather violently in (12): "then why do you say such rubbish?!". John apparently does not react to this sort of insult and continues with the problem-solving with a question: "what did we forget then?" (13). Susan then proposes an alternative solution in (14) in a very assertive way, being strongly implicated in her proposal, such as when she says, "it's obvious that it's like that". John rejects her proposal (15: "but that's not right!"), adopting a more impersonal formulation than Susan in 12, not saying "you are wrong" or "what you say is wrong" but rather "*that's* not right". Susan then rejects John's argument in (18) eschewing arguing herself, by saying, "I don't give a damn, for me that's the way it is".

First of all we need to note that the written transcription alone is not sufficient for exploring emotions in the interaction. We can find some relevant cues in the transcribed discourse (Andriessen, Baker & van der Puil, 2011) but we still are lacking:

(1) prosody, which is indicative of emotional movements;
(2) non-verbal expressions that we could observe on a video recording of the interaction, such as mimics, gestures, bodily postures and movements;
(3) the phenomenological description by the two participants of how they were feeling during this interaction; the best way to interview them is right after the interaction, by showing them the video or the audio trace of the interaction and asking how they felt during the exchanges, also by using the type of questioning proposed by Vermersch (1994) in a psycho-phenomenological perspective.

We have highlighted above how emotions are only partially expressed and socially shared, how they can be masked or even simulated; this explains why what is manifestly expressed is insufficient if we are interested in how the interaction was subjectively experienced by the persons. But still we can try to make several hypothesis based on the written transcription and try to illustrate some of the phenomena that we described earlier. We insist on the fact that we will propose here mainly hypothetical possibilities, since complementary data are lacking to unable a clear view of what the two participants are feeling here.

First of all we note that when Susan says, "then why do you say such rubbish?!", this is a discursive production which is potentially aggressive; the punctuation marks ("?!") indicate that the transcriber perceived a prosody indicating interrogation and exclamation at the same time; but still we do not know if the prosody was very aggressive or rather smooth. Also, if Susan had made this utterance whilst smiling at the same time, this would have attenuated the rude aspect of the utterance.

Notwithstanding, this utterance appears to be a bit rude and potentially threatening for John's face.

Nevertheless, the verbal reaction of John (here again, we do not know what his non-verbal behaviour would say) does not show any disturbance, following this quasi-insult. Two very different interpretations are thus possible:

(a) The appraisal that John produces of the situation at this moment is not one of being threatened by Susan's intervention; perhaps he is not offended at all by Susan's sentence because he knows that it is the way she is, and that she is partially joking, for instance. Otherwise, this is perhaps a usual way that these two students have of speaking with each other, which has become relatively conventional between them, as part of their relationship. In this case, John's internal reaction (personally experienced emotion) would correspond to the expressive reaction that he allows to be shown socially, or else, even indifference towards this potential aggression.

(b) Another possible interpretation would be that John has perceived this intervention negatively, that is quite rude towards him; he feels a little aggressed and, although he is not pleased with this exchange, he does not wish to show that he is affected or even annoyed by this assertion of Susan's, that accuses him of talking rubbish. In this case, his *appraisal* of the situation would be very different, and he would feel his face to be threatened. He prefers, nevertheless, to not show his feelings, and to control his sentiments that could have led him to verbally hit back in an aggressive way. He camouflages his emotions, pretending that nothing has happened, by ignoring the form of Susan's message, replying uniquely to its content. What motivates this absence of reaction is perhaps not conscious for John. It could be, for example, a matter of a vague fear of entering into an aggressive escalation with Susan, or a fear for the relationship between them, or else simply being centred on trying to solve the problem, which would mean that the relational aspect is less important for him at this point than the collaborative activity. In that case, there would be co-occurring affects, of the type "her tone annoys me, but we have to stay concentrated on the problem without wasting time". Other internal/personal reactions would undoubtedly be imaginable, and only John could describe for us his subjective feeling at this point in time, as well as what motivated him, in what respects that was linked to his past relations with Susan, or any other aspect concerning him personally, his goals, stakes, values and interests.

By these varied and plausible interpretations, we aim to underline the fact that only the subjective point of view of the person involved in the interaction can provide sufficiently complete information on what occurred for that person emotionally, that could have been obtained with post-interaction interviews (Cahour et al., 2007). Otherwise, one runs the risk of exploring interpretative routes that are not sufficiently founded. We also show that the emotions emerge from an appraisal which is highly subjective and dependent on the person's relation with the other participants, her objectives, her sensitivity, her desires and fears.

On the basis of the utterances in the interaction sequence reproduced above, one could also hypothesise that, after Susan had proposed an alternative solution with a very assertive or even peremptory tone of voice (line 14), the annoyance or tension of John would have been increased, thus leading him to exclaim, "yeah but that's not right!". Under this hypothesis, he would have rejected Susan's proposal since he was upset. However, it is known that it is not easy to reject a proposal of someone who is strongly associated with it (Cahour & Pemberton, 2001) because in that case, you would need to find strong arguments (which has a high cognitive cost) and because this would threaten the other person's face (which is risky for the overall interaction). It is much more easy to reject the proposal of someone who presents it whilst being distanced from it, saying for example, "perhaps this is another solution, but, it's not at all certain, it could be a possibility". In this case, we would have a potential illustration of the fact that, when one is in a negative mood, one judges things negatively to a greater extent. It is thus possible that John, being annoyed with the attitude of Susan with respect to him, was in a mood that led him to reject even more severely her alternative proposal, as a mirror movement, or tit-for-tat reply to the previous rejection of his own proposal by Susan. In other words, it is possible that John rejected Susan's proposal out of hand because she had aggressively rejected his own previous proposal.

Discussion

Our global conclusion is that affective movements orient cognitive and social activities, whilst conferring upon them a different quality (e.g. focusing attention, creativity, etc.). They create dispositions, orienting not only action but also thinking and the way of being in the world (openness, availability). The search for an equilibrium in affective states, and the avoidance of threats, not only for oneself but also for the persons with whom one interacts, or for the group itself, seems to be an essential process at work in social interactions, above all when the degree of intimacy is quite low.

The impact of affective dispositions on thought processes and persons' relations to the world that govern action is thus well established, but mostly in experimental settings. More work needs to be done on complex situations and ecologically valid contexts, in order to gain deeper understanding of these interactions between affects and complex human activities, notably in learning situations.

One difficulty in studying emotions is that, as we saw before, many experienced affective movements are masked and not socially expressed. This probably explains why most studies in the psychology of emotions are developed either through experimental settings, where contrasting emotional states are induced before observing differences in subsequent behaviour, or through the subjective feelings that the participants can verbalise following a natural(istic) situation, either with questionnaires or interviews. We have seen how, without the non-verbal behaviour during the exchange and without the subjective and phenomenological point of view of the participants, several hypotheses can be advanced, but not confirmed. External analytic visions are thus insufficient, and a first-person view is additionally required. This is a reason why appraisal theories seem particularly appropriate for studying emotions in groups of learners. We have seen with the John and Susan example that the subjective meaning that the participants in an interaction construct, turn-taking after turn-taking, is essential to the emotion that they will experience and then to the reaction that they will live and display during the collaborative process.

It does not seem possible to establish clear prescriptions for educational settings on the basis of learning and emotions research; but task design and organisation of collaborative learning can contribute to creating a certain mood; encouraging competition or co-construction, for instance, will not have the same impact on the emotional climate of a group; and we have seen how positive emotions tend to orient towards positive evaluations and towards creativity. Nevertheless, some tensions and disagreements, if they are not too intense and systematic, can also be fruitful for the collaborative learning by bringing controversies and critical views. More research needs to be carried out in order to understand how emotions circulate and interact with knowledge elaboration in natural settings, in a way that avoids applying simplistic principles to situations of life that are subtle and varied, according to the subjectivities of individuals who collaborate.

Notes

1 It is common to say that (schematically) for James, we are afraid because we escape, whereas for Cannon, we escape because we are afraid. The bodily automatic reaction is the first phenomenon for James, and he thinks that emotional reactions are nothing but awareness of physiological response patterns. Cannon argued that physiological patterns cannot differentiate all the emotions and that the emotion is first of all a cognitive phenomenon, followed by bodily effects.
2 Some authors also integrate the appraisal process (which can be considered as a source of the emotion or as a part of the emotion) and the tendency towards action, which can be considered as a consequence of the emotion or as part of the emotion itself.
3 Some authors also integrate the appraisal process (which can be considered as a source of the emotion or as a part of the emotion) and the tendency towards action, which can be considered as a consequence of the emotion or as part of the emotion itself.

References

Amabile, T.M., Barsade, S.G., Mueller, J.S. & Staw, B.M. (2005) Affect and creativity at work. *Administrative Science Quarterly*, 50, 367–403.

Andriessen, J., Baker, M. & van der Puil, C. (2011) Socio-cognitive tension in collaborative working relations. In S. Ludvigsen, A. Lund, I. Rasmussen & R. Saljo (Eds.), *Learning across Sites: New Tools, Infrastructures and Practices*, pp. 222–42. London: Routledge.

Arnold, M.B. (1960) *Emotion and Personality*. New York: Columbia University Press.

Averill, J.R. (1980) A constructivist view of emotion. In R. Plutchik & H. Kellerman (Eds), *Emotion, Theory, Research and Experience*, vol.1. San Diego: Academic Press.

Baron, R.A. (1987) Interviewer's mood and reaction to job applicants. *Journal of Applied Social Psychology*, 17, 911–26.

Barsade, S.G. (2002) The ripple effect: Emotional contagion and its influence on group behavior. *Administrative Science Quarterly*, 47, 644–75.

Barsade, S.G. & Gibson, D.E. (1998) Group emotion: A view from top and bottom. *Research on Managing Groups and Teams*, vol. 1, pp. 81–102.

Bono, J.E., Jackson Foldes, H., Vinson, G. & Muros, J.P. (2007) Workplace emotions: The role of supervision and leadership. *Journal of Applied Psychology*, 92(5), 1357–67.

Bower, G.H. (1981) Mood and memory. *American Psychologist*, 36, 129–48.

Brief, Arthur P., Weiss, Howard M. (2002) Organizational behavior: Affect in the workplace. *Annual Review of Psychology*, 53, 279–307.

Brunel, M.-L., Martiny, C. (2004) Les conceptions de l'empathie avant, pendant et après Rogers [The concepts of empathy before, during and after Rogers], *Carriérologie.uqam.ca*, vol.9, no 3.

Cahour, B. & Pemberton, L. (2001) A model of conversational positioning in collaborative design dialogues. *AI and Society*, 15(4), 344–58.

Cahour, B. (2006) Les affects en situation d'interaction coopérative: proposition méthodologique, *Le Travail Humain*/PUF, tome 69, no4/2006, 379–400.

Cahour, B., Brassac, C., Vermersch, P., Salembier, P., Bouraoui, J.L. & Pachoud, B. (2007) Etude de l'expérience du sujet pour l'évaluation de nouvelles technologies; l'exemple d'une communication médiée, *Revue d'anthropologie des connaissances*, 1.

Carnevale, P.J.D. & Isen, A.M. (1986) The influence of positive affect and visual access on the discovery of integrative solutions in bilateral negotiation, *Organizational Behaviour and Human Decision Processes*, 37, 1–13.

Damasio, A. (1994) *Descartes' Error: Emotion, Reason, and the Human Brain*. New York: Grosset/Putnam.

Decety, J. & Meyen, M. (2008) From emotion resonance to empathic understanding: A social developmental neuroscience account. *Development and Psychopathology*, 20, 1053–80.

Ekman, P., Friesen, W.V. & Ellsworth, P. (1972) *Emotion in the Human Face*. Pergamon: New York.

Forgas, J. P. & Moylan, S. (1987). After the movies. The effects of transient mood states on social judgments. *Personality and Social Psychology Bulletin*, 13, 478–489.

Freud, Sigmund. (1910) *Five Lectures on Psychoanalysis*. The Standard Edition, ed. by J. Strachey et al., vol.11. London: The Hogarth Press.

Frijda, N. H., Manstead, A. S. R., & Bem, S. (Eds.). (2000). Emotions and beliefs. How feelings influence thoughts. Cambridge, England: Cambridge University Press.

Frijda, N.H. & Zeelenberg, M. (2001) Appraisal: What is the dependent?, in K.R. Scherer, A. Schorr & T. Johnstone (Eds), *Appraisal Processes in Emotion: Theory, Methods, Research*, New York: Oxford University Press.

Frijda, N.H. (1987) *The Emotions*. Cambridge: Cambridge University Press.

Garcia-Prieto, P., Mackie, D., Tran, V., & Smith, E. (2007) Intergroup emotions in work groups: Some antecedents and performance consequences. In A. Mannix, M.A. Neale & C.P. Anderson, (eds), *Research on Managing Groups and Teams: Affect and Groups – vol. 10*, pp. 145–84. Dordrecht: Jai Press, Elsevier.

Goffman, E. (1967) *Interaction Ritual*. New York: Anchor Books.

Green, A. (1973) *Le discours vivant*. [Living discourse]. Paris: PUF.

Hoffman, M.L. (2000) *Empathy and Moral Development*. Cambridge: Cambridge University Press.

Isen, A.M. (1987) Positive affect, cognitive processes and social behaviour. In L. Berkowitz (Ed.), *Advances in Experimental Social Psychology* (vol. 20, pp. 203–53). New York: Academic Press.

Isen, A.M. (1993) Positive affect and decision making. In M. Lewis & J.M. Haviland (Eds.), *Handbook of Emotions*, pp. 261–77. New York: Guilford.

Izard, C. (1977) *Human eEotions*. New York: Plenum.

James, W. (1892) *Psychology*. Cleveland, OH: The Living Library.

Jouvent, R. (2009) *Le cerveau magicien; de la réalité au plaisir psychique* [The magician brain: from reality to psychological pleasure]. Paris: Odile Jacob.

Kelly, J.R. & Barsade, S.G. (2001) Mood and emotions in small groups and work teams. *Organizational Behavior and Human Decision Processes*, 86, 99–130.

Lazarus, R.S. (2001) Relational meaning and discrete emotions. In K.R. Scherer, A. Schorr & T. Johnstone (Eds), *Appraisal Processes in Emotion: Theory, Methods, Research*. New York: Oxford University Press.

Lazarus, R.S. (1991) *Emotion and Adaptation*. New York: Oxford University Press.

Linton, M. (1982) Transformations of memory in everyday life. In U. Neisser (Ed.), *Memory Observed: Remembering in Natural Contexts*. San Francisco: Freeman.

Martin, J.C., Abrilian, S., Devillers, L., Lamolle, L., Mancini, M. & Pelachaud, C. (2006) Du corpus vidéo à l'agent expressif [From a video corpus to an expressive agent]. *Revue d'Intelligence Artificielle*, numéro spécial sur les interactions émotionnelles, vol. 20, 4–5.

Merleau-Ponty, M. (1945) *Phénoménologie de la perception* [Phenomenology of perception]. Paris: Gallimard.

Oatley, K. & Johnson-Laird, P.N. (1995) The communicative theory of emotions: Empirical tests, mental models and implications for social interactions. In L.L. Martin & A. Tesser (Eds.), *Goals and Affects*. Hillsdale, NJ: Erlbaum.

Oatley, K. (1992) *Best Laid Schemes: The Psychology of Emotions*. New York: Cambridge University Press.

Oatley, K., & Jenkins, J.M. (1996) *Understanding Emotions*. Cambridge, MA: Blackwell.

Prinz, J. (2005) Are emotions feelings?, Special issue on "Emotion experience", *Journal of Consciousness Studies*, vol. 12, no 8–10, 9–25.

Ratcliffe, M. (2005) The feeling of being. *Journal of Consiousness Studies*, vol. 12, no 8–10, pp. 43–60.

Rimé, B. (2005) *Le partage social des émotions* [The social sharing of emotions]. Paris: PUF.

Rogers, C.R. (1975) Empathic: An unappreciated way of being. *The Counselling Psychologist*, 5, 2, 2–10.

Scherer, K.R. (1998) Analysing emotion blends. In A. Fischer (Ed.), *Symposia*, pp. 142–8, Würzburg: ISRE Publications.

Scherer, K.R., Schorr, A. & Johnstone, T. (2001) *Appraisal Processes in Emotion: Theory, Methods, Research*. New York: Oxford University Press.

Scherer, K., and Tran, V. (2001) Effects of emotion on the process of organizational learning. In M. Dierkes, J. Child & I. Nonaka (eds), *Handbook of Organizational Learning*. Oxford: Oxford University Press, pp. 369–92.

Schwartz, Y. (2007) Un bref aperçu de l'histoire culturelle du concept d'activité [A brief glimpse of the cultural history of the concept of activity], Revue *@ctivités*, vol. 4, no 2, pp. 122–33.

Tomkins, S.S. (1995) *Exploring Affect: The Selected Writings of Sylvan S. Tomkins*, ed. E.V. Demos. New York: Cambridge University Press.

Vermersch, P. (1994) *L'entretien d'explicitation* [Explicitation interviews], Paris: ESF.

Vygotsky, L.S. (1997) *Pensée et langage* [Thought and Language]. (French translation from 1934). Paris: La Dispute.

Wagenaar, W.A. (1986) My memory: A study of autobiographical memory over six years. *Cognitive Psychology*, 18, 225–52.

4

FEELING AND MEANING IN THE SOCIAL ECOLOGY OF LEARNING

Lessons from play and games

Jay Lemke

Introduction

A more integrated conceptualization of processes of feeling and meaning-making is needed if we are to understand their joint role in learning. In settings where the consequences of each successive action are amplified by the responses of social partners or computer programs, longer-term trajectories of learning become more unpredictable and the role of feeling, affect, and emotion in co-determining them becomes more evident.

From computer games to play and learning in an informal after-school program, a more integrated view of feeling and meaning offers both better opportunities for understanding and greater challenges for researchers. Feelings need to be reconceived as more active, interactive, distributed, situated, culture- and event-specific, and functioning on and across multiple timescales, just as we have similarly re-conceptualized meaning-making processes in recent years. Learning can no longer be defined as progress relative to fixed criteria when goals are not externally determined and activity trajectories are relatively unpredictable; such naturalistic learning needs to be identified retrospectively from actual outcomes and assessed by cultural value judgments.

I offer both a more unified theoretical model of meaning-and-feeling and accounts of research settings in which unpredictable learning is always occurring, but is also always subordinate to play, playfulness, and having fun. In these feeling-rich, free-choice settings, so unlike the affectively constrained, over-controlled conditions of classrooms and occasions of formal learning, we discover challenging opportunities to study the ways in which the minute-to-minute and month-to-month integration of social-affective feelings and semiotic meaning-making both do and do not cumulate into what we may retrospectively decide to call learning for the individual and for the group.

This chapter seeks to contribute to the overall aim of this volume: helping us to understand the role of our feelings as we work and learn together. I want to begin by making clear how I understand these phenomena and some of the terms we might use to describe them. Then I will present in some detail an effort to re-conceptualize feeling and meaning-making processes in a more unified way, in order to better understand the inevitable learning of everyday social life. Finally, I hope to raise some questions about the relation of play and learning, as seen in my own recent research with young students in an innovative after-school program.

A few beginnings

We live in a culture with a history. We inherit certain beliefs and attitudes about work and play, learning and living, reason and emotion that may not serve us well as we try to describe and understand what happens when people interact together, making old and new meanings, feeling in various ways about one another and their task, and coming away from it all changed in smaller or larger ways.

Academic culture, at least in the United States, and from my observation also in most of northern Europe, either acquiesces in or has to work against a very long-standing attitude that feeling and emotion is somehow opposed to reason and interferes with it. We also tend to inherit the view that learning is a kind of work, and therefore that it is distinct from and opposed to play. In this view, work should be difficult and tension-producing, while play should be easy, fun, and relaxing. These two sets of attitudes are closely interdependent in the discourses of our everyday culture, and I believe they permeate academic culture as well and make the work of truly understanding these phenomena more difficult. They lead us astray.

Because of this a certain care with terminology is required. For example, I use the term *feeling* as the most general correlate of *meaning*, and I use both to name processes (i.e. as present-tense, active gerunds). I take feeling to include not just the classical emotions (fear, anger, desire, disgust, etc.), but bodily feelings such as drowsiness or nausea, and also what I would term the higher affects, those most determined by culture such as remorse or *weltschmerz*. I do not want to reify feelings – they are processes with ebb and flow, duration, variable intensity, and frequently defy rational classification or naming. But the very grammar of our language makes it awkward to do this and still speak fluently on these matters. In what follows I will try to clarify these points regarding feeling and meaning as two aspects of what, I will try to argue, is a single unified bodily semiotic process.

Let me begin with the notions of reason and learning. Reason was one of the mental faculties in the psychology of an earlier day. It has been mostly replaced today by the notion of cognition, and the original sense of cognition as information processing, having proved inadequate, was later amended to include the notion of a broader sense-making or meaning-making, thus including the notion of active interpretation and the assignment of significance, and not merely the collecting and organizing of information. Likewise, cognition could no longer be regarded as a phenomenon or process that happened solely in the head or in the mind. Materialist commitments have required some of us to locate it in neuro-physiological processes and others to conceptualize it as taking place in the broader interactions of a body in an environment. Cognition has been re-imagined in the last decades as embodied, situated, distributed, and heavily culture-specific (Bickhard and Terveen 1995; Bruner 1990; Clark 2008; Hutchins 1995; Lave 1988; Lutz 1988; Sheets-Johnstone 2009). Personally, I no longer find the original term *cognition* suitable for this new view, and I prefer the term *meaning-making*.

Notice that insofar as meaning inherently involves significance, it is always the case that meanings carry some feeling-sense with them: we feel their relative importance (or lack of it), the desirability of any imagined state of affairs, whether it is ordinary or surprising, normative or transgressive, serious or humorous, and so on. There are no meanings without feelings, or perhaps more aptly, we do not make meaning without having some feelings about the process and its result. Nevertheless, we have not felt the need to revise our notions about feeling and emotion to bring them more in line with our new vision of meaning-making. Feelings and emotions are still for the most part not regarded as active, material, embodied, situated, distributed, and culture-specific. And so they remain all the more difficult to integrate into our analyses of cognition or meaning-making. (See Chapter 4 this volume, by Cahour, for an excellent review of current psychological theories of emotion and efforts to relate it to cognition.)

What happens to the notion of *learning* when we shift to the newer view of cognition as meaning-making? Logically, it also has to move from being some internal mental change to be something that is mediated by our interactions with people and artifacts, something that is situated and distributed. Should we say that brains learn? That computers learn? That systems learn? What is the right unit of analysis? The question is unanswerable, I think, unless we integrate the notion of learning into a view of meaning-making that is not strictly tied to persons or organisms. Whatever processes we choose to call learning are taking place in complex, extended systems, which include human organisms (for present purposes; of course, non-human organisms learn, too) in interaction with their environments. Such systems, we now know, are organized on and across multiple levels of organization in terms of processes on multiple timescales. If we wish to speak of cellular learning, we must equally speak of group learning and societal-scale learning. There is no preferred level: learning happens in fact across many levels in such systems (Lemke 2000a).

So the notion of learning itself becomes a bit shaky. Does all change count as learning? Only adaptive change? Is learning, at the whole-organism level, synonymous with development? Does change that lasts only briefly count as learning, or must the visible effects of learning persist over times long compared with the time of the learning process itself? What about kinds of learning that themselves require very long times, are intermittent, and perhaps cumulative over a lifetime? I believe it is in fact rather arbitrary what kinds of change we choose to call learning. What we seem to do, when we are being careful about this, is to identify a persistent pattern of "behavior" or "activity" (which itself has to occur on and across many organizational- and time-scales of a complex system going well beyond the organism), and then retrospectively trace contributing experiences, activities, events in which it or its putative precursors are visible (if we have the necessary over-time records) to some series of originary experiences. Whether we call just those supposedly initial experiences learning, or so name the whole sequence ("maintained learning"?) is again somewhat arbitrary, it seems to me. What is the point of "learning" that doesn't last? How long does it need to last? Does it last if we never see it again? How do we determine the beginning or the end of the sequence, which we might call the *learning trajectory*?

Much of the concern in this volume is with group, joint, or collaborative learning. We see multiple organisms interacting with one another and with bits of their immediate material environment. What we don't see but readily infer is that what is happening also depends on memories, habits, and the ways in which utterances and images are interpreted in relation to past experiences and imagined futures. We see a whole system evolving in time, even if we are culturally disposed to focus on just the individual human organisms in it, one at a time. We also see, as interpreting members of a culture, that all this activity also makes sense as a time-stream of feelings: the participants' feelings for one another, moment to moment and longer term; their feelings about their task and actions and the actions of others; their feelings about the tools and artifacts around them, about the topics and ideas and symbols and propositions, about the meanings being made, and about themselves. Nor can we neglect here to include our feelings as researchers and analysts about all these other elements of the dynamical system we join ourselves into, either in real time or virtually through our records of events.

Actions are being performed, meanings are being made, feelings are being produced, all in deeply interdependent ways that sometimes produce what seems to us a smooth flow of activity and sometimes one that seems more erratic, broken, interrupted and (sometimes) resumed.

In my own research, first on computer games as actively engaged with and powerfully experienced media, and then with young students playing with such games and with one another and some older adults, I have found it impossible to understand the sequences of actions, meanings-made, and feelings separately (Lemke 2009, in press-a, in press-b). An integrated analysis is simply necessary. But to make such an analysis we need to overcome the traditional separation and opposition between Reason and Emotion, cognition and affect, meaning and feeling. I turn now to a sketch of how I have been attempting to do this.

Is meaning a kind of feeling? Or is it the other way around?

What role do those phenomena we variously call emotions, affects, or most generally *feelings* play in the ways we make meaning, the ways we make sense of and with the world and one another? How can we analyze rich media data that document living activity without slighting either the feelings that incline us to particular actions or the meanings through which we interpret possible actions?

If a synthesis of approaches, heretofore separate, to both meaning (based in semiotics) and to feeling (from the phenomenology of experience) is to be possible, then I believe that a necessary first step is to re-conceptualize feeling along the same lines that we have done in recent decades for meaning.

Meaning is a process: meaning-making, or semiosis. It can no longer be regarded in sophisticated analyses as being in-the-head, or even mental in the old Cartesian sense of belonging to a plane of existence apart from the material. It should rather be recognized as being *distributed*: between organisms and environments, subjects and objects, cooperating persons and mediating artifacts. The material substrate, i.e. the dynamical system in and through which meanings are made, includes what have traditionally been distinguished as "subjects" (with a misconceived monopoly on agency and intentionality), "objects" (wrongly regarded as passive or merely reactive), and "meditational means" (tools, symbolic representations, etc.).

Likewise meaning-making is *situated*, both in the sense of being influenced by the context of situation (setting, participants, affordances of objects), and in the sense of being distributed throughout the situation (indeed in some sense relevance to meaning-making, and to feeling, defines what is or is not part of the "situation").

It is an *active* process, not specifically in the sense of conscious intention and agency attributed only to humans, but in the sense that it is not simply a reaction to external stimuli: through it situations are changed, actions imagined, possible and probable relevant events anticipated, transfers of energy, matter, and information initiated, evaluations made.

Moreover, its modes of operation are not psychological universals, despite the desire of Christian theological universalism and humanist moral universalism to have it so. The specific processes and their deployment vary: across human communities, individuals, situations, and moments. It is *locally specific*, and in common parlance *culturally specific*.

And so is feeling. If we are to bring the analysis of meanings and feelings into productive conjunction, we need to reject older elements of our own cultural tradition according to which feelings, and more specifically what we are taught to call "emotions", are in-the-head, mentalistic phenomena, purely individual and intra-organismic, passive reactions, and psychologically universal. We need to re-conceptualize feeling as an active process, distributed in a dynamical system that includes ourselves and others and the material elements of the settings and networks of mediating artifacts that make feeling, like meaning, happen as it does in each instance.

We need to re-conceptualize feeling as distributed, situated, active, material, and locally, including broadly culturally, specific.

I will generally use the term *feeling* rather than either *emotion* or the more fashionable *affect*, both to distance my discussion from these older prejudices, and to ground an approach to the "higher affects" (pride, sense of nobility, playfulness, reverence, etc.) and the classic emotions (love, hate, anger, fear, etc.) in more general, proprioceptive and animating processes (e.g. feelings of drowsiness or alertness, calm or frenzy). I do so in parallel with the broad usage of *meaning* to cover everything from attentional focus or salience to evaluations and interpretations.

I hope it is clear that I am also taking both meaning and feeling processes to be "embodied" – just not embodied solely within the limits of single human organisms, though obviously, for us experientially, they are both very significantly dependent on perceptual and motor processes, on neurological and biochemical processes that do occur in some sense "within" us, though never, I think, insofar as they are relevant to meaning and feeling, without necessary connections to our interactions in and with a larger material environment.

Indeed, the perspective being offered here requires us to re-think what we mean by organism and environment, in biological terms, and especially what we mean by person and environment, in meaning-and-feeling terms. I will discuss this in more detail below, but enough for now to recall von Uexkull's (1928, 1982) notions of *Umwelt* and its less-well-known partners (*Wirkwelt* and *Merkwelt*). In brief, the organism interacts with its material environments in ways that make some of their physical features more or less salient as elements relevant to particular processes, and more broadly, the basis on which any boundary is drawn between inside and outside, me and it/you, changes from species to species, organism to organism, and event to event. We are originally and always integral parts of larger ecological (including sociocultural) wholes, and our separability as individual persons or organisms is a very locally specific and variable construction. While I will refine this initial description later (see discussion of the 3-level Model below), for now we shall put wholes before parts, asking always what happens within wholes to differentiate out the parts.

Let me conclude this section by returning briefly to the initial question: if we re-conceptualize feeling to bring it more in line with newer understandings of meaning, then what sort of relationship between the two are we aiming at?

We could, for example, try to reframe feeling as a specific kind of meaning. This is done quite naturally in studies of the meaning of feelings, for example in analyses of the semantics of feeling terms in natural languages (Bednarek 2008; Martin and White 2005). It could also characterize the somewhat imperialistic efforts of the field of cognitive psychology to theorize emotions solely as evaluations, and thus as a specific variety of meaning-making (Frijda 2004; Lazarus and Lazarus 1994). There is, I believe, a certain usefulness in trying to understand what kinds of meaning-making are most convergent with active feeling processes. We can use the tools of linguistic semantics and more generally of multimodal semiotics to characterize the meanings that accompany, inform, call forth, modulate, interpret, and evaluate feelings.

On the other hand, we could try to reframe meaning as a kind of feeling, to ground the meaning-making process in what might seem to be phylogenetically earlier feeling processes, and to in fact imagine that bodily feelings were the first signifiers, prior to words, to gestures, and indeed to humans. I believe that this is also a useful exercise. But it happens not to be the case that feelings are phylogenetically prior. Semiosis is as old as life itself, if not older (Hoffmeyer 2008). And so are feelings. Not perhaps in the sense of experienced qualia, which require a relatively high degree of system complexity, but at least in the sense of consequential indices of system and subsystem conditions. In fact, it is in these simplest possible systems which can do both semiosis and aesthesis (i.e. feeling) that we find the very same processes functioning as both.

And so, I believe, is it likewise the case in all more complex systems: it is the same material dynamical processes that do both meaning and feeling, though the extended networks of intermediating sub-processes and their participant bits of matter get larger, longer, slower, and more complicated as we approach the case of people-in-settings, and perhaps go beyond it.

Origins and fundamentals: feeling

There is a certain rhetorical awkwardness in my project. Ultimately, I want to maintain that meaning and feeling are a single process. Minimally, my proposal is that it can be useful to think of them as two complementary and mutually inform-ing aspects of a single process. But we all begin with rather different ideas about what each of them is, and so for a time I will need to discuss them separately in order to connect with our separate initial ideas about them.

Let me begin with feeling, then, because the view of it I am offering here is more radically divergent from common opinion, although 20 years ago I think my view of meaning would have been regarded as equally unconventional.

Let's start with a little naïve phenomenology. Most of the time, we are not in the grip of strong, named emotions. We are not feeling angry or frightened. We may be feeling energetic or lazy, alert or tired, hungry or restless. For all these feelings, we recognize that they have some sort of onset, perhaps unnoticed at the time, some sense of duration-till-now, some degree of, perhaps variable, intensity. We always feel somewhere on the cline between elated and depressed, hopeful and despairing, energetic and fatigued, hungry and sated. And most often somewhere in the unmarked middle range, call it Satisfactory, or call it nothing; no warning bells, no special conditions. But even this middle state is a distinct feeling, as we know from its absence or replacement by something more unusual.

We are taught to think of these feeling-conditions as conditions of our Selves or of our Bodies. But in fact they are always indices of the condition of us-in-the-world, of our actual and potential interactions with what we think of as our environment: other people, things, circumstances, places. We inherit the Cartesian error of think-ing of our Minds or Selves as separate from our Bodies, as Descartes himself inher-ited it from centuries of Christian theology separating the Soul from the Body, the realm of Spirit from that of Matter. We do not sit inside our own bodies looking out. We *are* our bodies, actively scanning and looking *for*, looking around, reacting to visual impressions, anticipating them, comparing expectation to current impres-sions, etc. And of course we are a great deal more: all the rest that our bodies are doing in the process of being and staying alive, much of which is some sort of inter-action with, action upon, or anticipation and imagination of what is happening "outside" us.

Both physics and biology tell us not to take the notion of the isolated organism too seriously, even while law, commerce, and religion want us to take the notion of our individual personhood, soul, and moral-legal-financial responsibility very seriously. But living organisms are dynamic, open systems: they exist only by virtue of their (our) transactions with the environment, only by continuously exchanging matter (air, food, waste), energy (heat, nutrition), and information (perception, action, language) with other elements of the larger ecological and social systems to which we belong. Interrupt any of these for a short time and we rapidly become less human, less healthy, and finally much less (indeed not at all) alive.

What we are is the product of what we are doing now, and what we have done in the past that leaves its traces. But much of that is not "our" doing, but what has been done to us, has happened to us, has happened in fact in our interaction with the environment, each affecting the other, until it becomes impossible to say what came only from the doing of the organism and what came only from the doing of the environment. In developmental biology, each organism begins as an integral part of some other organism (for us, a mother), which is itself already tightly integrated into larger units (a family, a community, a culture or society), and we gradually become more specialized and differentiated as a part of the mother-ecology system.

After birth, the child gradually comes to function more independently of the mother, even while inheriting the mother's family, community, places, language, and culture as it comes to interact with these in ways that very gradually become less totally intermediated by the mother. So the child comes to have its own unique integration, still as a part, into the same larger wholes as the mother.

I am presenting this picture of organisms as units within larger wholes because it is essential to understanding that feelings monitor not simply the organism as a somewhat artificially separable unit, but rather the status of the organism-in-environment system. They monitor relations and interactions, actual and potential, and as part of that function, of course, they also monitor some aspects that we can think of as more "internal".

But why do we have such feelings? What are their actual and evolutionary (i.e. past, ancestral), adaptive functions? If we feel tired, why does that matter? It matters because it is a relevant aspect of our stance to the environment, our readiness to respond to danger or opportunity in and from the environment. Likewise if we feel nauseous, that too is a feeling about our condition relative to the environment, and perhaps also to what we should be ingesting from it or not.

It has long been accepted that the strong, visceral, named emotions, such as fear and anger, desire and disgust, are indicators of whether we should seek out or flee from something in the environment, whether we should attack or run away, swallow or spit out. In these cases even more clearly, feelings are about interactions and relations, they monitor the conditions of us-in-it, and not simply our imagined "interiors".

In this sense, feelings are most fundamentally signals or indices of part-in-whole relevant conditions. For us humans, in the right "external" circumstances, these signals or indices are "felt" as what philosophers call experiential "qualia". This is what we recognize as the feeling of our feelings, what anger or fear or nausea feels like, to us, on some particular occasion. But a system does not need to have the elaborate neurological-hormonal machinery of a human body to benefit from having and responding to such signals. A single cell certainly has feedback mechanisms, chemical signaling, sensitivity to local and protoplasmic concentrations of various chemicals, and ways of reacting to them, which serve the same function (Hoffmeyer 2008); and so on up the scale of organismic complexity throughout the whole kingdom of life, from unicellular to human. The qualia of feelings may differ from species to species, as they do, I believe, from person to person, and even from occasion to occasion.

I have so far in this account of feelings neglected somewhat one key aspect. Feelings are not passive, any more than perceptual processes are. We do not simply sit and absorb passing photons, sound waves and chemicals. We actively seek them out, we scan, we anticipate, we actively listen and sniff. The most unique property of living systems is that we are restless. We are constantly interacting with the environment, we are constantly actively doing. We are moving, we are animate. (For a brilliant discussion see Sheets-Johnstone 2009). We generate our feelings actively just as much as the environment provokes them in us as responses. Feelings do not just monitor, they are the products and indexical signs of our interaction with everything around us.

From this account it should already be clear that feelings too are distributed (arising in a material system that goes beyond the isolated organism), situated (i.e. specific to the context of setting, place, other persons and things present), active (initiating, interactive), material (processes in and among material systems), and locally and culturally specific (different in detail across species, communities, individuals, cultures, and occasions). It may also seem that feelings are phylogenetically more primitive than meanings, and so cannot really be aspects of the same processes by which we make meanings. But this view underestimates radically the scope of meaning-making, i.e. semiotic processes in material systems. And it is to this complementary topic that I now turn.

Origins and fundamentals: meaning

We have become accustomed to thinking of the term *meaning* as a noun, a sort of abstract thing. But I try to use it consistently as a verb, an action process, something we do when we mean something. To remind us of this I will for now use the synonym, *meaning-making*, for the (material) process. And meaning-making, in turn, is a less formal term for *semiosis*, provided we keep in mind that here semiosis will always mean the actual dynamical material processes of making meaning, and not simply the abstract phenomenon.

Perhaps the most useful starting point for understanding meaning-making or semiosis is Charles Sanders Peirce's (1992, 1998) basic account of it as a sign-process. Semiosis is the process by which something comes to stand for something else to someone (or some thing). Peirce's great contribution was to see semiosis as an inseparable unity of three, rather than two, elements. The more classic view of a sign was simply a relation between a signifier (the thing that stands for something else) and a signified (the something else), a binary relation. And the incoherent theories of representation, and even of truth, that many people still struggle with today, have never gotten very far past this misleading over-simplification (Bickhard and Terveen 1995).

There are a number of unsupportable assumptions in the binary view, beginning, as Peirce noted, with the simple fact that no signifier (he calls this the *representamen*) ever by itself points to what it is a signifier of, i.e. to its signified (which he calls its *object*). How are we supposed to know what the word "horse" refers to? Or a scribble on a piece of paper? How do we know which "real-world reality" some verbal proposition is supposed to represent or be "in correspondence" with? The signifiers can't tell us that. We have to interpret some signifier as being a sign of some particular signified or object, or someone else has to tell us how to do this, or do it for us. In every case of semiosis there must be what I shall call, updating Peirce's terminology a bit for my purposes, an Interpreting System or *System-of-Interpretance* (hereafter, the S.I.).

The S.I. is the crucial third element, the one that "construes" (a term from Halliday 1978) a specific kind of relationship (not just "correspondence"; Peirce catalogues a couple of dozen specific logical and material relationships) between signifier (representamen) and signified (object). In doing so, the S.I. produces a response, a reaction, an interpretation, a meaning, which Peirce calls the "interpretant".

So, what is the simplest material system that can do semiosis? Consideration of this question leads to some further basics for a material model of meaning-making.

How should we distinguish between simple material (Aristotle's "efficient") causation and a semiotically mediated response by some system: between a chair that tips over when kicked and a paramecium that swims in the direction of some potential food? What tests can we apply to say that some instance is an example of semiosis or not?

As we interact in the world we encounter a lot of perceptions, actions, phenomena, doings and happenings, processes and things, places and occasions. For some of them to count for us as signs of others, there has to be some set of associations (our nervous systems seems good at producing these), such that there is not, for us, an equal likelihood that anything can go with (i.e. follow closely in time, or appear nearby in space) anything else. There is not an equal probability or frequency of all possible combinations. There is not total chaos, but for us there is some degree of order. Mathematically, this means that there is some degree of "redundancy" or informational order: some things are more likely to go with (predict) some other things.

These more likely combinations can then be regarded as provisional units on a larger scale, and to them can then be associated still more elements that tend to more often be associated with them. If we then encounter some of these, we tend to expect the others. Our expectations come to be context-dependent. In seeing one thing, we take it as a sign of the whole cluster, or context; or alternatively, having recognized a whole, a context, from some of its signs, we then have a particular set of expectations different from what we would have in some other recognized context.

For any given item that we encounter (thing, happening, whatever), there are various associations it might have, predicting various other items, and *which predicts which* is itself a function of the context. This works both ways, of course: seeing a pattern of associations, we infer a context; and inferring a context, we adjust our expectations. A particular set of associations predicts a context, and vice versa. Indeed, a pattern of associations constitutes the context. In the language of semiotics, these are indexical relations: patterns of associations index contexts, and contexts index the various elements and associations that constitute them: symmetric indexical contextualization. We are almost to meaning-making.

Will every S.I. construe experience in the same way? No, of course not. There is not one meaning-world for all organisms, or indeed for all individual people. Jakob von Uexkull's famous analysis of the *Umwelt* of a species argued persuasively that different species "see" the world differently, not just because they have different sensory organs, but because different aspects of the environment are differentially relevant to them. Their worlds are different in terms of the *Merkwelt*, or what is perceptually salient (the "marks" we notice), the *Wirkwelt* (the action-world, how the world is for us in terms of how we act on it), and most generally the *Umwelt* (a notion of ecological "niche" that is more fundamentally interactive and less positivistic than the one that is often used).

If we now imagine variation across different systems for interpretance, then these systems are redundant with (i.e. index with some probability) the redundancy between contexts and relations between primary categories or classes of items that are thus contextually redundant with one another. This is then a second-order contextualization (indeed it implies an extensive hierarchy of potential contexts of contexts of contexts, etc.), which Bateson (1972) referred to as "meta-redundancy". This was my first clue to characterizing meaning-making as selective indexical meta-contextualization.

Yes, that is a mouthful, and very abstract. It is a logical formulation, following Peirce and Bateson, but it is also very specific: selective contextualizaton means the S.I. connects a particular signifier and a signified (representamen and object), that it more likely does so in a particular context, and how these combine with one another depends on the particular S.I. In fact, the S.I. is semiotically defined by how it does this. And if we have a lot of S.I.s, then the particular pattern of connections associated with each may itself constitute a still higher order (meta-meta-redundancy) pattern, which we might call the culture of a community, with its divisions among roles and types of people who make different sorts of sense of their experiences.

But we started out to answer the question of what would be the simplest material system that could do semiosis, that could do selective, indexical, meta-contextualization? And what do we know, then, so far about such a material system?

It has to be capable of distinguishing an A from a B, i.e. it must be able to selectively respond to, or do, different things and processes. But it cannot be locked into a mechanical, 100% predictable, way of doing this. It has to be able to recognize, classify, and respond differently in different contexts. Note that I mean these only functionally, I don't mean "consciously" or "intentionally". It has to behave as if it made differential recognitions, selective responses, taking some things or processes as the same for purposes of its functional response (same response to each member of a set), but still be capable of responding differently (to the whole set) in a different context.

Can we imagine that by this definition a system as simple as a paramecium or similar single-cell organism can do semiosis? Think of it as a system, a black-box, with inputs and outputs. Imagine that here is a molecule in the water around it; it reacts internally to that molecule in a way that starts its cilia moving faster. Which way does it move? Well, as it moves it encounters other molecules, and its membranes can "classify" these molecules as like or different from the first one. Spinning about a bit, there is a higher concentration of these molecules in "front" than "behind", and it moves that way, and so on, in effect following the concentration gradient of the molecules, as we would say, towards its source (say, a food object). But it is unlikely that a single-celled paramecium forms some sort of representation of the food source, the destination. Nevertheless, it is not moving as a mechanical response to the chemical reaction of the molecule(s) to its outer membrane. It is integrating "information" from multiple molecule-encounters across time and space. It is itself much, much bigger than these molecules. And if the situation is different: if it's not hungry, if it's not got much energy reserve for swimming, if it also encounters "threat" molecules en route, then it will behave differently. Its response is context-dependent.

Consider then the analogous case for humans. You walk into a room, you breathe in an aromatic molecule along with some oxygen, the molecule interacts with a membrane of your olfactory bulb, you smell "coffee", and you do what the paramecium does, tracking the scent to its source. Or not, if you don't like coffee, if you're feeling wired from already having had too much, if the social situation is such that it's not appropriate just then, if you're anticipating heartburn, etc.

What is striking in these cases is that the signified, or more exactly in Peirce's terms, the interpretant, and behaviorally the visible motor response to the interpretant, occurs at a vastly different space–time scale from the encounter with the signifier. A molecule interacts with a membrane on a tiny microscopic scale, but the reaction occurs at the whole-organism scale, many orders of magnitude larger. And indeed the effect of contextualization, of context-dependence, depends, materially, on this. The paramecium finds food by integrating contextual information across space and time ("evaluating" the gradient of the concentration, the presence of other molecules, its current organismic state in other respects). So do we. A molecule interacts with a membrane in our nose, on a vastly smaller scale than our response, which is integrated over our whole organism, and across time (in memory and through action); our response occurs adaptively and functionally (or not) on the whole-organism scale.

Materially, semiosis happens across space and timescales of at least a few orders of magnitude (powers of ten) and in complex living systems, across many more. And it must. The S.I. must be sufficiently larger, and more durable in time, than the signifiers (interactions with these), so that it can assess and classify contexts, situation-types, involving itself and its interactions in its environment, across space and time, at least up to its own organismic scale, and in some cases well beyond (the space of exploratory behavior, the timescale of long-term memory).

Theoretical biologists such as Jesper Hoffmeyer (2008), Howard Pattee (1995), Stanley Salthe (1993), and others have argued that the emergence of life, or at least of functional cells, is co-occurrent with the first semiosis. Functionally, single cells make meaning, even if they do not have the complexity to represent it to themselves. Single cells, and maybe even large stretches of membrane, operate as S.I.s. They do semiosis, they take A as standing for B in a context-dependent way. Presumably, they learn, in the sense that developmentally they come to effectively, functionally, recognize, classify, and contextualize.

I think we have here a model for the material process of semiosis, of meaning-making, in its most rudimentary form. It is not less primitive in evolutionary terms or system-complexity terms than the rudiments of feeling as we described them in the previous section. They are co-eval; they arose together in the very origin of life.

What is our human interpretant in the case of the coffee smell? In all, it's rather complex, and extends across time, but it would include not just the indexical sign relation of the (interpreted) smell to coffee (as substance and perhaps taste, in imagination), but also the feeling of, say, desiring coffee, the anticipation of the feeling of well-being from drinking the coffee. Or alternatively, the feeling of jitteriness and disinclination to the coffee, or the anticipation of embarrassment if going for the coffee would be socially inappropriate. If we were to exclaim, "Oh, great, coffee!" this response would be arising jointly from the feelings as well as the interpreted meaning of the smell-as-sign-of-coffee.

I am not denying that there are different specific mechanisms, neural routes, evoked hormonal and neurotransmitter secretions, associated actions (glancing about, looking to others for confirmation) and interactions, that engage some of the same and some different parts of the body and the environment in those aspects of this very fully integrated process that we conventionally think of as the meaning-interpreting side and the feeling side of it.

But there is no fundamental divide, either materially in terms of scales and participating body elements, or functionally in terms of sense-making, evaluation, imagination, and impulse to further action. We do not make sense without the integration of feeling. We do not imagine meanings without this imagining being accompanied by some feeling. We do not evaluate by either meaning-processes or feeling-processes alone, but only by their unitary integration. The continuous flow of action (even when action is inhibition of movement) proceeds jointly from meaning-interpreting and feeling processes. Feelings are dependent largely on the same contextual factors as meanings in any particular occasion. The contexts we defined for meaning-making and their anticipated associations of As and Bs also include the feelings of these situations and expectations.

The process of meaning-making itself always has a feeling. It may in some cases be the feeling of calm disinterested inquiry (rarely enough!), but it is always a feeling, and more often it is the feeling of curiosity, of anticipation, of effortfulness, or of frustration. It can be the feeling of surprise, or dismay. The very pursuit of Reason is driven by Desire.

Nor are feelings ever meaningless. The same processes that produce the feelings we feel are there to produce the meanings of these feelings for us. A feeling is an active process, very often an active engagement with the world that tells us something about the condition of our interactivity in that moment, or over some duration. What it tells us would not be useful if it was not also a meaning, and we can say that feelings are interpreted as signifiers of something more, some conditions and processes in the organism and between us and the environment on still longer timescales than those which generated the feeling initially.

I do not want to push too hard or too dogmatically for the identity of feeling and meaning processes. It is enough that we understand them to be of the same order, with no unbridgeable gulf or opposition between them, and always functionally integrated. Nothing that the one does can it do without the other. Feeling and meaning are co-eval, co-evolved, functionally complementary, co-determined, and co-determinative.

[For further discussion of the meta-contextualization model of semiosis and the role of cross-scale processes, see (Lemke 1993, 1995, 2000b).]

But have we lost the human interpreter here? Are we speaking only of interactions with the natural environment and neglecting the social? I hope not. I am instead trying to argue that humans are not the only interpreters, that interpretation in the sense of context-dependent construal of consequential and adaptive functional response is as widespread as life itself and perhaps found even more widely. Of course humans with our complex nervous systems learn to respond in much more finely calibrated ways, across contexts of contexts of contexts, classifications and evaluations of classifications and evaluations, etc., both in the meaning-making and the feeling dimensions of this process.

My effort here is to bridge between more structural-systemic views of meaning and feeling and more experiential-processual views. The former is the dominant tradition for semiotics, while the latter has been more influential in accounts of our feelings.

I have emphasized at the outset that feeling-and-meaning is not a purely individual phenomenon. Strictly speaking it never is. The material system in which meaning-making and feeling arise is always the organism-in-action-interacting-with-the-environment. The environment here significantly includes other humans and human-made, symbolically interpretable artifacts, and through them larger-scale, more slowly changing systems of cultural conventions, infrastructure processes, etc.

Group processes are a special case, and they invoke the biographical histories of the participating members, and so their social and cultural backgrounds, for each act of meaning- and feeling-mediated interaction. What is problematic, often enough outside laboratory studies and special cases, is: Who are the participating collaborators? What couplings of their trajectories of activity count as collaboration, insofar as our concern is with the role of joint activity in learning? And this applies to the group as well as the individual as a unit of analysis for learning. Groups certainly learn in ways that go beyond learning by individuals, but I believe that the "group" in the sense of the set of interacting individuals is the wrong unit. The right unit is a wider material system, including the individuals, but also the mediating artifacts; and as we extend this system over time, its relevant connections and inputs expand in ways that can be difficult to limit (e.g. to the noise-level or temperature of the ambient environment).

So we come finally to some actual cases of people working, playing and learning together. The contingencies of our individual meaning-and-feeling interpretations and construals of one another's actions, gestures, and talk multiply the space of possible meanings we can make together and the possible feelings we can share together or engender in one another.

Work, play, and learning

When people work together we make meaning together and we generate feelings, shared or not, of which we tend to be aware and which make some sort of difference in the probabilities for our next action. In this respect play and work do not differ. Particular instances may differ in the specific feelings involved, just as they do in the particular meanings at stake. All social activity leaves traces: in the participating organisms, in the material environment. Those traces are meaningful in the sense that they can usually be interpreted by members of a culture according to shared or at least complementary conventions. These may be memory traces in bodies, or they may be signs inscribed on paper, or they may just be a rearrangement of the furniture. But these meaningful traces should, by our prior arguments, always also be "feelingful": when we encounter them we do not simply interpret their meaning in terms of matters of fact or states of affairs, we also respond to them emotionally and evaluatively.

Over time, next processes (e.g. the next meeting of the group, or the next hour of the meeting) become more or less probable depending on the meanings we make, including those made on the basis of traces left by previous processes. Again, work and play are not different in these basic respects, neither semiotically nor as felt. If learning is persistent change in how meanings are made and how actions are performed, it is also persistent change in how we feel about actions and meanings (and persons, things, and ourselves). Does learning then take place in, or across, every action, every experience?

To some extent I think it does, if we focus not on isolated short-term events as being when learning occurs, but focus rather on over-time trajectories (over times long compared with what we might usually think of as a single learning event) that include everything that is happening in our lives. Some shifts in the probabilities of some kinds of future actions are always taking place. We decide, culturally and personally, which of these changes are important ones and which are not or only much less so. We look back from the vantage point of some important action or event and try to recapitulate which earlier events were the significant ones that initiated or sustained the trajectory leading up to this important one. Depending on what matters to us, we can say that we are never *not* learning. (Or at least that whatever we are experiencing is potentially changing the probabilities for future actions and events in some durable way.)

I am making this rather abstract argument because I want to be precise about what I mean by saying that work and play are no different as sites for learning. I don't believe we can know in advance whether what is learned in play or what is learned by serious work will ultimately prove to be the more important learning. Obviously every culture makes judgments about what kinds of learning are most important and, indeed, in complex societies like our own there are a lot of different systems of belief about such matters (religious, scholastic-academic, practical-everyday, professional, institutional-corporate, etc.). Even in our own dominant culture there are strong disagreements about the relative importance of school-learning, on-the-job learning, or learning from inspired experiences. But there is a widespread, and I believe quite erroneous, belief that what is learned in play or in experiences whose main aim is pleasure is of little value relative to serious learning.

This issue has immediate implications for the concerns expressed elsewhere in this volume regarding how feelings can enhance collaborative activity that has some sort of problem-solving or task-completion goal. Some authors here argue (and I would agree) that it is not just the smooth integration of collaborative contributions that advances the goal, but also, indirectly, the inevitable tensions and conflicts that arise during group activity. I would also argue that it is not just the serious, get-down-to-business activity that advances the goal, but also the playful, let's-have-a-laugh activity. Perhaps more significantly, there is also often in academic discussions of these phenomena an implicit commitment to the successful achievement of the goal, and an implied recommendation that feelings be "managed" so as to maximize the chances of success.

But that seems to me to be a potentially dangerous attitude. Very often participants in collaborative activity do not feel good about what is going on. We feel bored, frustrated, out of sorts. We would rather get up and leave. Our dominant culture teaches that we should suppress these feelings, that they are immature and that we ought to do our jobs anyway. But should we? The affective dimension of our experience is tuned by millions of years of evolution to provide us with a feel for opportunities and threats. We tend to marginalize such feelings when they conflict with modern institutional demands on the grounds that these instincts did not evolve under modern conditions. But neither did our faculties for meaning-making evolve under modernity, and we certainly do not believe we should ignore their import for our decisions. Insofar as these two faculties are in fact one, the conclusion, I think, ought to be that our feelings are also well adapted to modern conditions, that they operate just as well as our meaning-making does, and that they should just as much be taken into account in deciding on courses of action.

We do live in a society of injustice and widespread inhumanity, not just in distant parts of the world, or for the very poor, but for almost all of us. We live in an economic and political system which demands that in order to survive people do things they don't feel good about. And this is patently an artificial order of things. Societies do not need to be like this, certainly not nearly to the extent that our own is. Our feelings tell us what our reason confirms: that not all collaborative activity imposed on us by institutions is actually in our best interest, individually or collectively. From a research perspective, we need to understand when collaboration ought to fail rather than succeed, and paying attention to the role of feeling is essential for such an analysis.

When play comes first

In recent research conducted with colleagues and students at the University of California, San Diego in the Laboratory for Comparative Human Cognition (so named long ago by its founder, Michael Cole), the research team has been observing and participating in activities involving students aged 5 to 12 and university undergraduates at an after-school center in the city.

The young students stay on after the end of their formal school day to wait for working parents to come an hour or two later to pick them up. The undergraduates are enrolled in a class on communication and learning, which focuses on their own learning from field experiences in this after-school program. The school provides two staff members, the university provides two, and in addition members of the research team are regularly present. In fact roles often blur, with researchers, staff, and undergraduates interacting in often much the same ways with the kids. This model is a variant of the well-known "Fifth Dimension" model developed by Michael Cole and the lab over many years (Cole and Consortium 2006).

What we are all doing is playing: playing with each other and playing, in our part of the after-school center, with educational computer games. Of course a lot else is also going on, with the same or overlapping participants: laughter exercises in a large open-space room, arts and crafts activities, performance and drama activities, ball-playing, and innumerable playtime innovations of the kids' own devising. Some of it is chaotic. This is real life, not a controlled experimental laboratory.

What is happening is documented in part by fieldnotes, written on a daily basis (twice per week) by the undergraduates in an online database (a page or two per day for each of 12–20 undergraduates) as well as by the researchers, and by video and some audio-only recordings, made once or twice a week by the research team, but also at times by the undergraduates and even now and then by the kids themselves.

In the first nine months of this research we have been exploring basic phenomena. What is happening? What is important (to us, to the kids, to the undergraduates)? What kinds of learning are taking place? What kinds of activities? What sorts of meanings are being made? What sorts of feelings are being produced? How are these various elements or aspects integrated with one another?

We had originally planned something quite different. We were offered the chance to try out a well-known educational computer game, *Quest Atlantis*, developed at Indiana University by Sasha Barab and his team, (Barab et al. 2007, 2010) in a regular class in the 7th or 8th grade of the school. But the Grade 8 teacher was teaching this class for the first time and preferred to wait, while the undergraduates were already committed to the after-school program in terms of their time schedule. So we decided to see what would happen if we introduced a fairly serious (but also playful) learning game to a group of kids who were significantly younger than the age for which the game was designed.

The kids found the game fascinating. Especially the youngest ones were eager to go to the computer room at the school and try out something new. But this was after-school. It was not an academic program as such. These kids had already spent a long day in school and what they wanted to do was play. So they, and in time all of us, found ways to improvise around the original *Quest Atlantis* game to make it more fun.

The whole story is too long and interesting to be told here, but in short what happened was that the kids mostly played with each other and used the game and its virtual world as a springboard, a virtual play-space and inspiration for many kinds of play not specifically imagined by the creators of the game. In this, the undergraduates became their accomplices and play partners, as well as being their mentors and friends. The research team joined in to the extent we could do so and still manage to come away with some useful video records. What we saw was endless creativity, punctuated by briefer periods of boredom and sometimes outright rejection of the activity, but then resuming it when some further inspiration was found for fun and play.

We also saw a lot of learning, a lot of collaboration on tasks, serious problem-solving in the pursuit of play goals, and the energy, determination, creativity, and free spirit of kids at play. Play came first, but learning followed along.

When play comes first, the range and visible intensity of feelings is far greater than what you would see in a classroom or a well-organized, institutionally circum-scribed "serious" learning activity. So the essential role of feelings in everything that happens is correspondingly far more obvious. So also is their inseparability from meaning-making and the conduct of activity. In classrooms or most institu-tional settings in our society, the range of "appropriate" or permitted emotion displays is very narrowly limited, especially for adults. With younger children in a relatively free-wheeling setting where only total chaos and unsafe or morally dubi-ous activity are effectively policed by the staff, you see and hear everything from crying to whoops of joy and triumph, from close bonds of friendship to overt hos-tility; caring and tenderness to meanness and aggression, boredom and frustration to total concentration and engagement, silliness to insightfulness, anticipation to disap-pointment, simple selfishness to altruistic sharing and sacrifice.

Note that in my vocabulary of description I am mixing conventional emotion names with what are more usually activity names or qualities. I do this because the true range of feelings on display is vast. I have no sympathy for efforts to define a mere dozen or fewer primary or fundamental emotions. That is a cultural project of Western universalism and quite untrue to the experience of participation in these complex activities. While it is likely the case that there are some biologically well-grounded feelings, from hunger to fear, which we inherit from our primate and mammalian ancestors, what those feelings mean to us, and all the culturally newer feelings that arise from participation in our complex social and technological milieu, form a vast system of differentiated feelings equally as complex as the semantics of a language or the meaning system of a culture. Indeed we have many feelings which are "too specific for words", that are as un-nameable in language as the shapes of clouds or mountains are un-describable. If you want to find the semiotic representation of the specificity of human feelings, you need to turn to the writing of poets and the works of artists, rather than the classifications of psychologists or the linguistic primitives of semanticists. Just as text, not words, are the units of meaning in language, so the subtle over-time arcs of multi-dimensional feelings, not biological primitives, are the units of human feeling.

Does this mean that realistic analysis of human activity, including learning and collaborative working together, needs the skills of a poet or artist to sense and represent? It may be so. I am already persuaded that writing textual articles, even with a few exemplary photographs, will be wholly inadequate to telling this story. Feelings, even more so than meanings, are expressed, and felt, over time. To show them, video is a far more appropriate medium than text (with due deference to the poets) and is also richer in providing essential context than is the still photographic image. While academic publishers shy away from the costs of color plates in our books, and video on DVD discs remains a somewhat clumsy compromise for print works, online publishing makes multimedia presentations of research on human activity perfectly feasible today. It ought to become the norm in our field (Derry et al. 2010; Goldman et al. 2007).

Collaborative play and learning

By the spring of 2011 the kids in our after-school program had been playing with the *Quest Atlantis* gameworld for several months and were getting bored with it. The focus of their emotional interest continued to be on playing with one another and on their social relationships with their peers and with the university undergraduates. One of the undergraduates came up with an idea to renew interest in the game: use the gameworld as a backdrop for the kids to make a movie, with their game avatars as the actors. This would require them to move their avatars into a common virtual space and perhaps enact a script, or improvise. But what actually happened was far more unpredictable and spontaneous, and raises interesting questions about what counts as collaboration. Does there need to be a common goal for joint activity to count as collaboration? Can people learn together even if they are working against one another's goals, as in a competitive activity? Am I a collaborator if my only contribution is to offer encouragement or make a joke that defuses tension among others?

One undergraduate, Ian, was doing a side project to make a video of our work at the site and so had borrowed a professional-quality video camera, which he also planned to use to video-record a computer screen on which all the students' avatars would perform. But well before any script or plan could be worked out, I mentioned to the group that that day was Ian's birthday. Someone then proposed we hold a birthday party for him in the "Build World", a special area of the gamespace where the kids had built their own houses and castles, landscaping, domes and swimming pools. The chief architect of this space, an 11-year-old girl we will call Selena, proposed that the party take place around the pool she had attached to her treehouse, a central landmark in the Build World.

She was already there, and one by one three other kids, ages 8 and 9, "teleported" their avatars into the Build World and navigated their way to the treehouse and pool. One of them decided to start "dancing", an option in the avatars' behavioral menu. The others then asked him how to do this, and he both described it and moved over from his computer to theirs to show them. Selena also went over to show one of the other boys how. The four avatars now started dancing in and around the pool. Ian then asked if Selena, who was in effect the host of the party, had any "refreshments", and she shifted her avatar to a completely different "world" in the *Quest Atlantis* game to find what turned out to be pumpkin pie and used her skills as a virtual world builder to then place a pie near the pool.

A younger boy (Sean, age 9) now decided that one pie was not enough and used the building skills he had learned a few weeks before from Selena to duplicate the pie, eventually ending up with four identical pies (one for each of them). Throughout this, Ian was making video of the proceedings, and so was I. We were also both making suggestions, praising their dancing, talking about the pies and how other kids would be jealous they were not here for this, and more. The kids were commenting on each other's dancing, on the party, wishing Ian a happy birthday, and responding to each other and discussing the pies. This was the first time that four avatars had gathered in one virtual place and co-enacted a joint activity. It was a major collaborative accomplishment, given their general computer skills and current skills with this virtual world, and it was a culmination of much that had gone before, including the creation of the treehouse, learning initially how to find one another in the vast online world, and learning how to create and manipulate objects in it. The first time even two avatars had managed to interact in the virtual world had been only several weeks before and it was still a rare event. *Quest Atlantis* had been designed mainly as a single-player game, not as a multi-player cooperative space.

Was this truly collaborative activity? Was there a common goal? Or were the various participants each enacting their own activities: Ian making a video, me stimulating the kids to have fun, Selena playing hostess, Sean showing off what he could do, the other boys playing with the ability to dance? I think that it makes the most sense to see here a set of intersecting and interacting trajectories of play. Avatars came and went at different times, all being at the pool together only briefly. The kids themselves moved around during the event and were frequently paying attention to different visual spaces, different real people and computer screens. They were moving through a hybrid reality, part peopled computer classroom, part partially and temporarily shared virtual space.

And yet this was collaborative play, or joint play, and not simply kids on parallel and independent trajectories. The trajectories influenced one another, through spoken exchanges and watching others' avatars on screen, as well as through doing things meant to be seen or enjoyed by others. Emotionally, there was a great deal of laughter and shouting playfully at one another. Egging one another on, feeling pride in demonstrating a skill or showing off, concentrating on performing a desired action correctly (both technically and visually-for-others) in terms of timing, placement, movement, and enactment. There was a shared and collaboratively produced mood of celebration, laughter, and fun. The unity of the activity for all the participants was as much grounded in shared feelings as in shared meanings or actions.

Was there learning? By my earlier argument, we need to ask here how this event may have been part of one or more longer learning trajectories. Yes, two boys learned how to make their avatars dance, and learned it seemingly here and now. But Selena was also extending her trajectory of creating objects in one gameworld based on information found in another such world, and was learning to adapt it as a resource for social play in this situation. Sean was practicing duplicating an object and moving it around, a relatively new skill for him, and also adapting it in much the same way. All the kids were developing their skills of coordinating their avatars in time and space, and navigating to a common location, a process of learning extended over many weeks.

This last skill is one we can trace for two of the kids back to their first success at doing so seven weeks before, in yet another "world" of the game. And we can trace it forward for them in particular one week later when they initiated a game of hide and seek, or chase and catch, in that same world, in the middle of which they were joined by two others and briefly once again four avatars were in the same place, and this time they used another behavior menu option to have their avatars do karate moves and play at being ninjas. That option is in the same menu as the dance moves from the birthday pool party the week before.

There are other similarities between these events a week apart, primarily in the participants' social relationships and how they were using the game as a way to play with one another and challenge one another's competence, competing to see who could best the other in a game within a game. There was the same showing off, the same bravado and bravura, the same teasing of a friend who was also a sometime rival. And in both cases, this intimate competition did not take place face to face. The boys were at separate workstations, interacting visually through their avatars, though calling out to each other across the room. In the original experience several weeks previously, they had moved back and forth to each other's computer screens to see where the other was, but now they were competent enough and comfortable enough with their new virtual world skills to no longer need to do this. Once again there was a shared mood, different from the celebratory play of the birthday party, more one of playful competition.

There is no space here to present these events in detail, as I will hope to do elsewhere, but I believe that they illustrate both social and technical learning in collaborative play, where feelings are motivating actions whose consequences, including responses by others, engender further feelings along interacting feeling-and-meaning trajectories. (For further discussion see Lemke 2009; in press-a; in press-b).

I cannot, however, imagine any purely descriptive or discourse-analytic presentation of this material that would be sufficiently intelligible to convincingly demonstrate these points, without showing the video data itself.

Issues of evidence in the analysis of collaborative activity

If we accept that feeling and meaning-making are so entwined and integrated in collaborative social activity, whether work, formal learning, or play, that we need to analyze both dimensions to draw valid conclusions about either, then we need to consider what counts as appropriate evidence in such studies. When I look at transcripts of these interactions, I can hear the voices, the enthusiasms, the doubts and antagonisms, the degrees of engagement and disengagement. But a reader without access to the video cannot. No formal system of notation will convey such matters as well as our inherent empathic response to seeing a video or being present at the event. When I look at still images extracted from the video data, showing key moments, or facial expressions of strong emotion, I can feel again something of what the image captures, but a reader may well interpret the images very differently, lacking their real-time dynamical context.

Action taking place in time: movement, dynamic shifting of voice pitch, stress, loudness, pacings and rhythms and breaks with them, continuities and temporal cause – effect sequences – all contribute to a phenomenological feeling for the event in a way that the static representations of transcripts and still images cannot. No doubt these other, out-of-time inscriptions have their important uses, to allow us to more readily see patterns across time and which may not depend on temporal dynamics more than simply through sequencing. But our reliance on them is also a function of the older technologies of print, on which we are fortunately no longer dependent.

I believe that the feeling dimension of activity is particularly sensitive to real-time dynamics and requires real-time media for the evidentiary support of inferences and claims. And because I see feeling and meaning as so inseparable in the course of action, I believe that our accounts of even the meaning-making aspects of an activity lose reliability if we do not take into account the unitary real-time flow of feeling-and-meaning.

I do not want to push this argument too far. Certainly a great deal can be done without direct access to video records of activity, and through partial representations of speech alone or speech and gross annotations regarding contexts of co-occurring activity. But I do believe that we need to understand what we may be missing in order to have confidence that analysis based on such representations is sufficient for a particular purpose or correctly interpreted as evidence for some claim (see also Lemke 2007).

I hope that the arguments in this chapter will provide a useful perspective for the many researchers who today are devoting so much effort to the important study of affect in our learning together.

References

Barab, S., Dodge, T., Tuzun, H., Job-Sluder, L., Carteaux, R., Gilbertson, J., and Heiselt, C. (2007) "The Quest Atlantis Project: a socially-responsive play space for learning", in B. E. Shelton and D. Wiley (eds), *The Educational Design and Use of Simulation Computer Games* (pp. 159–86), Rotterdam, NL: Sense Publishers.

Barab, S., Gresalfi, M., and Ingram-Goble, A. (2010) "Transformational play: Using games to position person, content, and context", *Educational Researcher*, 39(7): 525–36.

Bateson, G. (1972) *Steps to an Ecology of Mind*, New York: Ballantine.

Bednarek, M. (2008) *Emotion Talk across Corpora*, New York: Palgrave Macmillan.

Bickhard, M. H., and Terveen, L. (1995) *Foundational Issues in Artificial Intelligence and Cognitive Science* (Vol. 109), Amsterdam: Elsevier/North Holland.

Bruner, J. (1990) *Acts of Meaning*, Cambridge, MA: Harvard University Press.

Clark, A. (2008) *Supersizing the Mind: Embodiment, Action, and Cognitive Extension*, New York: Oxford University Press.

Cole, M., and Consortium, D. L. (2006) *The Fifth Dimension: An After-School Program Built on Diversity*, New York: Russell Sage Foundation Publications.

Derry, S., Pea, R., Barron, B., Engle, R., Erickson, F., Hall, R., et al. (2010) "Conducting video research in the learning sciences", *Journal of the Learning Sciences*, 19(1): 3–53.

Frijda, N. (2004) "The psychologists' point of view" in M. Lewis and J. M. Haviland-Jones (eds), *Handbook of Emotions* (pp. 59–74), New York: Guilford.

Goldman, R., Pea, R., Barron, B., and Derry, S. (eds) (2007) *Video Research in the Learning Sciences*, Mahwah, NJ: LEA Publishing.

Halliday, M. A. K. (1978) *Language as Social Semiotic*, London: Edward Arnold.

Hoffmeyer, J. (2008) *Biosemiotics*, Scranton, PA: University of Scranton Press.

Hutchins, E. (1995) *Cognition in the Wild*, Cambridge, MA: MIT Press.

Lave, J. (1988) *Cognition in Practice*, Cambridge, UK: Cambridge University Press.

Lazarus, R., and Lazarus, B. (1994) *Passion and Reason*, New York: Oxford University Press.

Lemke, J. L. (1993) "Discourse, dynamics, and social change", *Cultural Dynamics*, 6(1): 243–75.

Lemke, J. L. (1995) *Textual Politics: Discourse and Social Dynamics*, London: Taylor & Francis.

Lemke, J. L. (2000a) "Across the scales of time: artifacts, activities, and meanings in ecosocial systems", *Mind, Culture, and Activity*, 7(4): 273–90.

Lemke, J. L. (2000b) "Opening up closure: Semiotics across scales", in J. Chandler and G. van de Vijver (eds), *Closure: Emergent Organizations and their Dynamics* (pp. 100–11), New York: New York Academy of Sciences.

Lemke, J. L. (2007) "Video epistemology in-and-outside the box: traversing attentional spaces", in R. Goldman-Segall, R. Pea, B. Barron and S. Derry (eds), *Video Research in the Learning Sciences* (pp. 39–52), Mahwah, NJ: Erlbaum.

Lemke, J. L. (2009) "Multimodality, identity, and time", in C. Jewitt (ed), *The Routledge Handbook of Multimodal Analysis* (pp. 140–50), London: Routledge.

Lemke, J. L. (2012) "Multimedia and discourse analysis", in J. P. Gee and M. Handford (eds), *Routledge Handbook of Discourse Analysis*, (pp. 79–89), London: Routledge.

Lemke, J. L. (2013) "Thinking about feeling: affect across literacies and lives", in O. Erstad and J. Sefton-Green (eds), *Learning Lives: Transactions, Technologies, and Learner Identity*, (pp. 57–69) Cambridge, UK: Cambridge University Press.

Lutz, C. (1988) *Unnatural Emotions*, Chicago: University of Chicago Press.

Martin, J. R., and White, P. R. R. (2005) *The Language of Evaluation: The Appraisal Framework*, New York: Palgrave Macmillan.

Pattee, H. (1995) "Evolving self-reference: matter, symbols, and semantic closure", *Communication and Cognition*, 12(1-2): 9–27.

Peirce, C. S. (1992) *The Essential Peirce: Selected Philosophical Writings* (Vol. 1), Bloomington, IN: Indiana University Press.

Peirce, C. S. (1998) *The Essential Peirce: Selected Philosophical Writings* (Vol. 2), Bloomington, IN: Indiana University Press.

Salthe, S. (1993) *Development and Evolution*, Cambridge, MA: MIT Press.

Sheets-Johnstone, M. (2009) *The Corporeal Turn*, Charlottesville, VA: Imprint Academic.

von Uexkull, J. (1928) *Theoretische Biologie*, Frankfurt: Suhrkamp.

von Uexkull, J. (1982) "The theory of meaning", *Semiotica*, 42(1): 25–87.

SECTION 2
Social relations and identities

5

KNOWLEDGE CO-CONSTRUCTION – EPISTEMIC CONSENSUS OR RELATIONAL ASSENT?

Crina Damşa, Sten Ludvigsen and Jerry Andriessen

> The affect arising from this cognitive synchrony is something human beings seem inclined to enjoy. In this setting it can serve to animate and sustain a cognitive exploration – to an extent that might be beyond what could be achieved in solitary conditions of learning. Yet that quality of affect is not an easy or an inevitable consequence of the contract for joint activity.
>
> (Crook, 2000: 166)

Introduction

Many collaborative learning tasks are complex, open-learning situations, for which the nature of collaboration itself is an adventurous process, with its outcomes requiring an exploration of new territory (Ludvigsen, Rasmussen, Krange, Moen & Middleton, 2011). Many learning activities are intended to happen in such situations of openness, and this can also be the case in highly structured knowledge domains within institutionalised education settings. When closely analysing what goes on in our daily actions, we realise that we must constantly foresee the uncertainty of the next moment. When individuals operate in a group, this capacity to foresee future developments and forward acting is part of a larger process we call meaning making, which we assume has a strong social component: the relations with others in the group and the emotions arising during interactions.

The idea of meaning making is employed here as the foundational concept that provides the basis to focus on specific aspects of the collaborative process. Meaning making is achieved through actions within specific contexts (Linell, 1998). Static descriptions of those meanings by researchers do not capture the streams of experience, knowledge and language activities of learners. Moreover, challenges, dilemmas, conflicts and tension are important in the meaning making process, such as when individuals participate in group activities. Although these meanings are vague, their vagueness supplies the power in regulating social and cognitive processes

(Valsiner, 2002). In collaborative learning situations, however, this regulation does not necessarily lead to shared understanding (Damşa, Kirschner, Andriessen, Erkens, & Sins, 2010), and sometimes the sharing of a learning situation does not entail a full involvement with the content by the participants. Hence, how participants build on ideas during interaction crucially depends on how they take the others' ideas into account and co-construct knowledge together with the others.

In this chapter, we attempt to describe and interpret co-construction of knowledge and how shared understanding is achieved in interaction between participants in a collaborative learning activity. Collaborative actions are distributed over time and space, while meaning evolves continuously. Hence, our study draws upon socio-cultural approaches (Vygotsky, 1978; Wertsch, 1995) in interpreting a series of interactional sequences extracted from the collaborative activities of a student group working on their bachelor thesis project. By taking social interaction as the main assertion, we choose not to take particular types of collaboration for granted but conceive it as a 'phenomenon' that must analytically be accounted for based on the empirical data at hand. In interpretation, we do not establish categories for analysis before we have sufficiently understood the interactions as displayed in the protocol. Our analytic procedure is described in more detail in the Method section.

In this chapter, we focus on depicting epistemic, social and relational aspects in students' interactions, and we attempt to understand how these aspects interrelate and, possibly, affect the interaction process. While various conceptualisations of collaboration capture important aspects of this process (e.g., people use each other and each others' expertise and skills to solve complex problems), they seem to overlook the idea of the gaps (see Graesser, Person, & Magliano, 1995) Ludvigsen et al., 2011) that participants often must cover in order to attain the state in which collaboration is beneficial for learning. The assumption in our study is that students come with different experiences and knowledge in relation to the knowledge domain. The implication is that there are gaps between students' knowledge and the desired level of knowledge required to solve a problem or task (see Graesser et al., 1995). These are gaps of epistemic nature. Furthermore, in collaborative settings, gaps can appear at social and relational level. Becoming aware of these gaps, closing them to some extent, is a fundamentally interactional process (Crook, this volume). It requires efforts from participants at all levels, during which they relate to each other, and deal with each other's goals and motives.

We will address gap-closing as an aspect of meaning making through an analysis of students' talk while they attempt to solve a specific problem within the field of educational research. To solve this problem, they must agree about a proper conceptualisation of the research problem and an operationalisation of the main concepts. The goal of our analysis is to understand and explain how students collaboratively deal with concepts and ideas inside this knowledge domain, how they co-construct their understanding of these concepts, and how they deal with each others' contributions, especially by closing gaps. The research questions we address are as follows: *How do students engage with concepts in order to solve an open problem? And: Which aspects − epistemic, relational and social − become activated in the interaction process and how do they affect this interaction?*

Perspectives on collaboration: social, epistemic and relational aspects

Various studies acknowledge the importance of the cognitive aspects in the collaborative process, but also of the social and relational aspects. The latter can, in some cases, determine the success or failure of the collaboration. These different aspects of collaboration are rarely studied as connected. We will here highlight a few studies that have included as least two of the aforementioned aspects. Roschelle and Teasley's study (1995) indicated that small group collaboration does not take place simply by putting people together and that interpersonal relationships need to be taken into account to understand the engagement of team members to coordinate their understanding. A case in point is the research of Barron (2000), which included multiple case studies of sixth-grade triads. These groups have to deal with what Barron calls both a relational space and a content space, which compete for limited attention. Her study on less successful groups indicates that relational issues, behaviourally expressed (e.g., violation of turn-taking norms, competing claims of competence, or difficulties in gaining the floor) can hinder or stimulate participants in dealing with and capitalising on the insights that are constructed in the group. She emphasises the complexity of the co-constructive process, since participants need to monitor and evaluate both their own individual and the others' epistemic processes. Moreover, she indicates that the relational aspects of collaboration are just as complex as the cognitive ones and that identity issues might be inherent to the relational ones. Engle and Conant's study (2002) on productive disciplinary engagement points at 'positioning' not only as a strictly socio-cognitive performance, but also as involving emotional displays, perseverance in having their ideas heard and attention over the sessions. Other studies too (Hogan, Nastasi, & Pressley, 2000) point at the less favourable effect of difficulties regarding relational aspects of the interaction. Higher rates of affirming, agreeing and accepting remarks within the group allowed successful groups to sustain a higher level of reasoning in a knowledge-building task, whilst discrepancy in willingness to understand one another led to ineffectual communication.

Although, in collaboration, diversity between people is considered a resource for generating new meaning or ideas, it can become difficult to channel the diverging, and sometimes opposing, stances towards a constructive interaction. In a collaborative setting, disagreements and breakdowns can occur when people press for conflicting answers about something that calls for resolution, when individuals experience difficulties in constructing a connection between the goals of their actions and the object and motive of the collective activity (Barab & Plucker, 2002), when diverging perspectives are proposed by partners in the collaboration (Barron, 2000), or when learners reflectively analyse their collaborative activities and questions. Disagreements are discussed by various studies (Engeström, 1999; Matusov, 2001; Wickman & Östman, 2002). Resolving disagreements in a productive manner involves, to an extent, addressing tensions of relational nature, thus employing the 'dialogic potential' of the participants, but ultimately in a way that creates a starting point for an interaction that assures epistemic progress. According to Wickman and Östman (2002), this process rests on learners noticing and filling gaps by construing new differences and similarities in relation to what is immediately intelligible to them; negotiation can be seen as the process that leads to achieving agreement among agents (Baker, 1995). Baker (1999; 2009) points out that achieving 'real' agreement presupposes joint understanding whereby two aspects are highly relevant. First, to create shared understanding requires co-construction; this cannot be done through simple accumulation of the contributions of individuals because each contribution is presumed to build on previous ones. Second, agreement needs to be established on the proposed meanings and solutions, and individual contributions – the 'bricks of knowledge' – must be mobile and open to changes and elaborations. Also Alpay, Giboin and Dieng (1998) emphasise that it is not sufficient that the proposed meanings are clarified; these meanings must also be accepted before they form the base for undertaking joint action. When interaction breaks down or misunderstandings appear, participants use repair strategies to continue communication and, if possible, close the gaps, or, more precisely, to create enough of a common understanding that allows them to continue their activity. This shared understanding can be related to the tasks and/or the content of the tasks.

When social relations become part of the scientific inquiry, institutional aspects also become part of the unit of analysis. In mathematics, socio-mathematical norms have been emphasised (Schwartz, Neuman, Gil, & Ilya, 2003), and in science education, the distinction between doing the lesson and doing science makes the institutional aspects visible (Jiménez-Aleixandre, Bugallo Rodríguez, & Duschl, 2000; Furberg & Ludvigsen, 2008). Institutional aspects (e.g., goals, curriculum, tasks, etc.) should not be understood as something given but realised in the social interaction by the participants involved. This aforementioned distinction clarifies how students orient themselves primarily towards the given task or the epistemic dimensions that are part of the tasks. At the empirical level, we can identify how the students move between these different orientations (Furberg, 2010). In educational institutions, students must interpret how they are expected to perform, as well as what they are expected to learn. Learning the content is part of the institutional contract and regulation. The content can be procedures, concepts or conceptual systems, or social attitudes and skills. The task structures and the task, the goals, the curriculum and the resources of the program give directions for students' work. Still, students must 'unpack' the tasks and task structure in order to make sense of what they will do, and they must choose how to define themselves as participants in the specific activities (Krange & Ludvigsen, 2009). In educational institutions and settings, this implies that students become accountable for learning some aspects of the content and the curriculum, with accountability also expressed in the fact that their work will be evaluated with a grade.

To conclude, we propose an interpretation of collaboration, wherein the roles of social and relational aspects during knowledge construction are taken into account.

We would argue that by taking the social interaction as the analytic starting point we can handle the variation (in experience and knowledge) among learners, variation that creates the contingency of the complex problems encountered by the participants in our study. This variation brings forward different types of knowledge, actions, attitudes and expectations, which characterise how collaboration is played out, and requires participants to align with the institutional demands.

The social cultural perspective

In this study, we build on a set of assumptions about how people co-construct knowledge by creating shared meaning and understanding when they take part in specific, domain-bound activities. Particularly, co-construction implies an invocation of resources that participants find relevant in a problem-solving situation, such as trying out ideas, providing arguments, giving examples and so on.

A multi-layered phenomenon

In our approach and analyses, we apply the socio-cultural perspective to analyse participants' meaning making and co-construction of knowledge. We assert this perspective as involving three interrelated layers: (1) participants' evolving (individual) understanding of concepts and their use; (2) social interaction; and (3) the social organisation of knowledge in institutional settings. The first layer depicts individual development and the way individuals construct knowledge in a social context. The social interaction layer encompasses knowledge construction through interaction between individuals. The third layer refers to how knowledge is organised, how it has become part of artefacts and tools, and how institutional settings have established rules, conventions and tasks to create social order (Ludvigsen, 2010). It is important to recognise that describing the socio-cultural perspective as three layers serves an analytic function; they are deeply interwoven. In order for the reader to better understand these layers, we refer to Linell's (2009) four dimensions of interaction: I, you, the object (it) and the socio-cultural setting (we). The 'I' dimension involves the individual's development, and it can be related to the layer denominating individual understanding. The 'you' and 'we' dimensions can be associated with the interactional layer, which involves more than one individual participant. 'You' represents the other participants involved in the interaction and it can be more than one individual; in that case, the 'I' and 'you' positions will be alternated during the communicative activities. 'We' refers to how language and knowledge create meaning potential in an interactional setting, with a given social-cultural basis to draw upon. The 'it' concerns the object of the interaction, which is constituted by how students talk about it, and tune their talk to institutional norms and demands. In interaction, participants coordinate and negotiate what to talk about and how to act. This depends on what each individual brings to the interaction (i.e., the meaning potential), such as new ideas, resources or particular skills. From this perspective, the situation requires that the resources are used to achieve 'something' and that the participants create what it takes to continue the activity. In interactional settings, participants' intentions and emotions play out, and the other participants can respond to what has become the focus of the interaction.

Thematic patterns

In institutional settings like education, the main intention is that students should learn a specialised discourse that includes concepts and categories (Akkerman, Overdijk, Admiraal & Simons, 2007). Concepts and categories in every knowledge domain are historically defined. The historical definition is based on what collectives have defined as acceptable with regard to the lexical aspects and how it could be used. Concepts have potential and properties, but they are dependent on how they are used in local dialogues; concepts are contingent in relation to discourse and activities. When participants are involved in learning scientific knowledge, the entire process of how they handle the domain-specific knowledge brings about a specific phenomenon. The concept of thematic patterns, introduced by Lemke (1990), reflects this specificity in the context of an institutionalised learning process. Thematic patterns are specific to the knowledge domain, but the thematic patterns in the context of students' science talk reflect the understanding of a concept or phenomenon as part of a particular dialogue, but not as part of the respective field of science. Lemke conceives a thematic pattern as a 'semantic relationship that describes the thematic content, the science content, of a particular topic area. It is like a network of relationships among the scientific concepts in a field, but described semantically, in terms of how language is used in that field' (Lemke, 1990, pp. 12–13). In a thematic pattern, conventions of the science field are used, but in the specific way that reflects how members of a community use and construe words on a particular subject, similarly from one text or occasion of speaking to another. In this context, creating thematic patterns during 'science talk' is related to reasoning in a scientific manner, which is learned, practiced and used by talking to other members of the community, as well as through writing or other complex activities (e.g., problem-solving).

We will look at participants' attempt to gain shared understanding and create conceptualisations of the domain knowledge they operate in, i.e., research-related concepts and their relationships. In addition, we look for illustrations of how they deal with each others' contributions and how the social-relational aspect plays a role in this co-construction process.

Method

Participants

Fourteen undergraduate university students attending the Bachelor Thesis course at a large Dutch university participated in an intensive follow-up, which provided data for in-depth case studies (Yin, 2003). Participants were members of five project groups supervised by the same tutor. In this study, we analyse the activities of one student group. The group in focus consisted of three full-time female students (average age 25.3, SD = 1.6).

Research context

The Bachelor Thesis is a 20-week course offered in the final year of the bachelor's degree study in Educational Sciences at a large university in the Netherlands. The aim of the course was to support students in integrating and applying previously acquired scientific research knowledge and skills. The course was organised according to a project-based model in which the participants were required to collaboratively, in groups of two to four students, set up and conduct a research project and to report on these research activities. The final group product was a common research report.

Groups were formed at the beginning of the course period, based on students' interest in the research topics proposed by external stakeholders. One of the research topics was submitted by a company that provides consultancy services on educational innovations. Using an electronic learning platform, this institution implements virtual action learning. This involves learners conducting assignments and uploading them to the system, where other learners provide feedback on these assignments and authors revise their products using this feedback. The group we focus on this study investigated the role of peer-feedback in the virtual action learning context.

Data sources, analysis approach and analytic concepts

For the purpose of this study, a case was defined as the research activities and the products of one group of students during the 20-week course period.

A variety of data were collected, consisting of field notes, interaction data (group talk and emails), reflective data (group interviews, reflective reports) and the group's products with all their iterations. This contribution discusses a cross-section of the data, drawing primarily upon the interaction data (recorded group discussions), observations and the group's meeting notes. Before the analysis, the recordings were transcribed verbatim and organised in chronological order. The extracts analysed below were selected after repeated reading of the data.

To operationalise the socio-cultural perspective we use a two-step analytic approach, as elaborated by Linell (2009). The *first order* analysis involves mapping what participants do during interaction, without making interpretations from an analytic perspective. This analysis was done, first, by creating a general description of the context and the process this group of students was engaged in, to provide a background for the interpretations that followed. Second, it involved describing students' actions as well as identifying the type of actions and how they fit in the larger scheme of the interaction process (see below a description of the analytic concepts used). We selected episodes, an episode corresponding to 'relatively bounded sequence' within a more comprehensive speech event or encounter (Linell, 1998: 187). The *second order* analysis served the purpose of systematically interpreting participants' (verbal) actions. For each excerpt, the interpretation is summarised and discussed in a section entitled 'Zoom out'. For interpreting the interactional sequences, we constructed an analytic scheme that reflects the multifaceted interactional processes under investigation, in which we employed three empirically sensitive concepts, i.e., orientation, elaboration, confirmation. These analytic concepts came forward after repeated analysis of the data, and were not conceived beforehand. The concept of *orientation* denominates *what* students are discussing, whether the talk is about the concepts belonging to the knowledge domain, or whether they are navigating the social-regulative aspects of the collaboration, or the affective-relational elements. The concept of *elaboration* depicts the way participants follow up on their orientation outcomes; in other words, *how* they act and interact. We study the language employed by the participants in order to grasp how they make sense of the topic, the knowledge related to it, individual students' ideas and arguments, and so on. Once students have oriented themselves in relation to the knowledge domain or each others' ideas, they elaborate on concepts, ideas, statements or stances using linguistic devices (i.e., to describe, clarify, or explain) to elaborate. The concept of *confirmation* is primarily reflected in how group members react to ideas, points of view, arguments or suggestions for action put forward by other members. It can take the form of either rejection or uptake. We aim here to find out what it takes to continue the process of co-construction, both regarding the epistemic (knowledge-related) and social-relational aspects of the interaction. We also used the notion of *disagreement,* taken up previously in the review, to pin down the elements of the interaction that express differences in participants' ideas, statements or contributions, and how participants deal with these differences at empirical level. We see disagreement as part of the processes that involve problematisation of ideas, concepts and content.

Analyses and findings

General description of the collaborative process

The client introduced the virtual action learning method during a session with student groups involved in this project, provided the groups with relevant literature on the method and pointed at the aspects that would require empirical investigation. At this point, our focus group decided that role and effects of feedback, and motivation to work in the electronic environment is an interesting topics for research.

The general collaborative strategy of the group was characterised by frequent face-to-face meetings, during which both logistics and content-related issues were discussed. Most of the ideas brought forward during these discussions were provisionally elaborated on the spot and provided with feedback by the others. One group member took notes, while the other two continued the elaboration verbally. When not able to meet face-to-face, they wrote down their ideas and emailed them, asking for feedback. However, division of labour was frequent. In the face-to-face discussions, after group members pinned down ideas and identified work ahead, they divided tasks among the members. Each of them worked on these tasks (e.g., sections of the literature review, theoretical framework for the research report, explanatory material for the client, etc.) and sent the resulting material to the others. The group did not produce many versions of the research report, but many notes were produced, during both group discussions and individually. In general, the group had difficulties in making decisions independently regarding the research topic and the direction of the investigation, and they relied frequently on their supervisor's opinion and input. This input determined rather frequent changes in the direction of their research. However, the group succeeded in setting up and conducting an empirical research, study and producing a research report that was assessed as of average quality.

Previous to the interaction sequences shown in the next section, the group collected relevant literature and explored the electronic platform. Based on this input, group members arrived at the point where they had to decide on the research topic. The interaction sequences were sampled from the period when students worked on the research proposal draft, which they were to present to their supervisor and the external stakeholder.

Sequences of interaction

We present our analysis of each of the excerpts below by first identifying students' actions, then by making our interpretation of what these actions mean. We use the analytic concept (orientation, elaboration, confirmation, disagreement), and finally, interpret these actions in the context of the interaction process.

Episode 1: Towards shared understanding of concepts

To be able to identify the research focus and to formulate adequate research questions, students needed a good understanding of the main concepts (*feedback* and *motivation*), of their mutual relationship, and of how they can be translated into 'researchable' variables (operationalised). The first episode shows the start of the discussion on the meaning of the two concepts, after group members recapped the ideas they came up with in a previous group discussion.

> *2 minutes' talk about logistic aspects*
> 1 Alice: Wasn't it so that we thought to measure feedback through motivation? The feedback can be measured through motivation ... we could especially look at how to measure feedback ... and that's again motivation ... I thought .... I thought we were to measure motivation ... and then you have ...
> 2 Elly: Motivation ...
> 3 Jane: There was that article ...
> 4 Alice: There was an article, which did it that way, investigated feedback through performance and motivation, and by performance you could include the click patterns ...

  5 Elly: Wait a second err

  6 Jane: But then you would have to look at both!!

  7 Alice: Motivation is, I think, easier to measure than feedback … what one thought back then, and then you could actually question people to find out those things.

  8 Elly: Motivation to learn …

  9 Jane: It's actually not clear to me how you reason. […]

10 Alice: But what they [students] do is, actually… err, give feedback to each other on papers, and motivate each other in this way. Thus you get more motivated when receiving feedback, which motivates you to go and look more often [au. on the VLC, the Virtual Learning Community]. Thus, feedback influences motivation.

11 Jane: Isn't that almost the other way around?

12 Elly: But then you investigate namely feedback and not motivation!

13 Jane: Yes. The way I see it is not feedback through motivation, but the other way around. Does feedback influence your motivation? . . . Something like that, it is simply the opposite of what we have here.

14 Alice: But that's an interesting way!

15 Jane: Yes, but then we have to change everything, all our initial ideas. Then is motivation the most important thing and not feedback, right?

16 Alice: I think you are quite wrong there.

17 Elly: But what you are saying now is that feedback leads to a higher motivation, that you will look on VLC more often.

18 Jane: Yes, but that is . . . wait. It's …

19 Alice: Searching for motivation.

20 Elly: Yes, true.

21 Jane: By using feedback. Then the question would be exactly the opposite of the one we have. Maybe we could turn it around . . .

22 Alice: No, no, no turning around! It's handier to ask about motivation . . . so we look at feedback, we have a good insight in the data . . . it's not realistic to look at all those . . . But then you would want to look at feedback, how would you approach that anyway?

23 Elly: Well, we have to think about that now.

In line 1, Alice summarises the conclusions of the last group discussion: '*Wasn't it so that we thought to measure feedback through motivation?*' This is an initial orientation in the group discussion towards domain-knowledge aspects. Alice does not wait for the others to confirm her orientation, but provides a first elaboration of her view on the research focus in the second sentence: '*The feedback can be measured through motivation, we could especially look at how to measure feedback, and that's again motivation . . . thought.*' This statement represents the trigger for the discussion that follows, but also a cause for disagreements between the group members.

This orientation towards understanding how the concepts relate to each other is evident also in the lines that follow (4, 7, 8, 10, 12, 14). This orientation, however, is rather tentative, as all three members pause hesitantly when they talk about these concepts and their relationship (line 2: *'motivation . . . I thought . . . I thought we thought to measure motivation . . . and then you have . . .'*; line 18: *'Yes, but that is . . . wait. Is . . .'*), make suggestions and wait for the others to confirm or (line 21: *'Maybe we could turn it around. . .'*), or trigger each other to elaborate more on their own ideas (line 17: *'But what you are saying now is that . . .'*).

The challenge to elaborate is taken on, and students use strategies such as: repeating ideas (see lines 1, 7, 10), reaching for sources that confirm it (lines 3–4), providing an example from practice (line 7) or filling in others' ideas (line 19). When elaborating on their ideas, students employ 'technical' research terms. However, the tone of conversation is informal, and we interpret this as the students' way to bring the abstract concepts closer to their 'world' and daily communication style. They use expressions such as *'But that's an interesting way'* (line 14), *'It's handier . . .'* (line 22) or express disagreement in a casual way: *'I think you are quite wrong there'* (line 16).

The interaction is mostly taking place *through* the object of discussion ('it'). Participants utter and exchange ideas all related to the concepts in discussion and make attempts to build on each other's account, despite disagreements at some point. The emotional load in the discussion is visible mostly in the way these expressions are uttered, but it does not affect the epistemic aspect of the conversation. Examples of utterances expressing disagreement are: *'Wait a second . . .'* (line 5), *'But then you investigate namely feedback and not motivation!'* (line 12), *'No, no turning around!'* (line 22). Alice is the one who has a diverging opinion; the other two group members attempt to not only understand her ideas but also to develop their own account of the concepts. Disagreements do not lead to conflict, but more to Alice being challenged to explain and to elaborate on her account (line 7) and to the other two members to provide their own account on the topic (lines 14, 18). In the end, Alice opens up for discussion by asking the others how they think feedback could be investigated. Elly replies with a reconciling tone and words (line 20), and this is the starting point of a new sequence of collaborative elaboration. Her choice of words (*'We have to. . .'*) indicates the intention to act together to further elaborate on this idea.

We observe that the participants are building on each others' ideas, even when these ideas are not always in accordance with their own views. When disagreements occur, they use repair strategies to bring the discussion back to its focus. An illustrative example is in 9–13 and 16–17. In line 9, Jane states, *'It's actually <u>not</u> clear to me how you reason.'* In later lines (13), it becomes clear that she is calling on Alice to elaborate on her idea. Alice takes up this call (line 10) and provides an account of the relationship between motivation and feedback. The other two students disagree with Alice's view, and Jane explains where Alice went wrong in her argument (line 13). But she builds on the view Alice provided, which indicates that they are able and willing to corroborate their epistemic discourse, despite the disagreement. In return, Alice verbalises her disproval of this new account (line 16) and her rather belligerent formulation is a potential source of disturbance in the conversation.

Elly makes a new attempt to understand Alice (line 14: '*But what you are saying now is . . .*'). By summarising Alice's ideas and by showing understanding of her diverging position, Elly keeps open the communication channel and avoids encouraging a potential argument. Furthermore, the group members reach for each others' confirmation of their ideas and intentions, linguistically expressed in using interrogatives ('*. . . right?*,' line 15).

Zoom out

The focus of this conversation sequence is the group members' attempt to create an account of the research concepts they need to work with, as well as their struggle to understand the relationship between these concepts. From the perspective of the knowledge domain, this hesitant discussion also represents a first attempt to create a thematic pattern (see Lemke, 1990). They construct this epistemic orientation on the thematic patterns by using concepts they know and domain knowledge they posses. As such, they have a degree of understanding of the concepts, but establishing the position and role of these concepts in relation to each other and to the investigated context seems more challenging. Nevertheless, the pattern is partly established here, and attempts to elaborate on it are visible in the next discussion section. Elaboration is employed at the linguistic level and as a function to develop ideas. Both aspects are visible at the micro level of the discourse, where students use language devices such as interrogatives, rhetorical means to state an opinion or to make themselves clear. Providing examples is a way to help the others understand their own points of view.

It is evident in the excerpt that disagreements here are task-related. The occurring disagreements could be explained by the fact that all three participants are rather unsure about the knowledge domain. This leads to a hesitant search for answers, through talking out loud and expressing 'raw' ideas, which sometimes oppose each other and lead to disagreement. Nevertheless, the disagreement emerges in a moderate tone and does not take over the conversation. It is addressed before it can evolve into a detrimental state of affairs; however, it is not clear in this sequence whether group members truly agree with each other or whether they go along with the group discourse, which leads to creating a rather shallow and partially shared understanding.

Episode 2: Searching for higher levels of conceptualisation

The excerpt that follows shows a sequel to the discussion presented above. Between these two sequences, students continued the discussion on the relationship of the two main concepts. The excerpt below shows the end of this discussion, where students attempt to settle for the concepts they will operationalise.

1 Jane: But we have rating [au. of feedback] now . . .
2 Elly: So, how feedback is rated, but . . . let me think . . . than we have the relationship of rating . . .

3 Alice: …with motivation.

4 Elly: Motivation for what, to learn?!

5 Alice: Yes, or motivation to participate.

6 Jane: To learn is just not concrete enough . . . or you specify, like, it's about continuing with a task or a product. And motivation is too abstract, too.

7 Elly: Yes, you are right; it must be more concrete.

8 Alice: But then the idea of 'persistence' is much better . . . it's, like, I give feedback and then I keep going back, that is thus . . . […]

9 Elly: Look at the relationship between persistence and … between rating . . .

10 Alice: The persistence . . .

11 Jane: In fact, you would look at rating the feedback and receiving feedback and presence in VLC, thus not only to the rating of feedback.

12 Elly: What kind of influence it has, for the persistence to keep working in VLC.

13 Jane: To keep performing well, I'd say. Performing well, that could mean that you place things on the [virtual] platform. Right? If someone, at some point, delivers less good products, gets lower ratings, right? He or she performs less. […]

14 Elly: … I am thinking now . . . we keep bringing in new concepts . . . I think we should stop doing that.

15 Alice: You're quite right. Feedback is important in the process in the VLC and we understand it somehow better. So, we don't drop that.

16 Elly: No, we don't. I want to investigate feedback. I find rating very interesting, then we can look at what happens if someone rates feedback as unimportant, is that the one still motivated to keep coming and working in the community? Just to give an example . . . we could process that.

The group makes attempts towards concretising and operationalising the concepts discussed. This is the main orientation of the group members at this point. Jane states what the group has chosen in terms of concepts and their relationship – '. . . *we have rating [of feedback] now*' – and also refers to the research framework (line 6: it is not about learning in general but '. . . *about continuing with a task or a product*'). However, this sequence of discussion shows that the group is not yet that advanced in their understanding and elaboration of the chosen concepts. In line 11, Jane reframes the initial orientation.

This excerpt shows an individual and collective elaboration effort in an attempt to shape the conceptual framework (see lines 2, 3, 6, 8, 9, 10, 13 and 16). There are some attempts at elaboration, such as Jane's in line 13: '*Performing well, that could mean that you place things on the [virtual] platform. Right? If someone, at some point, delivers less good products, get lower ratings, right? He or she performs less*'. Group members start their ideas and invite the others to think along. A relevant example can be found in lines

9 through 12, wherein each student continues to elaborate on the relationship between feedback, rating, presence and work in the VLC. Students concur in the decision to limit the investigation mainly to the concept of feedback (lines 15 and 16). They confirm the understanding of each others' ideas, based on the pragmatic arguments that . . . *it does seem that we somehow understand it better.*'

In their elaborations, group members use specific concepts, i.e., expressions and terms used in relation to the learning process (e.g., learning is not concrete enough; it's about a task, etc.). In terms of vocabulary, in the first part of the excerpt the use of the singular pronoun 'I' (e.g., '*I think*', '*I am not sure*') is rather frequent, which indicates a stronger orientation towards individual ideas. Comparably, in this section, the plural form 'we' is used more frequently (in expressions such as '*we don't drop that*', '*we can look what happens*', '*we could process that*'), which indicates the shift from rather individually oriented thinking to a more shared perspective. Also, rather more confirmative language is used in this sequence. Confirmation is asked for or given explicitly (line 13 '*Right? […] right*' or, line 15 '*You're quite right.*'). There is confirmation in the way group members take up and build on each others' ideas, expressed explicitly through language (line 7: '*Yes, you are right…*', line 15: '*Yes, you are quite right*').

Zoom out

In this section, too, the difficulties students encounter in their attempt to pin down the research concepts are noticeable; so is the group's struggle to reach a higher level of conceptualisation and, at the same time, operationalise the research variables. Although the meaning of the (main) concepts is clarified, the relationship between these concepts is still unclear. At epistemic level, the group does not seem to have made much progress.

Diverging opinions of the group members are visible here, too, but at some point, they are ignored in order to continue to work with the task. Although no absolute agreement was reached in that respect, the group members want to move on. This, however, leads to socially desirable actions, in which one of the members tries to bring in ideas that fit the others', despite having her own diverging ideas. The question arising here is whether the group members reached a sufficient level of conceptualisation, which allows taking the next step in their work on the research plan. They chose to resume the discussion after realising that it is not constructive to keep arguing about individual points of view and a high number of concepts.

It appears that group members realise that disagreement is not beneficial for advancing in their discussion and they make an attempt to address that by challenging each other to elaborate on the diverging points of view. This leads us to conclude that relational disagreements can, to some extent, enhance elaboration of epistemic nature. However, while solving this dilemma at relational level it does not necessarily lead, at least in the case of this group, to visible progress at epistemic level.

Episode 3: Settling for a decision

This last excerpt is selected from a discussion that took place a week after the previously shown one, and it illustrates how the discussion and negotiation around the concepts is resumed. This discussion sequence picks up at the point where the group members lay out a number of concepts they considered seminal for their research focus and variables.

1 Alice: We want to know the extent to which feedback influences motivation. That is what we agreed, right? Look at the notes.

2 Jane: [Checking the notes] OK.

3 Elly: But that motivation . . . which part of it?

4 Alice: The motivation to participate more often in the VLC.

5 Jane: And what is often? What is in fact often – every day, five times a day?

6 Alice: Then you should first look at what is normal, what is often . . .

7 Jane: What the average is.

8 Alice: Yes, what is normal, so to say. [. . .] What is the average and whether the more feedback you get, the higher your participation; you are there more.

9 Jane: Then you could say concretely, it is the average. In which way does feedback inside VLC correlate with the motivation to . . .

10 Elly: With the presence in VLC . . . if we look at how feedback correlates with presence in the VLC?

13 Jane: [. . .] But is it only presence? Or is it also what they do? You can be present but do nothing.

14 Alice: So . . . presence and . . .

15 Jane: . . . and what they do. Presence and activity. So, also look at what they are doing while they are present in the VLC. Right, the extent of presence . . .

16 Alice: But you base this on your own intuition.

17 Elly: No, we'll operationalise it. Can you write that up?

18 Alice: [Writing] . . . and level of activity. Here you can also only base it on your intuition. While motivation is reflected clearly in this [au. level of activity].

19 Elly: But we agreed this is a too complex concept.

20 Jane: Look, Alice, we can search for the average level of presence and activity and then check how it is in this group. Then we can interpret it, see if it's below or above the average. Then look at whether that has to do with feedback.

21 Elly: I see feedback as the most prominent here; it is part of the learning method and . . .

22 Jane: Yes, and it is very concrete. Right, Alice?

23 Alice: Mhmm, yeah. I still think it's a pity . . .

24 Jane: But otherwise it becomes too broad; you agreed with that yourself.

25 Alice: Yes, true.
26 Elly: Let's start brainstorming, OK?
27 Jane: Yes, exactly.

The group's orientation towards identifying feedback as an independent variable, shown in the previous excerpts, is definitive here. However, the quest for establishing the concepts' relationship continues, parallel with the effort to operationalise them. Alice recapitulates what the groups decided during the discussion that day (line 1: '*We want to know the extent to which feedback influences motivation*'), both for the purpose of concluding the previous discussions and of creating a starting point for the emerging discussion. This is also the point of view she tried hard to emphasise and wanted to have as a central aspect of their investigation. It appears that the relationship and position of the two concepts (feedback and motivation) became clearer, and the reader would expect that, from this point onwards, group members would make attempts to elaborate on this relationship. However, questioning starts again, this time by Jane (line 3: '*But that motivation . . . which part of it?*'). The questioning comes as a challenge to Alice's summary, but, in fact, it leads to clarification and elaboration of this summary. The orientation of the group towards particular concepts is supported by the individual and collaborative elaboration of these concepts. Group members elaborate freely, by thinking out loud and expressing their ideas (Alice in line 8 or Jane in line 15); they also ask each other explicitly to elaborate (line 5: '*What is in fact often – every day, five times a day?*') or leave sentences unfinished and, in this way, invite the others to fill in (line 9: '*In which way does feedback inside VLC correlate with the motivation to . . .*'). Such subtle invitations do not always have the expected effect (line 15 – invitation and line 16 – reply, but no elaboration). Moreover, the group finds the elaboration valuable and writes it down.

The language in this section of the discussion is notable through the more frequent use of the plural of the first person pronoun: '*we want to know*', '*we'll operationalise it*'. This indicates again the shared orientation towards concepts and action.

There is much explicit confirmation given and requested in this sequence. On the one hand is the mutual uptake of ideas when elaborating on the concepts, which validates the previous input; an example is line 9: '*Then you could say concretely, it is the average*' or lines 14–15 '*So . . . presence and . . . / . . . and what they do. Presence and activity.*' On the other hand, confirmation is asked or given explicitly, too, in lines 2 ('*OK*') or 8 ('*Yes, what is normal, so to say*'). However, one request for confirmation, addressed by Jane to Alice in line 22 ('*Right, Alice?*'), expresses in fact tension (line 20: '*Look, Alice . . .*'). It pressures Alice, who seems to have a relapse to her previous point of view regarding motivation (lines 18). To some extent, her tentative remarks show that, although Alice complied with the group's shared conception, she is still not convinced of the reasoning employed when developing this conceptual system. Elly and Jane explain their reasoning to Alice (lines 20 and 21) and appeal to earlier agreements by reminding her that she concurred with the common stance. Alice's vacillation indicates that she is not happy with this decision (line 23: '*Mhmm, yeah. I still think it's a pity . . .*' [she refers to the fact that the concept of motivation was thrown out of the system of variables]), but in the end, she hesitantly concurs with the group stance.

Zoom out

This excerpt closes the discussion session, and the group's struggle with clarifying the concepts and their relationship. Ultimately, the group moves on, showing a clear, goal-oriented attitude, which brings them closer to the solution to their problem. The question that arises is whether the group actually dealt with the previous disagreements in an appropriate way. As shown in this sequence, the disagreements around the concept of motivation surfaced again during the group's talk. The previous agreement was not necessarily attended through a full negotiation process and was guided more by pragmatic goals than by epistemic grounding and elaboration, and the unfinished negotiation process bounced back embodied in Alice's doubts. Jane's elaborated explanation is, potentially, an attempt to maintain the joint venture, which needs to be carried on beyond this specific discussion. This skill of pursuing their goals is not equalled by their conceptualisations at epistemic level, nor by how they deal with the unaddressed issues at relational level. There is also the plausible explanation that they resume and conclude discussion because they must move on with their work and proceed with writing the research plan. This implies that closure is not fully based on consensus, but partly on a deliberate and pragmatic decision, which is an important part of meeting the institutional demands.

Discussion

The first question addressed in this study was: *How do students engage with concepts in order to solve an open problem?* In an attempt to answer this question, we showed and discussed interaction sequences that illustrate participants' attempts and struggle to understand concepts they work with. The gaps identified in this material are of epistemic and relational nature. These gaps indicate students' different orientation, position in the interaction and also disagreement on how to understand and relate concepts to each other. This involves repeated attempts of the participants to make the others understand and accept their viewpoints, through using a knowledge domain-bound discourse and language. Viewed as an interaction trajectory, individual students' understandings of the concepts change over time, even if they do not reach a more fixed or firm understanding. The individual students' understanding is constituted by but not determined by the trajectory of the group (Ludvigsen et al., 2011).

The types of 'social science research talk' identified in the data are quite generic. This is because it entails establishing the logical relations existent between the concepts that belong to a particular conceptual system (Ludvigsen, 2010), which need to be not only understood but also applied to the given research context. Students attempt to construct and elaborate a thematic pattern (Lemke, 1990) by employing domain-specific language and terms (e.g., feedback, motivation, measuring, receiving positive or negative feedback, questioning people, higher motivation, etc.) learned in their previous courses or research modules. This endeavour requires not only expertise and sufficient information, but also intricate reasoning based on the knowledge domain in which they work. The construction of such patterns becomes visible through the interaction trajectory of the students (Furberg & Ludvigsen, 2008). Moreover, due to the collaborative nature of the type of research project, students are expected, according to the institutional norms, to engage in and perform this work in a joint manner. The interactional accomplishments are aimed at bridging the gaps between the institutional norms and students' activities. Chapter 10 by Andriessen, Pardijs and Baker in this volume illustrates a different possibility, where participants seem to resist the institutional demands, at the cost of further elaboration of their ideas.

The second question addressed in this study was *Which aspects – epistemic, relational and social – become activated the interaction process and how do they affect this interaction.* In an attempt to answer this question, we illustrated and discussed various ways of addressing the knowledge gaps identified in the excerpts. Examples are: posing one's own views and providing arguments, requesting elaboration from the others on new ideas, providing one's own elaboration or inviting the others to adjust or elaborate further. What appears as a condition is that (tacit) discrepancy and disagreements had to be explicated and acknowledged in a considerate way between collaboration partners to be able to cope with conflicting ideas.

This study showed that resolving different orientations and disagreements can be beneficial for the functioning of the group and for individual participation, but it did not necessarily lead to a superior understanding of the matter in discussion or a more advanced conceptualisation. Conscious decisions to overcome communicational or relational breakdowns caused by disagreement lead, as here, to a stricter commitment to the institutional demands than to epistemic elaboration as discussion progresses. It seems that this commitment to consensus diminishes, since the group members felt the urgency of their commission. We can argue here that task completion becomes the most important issue for the students. This institutional aspect gave direction and framed the historical given content at an overall level for the activities. Conversely, in Chapter 10 by Andriessen et al. (this volume), we see a case in which the activities were framed by social motives. The differences with our case may be explained by the role of the institutional setting, which is taken for granted by participants in our study.

Although it seems that at the relational and social levels the balance is still not achieved, the group has reached a decision regarding the epistemic aspect. Different ideas and disagreements do not lead to conflict or breakdown in the group's discourse, since the task completion becomes the primary aim for the students. Contrarily, they lead to participants (Alice, for example) becoming aware of the implications of their thoughts and ideas, explicating these (see also Stahl, Koschman & Suthers, 2006), and creating ground for joint epistemic efforts. In this sense, the disagreements are used as an arena for challenging the ideas expressed and for creating an understanding of the set of concepts they employ in their research. A team will benefit if divergence in meaning leads to further elaboration and negotiation. Through this negotiation by argument and clarification, the group works towards a convergence of meaning, and a partially shared account of the concepts at stake is constructed. Team members may diverge in their interpretation and tackle the situation from another point of view or perspective. Resistance to built understanding can lead to further elaboration of individual opinions and to negotiation of different meanings. De Dreu and Weingart (2003) claim that differences in the interpretation of the problem can be experienced as a personal, relational dismissal and, as such, can interfere with productive team activities. However, what we investigated here in relation to effects of disagreement is of a slightly different nature. Disagreement was employed by the group as a trigger for elaboration, but only up to a point. When the process of negotiation due to disagreements threatened to continue for too long, the group chose a pragmatic solution. Due to pressure to finalise their project and the difficulties in elaborating on the relationship between concepts, participants dealt in a rather simple way with the opinion of the one member who had a different stance. As claimed by Baker (1999, 2009) and Alpay, Giboin and Dieng (1998), meanings must also be *accepted* before they form the base for undertaking joint action. Generally speaking, meanings are accepted partially or not accepted, and co-construction of knowledge is determined by this choice. We can state that, in order to solve the problem, the group mobilised epistemic actions in which differences in view become transparent. When dealing with these differences, students built on each others' actions through confirmation and elaboration. One can say that the communication was at a level that was sufficient to solve the problem, even if it shows less evidence of deeper shared conceptual understanding, conceptualisation and elaboration. In a sense, the group reached an effective decision but not consensus.

We emphasised that co-construction of knowledge should be conceptualised and understood as a multi-layered phenomenon. In the analysis of the data, we identified the three layers within the interaction of the three students. We analysed these layers and the way they were enacted by employing three analytic concepts (orientation, confirmation, elaboration), which made these layers visible. The layer of students' individual ideas, conceptions and participation (the 'I' and 'you' in Linell's (2009) stance), here involves the participants bringing in different concepts – Baker's (2009) 'bricks of knowledge'– with a meaning potential. In this way, orientation towards particular stances is created. Whether the potential residing in this orientation and the concepts put forward is concretised, taken up and elaborated upon is up to the social interaction within the group. This is the second layer of the phenomenon analysed, conceptualised as the 'we' dimension by Linell, and the uptake is operationalised through confirmation at analytic level. At this layer, meaning is accepted, rejected, negotiated, or shared. The interaction involves different aspects: epistemic, social and relational, and is mostly facilitated by linguistic devices, which, in turn, carry a certain meaning potential. Furthermore, this is the context where the disagreements emerge and become materialised, but also where new potential meanings emerge. Elaboration of ideas leads to the construction of a thematic pattern (Lemke, 1990) and supports the shared understanding of the group. An example of such a thematic pattern is the discussion on feedback, together with the concepts and types of talk students employ in order to understand and explain this concept. The third layer brings in the institutionalised aspect of knowledge students deal with, the concepts that carry a generally accepted meaning, and the research project that embodies the institutional demands and framework wherein this inter-action takes place. Students' stronger orientation towards the institutional goals works to the detriment of appropriately dealing with problematic relational aspects (see also Barron, 2003; Furberg, 2010).

Concluding remarks

This study allowed us to explore how participants in interaction create meaning and new conceptual structures by employing institutionalised knowledge and lan-guage, but also by jointly co-constructing shared understanding and conceptualisa-tions. The experience of Alice, Elly and Jane teaches us that shared epistemic accounts may be the basis of a successful collaboration aimed at co-constructing knowledge. Previous research about collaboration has often made the claim that a shared goal is a condition for co-construction of knowledge (e.g. Baker, 1999). However, sharing a goal does not seem to be a condition, since the sharing of goals seems to be a part of the emerging process of working with the problem (see Krange & Ludvigsen, 2009). It became obvious that the social and relational aspects can contribute to or can impede joint elaborations and shared meaning making. By connecting the analysis of social, relational and epistemic aspects, we open ourselves to understanding how collaboration contributes to meaning making and co-con-struction of knowledge as a multi-layered phenomenon. The choices made when dealing with disagreement can determine, on short term, how shared understanding is emerging and gaining shape, how common knowledge is elaborated, and on long term, the outcomes and quality of the co-construction process. What disagreement means must be decided concretely at an empirical level in each study or even learn-ing situation. In other chapters of this book, various learning situations illustrate how the relational aspects of collaboration are embodied in a variety of manifesta-tions, and how these influence both the learning trajectories and participants' actions. Furthermore, the complex problem, the knowledge domain involved, and students' activities create a trajectory that is based on the contingencies analysed.

From the perspective of educational practice, in the current case we see a focus by the collaborating students on institutional norms as a guide to progress and evaluation. That led to epistemic consensus derived from supposed shared knowl-edge appeared to be less shared than expected. Moreover, while disagreements at the epistemic level were productive, dealing appropriately with the social-relational aspects of collaboration appeared as second to students' determination to meet the institutional norm. In general, educational institutions pose various norms that affect students learning trajectories, but those norms are often less explicit when it comes to collaborative learning. One main implication for educational practice that can be derived from these conclusions relates to educational design. If we want students to better understand how to make their collaboration productive, we need to enculturate them as to how collaboration might work, and how to deal with crucial aspects when collaborating about specific tasks, in our case, developing shared understanding and co-construction of knowledge. It should not be taken for granted that learners jointly develop common orientation and goals, bring in concepts, or generate elaborations. Also, and maybe foremost, collaborating learners need to better grasp the influence of social and relational concerns on their collaborative work. Another important implication concerns the relationship between the institutional demands and goals, the learning process of the participants involved and what they perceive as being important with regard to learning. In the current case, students' pragmatic decision to pursue the institutional norm is very evident; we assume that, when faced with different norms, they would have acted differently. Hence, we maintain that these norms should take into account not only the standards that must be met from a normative perspective, but also allow for space for students to pursue their learning interests and advance their knowledge, whether in collaboration or otherwise. Students' learning, the specific social organisation and the co-constructed knowledge should constitute a short history that becomes part of the longer-term history of the educational institution and of the students' trajectory.

Transcript notations

[au. text] Text in square brackets represents clarifying information
[…] Up to three utterances were removed from the original discussion
Underlined Emphasis in talk
(.) Short pause in the speech
… Long pause in speech
[*Italics*] Context descriptions

References

Akkerman, S., Overdijk, M., Admiraal, W. and Simons, R. J. (2007) 'Beyond imprisonment of meaning: Technology facilitating redefining', *Computers in Human Behavior*, 23(6), 29–98.

Alpay, L., Giboin, A. and Dieng, R. (1998) 'Accidentology: An example of problem solving by multiple agents with multiple representations', in M. W. Van Someren, P. Reimann, H. P. A. Boshuizen and T. de Jong (Eds.), *Learning with Multiple Representations*. Amsterdam: Pergamon, pp. 152–74.

Andriessen, J., Baker, M. and Van der Puil, C. (2011) 'Socio-cognitive tension in collaborative working relations', in Ludvigsen, S., Lund, A., Rasmussen, I. and Saljo, R., *Learning across Sites: New Tools, Infrastructures and Practices*, Routledge in the Early learning series.

Baker, M. J. (1995) 'Negotiation in collaborative problem-solving dialogues', in R. J., Beun, M. J. Baker and M. Reiner (Eds.), *Dialogue and Instruction: Modeling Interaction in Intelligent Tutoring Systems*, Berlin: Springer-Verlag, pp. 39–55.

Baker, M. J. (1999) 'Argumentation and constructive interaction', in G. Rijlaarsdam and E. Espéret (Series Eds.) and Pierre Coirier and Jerry Andriessen (Vol. Eds.), *Studies in*

Writing: Vol. 5. *Foundations of Argumentative Text Processing*, Amsterdam: University of Amsterdam Press, pp. 179–202.

Baker, M. J. (2009) 'Argumentative interactions and the social construction of knowledge', in N. M. Mirza and A.-N. Perret-Clermont (Eds.), *Argumentation and Education: Theoretical Foundations and Practices*, Berlin: Springer Verlag, pp. 127–44.

Barab, S. A., and Plucker, J. A. (2002) 'Smart people or smart contexts? Cognition, ability, and talent development in an age of situated approaches to knowing and learning', *Educational Psychologist*, 37(3), 165–82.

Barron, B. (2000) 'Achieving coordination in collaborative problem-solving groups', *The Journal of the Learning Sciences*, 9, 403–36.

Barron, B. (2003) When smart groups fail. *Journal of the Learning Sciences*, 12, 307–359.

Crook, C. K. (2000) 'Motivation and the ecology of collaborative learning', in R. Joiner, K. Littleton, D. Faulkner and D. Miell (Eds.), *Rethinking Collaborative Learning*. London: Free Association Press, pp. 161–78.

De Dreu, C. K. W. and Weingart, L. R. (2003) 'Task versus relationship conflict and team effectiveness: A meta-analysis', *Journal of Applied Psychology*, 88, 741–9.

Engeström, Y. (1999) 'Innovative learning in work teams: analyzing cycles of knowledge creation in practice', in Y. Engeström, M. R. Miettinen and R. L. Punamäki (Eds.), *Perspectives on Activity Theory*. Cambridge: Cambridge University Press.

Engle, R. A. and Conant, F. C. (2002) 'Guiding principles for fostering productive disciplinary engagement: Explaining an emergent argument in a community of learners classroom', *Cognition and Instruction*, 20(4), 399–483.

Hogan, K., Nastasi, B. K. and Pressley, M. (2000) 'Discourse patterns and collaborative scientific reasoning in peer and teacher-guided discussions', *Cognition and Instruction*, 17(4), 379–432.

Furberg, A. and Ludvigsen, S. R. (2008) 'Students' meaning-making of socioscientific issues in computer mediated settings: Exploring learning through interaction trajectories', *International Journal of Science Education*, 30(13), 1775–99.

Furberg, A. (2010) 'Scientific inquiry in web-based learning environments: Exploring technological, epistemic and institutional aspects of student's meaning making' (Doctoral thesis). University of Oslo, Norway.

Graesser, A. C., Person, N. A., Joseph, P. and Magliano, J. P. (1995) 'Collaborative dialogue patterns in naturalistic one-to-one tutoring', *Applied Cognitive Psychology*, 9(6), 495–522.

Jiménez-Aleixandre, M. P., Bugallo Rodríguez, A. and Duschl, R. A. (2000) 'Doing the lesson' or "doing science": argument in high school genetics', *Science Education*, 84(6), 757–92.

Krange, I. and Ludvigsen, S. (2009) 'The situated and historical nature of CSCL – Implications for design experiments', *Journal of Computer Assisted Learning*, 25(3), 268–79.

Lemke, J. L. (1990) *Talking Science. Language, Learning, and Values*, Norwood, NJ: Ablex.

Linell, P. (1998) *Approaching Dialogue: Talk, Interaction and Contexts in Dialogical Perspectives*. Amsterdam, The Netherlands: John Benjamins Publishing Company.

Linell, P. (2009) *Rethinking Language, Mind and World Dialogically: Interactional and Contextual Theories of Human Sense-Making*. Charlotte, NC: Information Age Publishing Inc.

Ludvigsen, S., Rasmussen, I., Krange, I., Moen, A. and Middleton, D. (2011) 'Multiplicity and intersecting trajectories of participation: temporality and learning', in S. Ludvigsen, A. Lund, I. Rasmussen and R. Säljö (Eds.), *Learning across Sites: New Tools, Infrastructures and Practices*, Routledge in the Early learning series.

Ludvigsen, S. (2010) 'Sociogenesis and cognition: the struggle between social and cognitive activities', in B. Schwarz, T. Dreyfus and R. Hershkowitz (Eds.), *Transformation of knowledge through classroom interaction*, Routledge in the Early learning series.

Mäkitalo, Å. (2003) Accounting practices as situated learning: Dilemmas and dynamics in institutional categorization', *Discourse Studies* 5, 495–516.

Roschelle, J. and Teasley, S. (1995) 'The construction of shared knowledge in collaborative problem solving', in C. E. O'Malley (Ed.), *Computer Supported Collaborative Learning*, Heidelberg: Springer-Verlag.

Säljö, R. (2002) 'My brain's running slow today. The preference for "things ontologies" in research and everyday discourse on human thinking', *Studies in Philosophy and Education*, 21, 389–405.

Schwarz, B. B., Neuman, Y., Gil, J. and Ilya, M. (2003) 'Construction of collective and individual knowledge in argumentative activity', *The Journal of the Learning Sciences*, 12(2), 219–56.

Stahl, G., Koschmann, T. and Suthers, D. (2006) 'Computer-supported collaborative learning', in R. K. Sawyer (Ed.), *The Cambridge Handbook of The Learning Science*, Cambridge: Cambridge University Press, pp. 409–26.

Valsiner, J. (2002) 'Beyond social representations: A theory of enablement' Invited lecture presented at the 6th conference on social representations, August, Stirling., UK.

Vygotsky, L. S. (1978) *Mind in Society: The Development of Higher Psychological Processes*, ed. M. Cole, V. John-Steiner, S. Scribner and E. Souberman, Cambridge, MA: Harvard University Press (Original work published 1930).

Wickman, P. O. and Östman, L. (2002) *Learning as Discourse Change: A Sociocultural Mechanism*, Wiley Periodicals, Inc.

Yin, R. (2003) *Case Study Research: Design and Methods*. (3rd edn), Thousand Oaks, CA: Sage Publications.

6

PAPER AND COMPUTERS

Gender differences in children's conversations in collaborative activities

Richard Joiner and Karen Littleton

Introduction

The opening chapter of this book (by Baker, Andriessen & Järvelä) starts by reporting an interesting extract of a discussion between two secondary pupils who are trying to solve a science problem. The discussion ends with little agreement and one child finishing with 'I don't give a damn'. For the authors of this chapter, one of the interesting aspects about this extract is that one student is a boy and the other student is a girl. The abrupt and uncooperative nature of the exchange is often characteristic of boy–girl interactions at this age. For a long time now theories of collaborative learning have ignored the social and affective dimensions of collaborative learning situations, such as gender. We know gender is an important part of a child's everyday life (Lloyd & Duveen, 1992). It determines the name of the child, the way a child is talked to and played with, the clothes he or she wears and the toys they play with. At school, gender influences the choices of subjects students choose to take and their performance at school. The aim of this chapter is to investigate the impact of social categories, such as gender, on the conversational dynamics of collaborative activity and how these are related to learning and development. We will then examine a number of explanations for these gender differences, before reporting a study which investigates these different theories in the context of collaborative problem-solving English-language task.

Gender differences in whole-class interaction

Research has shown that gender has an important impact on boys and girls' interactions in the classroom. Howe (2010), in her recent book, reviews the literature and draws three broad conclusions. The first was that on average boys contributed more than girls. Three major British studies (Bousted, 1989; French & French, 1984;

Swan & Graddol, 1988) and one Australian study (Dart & Clark, 1984) reported that boys' contribution dominated discussions concerning curriculum content, classroom management and problem behaviour. A recent study by Hardman (2008) replicated this finding for children in Kenya and Nigeria. The second conclusion was that the high predominance of boy contributions was the result of both teacher selection and pupil-initiated interactions (Bousted, 1989; Swan & Graddol, 1988). Duffy, Warren and Walsh (2001) in their large-scale study of Canadian High School Children found that boys were more likely to initiate interactions than girls in class. Sadker and Sadker (1985) reported that boys were eight times more likely to initiate interactions than girls. In terms of teacher selection, Swan and Graddol (1988) found that teachers were more likely to select boys than girls; a similar finding was reported by Duffy et al. (2001) and Altermatt, Jovanovic and Perry (1998). Also, boys received more attention than girls even before the question was asked. Swan and Graddol (1988) found that teachers gazed at them twice as often as at girls. The third general conclusion was that boys received more feedback than girls. Boys received more negative feedback (e.g. 'For the five hundredth time, seven times eight is not 58' and because they have been misbehaving) than girls (Good et al., 1973; Jones & Wheatley, 1989; Simpson & Ericson, 1983; Stake & Katz, 1984); however, they also received more positive feedback than girls (e.g. 'You're absolutely right' and 'What a great idea') (Good et al., 1973; Jones & Wheatley, 1989; Simpson & Ericson, 1988).

Gender differences in small group interaction

Furthermore, research has found that gender has an important impact on boys and girls' conversations in small groups. Leaper and Smith (2004) conducted three meta-analyses to examine the effect of gender on aspects of language which are thought to exhibit gender differences. These were talkativeness, affiliative speech (e.g. showing support, expressing agreement, or acknowledging the other's contributions) and assertive speech (e.g. directive statements, criticism, or giving information). They found that girls were slightly more talkative and used more affiliative speech than boys, whereas boys used more assertive speech; however, the effect size for these differences was either small or negligible.

Leaper (1991) in an earlier study investigated the influence of the speakers and partners' gender on conversation. He examined communication between pairs of children who were aged 5 and between pairs of children who were aged 7. He found that boys tended to use more assertive utterances than girls, but this was true only in all-boy pairings. Examples of assertive utterances are when one partner rejects the other (e.g. 'you jerk') and reluctant submission (e.g. 'I don't care'). Girls used more affiliative utterances than boys. Examples of affiliative utterance are mutual affirmation (e.g. 'I like playing with you') and willing submission (e.g. 'I don't mind let's do that'). All children modified their communication style depending on the gender of their partner. For example, boys and girls used more informing acts and fewer controlling and domineering acts when communicating with a girl. This study was replicated by Leaper et al. (1999) with an African American sample. Leaper's research shows that boys and girls use different communication styles (e.g. boys use a more assertive style and girls a more affiliative style) and they adapt these styles depending on the gender of the listener.

A similar finding was reported by Leman et al. (2005), who reported a study which investigated the relationship between gender and children's conversational styles in a problem-solving task. In this task children were given three different types of counters (triangles, squares and circles). Each type of counter had a different value. The children were asked in pairs to add the counters together to make 100. However, unbeknown to them, they had been told the counters had different values, which led to conflicts between the children. Leman et al. (2005) found that the children used gendered styles of communication. Girls' conversations were characterised with more affiliative talk than boys' conversations. However, he also found that boys and girls varied their conversational style depending on their partner. For example, boys tended to interrupt their partner more if their partner were a girl than if their partner were a boy, which had the effect of making the affective tone of the interaction very negative. A similar finding has been reported in a more recent study by Leman and Bjonberg (2010) where they compared differences in conversational style between girls and boys when they were discussing what constituted a fair punishment.

A further important consideration is the context of the conversation. Leaper and Smith (2004) in their meta-analysis found that the activity context moderated the gender differences in language use. For example, in feminine type games (e.g. playing 'mummy and daddy') girls would often take the lead, whereas in more masculine games (e.g. superheroes) boys would assume the lead role. Leman (2010) in his chapter argues that variations in the effects of gender in different contexts have important educational implications. For example, in a classroom task where boys are perceived as more expert they may dominate the interaction in mixed-gender group interaction; conversely, girls may dominate the interaction in tasks where they are perceived to be the expert.

Gender differences in collaborative learning

Finally, research suggests that gender has an important influence on boys and girls' learning in collaborative interactions. Psaltis (2011) noted that gender emerged as an important issue early in research on collaborative learning. Bearison, Magzamen and Filardo (1986), in a study on peer interaction and children's spatial reasoning, found that there was a curvilinear relationship between socio-cognitive conflict and development, but only found this relationship for boys and not girls. Furthermore, Cannella (1992), in a study concerning gender composition in pairs and spatial perspective taking, reported that female same-gender pairs disagreed more often and made fewer justifications than male same-gender pairs and mixed-gender pairs. Furthermore, male same-gender pairs progressed more than either female same-gender pairs or mixed-gender pairs. However, Barbieri and Light (1992) conducted a study investigating the effect of gender composition on children's computer-based problem solving and found that the gender composition of the pair did not have an impact on children's learning outcomes. These studies suggest there is no simple relationship between gender, collaboration and learning and development.

More recently, research has begun to investigate the impact of gender and knowledge asymmetry. Leman and Duveen (1999; 2003) investigated the impact of gender and knowledge asymmetry on a moral reasoning task. Their research is based on Piaget's (1932) distinction between asymmetric and symmetric relations. Asymmetric relations are characteristic of the relationships between adults and children and are based on an asymmetry of power, whereas relations of symmetry are found between children or peers and are based on an equality of power. Piaget argued that developmental progress is possible only through the resolution of inter-individual conflicts that occur in symmetric social relations (i.e. the relationships found between peers). In contrast, asymmetric relations inhibit the expression and/ or the resolution of conflicts and thus limit their potential for developmental progress. Leman and Duveen (1999; 2003) looked at two different sources of differential status, gender and knowledge, and compared four different types of pairs: (i) a more expert male paired with a less expert male; (ii) a more expert male paired with a less expert female; (iii) a more expert female paired with a less expert female and (iv) a more expert female paired with a less expert male. They found that there were differences between these four different pair types in terms of the conversations. The biggest differences were between pairs with a more expert male and a less expert female and the pairs with a more expert female and a less expert male. The discussions observed with the more expert male and less expert female pairs were often very short, with very little discussion. The male member would suggest an answer and their female partner would accept it. In contrast, the discussions observed in the female more expert and male less expert pairs were much more extended, with the female members having to persuade their male partner of the validity of their answer. Unfortunately, Leman and Duveen's (1999; 2003) studies did not include a post-test, and so it was not possible to determine whether these differences in conversation had a later impact on children's learning and development.

Fortunately, more recent research employing the same experimental paradigm has included a post-test. Psaltis and his colleagues investigated the impact of gender and knowledge asymmetry on a conservation task with a post-test and a control group who only worked individually (Psaltis & Duveen, 2006, 2007; Psaltis et al., 2009). They replicated the research reported above and found that pair type influenced the conversations and that these differences had an impact on later post-test performance. Male non-conservers who were paired with female conservers performed significantly better than males who were paired with other males and males who had only worked individually. Psaltis (2011) replicated the above finding with a study that investigated the effect of gender and knowledge asymmetry using a spatial transformation task.

Explanations for these gender differences in communication

We have seen, that there are gender differences in communication and these can have an important impact on children's learning and development. There are two possible explanations for these observed gender differences in communication. The first explanation is often referred to as the two cultures approach. Maltz and Borker (1982) explain gender differences by arguing that boys and girls grow up in different subcultures and develop different conversational styles, with males being more assertive and controlling and females being more affiliative and supportive. These two different conversational styles, assertive versus affiliative, relate to different types of interpersonal relationships that are gender-marked, and these colour the emotional tone of the interactions.

A second explanation is termed the status characteristic theory (Berger, Hamit, Norman & Zelditch, 1977; Berger, Rosenholtz and Zelditch, 1980), which proposes that in social interaction individuals evaluate themselves relative to the other participants (Cohen, 1994; Cohen, Lotan, & Catanzarite, 1990; James & Drakich, 1992; Lotan, 2006). If a group expects one of its members to be more competent or more expert, then the group will allow that individual to participate more and afford that member greater influence than others. Leman (2010) argues that the gender differences in conversation could be the result of gender differences in perceived expertise. If one gender is perceived as more expert in one domain than the other gender, then the gender perceived as more expert will take the lead role and the gender perceived as less expert will take the more supportive role. He also argues that these gender differences in conversation will be apparent in mixed-gender interactions only if gender is a relevant consideration in terms of expertise. If it is a not a relevant consideration, then there should be no gender differences in conversation. The status characteristic theory characterisation of expert–novices interaction is similar to Piaget's (1932) characterisation of asymmetrical social relations, with potentially the same negative impact on learning and development.

Both explanations are not necessarily mutually exclusive and they may both explain some or all of the differences observed; however, interestingly they do make differing predictions if we were to compare girls and boys' conversations in a collaborative activity where males are perceived more expert than girls compared with a collaborative activity where there are no perceived gender differences in expertise. The two cultures explanation would predict first that there would be differences in language between all boy pairs and all girl pairs in same-gender interactions because the different communication styles between girls and boys would lead girls to use more affiliative speech and boys to use more assertive or controlling speech. On the other hand, the status characteristic theory would predict, first, no difference in language between all-girl and all-boy pairs in same-gender interactions because in expertise terms children in a pair are comparatively equal. Second, there would be no differences in language between girls and boys in a collaborative activity where girls and boys are perceived to be equally expert.

Third, there would be differences in language between girls and boys in the mixed-gender interactions in a collaborative activity where boys are perceived to be expert because these gender differences in perceived expertise would lead boys to use more assertive and controlling language and girls to use more affiliative language.

The aim of this chapter is to report a study that compared boys and girls' conversations in a collaborative activity where boys are perceived as an expert with a collaborative activity where there is no gender difference in perceived expertise. The task was an English-language task and was the same for both activities. The difference was the method of presentation. In one collaborative activity the task was presented on a computer. Boys are generally perceived as more expert in computer activities than girls (Joiner et al., 1998; Robinson-Stavely & Cooper, 1990) and thus this computer presentation of the task was the collaborative activity where boys were perceived as the expert. In the other collaborative activity, the task was presented on paper and thus there were no expected gender differences in perceived expertise.

Method

We employed a three-factor mixed design, with gender (boy and girl) and type of pair (same and mixed) as the between-participants factors, and the mode of presentation (computer and paper) as the within-participants factor. There were 48 children (24 boys and 24 girls), aged between 13 and 14 years, who participated in the study. They were placed, with the teachers' consultation, into either boy–boy pairs, girl–girl pairs or boy–girl pairs. They were from a large state school in west London, which served a socially mixed catchment area. The children already had considerable experience of using computers and working in pairs and groups, including mixed-gender groups.

Two poems were used in this study. The first was the 'The Wife's Lament' written by Nikolay Nekrasov and translated by Juliet M. Soskice:

> My life is like daytime
> With no sun to warm it!
> My life is like night
> With no glimmer of moon!
> And I – the young woman –
> Am like the swift steed
> On the curb, the young swallow
> With wings crushed and broken;
> My jealous husband,
> Is drunken and snoring,
> But even while snoring,
> He keeps one eye open,

And watches me always,
Me, poor little wife!

The second poem was 'On a Cat, Ageing' written by Alexander Gray:

He blinks upon the hearth rug,
And yawns in deep content,
Accepting all the comforts
That Providence has sent.
Louder he purrs, and louder,
In one glad hymn of praise
For all the night's adventures
For quiet restful days.
Life will go on for ever,
With all that cat can wish:
Warmth and the glad procession
Of fish and milk and fish.
Only – the thought disturbs him –
he's noticed once or twice,
The times are somehow breeding
A nimbler race of mice.

The lines in the poems had been placed in a standard random order. The pupils' task was to discuss the order in which the lines should appear and move them into what they considered was the correct order. There were two versions of the task: (i) a paper version of the task, where the students used a pair of scissors to cut the lines into individual strips and move them until they were satisfied that they were in the correct order; and (ii) a computer version of the task where all the lines were visible on the computer screen and the students used the mouse to select lines and move them into what they thought was the correct order for the poem.

The study consisted of two sessions for each of which the children were taken to a quiet area of the school. The sessions lasted 20 minutes and they were recorded on audio tape. For the paper presentation of the task the children worked in pairs, seated at a table. In the centre of the table was a sheet of A3 paper, a copy of the poem, a pair of scissors and some glue. For the computer presentation the children worked in pairs and were seated at a computer placed on top of a trolley. The children were shown how to move the lines of the poem. On the top of the computer were instructions in case the children forgot how to move the lines. Before the students started the first session, they were given the following instruction:

We've talked a lot about spoken English and how your teacher has to assess this for the National Curriculum. Today I'm going to look at your discussion work when you're working with a partner. The paper/screen you see in front of you has a poem on it, but the lines are in the wrong order. What I'd like you to do, between you, is cut up/move the lines until you think the poem makes sense. Remember that we're not looking at who gets it right, but at how well you discuss things with your partner. I'm just going to watch and take a few notes, so I can't answer any questions once you start. Okay.

All students attempted both the computer and paper presentation of the task. In the first session they attempted one presentation of the task and in the second session they attempted the other. The second session was approximately two weeks after the first session. The order of presentation for both versions of the task (computer versus paper) and for each poem were counterbalanced (see Table 6.1).

In the second session, the students were given the following instructions.

> If you remember, a couple of weeks ago you looked at a poem that was mixed up and tried to put it in the right order. Well today, you are going to do a similar exercise, with a different poem only this time it's on paper/the computer.

During the sessions, the experimenter recorded the number of times the lines of poetry were moved by each student and the time each student had control of the mouse. The audio tape recordings of the interactions were transcribed.

The transcripts were analysed for number of utterances and type of utterance, which were dived into affiliative and assertive utterances. Four types of assertive utterances were identified, which were based on the categories used by Leaper and Smith (2004) for describing assertive utterances and they were as follows:

(i) Proposing: an utterance was classified as proposing when one of the pair suggested something they might do (e.g. cutting the paper). For example
    A   I'll cut and you sort.
  An utterance was also classified as proposing if it concerned a decision about where a line might go. For example:
    A   Oh. This is definitely the start. 'My life is like daytime. Where my life is like night'.
(ii) Disagreeing: an utterance was classified as Disagreeing when one member of the pair disagreed with or discouraged their partner's proposal. For example:
    A   That comes last.

TABLE 6.1 Order of presentation

Session	Order 1	Order 2	Order 3	Order 4
1	Computer	Paper	Computer	Paper
	The wife's lament	On a Cat ageing	The wife's lament	On a Cat ageing
2	Paper	Computer	Paper	Computer
	On a Cat ageing	The wife's lament	On a Cat ageing	The wife's lament

B   No, its got a comma.

Often these might have quite a negative tone:

A   Don't be silly that is completely wrong.

(iii) Seeking Information: an utterance was classified as seeking information when one or both members were trying to seek information from the other:

A   Where do you think that goes, before or after?

(iv) Repetition: an utterance was classified as repetition when one pair merely repeated the lines of the poetry. An example is shown below. The lines are repeated from 'On a cat ageing':

A   And watches me always.

B   But even while snoring.

The final category was classified as an affiliative utterance and was based on the categories identified by Leaper and Smith (2004).

(v) Supporting: an utterance was classified as supporting when one pair agreed or encouraged the other's proposal. The example below shows one child explicitly agreeing with the other:

A   Oh that's definitely first.

B   Oh yeah.

Other examples are when one child encourages the other child and exhibit quite a positive emotional tone:

A   Come on we can do it.

An independent coder performed a reliability check. The coder analysed 25 percent of the transcripts (i.e. 820 utterances) and agreed with all but three of the utterances.

Results

We first compared the number and type of utterances observed in the all-boy pairs and the all-girl pairs, regardless of whether the task was the computer version or the paper version. Tables 6.2 and 6.3 present the findings and show that there were a number of significant differences. Contrary to predictions, we found that girls in the all-girl pairs were more likely to disagree compared with boys in all-boy pairs both in the paper version and the computer version. Moreover, the boys were more likely to be supportive both in the paper version and the computer version than girls in all girl-pairs. Finally, the boys made more utterances and asked for more information than girls in the computer version. All other differences were non-significant.

The differences between boys and girls in mixed-gender interactions were analysed regardless of whether they using the paper or computer version of the task. We found that there were no significant differences in terms of either affiliative utterances or assertive utterances.

Next, we compared boys and girls' interactions in the computer version of the task in mixed-gender pairs. Table 6.4 shows that there were a number of significant differences. Boys overall made more utterances, they made more proposals, more

TABLE 6.2 Differences between all boy pairs and all girl pairs in computer interactions

	Boys		Girls			
	M	SD	M	SD	F	partial $\eta2$
Total Number of Utterance	39.6	6.9	35.5	4.3	4.1	0.12★
Assertive						
Proposing	18.1	3.1	17.3	2.9	0.5	0.02
Disagree	4.1	1.4	6.7	1.7	21.5	0.42★
Seeking Information	5.8	1.4	3.5	1.3	22.9	0.43★
Repetition	9.5	2.2	8.6	1.8	1.5	0.05
Affiliative						
Supporting	6.6	2.0	4.6	1.4	10.5	0.26★
Action						
Move	544.1	208.8	495.6	203.1	0.5	0.02

★ p < 0.05

disagreements and repeated more utterances than girls. They also controlled the mouse more than girls. Girls made more supportive utterances.

There were no significant differences between girls and boys in the mixed-gender interactions when they were using the paper version of the task on either the affiliative or the assertive utterances (see Table 6.5).

Discussion

The aim of the study reported in this chapter was to compare differences between the conversational dynamics of girls and boys in a collaborative activity where boys

TABLE 6.3 Differences between all boy pairs and all girl pairs in paper interactions

	Boys		Girls			
	M	SD	M	SD	F	partial $\eta2$
Total Number of Utterance	29.4	5.5	27.5	5.2	1.0	0.03
Assertive						
Proposing	13.8	3.5	13.0	13.8	0.4	0.01
Disagree	3.3	1.5	4.5	3.3	6.6	0.18★
Seeking Information	4.4	1.7	4.6	1.6	0.0	0.00
Repetition	8.1	1.9	7.6	1.4	0.7	0.02
Affiliative						
Supporting	5.7	1.4	4.6	5.7	4.6	0.13★
Action						
Move	11.6	3.0	11.8	11.6	0.0	0.00

★ p < 0.05

TABLE 6.4 Differences between girls and boys in the mixed gender computer interactions

	Boys		Girls			
	M	SD	M	SD	F	partial η2
Total Number of Utterance	51.5	7.0	31.0	6.8	35.2	0.71★
Assertive						
Proposing	26.3	4.7	12.1	3.9	42.6	0.75★
Disagree	9.1	2.7	4.5	2.4	12.6	0.47★
Seeking Information	4.0	1.8	4.4	1.7	<1	0.01
Repetition	12.8	2.7	9.3	2.4	7.5	0.35★
Affiliative						
Supporting	4.8	1.2	6.4	1.2	6.1	0.30★
Action						
Move	751.8	318.9	287.1	276.5	9.7	0.41★

★ p < 0.05

were perceived as more expert than girls, with a collaborative activity where there was no gender difference in perceived expertise. Consistent with our expectations, boys in all-boy pairs in the computer version of the task made more information-seeking utterances than girls in all-girl pairs. However, contrary to our expectations, girls in all-girl pairs in both the paper version of the task and the computer version of the task made more disagreeing utterances than boys in all-boy pairs. Furthermore, boys made more supportive utterances than girls in same-gender pairs in both the computer and paper version of the task. There was no difference in the language used by girls and boys when they worked in mixed-gender pairs on the paper version of the task; however, as expected, there were considerable differences in the language used by girls and boys when they worked in mixed-gender pairs on the

TABLE 6.5 Differences between girls and boys in the mixed gender paper interactions

	Boys		Girls			
	M	SD	M	SD	F	partial η2
Total Number of Utterance	30.4	5.4	29.9	4.5	0.0	0.00
Assertive						
Proposing	12.0	2.5	12.6	2.8	0.2	0.02
Disagree	4.8	1.6	5.6	1.9	1.0	0.07
Seeking Information	5.1	1.1	4.5	1.9	0.7	0.05
Repetition	8.0	2.0	8.3	1.5	0.1	0.01
Affiliative						
Supporting	5.0	1.3	4.6	1.4	0.3	0.02
Action						
Move	11.9	4.1	11.9	2.5	0.0	0.00

★ p < 0.05

computer-based version of the task. Boys made more assertive and controlling utterances (i.e. proposals, disagreements and repeated utterances) than girls, and girls made more supportive utterances than boys. The boys also dominated control of the mouse in the computer-based collaborative activity.

These findings replicate earlier research which has shown that social categories such as gender have an impact on the conversational dynamics of collaborative activity and that the impact of gender is moderated by the context of the activity in a similar way to that reported by Leaper and Smith (2004), who found that the conversational dynamics changes depending on the gender marking of the activity, although for conversations in same-gender collaborative activity our findings were not what we expected and were counter to those reported in the literature and to the two cultures explanation (e.g. Leaper & Smith, 2004). We expected that girls would make more affiliative and less assertive and controlling utterances, whereas we found that girls made more assertive and controlling utterances and boys made more affiliative utterances. However, the gender differences observed in mixed-gender interaction were consistent with the status characteristic theory and consistent with the literature on gender differences in collaborative computer-based activities (Howe, 1997). Boys in the computer-based version of the task, where boys are thought to be more expert, were expected to use more assertive and controlling utterances and girls more affiliative utterances and this is exactly what we found. In the paper-based version of the task, where there were no gender differences in expertise, no gender differences in conversation were expected or found.

The interesting question is whether these gender differences in conversation have any impact on children's learning. Recent research would suggest that they do. For example, Leman and Duveen (1999; 2003) in their studies on the impact of gender and knowledge asymmetry on conversation involving an expert child with a non-expert child, they found that, in the pairs where the female child was expert and the male child was less expert, the discussion was extended, and the female partners had to use a wide variety of arguments to convince their male partners of the validity of their answer. In contrast, the discussions of the pairs where the male was expert and the female was less expert were very brief and consisted of the male partner proposing an answer and the female partner agreeing with it. Psaltis (Psaltis & Duveen, 2006, 2007; Psaltis et al., 2009; Psaltis, 2011) found similar differences in conversation as a function of gender and knowledge asymmetry. Furthermore, they found this had an impact on later learning and development. The females who were less expert and paired with an expert male made the least progress, whereas the males who were less expert and paired with an expert female progressed the most. These findings suggest that the extended arguments, found in pairs with a female expert and a male who was less expert, may well be very beneficial for learning and development.

In the current study, we found that the female same-gender pairs disagreed more than the male same-gender pairs in both the computer and paper version of the task, but the males in the mixed-gender pairs in the computer version of the task disagreed the most. Unfortunately, we do not know whether the disagreement in either the same-gender pairs or the mixed-gender pairs were similar to the extended arguments observed by Leman and Duveen (1999; 2003) and Psaltis (Psaltis & Duveen, 2006, 2007; Psaltis et al., 2009; Psaltis, 2011) in pairs with the more expert female and the less expert male or the brief disagreements observed in the pairs with a more expert male and a less expert female. In addition, the study did not have a measure of learning and thus it was not possible to examine whether these differences had an impact on learning. Further work is necessary to examine gender differences in the nature of the disagreements and to analyse whether they were extended arguments or brief disagreements and whether the differences in conversation observed in this study would have an impact on learning. There may also be gender differences in how they are resolved. It might be the case that conflicts in the more assertive conversational styles are either not resolved at all or, if they are resolved, they are resolved in such a manner that it results in a very negative emotional tone with both partners not wishing to continue working together. On the other hand, a more affiliative style may lead to a more productive resolution of the conflict, which results in a more positive emotional tone.

Another area of future research would be to investigate the emotional tone of the discussions and whether that is influenced by the gender composition of the pairs. Very little research has investigated whether the emotional tone of the pairs is influenced by the gender composition of groups. Children at the age of the participants in this study tend to have friends of the same gender and therefore they are unlikely to be working with people who are their best friends. Therefore, the emotional tone is unlikely to be very positive. Research has reported that negative socio-emotional processes can have a negative impact on productive group work. Chiu and Khoo (2003) found that rudeness and especially rude criticisms undermine effective group work. Similarly, Webb, Nemer and Zuniga (2002) found that negative socio-emotional behaviour had a negative impact on productive group work. Further, research is required to investigate whether gender composition impacts on the emotional tone of collaboration. The first step would be to try and develop a way of measuring emotional tone during collaborative interaction. One possibility would be to use some form of self-report measure of the emotional tone of the interaction, possibly by the use of a questionnaire after the interaction; unfortunately this would suffer from the limitations of human memory and would provide only a global measure of emotional tone. An alternative and superior method would be to use real-time psychophysiological measures (e.g. galvanic skin response or levels of cortisol) and relate them back to the interaction and learning outcome. This method could potentially provide a more precise measure of emotional tone, enabling a precise linking of emotional tone, interaction and learning outcome.

In conclusion, this study showed that the gender and the gender marking of an activity had an impact on children's conversations. More specifically, it had an impact on the disagreements observed in the collaboration, which are known to be important in learning and development. More research is needed to further investigate the impacts of gender and gender marking on collaboration and how that in turn impacts on their learning development.

References

Altermatt, E. R., Jovanovic, J. and Perry, M. (1998) 'Bias or responsivity? Sex or achievement level effects on teacher classroom questioning practices.', *Journal of Educational Psychology*, 90: 516–27.

Barbieri, M. S. and Light, P. H. (1992) 'Interaction, gender and performance on a computer based problem solving task.' *Learning and Instruction*, 2: 199–213.

Bearison, D., Magzamen, S. & Filardo, E. K. (1986). Socio-cognitive conflict and cognitive growth in young children. *Merrill-Palmer Quarterly*, 32: 51–72.

Berger, J., Hamit, F., Norman, R. Z. and Zelditch, M. (1977) *Status Characteristics in Social Interaction: An Expectation States Approach*. New York: Elsevier.

Berger, J., Rosenholtz, S. J. and Zelditch, M. (1980) 'Status organizing processes', *Annual Review of Sociology*, 6: 479–508.

Bousted, M. W. (1989) Who talks? The position of girls in mixed sex classrooms. *English in Education*, 23: 41–51.

Cannella, G. S. (1992). Gender composition and conflict in dyadic sociocognitive interaction: Effects on spatial learning in young children. *Journal of Experimental Education*, 6, 29–41.

Chiu, M. M. and Khoo, L. (2003) 'Rudeness and status effects during group problem solving: Do they bias evaluations and reduce the likelihood of correct solutions?' *Journal of Educational Psychology*, 95: 506–23.

Cohen, E. G. (1994) *Designing Groupwork: Strategies for the Heterogeneous Classroom* (trans. F. Ouellet, 2nd edn). New York: Teachers College Press.

Cohen, E. G., Lotan, R., and Catanzarite, L. (1990) 'Treating status problems in the cooperative classroom.' In S. Sharan (Ed.), *Cooperative Learning: Theory and Research* (pp. 203–30). New York: Praeger.

Dart, B. and Clark, J. (1984) 'Sexism in schools: A new look.' *Educational Review*, 40: 41–9.

Duffy, J., Warren, K., and Walsh, M. (2001) 'Classroom interactions: gender of teacher, gender of student, and classroom subject.' *Sex Roles*, 45: 579–93.

French, J. and French, P. (1984) 'Gender imbalances in the classroom: an interactional account.' *Educational Research*, 26: 127–36.

Good, T., Cooper, H., and Blakely, S. (1973) 'Effects of teacher sex and student sex on classroom interaction.' *Journal of Educational Psychology*, 65: 74–87.

Hardman, F. (2008) Teachers' use of feedback in whole-class and group-based talk. In N. Mercer & S. Hodgkinson (eds.) Exploring Talk in School (pp. 131–150). London: Sage.

Howe, C. (1997) *Gender and Classroom Interaction: A Research Review*. Edinburgh: Scottish Council for Research in Education.

Howe, C. (2010) *Peer Groups and Children's Development*. London: Wiley/Blackwell.

James, D. and Drakich, J. (1992) 'Understanding gender differences in amount of talk: a critical review of the research', In D. Tannen (Ed.), *Gender and Conversational Interaction* (pp. 281–306). New York: Oxford University Press.

Joiner, R., Messer, D., Light, P. and Littleton, K. (1998) 'The effects of gender, expectations of success and social comparison on children's performance on a computer-based task.' *Educational Psychology*, 18: 319–25.

Jones, G. and Wheatley, J. (1989) 'Gender influences in classroom displays and student-teacher behaviour.' *Science Education*, 73: 535–45.

Leaper, C. (1991) 'Influence and involvement in children's discourse: Age, gender, and partner effects.' *Child Development*, 62: 797–811.

Leaper, C. and Smith, T. A. (2004) 'A meta-analytic review of gender variations in children's talk: Talkativeness, affiliative speech, and assertive speech.', *Developmental Psychology*, 40: 993–1027.

Leaper, C., Tenenbaum, H. R. and Shaffer, T. G. (1999) 'Communication patterns of African-American girls and boys from low-income, urban backgrounds.' *Child Development*, 70: 1489–503.

Leman, P. J. (2010) 'Gender, collaboration and children's learning.' In K. Littleton and C. Howe (eds.), *Educational Dialogues: Understanding and Promoting Productive Interaction* (pp. 216–39). London: Routledge.

Leman, P. J. and Bjornberg, M. (2010) 'Conversation, development, and gender: A study of changes in children's concepts of punishment.' *Child Development*, 81: 960–73.

Leman, P. J. and Duveen, G. (1999) 'Representations of authority and children's moral reasoning.' *European Journal of Social Psychology*, 29, 557–75.

Leman, P. J. and Duveen, G. (2003). 'Gender identity, social influence and children's conversations.' *Swiss Journal of Psychology*, 62, 223–35. doi:10.1024//1421-0185. 62.3.149.

Leman, P. J., Ahmed, S. and Ozarow, L. (2005) 'Gender, gender relations, and the social dynamics of children's conversations. *Developmental Psychology*, 41: 64–74.

Lloyd, B. and Duveen, G. (1992) *Gender Identities and Education: The Impact of Starting School.* Hemel Hempstead: Harvester Wheatsheaf.

Lotan, R. A. (2006) 'Managing groupwork in the heterogeneous classroom.' In C. M. Evertson and C. S. Weinstein (Eds.), *Handbook of Classroom Management: Research, Practice, and Contemporary Issues* (pp. 525–39). Mahwah, NJ: Lawrence Erlbaum Associates Publishers.

Maltz, D. and Borker, R. (1982) 'A cultural approach to male-female mis-communication.' In J. Gumperz (Ed.), *Language and Social Identities* (pp. 196–216). Cambridge, England: Cambridge University Press.

Piaget, J. (1932). *The moral judgment of the child.* London: Routledge & Kegan Paul.

Psaltis, C. (2011) The constructive role of gender asymmetry in social interaction: Further evidence. *British Journal of Developmental Psychology*, 29: 305–12.

Psaltis, C. and Duveen, G. (2006) 'Social relations and cognitive development: The influence of conversation type and representations of gender.' *European Journal of Social Psychology*, 37: 407–30.

Psaltis, C. and Duveen, G. (2007) 'Conversation and conversation types: Forms of recognition and cognitive development.' *British Journal of Developmental Psychology*, 25: 79–102.

Psaltis, C., Duveen, G. and Perret-Clermont, A. N. (2009) 'The Social and the Psychological: Structure and Context in Intellectual Development.' *Human Development*, 52: 291–312.

Robinson-Stavely, K. and Cooper, J. (1990) 'Mere presence, gender and reactions to computers: Studying human computer interaction in social context.' *Journal of Experimental Social Psychology*, 26: 168–83.

Sadker, M. and Sadker, D. (1985) 'Sexism in the schoolroom of the 80s. *Psychology Today*, 54–7.

Simpson, A. W. and Ericson, M. T. (1983) 'Teacher's verbal and nonverbal communication patterns as a function of teacher race, student, gender, and student race.' *American Educational Research Journal*, 20: 183–98.

Stake, J. and Katz, J. (1984) 'Teacher-pupil relationships in the elementary school classroom: Teacher-gender and pupil-gender differences.' *American Educational Research Journal*, 19: 465–71.

Swan, J. and Graddol, D. (1988) 'Gender inequalities in classroom talk.' *English in Education*, 22: 48–65.

Verba, M. and Winnykamen, F. (1992) 'Expert novice interactions: influence of power status.' *European Journal of Psychology of Education*, 7: 61–71.

Webb, N. M., Nemer, K. M. and Zuniga, S. (2002) 'Short circuits or superconductors? Effects of group composition on high-achieving students' science performance.' *American Educational Research Journal*, 39: 943–89.

SECTION 3
Emotion and motivation

7

MOTIVATION AND EMOTION SHAPING KNOWLEDGE CO-CONSTRUCTION

Dejana Mullins, Anne Deiglmayr and Hans Spada

Introduction

When students co-construct knowledge while collaborating on a task, cognitive processes interact with motivational and emotional processes at both the individual and the group level. Important influences between motivation/emotion and cognition can be observed in both directions: Students' individual motivation influences how deeply they are willing to engage in the joint task. Individual task commitment is also affected by volitional regulation at the group level. Higher task commitment, in turn, typically leads to more effective knowledge co-construction, which then constitutes a positive learning experience with the potential to foster students' interest and self-efficacy in the learning domain, their positive valuing of knowledge co-construction as a worthwhile learning activity, as well as their identification with their group. Despite these important interactions, studies of collaborative learning often focus on either cognitive or motivational-affective aspects. Even worse, the role of motivation and emotion in knowledge co-construction has often been neglected in favor of cognitive aspects.

The goal of this chapter is to show how we can expand our understanding of effective collaboration by including aspects of motivation and emotion. To this purpose, we draw on the extensive research literature on motivational-affective aspects in individual learning contexts, which is still waiting to be applied to collaborative learning settings. We elaborate which roles these "individual" motivational-affective concepts may play in a collaborative learning context, and provide examples from several of our own studies in which motivation and emotion interacted with cognitive processes in collaborative knowledge construction. In this chapter, we interpret our findings in light of the motivational-affective concepts introduced in the theoretical section. The examples show how these concepts, which were initially developed for individual learning settings, can help to develop a scientifically targeted motivational-affective perspective on collaborative learning. The examples from our research focus on collaboration in dyadic settings, but some may be transferred to larger groups. The collaborative settings realized in the experimental studies we report on vary from face-to-face to virtual collaboration, and from collaborative problem-solving between peers with diverse expertise to the collaborative drawing of inferences based on distributed information. In all examples, our unit of analysis is the individual student within the group; for a group-level perspective, including a discussion of possible tensions and differences in motivational attitudes between group members, we refer the reader to Järvenoja and Järvelä, "Regulating emotions together for motivated collaboration" (Chapter 8, this volume).

Theoretical background

It is commonly assumed that students' motivation influences how deeply they are willing to engage in learning. What yields high student motivation? Many motivational theories consider motivation as an interaction between people's values (e.g. the subjective value of a good grade) and their expectancies of success (e.g. the expected likelihood that studying hard for a test will lead to a good grade). In the following review, we will follow this lead and look at the factors that influence the value and the expectancy component of the motivation equation. That is, we will look at some factors that influence which goals students are motivated to obtain when engaging in (collaborative) learning, and we will consider factors that contribute to their confidence that putting effort into the (collaborative) learning activity will help them reach their goals. Thereby, we will particularly focus on the role of individual learner differences, and how these interact with the learning situation (cf. Dweck & Leggett 1988; Rheinberg, Vollmeyer, & Rollett 2000). The last section of the theoretical background reviews the role of affective factors that contribute to students' motivation. While most of the concepts introduced in this section originate from research on individual learning, we will frequently point out the role of the collaborative context, for instance the interplay between interpersonal feedback and the motivational-affective dimension.

Subjective value in (collaborative) learning

What is it that students value about learning activities – be they individual or collaborative? One widely accepted notion is that students can be motivated to engage in an activity either by pure interest in the activity itself (see Chapter 2, this volume), or by some outcome of that activity, for instance, a reward or the activity's instrumentality for some other goal. This has been most clearly described in Ryan and Deci's (e.g. 2000) *self-determination theory*. Ryan and Deci distinguish two qualities of motivation: intrinsic and extrinsic motivation. *Intrinsic motivation* refers to behavior that is self-determined and performed out of interest in and enjoyment of the task itself. Intrinsic motivation to engage in (collaborative) learning activities can be particularly expected if those activities "have the appeal of novelty, challenge, or aesthetic value" (Ryan & Deci 2000: 60f.). However, learning environments that exercise high amounts of external control can undermine intrinsic motivation.

In contrast to intrinsic motivation, *extrinsic motivation* is directed towards behavior that is instrumental to a specific outcome, for instance a better grade or the appreciation by teachers or peers. Depending on the degree of autonomy perceived by the learner, it is possible to further distinguish different kinds of extrinsic motivation. Behavior that is purely externally regulated is typically accompanied by emotions of resentment and disinterest. One example would be that a student mainly performs a task to avoid sanctions. On the other hand if learners identify with and integrate the goals of the learning activity, they will demonstrate persistence and engagement in learning (Ryan & Deci 2000). Since many learning tasks are not inherently interesting to students, "knowing how to promote more active and volitional (versus passive and controlling) forms of extrinsic motivation becomes an essential strategy for teaching" (Ryan & Deci 2000: 55). A major factor in this context is the feeling of *relatedness to others*: Students are more motivated to engage in a learning activity when they know that their activities are valued by significant others, for instance, by their teacher or peers. The collaboration with a partner increases the feeling of relatedness; the collaboration thus has the potential to yield an integrated form of extrinsic motivation if the learning activity is valued by the peer. Another important factor for the internalization of extrinsically motivated behavior is the *competence* perceived by the learner. For instance, positive performance feedback will increase a students' perceived competence and thus yield higher motivation and engagement. On the other hand, negative feedback may reduce motivation and promote frustration. In a collaborative situation, the learning partners are a crucial source for feedback. This feedback may have both positive and negative effects: From a cognitive point of view, the feedback of learning partners can support knowledge acquisition by pointing out misconceptions and providing informative feedback (Webb 1989); on the other hand, from a motivational-affective perspective, the feedback may also be detrimental, particularly if the social comparison with learning partners reveals own deficits and yields frustration.

Other influential theories of motives and goals that underlie learning motivation have focused on the kinds of goals students pursue when engaging in (collaborative) learning activities. For instance, the theory by Dweck and Leggett (1988) distinguishes between performance and learning goals. Students who pursue a *performance goal* aim at being judged as competent (e.g. receiving good grades) and want to avoid situations that show their inadequacy. When they are concerned that their ability might be insufficient, they avoid potential learning opportunities and display a helplessness that is reflected both in their actions and their emotions: They express negative affect towards the task, such as boredom, and do not apply effective learning or problem-solving strategies. In contrast, learners who pursue a *learning goal* aim at improving their competences and want to acquire new skills. When they are faced with a challenging situation, they are motivated to master the challenge. While students differ in their dispositional *goal orientation*, the goal orientation can also be influenced by characteristics of the learning situation. For instance, learning goals can be influenced through vicarious learning from a model. Particularly if the student perceives a great similarity between him- or herself and a model, such as a more competent peer, it is likely that he or she will adopt the learning goals and the performance standards of the model (cf. Schunk 2003). This modelling effect is particularly relevant in a collaborative setting as the learning partners may influence one another. For instance, one student may adopt the learning goal orientation by his or her learning partner and as a consequence show increased learning efforts.

A dichotomy similar to learning and performance goals is proposed by Higgins' (1997) *regulatory focus theory*. Higgins distinguishes between two different foci that drive a learner's goals: promotion focus versus prevention focus. *Promotion-focused* students are motivated by strong ideals, striving to reach their aspirations and hopes. *Prevention-focused* students, on the other hand, are motivated by strong oughts, striving to fulfil their felt duties and responsibilities. The same goal (e.g. receiving an "A" on an upcoming math test) will lead to different strategic behaviors when perceived from a promotion versus prevention focus: promotion-focused students will use eager strategies that help them advance towards their goal (e.g. additional practice with math problems they find particularly challenging), while prevention-focused students will use vigilant strategies that will help them ensure they do not mismatch a given standard (e.g. being careful not to miss a class and to do all the assigned homework; cf. Higgins 2000). Promotion focus leads to greater *perseverance* in the face of difficulties (Higgins 1997) and fosters creative problem-solving (Friedman & Förster 2001). On the other hand, a prevention focus leads to better performance if a task requires great self-control, such as working on an assigned problem in the face of a tempting distraction (Freitas, Liberman, & Higgins 2002). While people differ in their dispositional tendency to be promotion- versus prevention-focused, regulatory focus can also be induced by the learning situation. In particular, feedback and rewards that emphasize advancement towards a goal foster a promotion focus, while feedback and rewards that emphasize the mismatch to a goal or standard foster a prevention focus (cf. Brockner & Higgins 2001; Higgins 1997). Just like learning goals, regulatory focus may also be modelled by figures of authority or by one's peers (Brockner & Higgins 2001). Furthermore, the history of successes and failures in working on a particular type of task may lead to the adoption of either a promotion focus (if feedback has been predominantly positive) or a prevention focus (if feedback has been predominantly negative; cf. Higgins 1997). Solving problems with a partner rather than alone will often lead to more successful performance and thus more positive feedback, and may in this way induce students with a promotion focus.

Particularly in collaborative learning activities, relevant goals and values concern not only the task or learning domain, but also social and interpersonal aspects. Students might be motivated to collaborate with their peers not (only) to solve a joint problem, but also because they value their group. For example, students' self-identity is strongly influenced by the accomplishments of groups that they feel part of (Karau & Williams 1995). Engaging in successful collaborative problem-solving therefore is prone to enhance students' feelings of belonging to their group. Students then identify more strongly with group norms and goals, such as rules and standards regarding collaborative learning and problem-solving.

Self-efficacy, collective efficacy, and indispensability

So far, we have reviewed factors that influence the subjective value of a learning activity. However, a high subjective value is not sufficient to yield a high learning motivation. In fact, even if a collaborative learning activity could potentially yield outcomes that are valued highly by a student, he or she will be motivated to perform them only if he or she also expects his or her efforts to be effective. A very relevant concept in this respect is *self-efficacy*: the belief that one is able to perform well on a given task. The concept of self-efficacy was first introduced by Albert Bandura (1986). Similarly, *collective efficacy* refers to group members' conviction that their group is able to perform a given task. Learners who are convinced that they and/or their group can master a task will show greater persistence and better achievement (Bandura 1993; Schunk 2003). On the other hand, the successful completion of a task can also positively affect self-efficacy.

In collaborative learning settings, many tasks are collective tasks, that is, the group members' individual contributions are combined into a single group product, and only the final group product is evaluated. In these settings, valued goals and high efficacy beliefs may not be sufficient to motivate students; in addition, students need to feel that their individual effort is essential, that is, *indispensable* for the group's success. Otherwise, the frequently documented phenomenon of social loafing is likely to occur: Students reduce their individual effort and rely on their team members to do the work (Salomon & Globerson 1989; Karau & Williams 1995). This is particularly the case if individual contributions cannot be identified. Further, high-performing students often expect their group members to loaf and may therefore withhold their own effort in order not to be the "sucker" who is exploited by the group (sucker effect: cf. Salomon & Globerson 1989). Students are more motivated to contribute to collective tasks if they perceive their individual contribution to be indispensable, for example because they hold specific expertise on a part of the task, and if their costs for contributing to the group's effort are not very high (cf. Shepperd 1993).

Affective aspects contributing to motivation

In addition to motivation, students' emotions during learning can have an impact on their knowledge co-construction. In a literature search on academic emotions, Pekrun, Goetz, Titz, and Perry (2002) found that the emotion that was most often considered in studies on achievement and learning is anxiety, more precisely *test anxiety*. Anxiety may increase task-irrelevant thinking and thus reduce beneficial cognitive processes. However, as our everyday experience tells us, anxiety is certainly not the only emotion that can influence students' motivational and cognitive processes and thereby affect their achievement. Students experience a variety of emotions in an academic setting: positive emotions such as enjoyment of learning, hope, pride, and relief, and negative emotions such as anxiety, anger, and shame. These emotions are related to student motivation and achievement (e.g. Pekrun et al. 2002). It is often assumed that positive emotions promote motivation and achievement, while negative emotions are detrimental for learning. However, this conceptualisation is too simplistic (e.g. Kort, Reilly, & Picard 2001). For instance, anxiety has a different impact on learning for different students: While for some students, it correlates negatively with motivation, for others, it is positively related to motivation (Pekrun et al. 2002). One possible explanation may be that some students appraise a test situation as a *threat*, thus yielding disengagement and withdrawal, while others view it as a *challenge*, yielding increased motivation to master the challenge (Lazarus & Launier 1978). So far, the impact of emotions on student learning has often been addressed only indirectly in the context of motivation theories (*Greder-Specht 2009*). Several examples of the interplay between motivational and affective factors were already mentioned in the previous sections. A first example is the concept of *relatedness*: Emotionally positive relations with peers can promote student motivation and thus increase their learning. Similarly, positive emotions such as joy and pleasure are closely related to intrinsic motivation (Ryan & Deci 2000). Finally, emotions are closely linked to students' self-efficacy and collective efficacy: Students' evaluations of themselves and their group regarding the effectiveness of their actions for reaching a given goal can influence their emotional experiences during learning, with high effectiveness leading to positive emotions and low effectiveness leading to negative emotions (e.g. Bandura & Cervone 1983).

Emotions also play an important role in a collaborative learning setting as another source for affective experiences is added: the social environment. For instance, if students do not get along well with their learning partners and show negative emotions towards them, they may decrease their engagement in the learning activity. However, if they are positively attached to the group, they will be more likely to adopt the partners' goals and be motivated to succeed in the learning activity. The other way around, successful collaboration is prone to elicit positive affect (for example, shared *"Eureka" moments* during collaborative problem-solving, Bühler 1907). This may be one reason why a history of successful collaboration often results in improved interpersonal relations between students (e.g. Tolmie et al. 2010).

Examples of interactions between cognition and motivation/emotion in knowledge co-construction

In the previous section, we reviewed theories of learning, motivation and emotion. These theories were mainly developed for individual learning settings, but have relevance also for collaborative learning and knowledge co-construction. In the following section, we give examples from our own research that provide insights into the interplay of motivational-affective and cognitive factors during knowledge co-construction. For each example, we first provide some background information on the experimental study it was taken from. In particular, we describe the collaborative setting and highlight the main cognitive aspects targeted by the instructional intervention under study in the experiment. Then, we describe in which way motivational-affective factors interacted with cognitive aspects in shaping the process of collaborative knowledge construction. All of the examples are taken from experimental studies emphasizing the cognitive dimension of collaborative learning (e.g. following a collaboration script; exchanging information with a partner; elaborating on information). All examples are re-analysed based on some of the theories and concepts introduced in the theoretical background section. These re-analyses demonstrate that much can be gained by taking into account motivational-affective factors as a relevant analytical dimension when trying to understand the interplay of individual and group-level phenomena in collaborative learning.

Effects of instruction on motivation to engage in knowledge co-construction

The first research example demonstrates how the effectiveness of instruction on knowledge co-construction can be mediated by motivational effects, in this case, an instance of "overscripting" collaboration. While instruction with the help of a collaboration model promoted student motivation and self-efficacy, instruction through a collaboration script was too coercive and thus demotivated students.

The collaboration setting

In one of our projects (the Netcoop project, e.g. Rummel & Spada 2005), dyads consisting of a medical student and a student of psychology from the University of Freiburg, Germany, collaborated via a desktop videoconferencing system. They worked on hypothetic patient cases that had been designed to require the combined application of both medical and psychological expertise to be solved correctly. During the experiment, participants were seated in two separate rooms at our research lab. The desktop videoconferencing system allowed participants to see and hear each other while discussing the case. It included a shared workspace they could use to prepare a written joint solution as well as two individual text editors. In total, 76 dyads participated in the project (in two separate experiments). Each collaboration lasted for about 120 minutes.

The cognitive dimension

In order to improve collaboration, an instructional approach was taken: Dyads first underwent a learning phase (experimental phase) before they collaborated freely during a test phase (application phase). The main goal was to evaluate two methods of instructional support that were implemented in the learning phase. In the model conditions, participants observed a model collaboration in which two collaborators solved the first patient case. The model presentation consisted of recorded dialogue and animated text clips that allowed participants to follow the development of a model solution in the shared text editor. In the script conditions, participants were provided with a script guiding them through their collaboration on the first case.

Interplay with motivational-affective dimension

In a first study of the Netcoop project, the model condition significantly outperformed the script condition. Observations during the study and remarks of the participants indicated that this effect was mediated by student motivation (cf. Rummel & Spada 2005).

In the model condition, the two model collaborators displayed effective collaboration strategies and provided criteria for a successful problem solution. Furthermore, they were motivated to solve the task and to collaborate with each other. The similarity between the models and the study participants (similar age; models displayed a similar level of expertise) may have contributed to the fact that the study participants adopted not only the collaboration strategies, but also the positive attitude towards the task and the collaboration (cf. Schunk 2003). Indeed, dyads from the model condition collaborated with much enthusiasm and showed a great persistence to reach a good outcome. Furthermore, the success of the model may have encouraged the participants that they would also be able to master the problem, thus increasing their *self-efficacy* and *collective efficacy* (cf. Bandura 1986).

In contrast, in the scripted condition, students showed *reactance* towards the script and displayed motivational problems at the beginning of the application phase. They were frustrated with the script, which they experienced as coercive. The frustration and reactance is reflected in a statement of a medical student during the application phase: "I think we don't have to proceed as rigidly as the first time". Rummel and Spada (2005) explained this negative effect by referring to *self-determination theory* (Deci & Ryan 2000): Participants perceived the script as too coercive, not allowing them to self-regulate their problem-solving and learning; thus, they did not internalize the collaboration skills that were emphasized in the script.

Additionally, the script instructions might have induced a *prevention focus* by prescribing a sequence of problem-solving steps from which students where expected not to deviate (an ought). On the other hand, the model instruction might have induced students with a *promotion focus* (cf. Higgins 1997), i.e. an aspiration to collaborate just like the model dyad (an ideal). As a promotion focus fosters intrinsic motivation, perseverance in the face of difficulties, and creativity in problem-solving, the *regulatory focus* that was induced in students by the instruction during the learning phase may be partially responsible for the model condition's success (Friedman & Förster 2001; Higgins 1997).

A potential negative motivational effect of coercive collaboration scripts is by now well known in the literature, and is often referred to as "overscripting collaboration" (Dillenbourg 2002). In the first study, we did not directly assess student motivation, but merely assumed from observations that motivational influences can explain the observed differences between learning from observing a model versus learning from following a collaboration script. Therefore, we conducted a second study that directly evaluated the impact of motivational factors in the described learning scenario. This study furthermore introduced an additional variation to the two experimental conditions: Half of the participants in the model and script conditions were asked to reflect on the instruction at several points during the learning phase, enabling them to better understand the value of the instructed collaboration skills and thus facilitating their internalization (cf. Ryan & Deci 2000).

We assessed the collaboration quality with a multidimensional rating framework for assessing net-based collaboration (Meier, Spada, & Rummel 2007; Rummel, Deiglmayr, Spada, Kahrimanis, & Avouris 2011), which included a total of eleven dimensions for assessing the quality of the "cognitive" aspects of communication, coordination, and joint information processing, as well as the quality of the "motivational" aspects of interpersonal relationship management and individual task orientation. For each dimension, a rating handbook described positive and negative indicators of effective collaboration. Based on this handbook and following a careful rater training, each dimension was evaluated on a 5-point rating scale. Again, both model conditions (with and without elaboration) outperformed the script conditions in the joint outcome (Rummel, Spada, & Hauser 2009). Furthermore, the rating analysis confirmed the differential effect of the instruction on student motivation: Students in the model conditions showed significantly higher ratings in individual task orientation than students in the scripted conditions (Meier et al. 2007). Furthermore, high student motivation was positively correlated to the participants' knowledge about good collaboration as assessed in an individual post-test. These results demonstrate how instruction can shape learning outcomes by affecting students' motivation, thus stressing the relevance of motivation in the context of computer-supported knowledge co-construction.

Interplay of collaborative engagement and elaboration on knowledge co-construction

The following example demonstrates the necessity of high motivational engagement for the instruction to be successful. While in some dyads in this collaborative learning study students were motivated to follow the instructions to mutually elaborate on the learning content, in other dyads students rather tried to proceed through the learning environment as quickly as possible. These motivational differences helped explain why instruction was successful only for some dyads and not for others.

The collaboration setting

This example comes from a project on algebra learning that evaluated the effect of collaboration on students' knowledge acquisition in mathematics (Mullins, Rummel, & Spada 2011; Rummel, Mullins, & Spada 2012). During instruction, two students worked together on one computer (face-to-face setting), using an intelligent tutoring system (Koedinger, Anderson, Hadley, & Mark 1997). The learning environment provided adaptive feedback in the form of error-flagging and hints. Students' knowledge acquisition was assessed with individual and collaborative post-tests. One experiment evaluated the effect of a collaboration script as an instructional support method (Diziol et al. 2008; Rummel et al. 2012). The script structured student interaction and provided adaptive feedback when ineffective collaborative learning behavior was detected: Trial and error (multiple errors at one step within a short time interval), or hint abuse (students clicking through several consecutive hints in order to copy the correct answer that was provided eventually). The study was a classroom experiment with 106 participants of the age of 16. It compared scripted collaboration with a collaborative condition without script support and an individual condition. It took place on three days – two instruction days and one test day – during regular math instruction.

The cognitive dimension

The effects of the script instruction on students' learning outcome were mixed: Scripted dyads outperformed unscripted dyads in a post-test that evaluated preparation for future collaborative learning situations. However, the scripted condition showed low test results in a retention test that was composed of problems isomorphic to the problems of instruction (Rummel et al. 2012). A high variance in the post-test performance indicated that some dyads benefited from scripting while others did not. To better understand the differences between more and less successful dyads, we analyzed the quality of the dyads' collaborative problem-solving. As the following paragraph shows, taking into account the motivational-affective dimension was again helpful to better understand the differential effects of instruction on students' cognitive outcomes.

Interplay with motivational-affective dimension

To evaluate the collaboration quality during students' collaborative problem-solving, we adapted the multidimensional rating framework described above (cf. Meier et al. 2007) to the algebra project's learning environment (Diziol et al. 2008). We added one dimension evaluating students' mathematical understanding and one dimension evaluating students' capitalization on the system resources, that is, immediate error feedback and hints. As in the original framework, one dimension assessed motivational aspects of the collaboration, more specifically, the collaborative engagement of the dyad. The dyads' performance on each dimension was rated with a 5-point rating scale. Collaborative engagement was rated as high when both partners showed interest and a positive attitude towards the task and were symmetrically involved in the problem-solving process.

The analysis revealed that scripted dyads who showed higher motivation and were more actively engaged in the collaboration also showed more elaboration and less frequently employed ineffective learning strategies such as trial and error and hint abuse (Diziol et al. 2008). Particularly, dyads who were high in collaborative engagement overall also showed higher compliance with the adaptive feedback following detected hint abuse. This feedback asked them to first elaborate on the hint messages provided by the tutoring system before asking for yet another hint. That is, when prompted, these dyads were more motivated to try and find a solution on their own. In contrast, dyads with low collaborative engagement less often followed the advice provided by the adaptive feedback and were more likely to ask for the final hint message in order to simply copy the answer it gave. This indicates that the adaptive feedback interacted with the goal structure displayed by the dyads. While some dyads adopted a *learning goal* and engaged in effortful elaboration activities, others rather followed a *performance goal*, that is, they tried to proceed through the learning environment as fast as possible (Dweck & Leggett 1988). Importantly, the evaluation of the post-test results of motivated dyads revealed that the increased collaboration quality also yielded a higher learning outcome when compared to less motivated dyads.

An interesting question for future research would be to evaluate what yields high versus low collaborative engagement. One possible explanation may be that *intrinsic motivation* (Ryan & Deci 2000) and the desire to understand the learning content are prerequisites for high collaborative engagement. Another possible explanation may be that a high *collective efficacy* (Bandura 1993), that is, a strong belief of the learning partners that their combined knowledge will be sufficient to solve the tasks, is necessary for a high collaborative engagement as it might encourage students to show higher persistence in their learning efforts. For future studies, it would therefore be beneficial to take students' motivational state prior to collaboration into account.

Interplay of emotional and motivational factors on elaboration after receiving feedback

A second study within the algebra project provided various insights concerning the importance of the motivational-affective dimension for knowledge co-construction (Mullins et al. 2011). First, when students solved very demanding tasks in which the discussion with a partner was beneficial for gaining deeper understanding, collaboration reduced unmotivated behavior such as trial and error. This may be explained by a higher level of collective efficacy. However, when the tasks invited task division and when individual effort was dispensable for the group's success, the positive effect of collaboration on student motivation was reduced. Second, the example demonstrates how differences in students' emotional reactions to corrective feedback can influence their learning success.

The collaboration setting

The second study of the algebra project was conducted in a lab environment with 79 participants at the age of 13. The experiment lasted about 140 minutes. The study evaluated whether collaboration with a learning partner would be equally effective for different types of learning material (see Diziol, Rummel, Spada, & Haug 2010; Mullins et al. 2011): conceptual tasks that require deeper elaboration, and procedural tasks that can be solved with step-by-step procedures. To evaluate this question, we compared individual and collaborative learning with conceptual tasks, and individual and collaborative learning with procedural tasks, respectively. For conceptual instruction, we used word problems that asked students to translate between verbal and algebraic representations of algebra concepts. For procedural instruction, we used problems that asked students to solve algebraic equations. Students worked in a learning environment that provided adaptive feedback in the form of immediate performance feedback and hints. In the collaborative conditions, two students worked together on one computer. For the performance feedback, correct answers were marked in green, and incorrect answers were marked in red. Only once a step had been solved correctly were the students able to proceed to the subsequent step. Hint messages served to ensure that students would not get stuck during problem-solving: The learning environment automatically launched a hint after the third incorrect student attempt. The hint message told students the correct solution to the current problem-solving step.

The cognitive dimension

We evaluated student learning separately for conceptual and procedural knowledge acquisition. Results from the conceptual post-tests showed that collaborative learning with conceptual tasks benefited students' conceptual understanding. However, this positive effect could not be found for procedural knowledge acquisition: In the procedural post-tests, students who had learned collaboratively showed even slightly lower test results than students who had learned on their own. To better understand this differential effect of collaboration, we evaluated students' problem-solving following performance feedback. On the one hand, we coded their problem-solving behavior after performance feedback, for instance: Were students able to correct the error in the next step, did they elaborate on the error, or did they engage in trial and error? On the other hand, we evaluated if both students participated in the error correction and collaborated in trying to understand the hints. This behavior can provide an indirect assessment of their motivation: While unmotivated students tend to engage in trial and error to receive the hint message and copy the correct answer, students with a learning goal and a high promotion focus show greater perseverance in trying to correct errors.

Interplay with motivational-affective dimension

First, the results of our study indicated that the differential effectiveness of individual vs. collaborative learning was mediated by motivational-affective aspects of student interaction. In the conceptual conditions, collaboration positively influenced students' learning motivation. During the instruction phase, collaboration with a partner reduced unmotivated behavior such as trial and error and hint abuse, and increased students' *perseverance* in trying to correct the error (cf. Mullins et al. 2011). Furthermore, dyads engaged in elaboration more often than students working individually. A possible explanation may be that learners felt more competent when they worked with a partner and perceived higher self-efficacy – or more precisely, higher *collective efficacy* – when compared with students who had to solve the problems on their own (Bandura 1993). However, in the procedural conditions, this positive effect of collaboration could not be found. Dyads engaged more often in unmotivated trial and error behavior than students learning individually. Furthermore, students often took turns when correcting errors, and thus their individual practice opportunities were reduced. An explanation for the reduced student motivation may be seen in the type of task: While the conceptual tasks were very demanding and thus the individual's effort was essential to find the correct solution, this was less the case for the procedural tasks where the individual effort was more dispensable (cf. Salomon & Globerson 1989).

Second, observations from student behavior after errors demonstrated how positive and negative performance feedback can yield emotional reactions of the collaborating students which influence student motivation and achievement. Positive performance feedback yielded positive emotional reactions. Learners in successful dyads reinforced each other by pointing out that they hadn't made any errors so far. Particularly, they expressed joy when they succeeded in a particularly difficult problem-solving step ("Yes, we are good, are good, are good, …"). The positive feedback also seemed to positively influence students' *self-efficacy* (cf. Bandura 1986). For instance, one student expressed her joy that she finally was able to correctly solve this kind of math problem. According to Ryan and Deci (2000), these feelings of competence can promote student motivation as they increase the perceived autonomy and competence in the learning situation.

In contrast, negative performance feedback had mixed effects on students' emotions and their subsequent motivation. Some students appraised the situation as a *challenge* and showed persistence in trying to correct the error (cf. Lazarus & Launier 1978). For instance, one student pointed out to her partner that they had to solve the step correctly in the next attempt, because otherwise they would receive a hint providing them with the correct solution. However, for other students, the negative performance feedback yielded increased frustration and thus promoted unmotivated behavior. For instance, after two unsuccessful attempts, one student suggested "come on, let's just try something", and the learning partner agreed to engage in trial and error. The differences in behavior after negative performance feedback could be explained by differences in students' *goal orientation*. Some students adopted a learning goal and thus showed perseverance in trying to understand what they did wrong (cf. Dweck & Leggett 1988). Other students adopted a performance goal. When they did not feel competent enough to solve the task, they displayed helplessness and did not make an effort to correct the errors or to understand the hint messages provided by the system, as reflected in the following student statement in response to a hint message: "What? Never mind. At least, we understood the previous task".

Positive motivational and emotional effects of successful knowledge co-construction

The final example on the interplay between cognitive and motivational-affective dimensions in collaborative learning comes from a project in which students solved problems on the basis of complementary expertise. In doing so, they had to generate new knowledge through collaborative inferences, that is, inferences that bridged their individual knowledge resources. Training, based on a feedback from a specifically designed inference tutoring tool, was shown to be effective in increasing students' ability to draw such collaborative inferences. Here, we will discuss how the training's effectiveness was brought about through an interplay of cognitive and motivational effects. Finally, we will discuss how the drawing of collaborative inferences, as an example of a cognitive accomplishment, also has very positive motivational and affective consequences.

Collaboration setting

This final project we introduce studied the effects of information distribution and of instructional support and training on collaborative problem-solving (Deiglmayr & Spada 2010a; Deilgmayr & Spada 2011). Dyads of university students had to find the guilty person among four suspects in a fictitious homicide investigation (murder-mystery task). Each student first read a set of information sheets, handed back his/her materials, and then discussed the case with his/her partner who had received a systematically different set of information. Students collaborated remotely, making use of an audio connection (headsets) and a shared text editor for writing up their joint solution. To find the optimal solution to their joint problem, students had to draw several inferences, e.g. by inferring motives or alibis for the suspects in the murder-mystery task. Our focus was on those inferences that students had to draw collaboratively because the pieces of information enabling an inference were distributed between students (collaborative inferences). Collaborative inferences are a prime example of synergy effects from pooling and integrating group members' complementary knowledge resources (Deiglmayr & Spada 2010a). They are particularly important in settings in which students come from different areas of expertise, such as psychology and medicine (Rummel & Spada 2005), or in learning arrangements designed to create resource interdependence, such as the jigsaw method (Aronson et al. 1987).

The cognitive dimension

In our experiments, we compared three types of inferences (as a within-dyads factor): collaborative inferences (based on distributed information), individual inferences (based on individual information), and shared inferences (based on shared information). During the first, individual reading phase, in which students studied their individual sets of information, we realized the possibility for the three types of inferences by systematically distributing the available information between students.

For a *collaborative inference*, the experimental information distribution was as follows: a student held a piece of information (e.g. that the murderer did not know the victim was left-handed) that led to a solution-relevant inference only when combined with a piece of information that was held by his or her partner (e.g. the fact that suspect Horst knew that the victim was left-handed). Thus, the inference could not be drawn by either of the students alone, but had to be drawn collaboratively. On the other hand, the opportunity for drawing an *individual inference* was realized by assigning interdependent information to one and the same student, while the opportunity for a *shared inference* was created by handing the same set of interdependent information to both students. In a first experiment, we could show that collaborative inferences were much less likely to be drawn than individual and shared inferences (Deiglmayr & Spada 2010a). In a second experiment, training employing an adaptive tutoring tool was designed and proven to be effective for enhancing collaborative inferences during a transfer task (Deiglmayr & Spada 2010b; Deiglmayr & Spada 2011).

Interplay with motivational-affective dimension

We would like to highlight two aspects in which the interplay of cognitive and motivational-affective factors could be observed. First, cognitive and motivational mechanisms worked together in students' processing of the adaptive tutoring tool's feedback in the training experiment (Deiglmayr & Spada 2011), and presumably led to an increase in both students' ability and their motivation to draw collaborative inferences. Second, the drawing of collaborative inferences, as a cognitive accomplishment, also has positive motivational and affective consequences.

Our experiment (Deiglmayr & Spada 2011) demonstrated the effectiveness of a training technique designed to foster the acquisition of relevant skills for drawing collaborative inferences. In particular, receiving feedback and hints from an inference tutoring tool while solving a training task was effective in enhancing students' ability to draw collaborative inferences when collaborating on a subsequent testing task (without the feedback tool). The inference tutoring tool was controlled by a human observer who monitored students' discussion and gave immediate and adaptive feedback through the tool, choosing from several pre-defined messages (wizard-of-oz design). The tool provided two kinds of simple feedback: First of all, it guided students' attention towards new pieces of information and assisted them with their integration. That is, whenever a student mentioned a relevant piece of information for the first time, the tool would immediately provide "new information" feedback, accompanied by a hint telling who held complementary information that would enable an inference. Second, the tutor informed students whenever they had drawn a correct inference. That is, as soon as one student mentioned a correct inference for the first time, the tool would provide "correct inference" feedback.

The tutoring tool's feedback aimed at the cognitive skills of the trained students. For example, the "correct inference" feedback informed students about the correctness of their reasoning (informational value), and thereby fostered the learning of the rule-like strategic knowledge making up the necessary collaboration skills for drawing collaborative inferences (Deiglmayr & Spada 2010b). As part of this knowledge, students for example needed to learn to take up new information mentioned by their partner and integrate it with their own information. This was further facilitated by the information provided with the tool's "new information" feedback. However, positive feedback, like the "correct inference" feedback, always has both informational and incentive value, and thus has cognitive as well as motivational consequences (Spielberger & DeNike 1966). First of all, being praised for each successful inference added incentive value to successful collaborative inferences, and thus might have increased students' motivation to draw more collaborative inferences. Further, because students had been told that their task required them to pool their information they may already have interpreted the "new information" feedback as a sign of effective collaboration and thus may have experienced this feedback, too, as positively reinforcing. Therefore, when students processed the tool's feedback, motivational factors likely played an important role in enhancing its positive effects on learning.

In addition, we would like to discuss an observation regarding potential positive motivational-affective effects of collaborative inferences. As elaborated above, collaborative inferences are important for finding problem solutions and making decisions that integrate group members' unique knowledge. However, when observing our study participants collaborating on their problem-solving task, it became apparent that collaborative inferences may also foster the subjective value attached to collaboration by enhancing *task enjoyment*, *collective efficacy*, and *group cohesiveness*. This is because a collaboratively drawn inference exemplifies what people typically consider as prototypic for successful collaboration: From a collaborative effort, a synergy is reached that could not have been obtained by any person working alone. The *"Eureka"-experience* (cf. Bühler 1907) associated with drawing an inference and arriving at a new insight into the joint problem makes this synergy very tangible. Table 7.1 gives an example of a successful collaborative inference during which students seem to have experienced such a "Eurekamen"-moment ("Ah, wait!...", "Now we've got it!").

Exploratory analyses of successful collaborative inferences showed that students often reacted very excitedly to new information that enabled them to draw a collaborative inference, and seemed very pleased once an inference had been drawn. In a few cases, students even explicitly expressed their satisfaction with their accomplishment and with the progress of their collaboration in general as a reaction to a successful collaborative inference. However, most of the time, their heightened motivational-affective state could only be inferred from their nonverbal and paraverbal behavior. In future studies, we plan to investigate in more depth the verbal and, in particular, nonverbal and paraverbal indicators of particularly satisfying moments of collaboration, such as the successful drawing of a collaborative inference.

What effects might the satisfying experience of successfully integrating one's own information with that of a collaboration partner have? First of all, experiencing success in drawing collaborative inferences should strengthen group members' confidence that they are collaborating well (i.e. increased *collective efficacy*, Bandura

TABLE 7.1 Example of a collaborative inference taken from a transcript (translated to English and shortened for better readability) from the study by Deiglmayr and Spada (2011)

Student A:	It was supposed to look like suicide, but the gun was in Doppler's [the victim's] right hand, even though he is left-handed.
Student B:	Ah! Okay, that was one of the facts I could not make sense of, that he was left-handed.
A:	[…] With Wolfgang, I don't know whether he knew that [Doppler was left-handed]. But the gun was in his right hand, and he shot into his right temple.
B:	And if he was left-handed, that would not have been possible.
A:	Yes, and the gun was-
B:	Ah, wait! Yes! Somebody did know that he was left-handed
A:	Oh, Now we've got it! Who was it?
B:	[…] I believe Horst knew it, because Horst said that Doppler had been his "left hand", because he was left-handed. I believe Horst said that. Yes, pretty sure it was Horst.
A:	Horst. Okay, then it wasn't Horst [who committed the murder], I guess.
B:	Yes, it's not Horst, we can cross him off.

1982). According to Bandura "perceived collective efficacy will influence what people choose to do as a group, how much effort they put into it, and their staying power when group efforts fail to produce results" (Bandura 1982: 143). That is, dyads with high collective efficacy can be expected to set more ambitious goals, be more committed to reaching these goals, and be more persistent in trying to solve their joint problems in the face of obstacles. Additionally, a history of collaboration that has been experienced as satisfying and successful may also lead to increased group cohesiveness, which in turn enhances group performance (Beal, Cohen, Burke, & McLendon 2003). Thus, effective collaboration that is experienced as satisfying and rewarding, may set in motion a positive circle of success, in which cognitive collaborative accomplishments foster motivation to collaborate, and vice versa.

Summary and outlook

As the examples given above illustrate, there is much to be gained from considering the interplay of cognitive and motivational-affective aspects when analysing collaborative learning, even in settings that aim predominantly at cognitive outcomes such as knowledge and skills. The last section of our chapter summarizes our main findings, provides some practical implications, and discusses research questions that should be addressed in the future.

Motivational-affective factors in collaborative knowledge construction

First of all, high student motivation to engage in the learning activity is a crucial *prerequisite* for the success of the interaction. For example, in the first algebra study, we could see that dyads differed in their collaborative engagement. Dyads with a high collaborative engagement elaborated more deeply on the learning content and on the hints and the error feedback they received from the learning environment, and the increased elaboration was positively related to students' learning gains. Students may differ in the motivational predispositions they bring into the collaboration (e.g. some may hold predominantly performance goals, while others hold predominantly learning goals). In practical application, this means that teachers should take the individual's motivation into account when composing student groups. For instance, grouping two students who predominantly hold a performance goal may reduce the amount of dyad elaboration, while mixing students with different motivational background may increase perseverance and thus yield improved learning. Of course, students' motivation to engage in a specific collaborative learning task also depends on the dynamics of the situation, in particular, on their appraisal of the ongoing collaboration, and on characteristics of the learning environment. It therefore might be a worthwhile instructional goal to enhance students' skills for self-regulating – and co-regulating – motivation and emotion in the service of collaborative learning activities. For example, sustaining beneficial goal orientations in oneself and in others, such as learning (instead of performance) goals, might be considered such a motivational-affective collaboration skill. Collaboration skills may also include the ability to choose appropriate models from whom to adopt behaviors, standards, and goals. Research on effective ways of fostering such motivational-affective collaboration skills would be very relevant also for educational practice.

Collaborative engagement is not simply the sum of the motivation levels across all group participants; instead, it is *influenced by dynamics within the learning group*. Most importantly, when students experience the collaboration with their peers as successful, this can increase their (collective) efficacy, that is, their belief that the group can master the task, along with an increase of their task enjoyment and commitment. This effect was most clearly seen in the example from our studies on collaborative inference drawing (Deiglmayr & Spada 2010a; Deiglmayr & Spada 2011), in which students' spontaneous verbal and nonverbal reactions to the successful drawing of collaborative inferences indicated that they experienced these as inherently rewarding. In the algebra study, too, collective efficacy may have played a major role in promoting collaborative engagement. While the tasks were quite challenging for individual students, the collaboration with a peer may have encouraged some students that they would be able to find the solution by combining their individual efforts. The importance of collective efficacy is also illustrated by the second algebra study where the collaboration with a peer increased students' perseverance in trying to correct errors when compared to individual learners. On the other hand, collaborating with others can also have negative motivational consequences. For instance, if a student's individual effort is not essential for the group's success, he or she may reduce the individual engagement and task orientation (cf. procedural tasks in the algebra project). From a practical perspective, it is therefore important that the instructor chooses tasks where the collaboration with a partner can bring a real benefit. In addition, collaborative problem-solving tasks should be prepared by preceding assignments that allow students to acquire basic motivational-affective collaboration skills for co-regulation. As an example, students will benefit more from collaborative learning tasks when they know how to enhance one another's commitment and perseverance by giving and processing feedback in ways that promote their own and their peers' self- and group-efficacy (e.g. by self- and group-serving attributions of successes and failures).

Finally, our examples show that *characteristics of the learning environment* can influence the interplay of cognitive and motivational-affective aspects of knowledge co-construction. As was demonstrated in the script condition of the Netcoop project, effects of instruction are often mediated by their influences on motivation. A learning environment that is too coercive can reduce student motivation and thus negatively influence students' learning outcome (cf. overscripting; Dillenbourg 2002). As the study shows, the negative motivational effects of such overscripting may endure even after the script has been removed. Teachers and experimenters should therefore keep in mind that well-intentioned instruction targeting the cognitive dimensions of collaboration may have negative side effects on the motivational-affective dimension of collaboration. Feedback that is built into the learning environment also influences students' academic emotions: As demonstrated in the algebra project example and the inference tutoring tool example, positive performance feedback can yield joy and thus increase students' engagement in the collaborative activity, whereas negative performance feedback can either motivate students to increase their efforts or yield frustration and helplessness. In a collaborative learning environment, learning partners will typically discuss the feedback with one another, complain to each other if instruction is too coercive, and share their joy about successful collaborative experiences. Due to this collaborative processing and elaboration, the effect of motivational-affective reactions in a collaborative learning setting may be even stronger and more influential than in individual learning. Consequently, in a collaborative learning environment, it may be even more important that a teacher tries to anticipate effects of instruction both on the cognitive and on the motivational-affective level.

Further considerations

In the examples reviewed above, we reasonably assumed that students essentially shared the goal of solving their joint task. However, in collaborative learning settings, collaborators may differ in their motivational dispositions as well as in the concrete goals they have for a given learning situation (see also Chapter 8, this volume). There is a growing body of literature, particularly from social psychology, which shows that the differences in the individual orientations and goals of group members play a crucial role in shaping how individuals contribute to collaboration, and how they process what they learn from their collaboration partners. This literature focuses on small groups engaged in solving problems that require a substantial amount of information exchange and shared decision making – thus, problems that closely resemble typical collaborative learning tasks. For example, Wittenbaum, Hollingshead, and Botero (2004) point out that group members will communicate or withhold information in line with their personal goals, which may not be the same as the group's goals. In their *motivated information processing in groups* model, De Dreu, Nijstad, and Knippenberg (2008) point out the important mediating role of individual group members' social and epistemic motivation. *Brodbeck, Kerschreiter, Mojzisch, and Schulz-Hardt (2007)* review empirical evidence of how preference-consistent information processing (e.g. concerning preferences for a certain solution to a joint problem) often shape both an individual's sharing of information with the group, as well as his or her evaluation and processing of information learned from other group members. These models and findings are still waiting to be explored and adapted by researchers focusing on collaborative learning. For example, in a project building on the "collaborative inferences" studies reviewed above (Deiglmayr & Spada 2010a, Deiglmayr & Spada 2011), we (Hans Spada, Sören Pape, & Anne Deiglmayr) are currently designing an experiment in which dyads of learners will start out with different preferences towards the learning task that presents them with scientific information which is partially conflicting and/or tentative. Specifically, the task is to sight evidence speaking in favor of and against artificial snowmaking in a (fictitious) ski resort in the Alps. We aim to explore the ways in which preference-consistent information processing in this setting influences, among other things, the drawing of collaborative inferences, the detection of conflicts within the available information, the quality of the collaborative problem-solution, and individual learning. We hope that this research will contribute to the growing knowledge base on how students' prior knowledge and attitudes towards given topics (which may operate on an affective rather than a cognitive level) affect the ways in which they process information and communicate it to peers in collaborative settings, and how instruction can be designed to reduce bias and increase open consideration and discussion of alternative views. A simple implication of existing research for educational practice is, for example, to have students collaborate in heterogeneous rather than homogenous groups in order to prevent premature consensus building on controversial topics (cf. Brodbeck et al. 2007).

Another open research topic is the assessment of motivation and affect in collaborative learning. For example, it would be interesting to study the effects of specific events in the process of knowledge co-construction (e.g. positive vs. negative feedback from the system or from one's partner or jointly achieved insights) on a moment-to-moment basis, and as unobtrusively as possible. With such an analysis, it would, for example, be possible to capture the dynamic and mutual influences between motivational states, cognition, and communication of group members, and to relate these dynamics to overall effects of collaborative learning on individual motivation (e.g. beliefs concerning self-efficacy and collective efficacy) and cognition (e.g. knowledge acquisition). For educational practice, being able to identify milestones (such as successful collaborative inferences, persistence-enhancing mutual encouragements, or co-constructed insights) as well as detours (such as mutually enhanced misconceptions or feelings of incompetence and low efficacy) in students' cognition and motivation during collaborative learning would provide valuable anchoring points for formative assessment and adaptive instruction.

We hope that the theoretical impulses from individual learning settings and the collaborative learning examples we have assembled in this chapter may help to better understand collaborative knowledge acquisition. However, in the future, we will need more specific theoretical models that explicitly address the interplay between individual cognition, motivation and emotion, with interpersonal communication and regulation, in the context of a given learning environment.

References

Aronson, E., Blaney, N., Sikes, J., Stephan, C., and Snapp, M. (1987) *The Jigsaw Classroom*, Beverly Hills, CA: Sage.

Bandura, A. (1982) "Self-efficacy mechanism in human agency", *American Psychologist*, 37: 122–47.

Bandura, A. (1986) *Social Foundations of Thought and Action: A Social Cognitive Theory*, Englewood Cliffs, NJ: Prentice Hall.

Bandura, A. (1993) "Perceived self-efficacy in cognitive development and functioning", *Educational Psychologist*, 28(2): 117–48.

Bandura, A. and Cervone, D. (1983) "Self-evaluative and self-efficacy mechanisms governing the motivational effects of goal systems", *Journal of Personality and Social Psychology*, 45(5): 1017–28.

Beal, D. J., Cohen, R., Burke, M. J., and McLendon, C. L. (2003) "Cohesion and performance in groups: A meta-analytic clarification of construct relation", *Journal of Applied Psychology*, 88: 989–1004.

Brodbeck, F., Kerschreiter, R., Mojzisch, A., & Schulz-Hardt, S. (2007) Improving group decision making under conditions of distributed knowledge: The information asymmetries model. Academy of Management Review, 32: 459–479.

Brockner, J. and Higgins, E. T. (2001) "Emotions and management: A regulatory focus perspective", *Organizational Behavior and Human Decision Processes*, 86: 35–66.

Bühler, K. (1907) Tatsachen und Probleme zu einer Psychologie der Denkvorgänge. Über Gedanken."[Facts and Problems of a Psychology of Cognitive Processes. On Thoughts.]", *Archiv für Psychologie*, 9: 297–365.

Crook, C. (2012) "Varities and 'togetherness' in learning – and their mediation", in M. Baker, J. Andriessen, and Järvelä, S. (eds), *Affective Learning Together: Social and Emotional Dimensions of Collaborative Learning*, London: Routledge.

Deiglmayr, A. and Spada, H. (2011) "Training for fostering knowledge co-construction from collaborative inference-drawing", *Learning and Instruction*, 21: 441–51.

Deiglmayr, A. and Spada, H. (2010a) "Collaborative problem-solving with distributed information: The role of inferences from interdependent information", *Group Processes and Intergroup Relations*, 13: 361–78.

Deiglmayr, A. and Spada, H. (2010b) "Developing adaptive collaboration support: The example of an effective training for collaborative inferences", *Educational Psychology Review*, 22: 103–13.

Dillenbourg, P. (2002) "Over-scripting CSCL: The risks of blending collaborative learning with instructional design", in P. A. Kirschner (ed.), *Three Worlds of CSCL. Can We Support CSCL?* Heerlen: Open Univeriteit Nederland.

Diziol, D., Rummel, N., Kahrimanis, G., Guevara, T., Holz, J., Spada, H., and Fiotakis, G. (2008) "Using contrasting cases to better understand the relationship between students' interactions and their learning outcome", in G. Kanselaar, V. Jonker, P. A. Kirschner, and F. Prins (eds), *International Perspectives of the Learning Sciences: Cre8ing a Learning World. Proceedings of the Eighth International Conference of the Learning Sciences (ICLS 2008), Vol 3.* International Society of the Learning Sciences.

Diziol, D., Rummel, N., Spada, H., and Haug, S. (2010) "Learning in mathematics: Effects of procedural and conceptual instruction on the quality of student interaction". Poster presented at the International Conference of the Learning Sciences 2010, Chicago.

Dweck, C. S. and Leggett, E. L. (1988) "A social-cognitive approach to motivation and personality", *Psychological Review*, 95(2): 256–73.

Freitas, A. L., Liberman, N., and Higgins, E. T. (2002) "Regulatory fit and resisting temptation during goal pursuit", *Journal of Experimental Social Psychology*, 38: 291–98.

Friedman, R. S. and Förster, J. (2001) "The effects of promotion and prevention cues on creativity", *Journal of Personality and Social Psychology*, 81: 1001–13.

Greder-Specht, C. (2009) *Emotionen im Lernprozess* [Emotions during learning], Hamburg: Verlag Dr. Kova.

Higgins, E. T. (1997) "Beyond pleasure and pain", *American Psychologist*, 52: 1280–300.

Higgins, E. T. (2000) "Making a good decision: Value from fit", *American Psychologist*, 55: 1217–30.

Järvenoja, H., and Järvelä, S. (2012) "Regulating emotions together", in M. Baker, J. Andriessen, and Järvelä, S. (eds), *Affective Learning Together: Social and Emotional Dimensions of Collaborative Learning*, Crook (2012).

Karau, S. J. and Williams, K. D. (1995) "Social loafing: Research findings, implications, and future directions", *Current Directions in Psychological Science*, 4(5): 134–40.

Koedinger, K. R., Anderson, J. R., Hadley, W. H., and Mark, M. A. (1997) "Intelligent tutoring goes to school in the big city", *International Journal of Artificial Intelligence in Education*, 8: 30–43.

Kort, B., Reilly, R., and Picard, R. W. (2001) "An affective model of interplay between emotions and learning: Reengineering educational pedagogy – building a learning companion", in T. Okamoto, R. Hartley, Kinshuk, and J. P. Klus (eds), *Proceedings IEEE International Conference on Advanced Learning Technology: Issues, Achievements and Challenges*. Madison, Wisconsin: IEEE Computer Society.

Lazarus, R. S. and Launier, R. (1978) "Stress-related transactions between person and environment", in L. A. Pervin and M. Lewis (eds.), *Perspectives in Interactional Psychology*. New York: Plenum Press.

Meier, A., Spada, H., and Rummel, N. (2007) "A rating scheme for assessing the quality of computer-supported collaboration processes", *International Journal of Computer-Supported Collaborative Learning*, 2: 63–86.

Mullins, D., Rummel, N., and Spada, H. (2011) "Are two heads always better than one? Differential effects of collaboration on students' computer-supported learning in mathematics", *International Journal of Computer-Supported Collaborative Learning*, 6(3): 421–43.

Pekrun, R., Goetz, T., Titz, W., and Perry, R. P. (2002) "Academic emotions in students' self-regulated learning and achievement: A program of qualitative and quantitative research", *Educational Psychologist*, 37(2): 91–105.

Rheinberg, F., Vollmeyer, R., and Rollett, W. (2000) "Motivation and action in self-regulated learning", in M. Boekaerts, P. Pintrich, and M. Zeidner (eds), *Handbook of self-regulation*. San Diego: Academic Press.

Rummel, N., Deiglmayr, A., Spada, H., Karimanis, G., and Avouris, N. (2011) "Analyzing collaborative interactions across domains and settings: An adaptable rating scheme", in S. Puntambekar, C. Hmelo-Silver and G. Erkens (eds), *Analyzing Interactions in CSCL: Methods, Approaches and Issues*. Berlin: Springer.

Rummel, N., Mullins, D., and Spada, H. (2012) "Scripted collaborative learning with the Cognitive Tutor Algebra. An experimental classroom study", *International Journal of Computer-Supported Collaborative Learning*, 7(2): 307–39.

Rummel, N. and Spada, H. (2005) "Learning to collaborate: An instructional approach to promoting problem-solving in computer-mediated settings", *The Journal of the Learning Sciences*, 14: 201–41.

Rummel, N., Spada, H., and Hauser, S. (2009) "Learning to collaborate while being scripted or by observing a model", *International Journal of Computer-Supported Learning*, 4(1): 69–92.

Ryan, R. M. and Deci, E. L. (2000) "Intrinsic and extrinsic motivations: Classic definitions and new directions", *Contemporary Educational Psychology*, 25: 54–67.

Salomon, G. and Globerson, T. (1989) "When teams do not function the way they ought to", *International Journal of Educational Research*, 13: 89–99.

Schunk, D. H. (2003) "Self-efficacy for reading and writing: Influence of modelling, goal setting, and self-evaluation", *Reading & Writing Quarterly: Overcoming Learning Difficulties*, 19(2): 159–72.

Shepperd, J. A. (1993) "Productivity loss in performance groups: A motivation analysis", *Psychological Bulletin*, 113(1): 67–81.

Spielberger, D. and DeNike, L. (1966) "Descriptive behaviorism versus cognitive theory in operant conditioning", *Psychological Review*, 73: 306–23.

Tolmie, A. K., Topping, K., Christie, D., Donaldson, C., Howe, C., Jessiman, E., Livingston, K., and Thurston, A. (2010) "Social effects of collaborative learning in primary schools", *Learning and Instruction*, 20: 177–91.

Webb, N. M. (1989) "Peer interaction and learning in small groups", *International Journal of Education Research*, 13: 21–39.

Wittenbaum, G., Hollingshead, A., & Botero, I. (2004). From cooperative to motivated information sharing in groups: moving beyond the hidden profile paradigm. Communication Monographs, 71, 286–310.

8

REGULATING EMOTIONS TOGETHER FOR MOTIVATED COLLABORATION

Hanna Järvenoja and Sanna Järvelä

Introduction

Imagine an ideal situation where you have found a perfect group of people to work with. Each member of your group has had unique experiences and possesses unique skills that make your group more powerful and effective than you would be separately in terms of your common aims and goals. You value each others' expertise and feel appreciated by other group members. You have never been as creative and productive as you are now, as a part of this special group. It seems that together you bring out the best in each other and the others make you achieve things you could not have done alone. Best of all, you really enjoy working with these people and the feeling is mutual.

It is not only imagination, but research provides evidence to support the benefits of group processes and social interaction. The power of collaborative learning is in bringing together people with different experiences, values, and knowledge to solve complex and undefined problems (Light, Littleton, Messer, & Joiner, 1994; Van den Bossche, Gijselaers, Segers, & Kirschner, 2006). In true collaboration students engage in shared knowledge construction, coordination of different perspectives, commitment to joint goals, and shared evaluation of collective activities (Roschelle & Teasley, 1995). At its best, a collaborative group is able to create something that exceeds what any one individual could achieve alone.

Unfortunately, true collaboration does not happen as frequently as could be expected. Usually it takes time and effort to accomplish such a good collaborative group; you can reach this special kind of "flow" of collaboration only occasionally. Learning through collaboration is not something that just takes place whenever learners with adequate cognitive capacity come together. Empirical studies have shown that, while members of a group may cooperate, the group itself, as a social entity, does not always follow the mutually shared cognitive and social processes of collaboration (Barron, 2003; Järvelä & Häkkinen, 2002). In any joint venture, team members need to be committed to a shared goal, to on-going negotiation, and to the joint monitoring of progress and achievement. This involves not only cognitive capacity and engagement in social interaction but also motivational and emotional engagement (Dillenbourg, Järvelä, & Fischer, 2007). Motivation, in fact, is the fuel that mobilizes students to use the potential of their cognitive capacity and skills. Individual and social processes are influenced, shaped and directed by motivation and emotions.

The importance of optimum motivational and emotional conditions for collaboration is widely acknowledged (Järvelä, Volet, & Järvenoja, 2010). The role of these conditions is clear when one considers how learning something new often requires challenging yourself or putting yourself in situations where (cognitive) conflicts can emerge; not everything is controllable and, often, you may not even know what it is that you are expected to accomplish. One idea in collaborative learning designs is to create sought-after challenges that require a group of people to fully use their potential, but these requirements can challenge group members' motivation and are a potential source of different emotional reactions. It is reasonable to say that motivation and emotions are functional factors in the creation of successful collaboration. Several questions raised from collaborative learning research, such as students' engagement in collaboration (Van den Bossche et al., 2006) and co-regulation (Volet, Summers, & Thurman, 2009), cognitive and motivational coping (Järvelä, Hurme, & Järvenoja, 2010), students' motivational profiles in virtual collaboration (Veermans & Lallimo, 2007) and socio-emotional challenges in collaboration (Järvenoja & Järvelä, 2009). What is still missing is a bridge between motivation and emotion research and collaborative learning research so that we can better understand motivation and emotion in collaboration. Until now, the role of motivation – which is affected by emotions – in either hindering or supporting collaborative processes has emerged mainly as an outcome or as a possible explanation for certain types of group dynamics (Dillenbourg, Järvelä, & Fischer, 2007), and less frequently as a focus of studies on prerequisites and processes of collaborative learning.

This chapter focuses on the socio-emotional aspects in collaboration. It aims to create a link from motivation and emotions in learning research (Järvelä & Volet, 2004; Schutz & Pekrun, 2007) to research on collaborative learning processes. In order to demonstrate the connection the chapter targets emotions and motivation as they operate in collaborative learning. The ideas presented in the chapter rely on self-regulated learning theory (Zimmerman & Schunk, 2008) and especially on research on the regulation of motivation and emotions. It is argued that successful collaboration involves the regulation of emotions to ensure a favorable affective atmosphere for collaboration and motivation to ensure goal-directed learning. Furthermore, when an affective atmosphere is challenged, group-level regulation is needed to complement individual regulation so that motivated activity can continue.

This chapter focuses on the socio-emotional aspects in collaboration. It is composed of three parts. The first part introduces the role of emotions in motivated collaborative learning.

In the second part "regulating emotions together" will be demonstrated with an example from empirical video-data, from which one extract is selected for a detailed illustration that shows how regulation of emotion is manifested in authentic collaborative learning situations. The situation is selected from a collaborative learning task, where a group's affective balance and motivation was challenged. The example will follow the groups' interactions as they regulate the situation to restore good conditions for their collaboration. The situation presented in the example was discovered as a result of several cycles of process data analysis where meaningful episodes that reflected motivation and emotions were first sequenced on a general level from the whole set of data. The next cycles of analysis expanded on more details to determine the meaningful situations which exemplified socially shared regulation.

The third part concludes the chapter by raising questions regarding the implications of motivation and emotion regulation in collaborative learning. It is suggested that, just as contemporary computer-supported learning technologies are implemented in many sophisticated ways to orchestrate and scaffold collaborative interactions and cognitive knowledge construction, so technological tools similarly could also be a powerful way to support individual and group regulation of motivation and emotions.

Emotions in social learning situations

Learning not only involves cognitive operations, but also includes aspects of how learners feel in the situation, in other words, emotional reactions aroused by the conditions and context. *Emotions* are intense reactions to something, usually directed toward an object or achievement dispositions (Goetz, Zirngibl, Pekrun, & Hall, 2003). The emotional reactions that are awakened or otherwise related to the learning situation, such as the emotional atmosphere within a learning context as well as the interaction between learners, all contribute to the learning process especially through learners' motivation to learn (Meyer & Turner, 2006). *Motivation*, in turn, arouses, directs, maintains, hinders, or inhibits behavior. The motivational structures, which include emotions, are internal part of the learning process.

The social context, which is built on the relationships of "feeling" human beings, is filled with different affective experiences and emotional reactions. Many of these emotional reactions relate to interpersonal interactions, and require the considerations of other people or social norms (Andersen & Guerrero, 1998; Dowson & McInerney, 2003; Goetz, Zirngibl, Pekrun, & Hall, 2003; Hareli & Weiner, 2002; Isaac, Sansone, & Smith, 1999; Järvenoja & Järvelä, 2005). More specifically, both negative and positive emotions experienced within the group derive from multiple sources that encompass a variety of factors from personality differences to the dynamics and processes experienced within the collaborative group (Mäkitalo, Häkkinen, Järvelä, & Leinonen, 2002; Van den Bossche et al., 2006; Volet & Mansfield, 2006). When socio-emotional challenges emerge, the collaborative group encounters them with the means they possess in that specific context and time. The group's reactions to the challenges will further influence and shape the group's emotional and motivational atmosphere. The result can be positive and thus lead to increased motivation in group activities; alternatively, it can be negative and lead to de-motivation and withdrawal. Overall, when aiming for true collaboration with shared understanding, it is likely that conflicting views emerge and put emotional pressure on individuals in a group to restore well-being and motivation (Boekaerts & Corno, 2005; Järvenoja & Järvelä, 2009). The socio-emotional experiences and reactions among the group members give rise to unique group dynamics and situational motivation.

Groups can face multiple types of situations where collaboration and task completion is compromised or endangered. During a group learning activity, for example, challenges can arise due to differences in respective goals, priorities and expectations, or conflicts can be generated by interpersonal dynamics (Blumenfeld, Marx, Soloway, & Krajcik, 1996; Webb & Palincsar, 1996), such as different styles of working or communicating, the tendency of some individuals to rely on others to do their share of the work and power dynamics among members (Arvaja, Salovaara, Häkkinen, & Järvelä, 2007). Groups that are culturally diverse can face further challenges due to greater differences in background characteristics. These can include language and communication style, as well as prior cultural-educational experiences that leave students unprepared to break out of their zone of comfort and interact with less familiar peers (e.g., Summers & Volet, in press; Volet & Karabenick, 2006).

As an example of socio-emotional challenge, imagine a situation where, in your opinion, you have put a lot of effort into preparing good ground work for a task your group has agreed the previous day to complete. You come to a group meeting with great ideas and plans, but so do the others. After a while, your group seems to disagree with the whole thing, even though yesterday it seemed to be so clear and straightforward. On a cognitive level, collaborative learning aims to create cognitive conflicts which can lead to creating something new and elaborated learning results. Now, however, it seems that in your group this is not going to happen because everyone seems to be so frustrated with each other and offended by other peoples' critiques that no one is motivated to continue.

As a previous imagined example points out, a clash of individual viewpoints and interpretations of situations or task requirements can lead to conflicts and negative emotional arousal. To overcome these challenges, group members are forced to exercise control over their emotions, their motivation, and sometimes their social environment to be successful with learning and interaction (Wolters, 2003). Emotion and motivation regulation processes aim to address a variety of distractions and disturbances, which may interrupt the activity, so that motivated, productive engagement can be maintained. Given the challenging nature of most group activities, strong regulation strategies to control emotions are often needed from all the group members for continued productive engagement toward goal achievement (Järvenoja & Järvelä, 2005). In the imaginary situation described above, the regulation could, for example, go like this:

Your group realizes that you have come to a dead-end and that something has to be done, if you want to complete your joint task. Luckily you have built a solid emotional ground in your earlier working sessions. Everyone feels safe enough to express his or her frustrations, but even more importantly, all of you are committed to the group. You want to solve the socio-emotional challenge you are facing as a group. That enables you to work through the socio-emotional challenge by regulating the situation. As a result, everyone is ready to soften their opinions, compromise and see positive sides in each others' ideas and comments; little by little, you restore the favorable emotional balance. Actually, when you get home in the evening, you suddenly realize that you managed to come up with a much better idea and much better results as a group than the one you had in mind in the morning. And all of this would have been missed if your group members had not been able to regulate their emotions in a challenging situation.

Regulating motivation and emotions during collaborative learning

Self-regulated learning (SRL) refers to the processes through which learners control their thoughts, feelings and actions. Models of SRL emphasize that students are more effective when they assume a purposeful role in their own learning (Boekaerts, Pintrich, & Zeidner, 2000). This is to say that self-regulated learners are autonomous, reflective and efficient and have the cognitive and metacognitive abilities as well as the motivational beliefs and attitudes needed to understand, monitor and direct their own learning. Accordingly, different studies on SRL have stressed different aspects: metacognitive processes (Winne & Hadwin, 1998), learning strategies (Zimmerman & Martinez-Pons, 1990), self-efficacy (Schunk & Zimmerman, 1997), motivational regulation (Corno, 2001; Wolters, 2003) and emotion regulation (Pekrun, Goetz, Titz, & Perry, 2002).

Self-regulated learning theory provides a relevant framework for understanding the "will and skill" of learning. As the previous example illustrated, learning in general, and collaborative learning in particular, can be beneficial only when skills (cognitive and social aspects) and will (motivational and emotional aspects) are well in balance. Furthermore, when this balance is endangered, aspects of the learning process need to be regulated. The need for active motivation and emotion regulation in collaborative learning situations is evident because of complex and challenging interactions in changing learning contexts (Järvelä, Volet, & Järvenoja, 2010).

By definition, *regulation of motivation* refers to strategies that are used purposefully and in a willful manner to initiate, maintain, or supplement motivation in efforts to complete a particular activity or goal (Wolters, 2003). Motivation regulation strategies can be classified based on what motivational aspect is being controlled.

Self-talk, for example, may aim to enhance interest or self-efficacy or it can aim to support mastery or performance goals. Hence, self-talk, as a strategic activity, can be used as an interest enhancement strategy, a mastery and performance goals-inducement strategy, or a self-efficacy control strategy aiming to calibrate or bolster feelings of confidence and competency.

The purpose of *emotion regulation strategies* is to manage feelings and emotional reactions that may disrupt learning (Corno & Kanfer, 1993). Emotion-regulation strategies are used to cope with stressful situations, reduce negative affective responses in learning situations, and control harmful emotional experiences associated with performance. These strategies can be problem- or task-focused, but they can also be avoidance-focused and used to escape from emotionally unpleasant situations at the expense of learning and performance (Op't Eynde, De Corte, & Verschaffel, 2007). Emotion regulation, therefore, can focus on ensuring the appropriate motivation to learn or, instead, on restoring emotional well-being (Boekaerts & Corno, 2005). Self-handicapping, for example, can serve as a strategy to protect emotional well-being at the expense of learning. When the use of a particular emotion regulation strategy aims to ensure a favorable atmosphere and adequate effort for completing an academic task it is, in fact, a strategy for regulating motivation (Wolters, 2003).

The social context is a source for emotional reactions and motivations for both an individual and a group (Järvenoja & Järvelä, 2009). This means that social learning situations also call for both individual- and group-level regulation. Researchers have introduced varying definitions and constructs to analyse social influence on regulation processes, such as co-regulation (McCaslin & Hickey, 2001; Volet et al., 2009), communal regulation (Jackson, McKenzie, & Hobfoll, 2000), social self-regulation (Patrick, 1997), or shared regulation (Järvelä et al., 2010). Socially shared regulation refers to a process where a group forms a social entity that regulates its learning consensually so that regulatory processes are co-constructed in reciprocal interaction. One option to differentiate between the different forms of regulation (individual or self and group or social) is to define the intended target or motive of regulation. Group members can engage in individual regulation where they aim to ensure their own emotional balance or motivation, or alternatively they may engage in regulation processes which aim to ensure successful group work. According to Hadwin, Järvelä, and Miller (2011), socially shared regulation is interdependent and is based on collectively shared regulatory processes, beliefs and knowledge orchestrated in the service of a co-constructed or shared product. Shared-regulation may occur in cooperative and collaborative tasks. From this perspective the ultimate goal of learning together is for multiple, individually regulating individuals to co-construct and synthesize strategies, monitoring, evaluation, goal setting, planning, and beliefs toward shared outcomes. Shared knowledge construction or shared outcomes are often desired, but it does not imply shared regulation of learning.

In practice, regulation of motivation and emotion includes various strategies which attempt to bolster the task completion, the beliefs in one's own competency, the importance or relevance of the task, or, purely, the importance of coping with negative emotional experiences. Research has named several strategies that learners use to self-regulate their motivation and emotions (Wolters, 2003). Whether and how the group members can use these or some other strategies together is still not clear. The present study investigates individual regulatory processes as part of collaborative learning. It attempts to identify socio-emotional challenges in collaboration and the motivation regulation activated to overcome the challenging situations (Järvelä et al., 2010) as well as metacognitive regulation in group problem solving (Hurme, Merenluoto & Järvelä, 2009). The results show that socially constructed self-regulation emerges when learners work in collaborative learning groups and make consistent efforts to regulate their learning and engagement. Students shaped their use of motivation and emotion regulation strategies to fit specific situational challenges (Järvelä, Järvenoja, & Veermans, 2008; Järvenoja & Järvelä, 2009).

During the past years we have been studying the regulation of motivation and emotions in different collaborative learning environments. This chapter builds on findings from a study designed to demonstrate socially shared regulation of motivation and emotions in practice. The study examined how motivation and emotion regulation emerge when university students collaborate on a study activity, namely the completion of a collaborative learning project, perceived as particularly motivationally and emotionally challenging. The illustration presented here is based on and continues analyses carried out in our previous work (see Järvelä et al., 2008; Järvelä & Järvenoja, 2011; Järvenoja & Järvelä, 2009 for more detailed description the study).

Illustrating "Regulating Emotions Together" – An extract from video-data

As stated above, the focus of this section is to gain an understanding of the socially shared regulation of motivation and emotions in practice, by presenting an illustrative data example. The example derives from empirical data collection, where 99 first-year educational psychology students (74 females and 25 males, average age 24) studied together on three different tasks following the principles of collaborative learning. Each of the tasks lasted over two to three lessons, each lesson lasting 90 minutes.

The data example targets a specific moment where a group of four students regulate the emotional atmosphere in the group. The example group had four members, Jari, Riitta, Timi and Anna. The collaborative learning task was designed to promote discussion and a sharing of different views and understanding (Brown & Campione, 1994). In practice, the students were first asked to read articles dealing with the theoretical basis of motivated learning. Every group member read a different piece. The reading preceded construction of a real-life case example of the phenomenon the group was studying. Once agreement was reached regarding the case, the group members "analysed" the case. Every member was expected to contribute to the analysis based on the unique expertise gained from the different articles. As part of the task, all groups were also required to comment on a case created by another group and, reciprocally, to receive and discuss the comments from that other group on their own case.

The example group's work session during the collaborative learning task was videotaped. The illustration presented here is based on an extract from a specific situation, where the example group faced a socio-emotionally challenging situation but managed to restore emotional balance into the group and assure solid ground for collaboration by regulating the situation together. That is, the illustration outlines a situation where a need for a socially shared regulation of emotions arises within the group and discusses group members' reactions and actions in that specific situation.

The extract from video-data was located through three preceding video-data analysis cycles. Each cycle of the analysis had its own focus and the entire process is presented in Figure 8.1. The first cycles of the analysis were part of the earlier, larger-scale analyses, and worked as facilitation in locating actual interactive moments through which the group members composed socially shared regulation in interaction with each other. When the analysis proceeds, the focus of the analysis moves to a more micro level.

The first cycle of the analysis identifies motivationally/emotionally meaningful episodes in the course of the collaborative learning task. The second cycle focuses on shared-regulation strategies that may occur within the motivationally/emotionally meaningful episodes identified in step one. The analysis of this cycle is based on the knowledge gained from the research on self-regulation strategies. The third cycle outlines the circumstances and development of a shared regulation process within each of the situations. Finally, the fourth cycle traces and presents verbal and nonverbal interactions through which shared regulation is manifested within the example group. Cycles three and four demonstrate how shared-regulation can

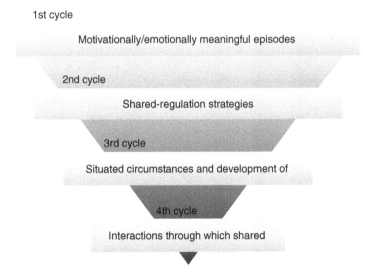

1st cycle

Motivationally/emotionally meaningful episodes

2nd cycle

Shared-regulation strategies

3rd cycle

Situated circumstances and development of

4th cycle

Interactions through which shared

FIGURE 8.1 The four cycles of video data analysis

include some similarities with self-regulation strategies but is unique as it is composed in the specific situation and in interaction between the group members. All together, the focus in this chapter is on micro-level analysis, namely on the two last cycles.

Cycles 1 and 2 of analysis

In the first cycle of the analysis, the example group's videotaped working session was sequenced into meaningful episodes in terms of motivation and emotion within the group (Järvelä et al., 2008). One meaningful episode could have been, for example, a phase where the group discussed their joint goals, or when they had difficulties moving to the next phase of learning. Each episode was described briefly from the perspective of motivational or emotional aspects in that specific situation. The average of these episodes was about five minutes, but it varied from about two minutes to almost thirty minutes. This cycle of the analysis provided the possibility to gain an overview of the situational motivations and emotions within the group.

During the second cycle of the analysis, selected episodes that included regulation of motivation and emotions were identified. From these episodes, the group's (possible) emerging socially shared regulation was coded into six categories. The categories were based on the existing literature on individual regulation of motivation and emotions (Corno & Kanfer, 1993; Wolters, 2003), but they were modified to adapt to collaborative learning situations where regulation was assumed to be socially shared at times (Järvelä & Järvenoja, 2011). The final categories were task structuring, social reinforcing, self-efficacy management, interest enhancement, socially shared goal-oriented talk, and handicapping of group functioning strategy. Table 8.1 presents a description and example of each strategy type. This phase of the analysis provided a general overview of the groups' motivation and emotion regulation, and specified the episodes where it was possible to trace socially shared regulation of motivation.

TABLE 8.1 Socially shared regulation strategies

Regulation strategy	Definition	Example
Social reinforcing	Identification and administration of reinforcements influencing motivation and shaping joint behavior.	The students make reciprocal suggestions of how to plan the poster. Kalle suggests an idea and Mari completes "why don't we add…". The other two support the plan.
Socially shared goal oriented talk	Using goal-oriented dialogue; thinking about various reasons for persisting in or completing a task.	The students discuss which topic to take for the poster-task. Let's take the topic "metacognition". That is also a good choice concerning the exam".

(Continued)

TABLE 8.1 Cont'd

Regulation strategy	Definition	Example
Interest enhancement	Increases aspects of intrinsic motivation or situational interest while completing an activity.	"This is a brilliant idea!" The students express concrete examples to increase joint interest "I can describe my example…."
Task structuring (environmental structuring)	Decreasing the possibility of off-task behavior by structuring task or environmental conditions.	In a situation where students have difficulties making progress with the task, one student says "Let's make a list of the five most important points."
Self-handicapping	Manufacture of obstructions before or during a task that make performing difficult.	"This text is so complicated…" "The other group has a much better poster than we have."
Efficacy management	Ability to monitor, evaluate and control expectations, perceptions of competence, or self-efficacy.	"The task is not easy and this group is not working well" or "The discussion today has been productive. We progressed well!"

Figure 8.2 shows that the example group had opportunities to employ all six types of shared-regulation strategies during the three tasks. The distribution of the strategies varied between the three tasks, but, together, they seemed to have a lot of opportunities to use task structuring strategies (especially during the third task), and there were only a few times when they may have engaged in activities that aimed to handicap motivated collaboration.

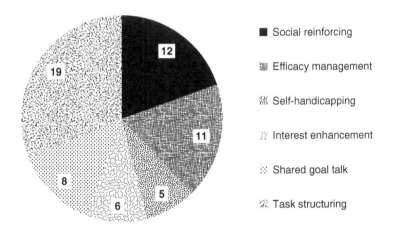

FIGURE 8.2 Coding entries to each of the shared-regulation categories from the three collaborative tasks of the four-student case group

Cycle 3 of analysis

The third cycle of the analysis "dived" to the episodes that probably triggered or demanded activation of socially shared regulation processes. The aim of this cycle of the analysis was to find the situations from which the actual use of shared regulation strategies could be traced. Each phase is described in a story line, drawing a picture of the causes, actions and effects of regulation of motivation and emotions within the situation (see an example story line below). The group's activities during an episode were divided into more detailed narratives on the phases. The narratives on the phases described the starting point in the motivationally/emotionally meaningful episode, the cause or trigger that invited group members to engage in shared regulation, the moment of shared regulation, and the end point of the episode.

The example story line describes an approximately fifteen-minute episode where the example group was working on a task. The group was in the final phase of the task, commenting on the work (a real-life case example) created by another group. The case dealt with an eight-year-old boy described, on the one hand, as an underachiever and, on the other hand, as energetic and talkative. When the narrative of the episode was created it was considered how the verbal interactions and body language of the group members affected how they created, maintained and restored their motivation throughout the challenging task. This is was also further elaborated in the cycle four analysis. The collective activity shown in the video makes it possible to interpret the group's social interactions and infer meaning from the members' collective actions.

An example of a story line:

PHASE 1 (time 00:54:03–00:56:30)
The episode illustrates how the group members established an emotional and cognitive common ground to facilitate the group activity when they started a new phase of collaboration.

The group is about to start commenting on the case that was generated by another group. Through shared jokes, the opening comment by Jari and the other group members' reactions to it, the group establishes an emotional and cognitive common ground (Clark & Brennan, 1991) to facilitate the group activity. In forthcoming phases, the group continues regulating its working and collaboration by telling jokes, sharing first impressions and being sensitive to others' reactions and comments.

PHASE 2 (time 00:56:30–01:02:30)
The episode describes the collective activity of the group in a situation where there is no need for active motivation regulation among members because the group appears to be working intentionally towards a shared goal.

The participation of the group members seems relatively equal in the sense that every member expresses his or her own ideas. They support each other's expertise, ask questions and interrupt others which may signal confidence among the members. The style of interaction is in contrast with the first phase, where students were more careful to make sure they did not offend each other.

PHASE 3 (time 01:02:30–01:04:20)

The episode highlights how the seemingly firm emotional grounding can easily be disturbed. The situation results in an immediate change in the group members' motivation and social interactions, and requires deliberate collective activity to reconstruct the motivation of some members, as well as to rebuild the emotional common ground within the group.

In this short period of time the group members' conversation gets side-tracked. Soon they realise that the earlier joint, secure emotional atmosphere has vanished. Gestures and body language change, momentarily, when Jari cocks his eyebrows and leans backwards away from Anna. The other two support Jari's comment and Anna also turns away from the group. Even though this unsettling moment is brief, every group member begins to adopt regulatory strategies to deal with the socio-emotionally challenging situation (e.g., react with gestures and soften their opinions).

PHASE 4 (time 01:04:20–01:09:30)

The episode describes how the group, who had previously created a sense of shared understanding and commitment, manages to restore motivation and collective activity after a socio-emotionally challenging interaction.

After the socio-emotionally challenging situation experienced in the previous phase, in this phase the group members still struggle a little to restore their positive emotional atmosphere. Interestingly, this is done by using the same kind of regulation strategies adopted at the beginning of their group task. The sense of togetherness is created by joking and by responding positively to each other, as well as by contrasting their own group with the other group. One could argue that this is possible because they had developed "a joint history" of shared motivation and emotional grounding a little earlier.

The storyline above describes a situation where a seemingly firm emotional balance and a sense of group identity can unexpectedly be disturbed by situational circumstances, in this case group members' spontaneous reactions to each other. The first two phases described situations where group members established and maintained motivated activity. In phase 1, the group was starting a new stage straight after they had finished the previous working phase. Since the overall task commitment had already been created earlier in the group's collaboration, it didn't take long to establish motivational ground for this particular phase. The group moved quickly to phase 2 in which they started a focused discussion according to their shared goal. In phase 3, however, this smooth and coordinated interaction was suddenly jeopardized. This phase described the trigger that created the disturbance within the group, group members' reactions and attempts to restore the emotional balance to the group. Finally phase 4 dealt with how the group had managed to restore emotional balance and a motivated, goal-directed working mode after a socio-emotionally challenging situation, which had had the potential to lead to a more serious conflict within the group.

In the third cycle of the analysis, a situation that triggered socio-emotional challenges and called for shared emotion regulation was framed. As a result, it was possible to limit the exact time frame from which to trace the regulation activity as it proceeded in the group members' interactions.

Cycle 4 of analysis

In the fourth cycle of the analysis, the aim was to trace the process of shared regulation, from the group members' verbal and non-verbal interactions, as it evolved within the situation. This was done by analysing the utterances and reactions the group members externalized in the situation described in "phase 3" of the Cycle 3 of analysis, where socially shared regulation strategies were located. The idea was to code each group member's utterance/reactions to the interaction. Table 8.2 illustrates how the group members' actions were traced as they unfolded over time to provide more detailed evidence on how the shared regulation process manifested in one authentic situation. The same information is presented in a descriptive narrative below. Whereas the information presented in Table 8.2 focused on turn taking and the tone of the interactions between the group members, the narrative includes a detailed description of each phase of the storyline and full transcriptions of the utterances that are marked into Table 8.2 with numbers.

TABLE 8.2 The example group's interaction process in regulating a socio-emotionally challenging situation

Storyline (time 01:02:30–01:04:20)	JARI	RIITTA	TIMI	ANNA	OTHER GROUP
(01:02:30–01:02:57) The group is communicating with another group.	X				X
	X				X
	X				
				X	
			X		
		X			X
	X				
		X			
			X	X	
(01:02:59–01:03:13) A socio-emotional challenge emerges (1–4 see utterances in narrative below) (01:03:14–01:04:20) (5-6 see utterances in narrative below)		[−2 ↑ / −3 −4 ← +]	R5	+1 +6	

(*Continued*)

TABLE 8.2 (Cont'd)

Storyline (time 01:02:30–01:04:20)	JARI	RIITTA	TIMI	ANNA	OTHER GROUP
The group members start to regulate the situation.	R				
			R		
	R				
		R			
	R				
		R			
			R		
(7–9 see utterances in narrative below)			R7		
			R		
		R8			
Emotional balance is restored	R9				

X = objective utterance, + = positive utterance, – = negative utterance, R = regulative utterance

A descriptive narrative of the example group's activity in a socio-emotionally challenging situation:

01:02:30–01:04:20
The group is having a short discussion with another group about some detail regarding the case. After clarifying the details, they turn to internal group discussion. Soon Anna's mention of her childhood recollection leads the group to discuss a new topic based on her memory. Anna's recollection means that she is sharing a subjective experience from her childhood. In addition, Anna's way to present this memory includes a heavy opinion about human memory systems, since it includes a claim that relatively small children can have concrete memories from their early childhood.

1: ANNA: You can remember things from the time you were three years old… At least I can remember lots of things already from my early childhood. A child can….

Other group members' spontaneous reactions are not what Anna may have anticipated based on the firm emotional atmosphere present in the group. Jari, Riitta and Timi all react negatively to Anna's comment, and back up each other. Riitta bursts into laughter and Timi rolls his eyes. In that exact moment Jari is the only one who keeps any eye contact with Anna. With both their verbal and non-verbal reactions, the other three members question Anna's ability to remember things from early childhood.

2: RIITTA: I don't…

3: TIMI: I do not agree with that opinion!

4: JARI: I'm lucky if I remember things from last week.

Anna reacts negatively towards other group members' reactions. Timi reacts to Anna's negative non-verbal expression immediately and starts to regulate the situation by making a mediating comment. Encouraged by Timi's regulative action, Anna's

counteraction is to verify her earlier opinion by presenting another memory which is even more extreme than the first.

5:TIMI: Maybe you can have small memories… Some kind of understanding or idea of different situations. So that you can be outdoors by yourself, without your mum.

6:ANNA: I have my first memories from when I was less than two years old. I was sleeping in my crib.

Again, Anna is questioned by the other group members. After this episode, Anna's reaction is even more negative. She turns her head away from the group and does not participate in the conversation anymore. The others try to make up for their earlier reactions which may have hurt Anna's feelings. They explain and soften their negative remarks hoping to re-engage Anna by bringing in examples from their own experiences and through humor. At first their comments were harsher, but, as a reaction to Anna's non-verbal cues, they soften their opinions little by little.

Timi acts as a change agent (again) by turning the discussion to a more objective and humorous level. Riitta and Jari evolve themselves to this line of discussion.

7:TIMI: It's kind of like when you have a dream and afterwards you are not sure whether it really happened or not… I talked with my psychology teacher… I first had a dream and then really experienced the same situation.

8: RIITTA: It's really scary. You don't know whether or not you have actually done something already before

9:JARI: And then you can say that soon someone will enter from the door…

The situation ends up with a joke and laughing. Finally, even though the difference in the opinion is not solved thoroughly, everybody is involved in the "objective" joking and Anna is returned back to the group. The group returns back to the task-oriented work and equal participation.

Summary

The aim of the previous example was to illustrate "regulating emotions together" by presenting a detailed analysis of an extract from an example group's videotaped collaborative working session. In the presented extract, four group members, Timi, Riitta, Jari and finally also Anna, engaged in a shared activity that aimed to regulate disturbing emotions within the group.

What is it that makes some of the activity in this episode an implementation of socially shared regulation of emotions? As such, not a single one of the reactions or utterances can be interpreted as regulation strategy alone. Nor is there any single action that could indicate individual regulation of emotions, such as counting to ten or turning something negative into something positive in terms of learning. Rather, the socially shared process of regulation is embedded in the collaborative learning context, in group members' reactions to each other and in the nuances of these reactions. The example suggests that socially shared regulation of emotion is situated within the group and cannot be assigned to any individual alone.

The group's history, the needs of the group, and group members' reactions in different situations all contribute to how a group is able to activate a socially shared regulation process. In the present example, indicators of meaningful behaviors and interactions include: individual body language, facial expressions, nature and intensity of eye contact, sudden momentary changes in gestures as members relate to each other, and collective movements of members shifting closer or further apart from each other, as well as consistency in verbal and non-verbal interactions at both individual and collective levels.

The recognition of socially shared regulation of emotions presented in the example was built on several indicators. First, a situation arose where socio-emotional challenge emerged and was identified. Second, there was the realization that the students in the example group needed to regulate the socio-emotionally challenging situation. Third, there was evidence of regulation in order to restore the emotional balance. Because of the shared willingness and reciprocal activity of the group, group members were ultimately able to restore a secure emotional atmosphere.

Discussion

The development of socio-emotional strengths will become increasingly important in a rapidly changing society, which demands coping with multiple challenges, stressful situations, and competing goals. Therefore, understanding how to manage with affective experiences, so that they can be resources rather than constraints, would be beneficial for people who are overwhelmed with numerous demands and expectations. Coping with emotional challenges is not an easy task, but it is possible to learn and to develop strategic emotion regulation, especially if you are provided with appropriate scaffolding (Turner & Patrick, 2004), whether by other people or different tools (Azevedo, 2005).

Since emotions often have a social origin and collaborative learning is increasing in many fields in education and working life, there is especially a need to develop practical solutions for people to "regulate emotions together" in various collaborative learning settings. Future research is challenged with questions such as: What kind of new opportunities can technology provide to group members to support the construction and maintenance of engagement, which actually involves core processes of self-regulated learning? How can various technological tools be used to promote and scaffold regulation processes in social learning situations?

Until now, different pedagogical models and technology-based regulation tools have been developed to support collaboration between participants. One way to enhance the process of collaboration as well as to integrate individual and group-level perspectives of learning is to structure learners' actions with the aid of scaffolding or scripted cooperation (Weinberger, Stegmann, Fischer, & Mandl, 2007). Pedagogical structuring and regulation tools built into the learning environment can both be considered as means for supporting self-regulated learning.

In addition to scripting, one mechanism for structuring collaboration, structuring can be enriched with various technology-based emotion and motivation regulation tools, which offer a group of learners visual representations or prompts to support them in self-regulating their collaborative learning processes. Järvenoja, Järvelä, and Malmberg (2009) investigated ways of scaffolding motivation in computer-supported collaborative learning. Their study explored students' situational motivation during classroom learning. A "motivation scaffold sheet" was designed to prompt students' awareness of their emotions and motivation in situations that required self-regulation. The results showed that the students' situational motivation varied during the two months within all the students. However, there were differences in how the students with a different situational motivation profile explained their use of motivation strategies as well as differences in how they performed in the research skills learning test. In general, the study suggested that tools that aim to scaffold awareness of situational emotions and motivation can be promising in helping individuals and groups to recognize critical situations involving motivation loss or emotional conflicts.

The challenge in the future is to investigate whether motivation and emotion scaffolds or other tools that aim to increase learners' awareness of these processes can be used to prompt students to regulate their situational motivation and enhance the possibilities for them to take responsibility in the learning process. Different technologies can offer powerful solutions to support individual and group regulation of motivation and emotions. We have a long tradition for developing various cognitive supports and knowledge building tools for collaboration (e.g. Scardamalia & Bereiter, 2006). The contemporary computer-supported learning technologies are often sophisticated in terms of orchestrating and emphasizing collaborative interactions and cognitive knowledge construction. But, without engagement, these cognitive processes will come to an unsatisfactory end or will not take place at all. Emotion and motivation cannot be neglected. The potential of technological tools for motivation and emotion regulation still requires more understanding about how regulation is manifested, especially as a shared activity.

References

Andersen, P. A., & Guerrero, L. K. (Eds.). (1998). *Handbook of Communication and Emotion: Research, Theory, Application and Contexts*. San Diego: Academic Press.

Arvaja, M., Salovaara, H., Häkkinen, P., & Järvelä, S. (2007). Combining individual and group-level perspectives for studying collaborative learning in context. *Learning and Instruction*, 17, 448–59.

Azevedo, R. (2005). Using hypermedia as a metacognitive tool for enhancing student learning? The role of self-regulated learning. *Educational Psychologist*, 40, 199–209.

Barron, B. (2003). When smart groups fail. *The Journal of the Learning Sciences*, 12(3), 307–59.

Blumenfeld, P., Marx, R., Soloway, E., & Krajcik, J. (1996). Learning with peers: From small group cooperation to collaborative communities. *Educational Researcher*, 25(8), 37–40.

Boekaerts, M., & Corno, L. (2005). Self-regulation in the classroom: A perspective on assessment and intervention. *Applied Psychology: An International Review*, 54(2), 199–231.

Boekaerts, M., Pintrich, P. R., & Zeidner, M. (Eds.). (2000). *Handbook of Self-Regulated Learning*. San Diego; CA: Academic Press.

Brown, A. L., & Campione, J. C. (1994). Guided discovery in a community of learners. In K. McGilly (Ed.), *Classroom lessons: Integrating Cognitive Theory and Practice* (pp. 229–70). Cambridge, MA: MIT Press.

Clark, H. H., & Brennan, S. E. (1991). Grounding in Communication. In L. Resnick, J. Levine & S. D. Teasley (Eds.), *Perspectives on Socially Shared Cognition* (pp. 127–49). Washington, DC: American Psychological Association.

Corno, L. (2001). Volitional aspects of self-regulated learning. In B. J. Zimmerman & D. H. Schunk (Eds.), *Self-Regulated Learning and Academic Achievement: Theoretical Perspectives* (pp. 191–225). Mahwah, NJ: Lawrence Erlbaum.

Corno, L., & Kanfer, R. (1993). The role of volition in learning and performance. In L. Darling-Hammond (Ed.), *Review of Research in Education* (pp. 3–43). Washington, DC: AERA.

Dillenbourg, P., Järvelä, S., & Fischer, F. (2007). The evolution of research on computer-supported collaborative learning: From design to orchestration. In N. Balacheff, S. Ludvigsen, T. de Jong, A. Lazonder & S. Barnes (Eds.), *Technology-Enhanced Learning: Principles and Products*. Kaleidoscope Legacy Book (pp. 3–19) Springer.

Dowson, M., & McInerney, D. M. (2003). What do students say about their motivational goals?: Towards a complex and dynamic perspective on student motivation. *Contemporary Educational Psychology*, 28, 91–113.

Goetz, T., Zirngibl, A., Pekrun, R., & Hall, N. (2003). Emotions, learning and achievement from educational-psychological perspective. In P. Mayring & C. V. Rhoeneck (Eds.), *Learning Emotions: The Influence of Affective Factors on Classroom learning* (pp. 9–28). Frankfurt/M: Peter Lang.

Hadwin, A., Järvelä, S., & Miller, M. (2011). Self-regulated, co-regulated, and socially shared regulation of learning. In B. Zimmerman & D. Schunk (Eds.), *Handbook of Self-Regulation of Learning and Performance* (pp. 65–84). New York: Routledge.

Hareli, S., & Weiner, B. (2002). Social emotions and personality inferences: A scaffold for a new direction in the study of achievement motivation. *Educational Psychologist*, 37(3), 183–93.

Hurme, T.-R., Merenluoto, K., & Järvelä, S. (2009). Socially shared metacognition and feeling of difficulty in the process of mathematical problem solving in CSCL context. *Journal of Educational Research and Evaluation*, 15, 503–24.

Isaac, J. D., Sansone, C., & Smith, J. L. (1999). Other people as a source of interest in an activity. *Journal of Experimental Social Psychology*, 35, 239–65.

Jackson, T., McKenzie, J., & Hobfoll, S. E. (2000). Communal aspects of self-regulation. In M. Boekaerts, P. R. Pintrich & M. Zeidner (Eds.), *Handbook of Self-Regulation* (pp. 275–300). San Diego: Academic Press.

Järvelä, S., & Häkkinen, P. (2002). Web-based cases in teaching and learning – the quality of discussions and a stage of perspective taking in asynchronous communication. *Interactive Learning Environments*, 10(1), 1–22.

Järvelä, S., Hurme, T.-R., & Järvenoja, H. (2011). Self-regulation and motivation in computer supported collaborative learning environments (pp. 330–45). In Ludvigsen, S., Lund, A., Rasmussen, I. & Säljö, R. (Eds.), *Learning across Sites: New Tools, Infrastructures and Practices*. Oxford: Routledge.

Järvenoja, H., & Järvelä, S. (2009). Emotion control in collaborative learning situations - do students regulate emotions evoked from social challenges? *British Journal of Educational Psychology*, 79(3), 463–81

Järvelä, S., & Järvenoja, H. (2011). Socially constructed self-regulated learning in collaborative learning groups. *Teachers College Records*, 113(2), 350–74.

Järvelä, S., Järvenoja, H., & Veermans, M. (2008). Understanding dynamics of motivation in socially shared learning. In special issue "Application of qualitative and quantitative methods to enrich understanding of emotional and motivational aspects of learning". *International Journal of Educational Research*, 47(1), 122–35.

Järvelä, S., & Volet, S. (2004). Motivation in real-life, dynamic and interactive learning environments: Stretching constructs and methodologies. *European Psychologist*, 9(4), 193–97.

Järvelä, S., Volet, S., & Järvenoja, H. (2010). Research on motivation in collaborative learning: Moving beyond the cognitive-situative divide and combining individual and social processes. *Educational Psychologist*, 45(1), 15–27.

Järvenoja, H., & Järvelä, S. (2005). How students describe the sources of their emotional and motivational experiences during the learning process: A qualitative approach. *Learning and Instruction*, 15(5), 465–80.

Järvenoja, H., & Järvelä, S. (2009). Emotion control in collaborative learning situations – do students regulate emotions evoked from social challenges? *British Journal of Educational Psychology*, 79(3), 463–81.

Järvenoja, H., Järvelä, S., & Malmberg, J. (2009). Scaffolding primary school students awareness of situational motivation and emotion in self-regulated learning. A paper presented in EARLI conference, Amsterdam, the Netherlands.

Light, P., Littleton, K., Messer, D., & Joiner, R. (1994). Social and communicative processes in computer-based problem solving. *European Journal of Psychology of Education*, 14(1), 93–109.

Meyer, D. K., & Turner, J. C. (2006). Reconceptualizing emotion and motivation to learn in classroom contexts. *Educational Psychology Review*, 18, 377–90.

Mäkitalo, K., Häkkinen, P., Järvelä, S., & Leinonen, P. (2002). The mechanisms of common ground in the web-based interaction. *The Internet and Higher Education*, 5(3), 247–65.

McCaslin, M., & Hickey, D. T. (2001). Self-regulated learning and academic achievement: A vygotskian view. In B. Zimmerman & D. Schunk (Eds.), *Self-Regulated Learning and Academic Achievement: Theory, Research, and Practice* (2nd edn, pp. 227–52). Mahwah, NJ: Erlbaum.

Op't Eynde, P., De Corte, E., & Verschaffel, L. (2007). Students' emotions: A key component of self-regulated learning? In P. A. Schutz & R. Pekrun (Eds.), *Emotion in education* (pp. 185–204). Burlington, MA: Elsevier.

Patrick, H. (1997). Social self-regulation: Exploring the relationships between children's social relationship, academic self-regulation, and school performance. *Educational Psychologist*, 32, 209–20.

Pekrun, R., Goetz, T., Titz, W., & Perry, R. P. (2002). Academic emotions in students' self-regulated learning and achievement: A program of qualitative and quantitative research. *Educational Psychologist*, 37(2), 91–105.

Roschelle, J., & Teasley, S. (1995). The construction of shared knowledge in collaborative problem solving. In C. E. O'Malley (Ed.), *Computer Supported Collaborative Learning* (pp. 69–97). Heidelberg: Springer-Verlag.

Scardamalia, M., & Bereiter, C. (2006). Knowledge building: Theory, pedagogy, and technology. In K. Sawyer (Ed.), *Cambridge Handbook of the Learning Sciences* (pp. 97–118). New York: Cambridge University Press.

Schunk, D. H., & Zimmerman, B. J. (1997). Social origins of self-regulatory competence. *Educational Psychologist*, 32, 195–208.

Schutz, P. A., & Pekrun, R. (Eds.). (2007). *Emotion in Education*. San Diego: Academic Press.

Summers, M., & Volet, S. E. (in press). Group work does not necessarily equal collaborative learning: Evidence from observations and self-reports. *European Journal of Psychology of Education*.

Turner, J. C., & Patrick, H. (2004). Motivational influences on student participation in classroom learning activities. *Teachers College Record*, 106(9), 1759–85.

Van den Bossche, P., Gijselaers, W., Segers, M., & Kirschner, P. A. (2006). Social and cognitive factors driving teamwork in collaborative learning environments: Team learning beliefs & behaviors. *Small Group Research*, 37(5), 490–521.

Veermans, M., & Lallimo, J. (2007). Analyzing students' motivational profiles in virtual collaboration. *Qwerty*, 1, 17–30.

Volet, S. E., & Mansfield, C. (2006). Group work at university: Significance of personal goals in the regulation strategies of students with positive and negative appraisals. *Higher Education, Research and Development*, 25(4), 341–56.

Volet, S. E., & Karabenick, S. (2006). Help-seeking in cultural context. In S. Karabenick & R. Newman (Eds.), *Help Seeking in Academic Settings: Goals, Groups and Contexts* (pp. 117–50). Mahwah, NJ: Erlbaum.

Volet, S. E., Summers, M., & Thurman, J. (2009). High-level co-regulation in collaborative learning: How does it emerge and how is it sustained? *Learning and Instruction*, 19(2), 128–43.

Webb, N. M., & Palincsar, A. S. (1996). Group processes in the clasroom. In D. C. Berliner & R. C. Calfee (Eds.), *Handbook of Educational Psychology* (pp. 841–73). New York: Simon & Schuster Macmillan.

Weinberger, A., Stegmann, K., Fischer, F. & Mandl, H. (2007). Scripting argumentative knowledge construction in computer-supported learning environments. In: F. Fischer, H. Mandl, J. Haake & I. Kollar (Eds.), *Scripting Computer-Supported Communication of Knowledge – Cognitive, Computational and Educational Perspectives* (pp. 191–211). New York, USA: Springer.

Winne, P. H., & Hadwin, A. (1998). Studying as self-regulated learning. In D. Hacker, J. Dunlosky & A. Graesser (Eds.), *Metacognition in Educational Theory and Practice* (pp. 277–304). Hillsdale, NJ: Erlbaum.

Wolters, C. A. (2003). Regulation of motivation: Evaluating an underemphasized aspect of self-regulated learning. *Educational Psychologist*, 38(4), 189–205.

Zimmerman, B. J. (2000). Attaining self-regulation. A social cognitive perspective. In B. Boekaerts, P. R. Pintrich & M. Zeidner (Eds.), *Handbook of Self-Regulation* (pp. 13–39). San Diego, CA: Academic Press.

Zimmerman, B. J., & Martinez-Pons, M. (1990). Student differences in self-regulated learning: Relating grade, sex, and giftedness to self-efficacy and strategy use. *Journal of Educational Psychology*, 82, 51–9.

Zimmerman, B. J., & Schunk, D. (2008). Motivation an essential dimension of self-regulated learning. In D. Schunk & B. Zimmerman (Eds.), *Motivation and Self-Regulated Learning: Theory, Research and Applications* (pp. 1–30). New York: Lawrence Erlbaum.

SECTION 4
Tensions in groups

9

IDENTIFYING AND OVERCOMING TENSION IN INTERDISCIPLINARY TEAMWORK IN PROFESSIONAL DEVELOPMENT

Patrick Sins and Klas Karlgren

Introduction

Rapid changes in current networked and knowledge-based society present cognitive, social, and motivational challenges to human competence and flexibility. Productive participation in knowledge-intensive work requires that practitioners, their professional communities, and their organizations develop new practices, advance their knowledge and their understanding as well as produce innovations. This is reflected in developments in professional communities wherein work is increasingly focused on the deliberate advancement of knowledge rather than on the mere production of material artifacts. In order to cope with these challenges, tools and pedagogical methods are needed that open up opportunities for practitioners to transform their knowledge practices accordingly.

Based on the works of Engeström (1987), Schatzki (2002) and Reckwitz (2002) we define a knowledge practice as follows: *a social-historically created and shared behavioral pattern consisting of an interconnected and inseparable array of recurrent activities, conventions, rules and norms that play part in the creation of knowledge artifacts.* According to this conceptualization, practices are characterized by their social nature, which means that practices are shaped by and evolve within a particular community, ultimately becoming part of its identity. This implies that a knowledge practice such as collaborative scientific inquiry is a situated and socially mediated set of activities that is focused towards the gradual and iterative advancement of particular knowledge artifacts (e.g. meeting notes, reports and scientific publications) within a certain knowledge community with its own rules, values and norms for collaborative work (Kaptelinin, 2002). Moreover, the concept of knowledge practice entails stability since it is reflected as routines, procedures, conventions, underlying beliefs and values, epistemological conceptualizations and the set of available tools.

By definition, practices are thus difficult to change because such transformation involves a period of disorientation while old practices are gradually unlearned and new practices are gradually developed (Eraut, 2004). During this period practitioners feel like novices, but without having the excuses or discounts on performance normally assigned to novices. The pain of transformation lies in the loss of control over one's practice when one's tacit knowledge ceases to provide the necessary support. In addition, Little (1990) reports that practitioners view transforming practices as involving high transactional costs to participatory work in time. According to Argyris and Schön (1978) the central problem for most practitioners is that they are intellectually and emotionally committed to espoused theories, which describe the world as they would like it to be, but which do not necessarily accurately describe their own activities constraining possibilities for transforming their practices. Moreover, practices are similar to physical infrastructures in a sense that when everything is working well one does not pay attention to them. Consequently, practitioners rely on them even though they are not fully aware what constitutes them.

A central interest in developing professionalism resides in the potential for practitioners to learn from and with one another in ways that support transformations of their knowledge practices. Several authors have been arguing that diversity in collaboration between practitioners is a significant resource for creating awareness of the need to change their practices (de Dreu & van de Vliert, 1997; Engeström, Engeström & Kärkkäinen, 1995; Gutiérrez, Baquedano-López & Tejeda, 1999; Wenger, 1998). However, the consequence of this diversity is that negotiation between multiple perspectives, interests, practices and traditions takes place, which may lead to tension. While tension can disable learning, in this chapter we argue that identifying these tensions should be viewed as a significant source for change and development of practitioners' knowledge practices.

Our argument is that, although practices tend to remain stable, this stability is altered as internal or external disturbances produce various forms of tensions within activity systems. Based on the works of De Dreu & Van de Vliert (1997) and Kuutti (1996) tensions are conceptualized as *collectively explicated and acknowledged manifestations of a misfit within and between actor, tools and/or objects, between different activities or between different developmental phases of a single activity.* An example of a tension as described in Yamagata-Lynch and Haudenschild (2009) is that teachers articulated that their motivation and goals for participating in professional development were not in alignment with those of their school district and the universities that designed and facilitated professional development activities. Often, tensions are not about the issue at hand but rather about what they represent. This means that the misalignment articulated by teachers can be found to be rooted in the conflict between the value systems of individual teachers, school districts and universities on how to spend resources on professional development activities.

Several prominent scholars in collaborative learning have maintained that tension is more than a simple disruption of ongoing collaboration; it is a vital precursor to learning and development (Barab, Barnett & Squire, 2002; Dewey, 1966;

Engeström, 1987; 1999; Koschmann, Kuutti & Hickman, 1998). The underlying presumed mechanism that explains how tensions lead to practice transformation is based on the premise that awareness of ignorance motivates learning (Nevis, DiBella & Gould, 1995). This means that in order to overcome tensions, practitioners have to analyze their collaborative activities and question and deviate from established practices. By definition, tensions take place on an affective level and may turn into resistance on the socio-cognitive level. As argued by Giddens (1984), the subsequent collective search for solutions to overcome this resistance may lead to creative externalization or new ways of doing. These new ways of doing can consequently become materialized as artifacts that serve to mediate the new practice. This suggests that tensions are not only an opportunity to improve, but they are also of crucial importance to coordinate this improvement. In sum, tensions help learners to counter the blindness that is inherent in the way things are normally done and they may uncover a space for alternative actions in taken-for-granted activity.

However, what is still lacking in accounts and studies of tensions as conditions for practice transformations to occur is a description of patterns of tension resolution that lead to productive changes and development. Therefore, in this chapter two cases are presented that show similar patterns in the resolution of tensions. The first case involves tension resolution in collaborative medical simulation training whereas the second investigated teacher–researcher collaboration at a secondary school. The two cases involved ethnographic studies with participatory observation, developmental intervention approaches, interviews and event sampling to follow processes towards new practices. Our analyses took tensions in professionals' activities as a point of departure. We looked for episodes in the material that express problems and materialize as developmental tensions. Then we investigated discursive activities between professionals (micro-level), elaborated on episodes of tension resolutions over time (meso-level) and examined how patterns of tension resolution relate to transformations of practices at the level of trajectories (macro-level).

Case 1: Analyzing medical teamwork in simulation training course

At the Södersjukhuset hospital in Stockholm, simulation courses are organized aimed at training medical teams in neonatal resuscitation. The participants are pediatricians, anaesthetists, obstetricians, nurses, and midwives. The courses start with lectures and are followed by simulations and debriefing and feedback sessions. The participants work in teams to practice solving complex, authentic cases: the medical teams provide newborns (a small manikin) arriving from the delivery room with intensive care. Emphasis is on learning the medical guidelines, resuscitation procedures, and equipment but also on medical teamwork, leadership and communication skills. During the course the participants take part in several simulations that are recorded on video and watched and analyzed together with instructors in debriefing sessions following each simulation.

The focus here was on tensions that occurred during the debriefing sessions. Various approaches exist for how to conduct debriefing and judgmental approaches which involve harsh criticism risk, having serious costs such as humiliation, dampened motivation and exit of talented trainees (Rudolph, Simon, Dufresne & Raemer, 2006). On the other hand, non-judgmental approaches where direct criticism is withheld have been questioned as well – sugar-coated criticism and asking leading questions as a method to help learners discover on their own without expressing critical opinions will cause confusion and even suspicion among learners since the instructors' opinions will "leak" to the participants. Rudolph and colleagues (2006) have instead suggested an approach (called Debriefing with Good Judgment) that encourages instructors to share their critical insights, not as ultimate truths but rather as hypotheses open for testing and exploration. In this study, several teams have been observed and video recordings of debriefing sessions have been analyzed using an interaction analysis approach with a specific focus on what the participants discuss (and do not discuss) in the debriefings, their roles in the team (leader or member), professional role (profession) and role in the simulations (participant, observer). The kinds of analyses that are created in the debriefing discussions and how these develop during courses have been of especial interest.

Empirical findings

The characteristics of the teams' discussions and analyses varied depending on the team, its participants and the character of the simulated case. However, some typical recurrent trends have been discerned in the debriefings of the many courses that have been studied. The initial analyses made by the participants were often not so well-structured and, instead, were imprecise and overly positive about any achievements made by the team, with participants tending to overlook serious mistakes and safety-critical habits, revealing ignorance of many critical issues regarding teamwork in critical care.

To exemplify this: a team has taken part in a simulation where, for a while, they had lost focus of one of the most important activities during resuscitation, namely ventilating the child properly. In addition, they failed to call for an anaesthetist in time, failed to document their work, and a couple of the team members entertained ideas which could have helped the team avoid some problems but failed to share these with the rest of the team, as is revealed later. Despite these serious issues, the team displayed a positive attitude to the team's performance:

Excerpt 1	*Debriefing after a first simulation*	
1 Instructor	What do you say about this?	
2 Pediatrician	I felt positive support, because I got so many suggestions, I thought	
	(continued discussion)	
3 Midwife	Yes, it was good, if not very good	
4 Obstetrician	Our thinking was good	

The excerpt above shows the absence of any critical views on the performance of the team. This kind of positive attitude is common after the first simulations and there is a risk that teams are overly positive and overlook the problems and difficulties which actually take place. The analyzing was thus not so productive at this stage but later this team realized several of the problematic issues. But at this stage there was an *unawareness* of many of the problems which the team members did not seem to notice. This is problematic because such an attitude is unlikely to contribute to developing the practices of the team.

One way that the instructors addressed such unawareness was by continuously asking questions about the priorities of the teams and asking them to describe the most important activities with regard to the patient's health. Another approach used by instructors was to summarize the many activities that had been taking place in an attempt to create an overview which could help the teams to create a picture of what they had been involved in. Yet another way was to directly question the motivation behind specific activities.

Excerpt 2		*Debriefing after a first simulation*	
1	Instructor	Much happening now, many of you working intensely. What is most important now? (Silence)	Question about priorities
2	Instructor	If we put it this way: you are ventilating with the Neopuff, you have applied the ECG-electrodes, you are working with the pulse oximeter, applying it, you have blood gas – only examples of all the things that are going on! – which is the most important? (continued discussion)	A summary of all activities followed by a question about priorities
3	Instructor	If you have to choose between all the things that you are doing, what would you take away right now? You can not take away the ventilation. (continued discussion)	Question about priorities
4	Instructor	What are you going to use the intravenous access for? (continued discussion)	An activity is questioned

The questions from the instructor concerned which part of the work the team viewed as being most important and prioritized, i.e., to decide which activities were most crucial for the resuscitation of the patient. The instructor summarized some of the things going on and asked the team several times to prioritize between these. The discussion had been without any noticeable tensions so far, but these questions were likely to create some tension. A consequence was that the questioning eventually led to a lengthy discussion about the activities and the need for them in the case.

After a while the team arrived at identifying a couple of problems which had not been brought up before:

Excerpt 3	*Debriefing after a first simulation*	
1 Pediatrician	I realize that now. The child was blue, we should have given more oxygen	A problem is identified
2 Instructor	OK, you might now at the age of 3–4 minutes consider adding some oxygen. You are ventilating the child and you still have central cyanosis.	
3 Pediatrician	And at this stage we should have called for an anaesthetist. (We had) a child which does not react correctly to ventilation	A problem is identified

The continuous questioning about the priorities of the team possibly caused some tension in the team which initially had been rather satisfied with its performance. However, the questioning led to the positive result that the team *identified* a few problems which had gone unnoticed; they had not been ventilating the patient adequately and they should have called for help earlier. At this point it is not uncommon that team members put the blame for the problem on themselves as individuals, as is clear in this quote from the midwife of the team:

Excerpt 4	*Debriefing after a first simulation*
1 Midwife	It is I who should have done that immediately

Such a self-critical reaction is initially not uncommon among individual team members – it is, however, not constructive for the team in the sense of preparing for avoiding the problems in the future since it only focuses on what should have ideally been done without providing any explanations as to how the problem could take place nor how it could go unnoticed by the team. The team had not arrived at any explanations to why they acted as they did – they just established that they "should have" given more oxygen and that they "should have" called for help and that they didn't, but not *why* this could happen.

This kind of self-blame lacked explanations and solutions to the problem and therefore the instructors needed to continue advancing the analysis. The team's learning from the case was still quite limited. Without better ideas of why the problems took place it was unlikely that they would come up with constructive ideas about how to avoid the problems from showing up again. Without explanations to the problems there was little chance of the teams suggesting ways to transform their practices.

The next excerpt shows how the instructor continued to question priorities and how he prompted for explanations in order to encourage the participants to create *explanations* for another problem that they had identified and suggestions for *alternative strategies* (solutions) to avoid it. In this example the questioning eventually gave the desired results; the team began to give explanations to a problem and alternative suggestions for how to behave.

Excerpt 5	*Debriefing after the last simulation*	
1 Anesthesiologist	The blood gas is coming at the same time	A problem is identified
2 Instructor	Yes, and exactly in this situation a distraction takes place, we will see what happens.	
3	(They watch the video for a few seconds)	
4 Instructor	The blood gas, what's with the blood?	
5 Pediatrician	Yes, there is a delay with the (paper) note and all	Problem identified
6 Instructor	Ye-es. We see that. And why did this happen then? How can this come to take place?	Prompts for explanations
7	Silence	
8 Pediatrician	Because I was distracted by the paper note of course, otherwise …	Explanation suggested
9 Instructor	Instructor: Can this happen in real life do you think?	Prompts for elaboration of the explanation
10	Yes	
11	Absolutely	
12 Anesthesiologist	The midwife coming in with the paper maybe checks what is going on and does not put it in your fist, it's a bit like that, is this the right occasion?	A solution is suggested
13 Pediatrician	…or I should have said: "Wait a second" and put up my hand to illustrate.	Another solution is suggested

The excerpt is from the last debriefing from a course. Here the team has identified a problem (lines 1 and 5) and the instructor prompts the team to come up with explanations about why the team behaved in the way it did (6, 9). An explanation was suggested (8) which eventually led to two different suggestions about alternative behaviors (12, 13) which could be ways of avoiding the distraction that disturbed the team and which could have kept the team focused on what they considered most prioritized.

The next excerpt displays an incident that concerned the documentation of the patient's status, this being a task that was neglected. One participant had an idea about documenting but did not dare disturb the rest of the team and kept quiet instead. Also, different views existed in the team concerning the importance of documentation but these views were not discussed explicitly during the simulation and not until the instructor had asked several questions about the issue during the debriefing did the team members express their views. The different views were a potential tension. As can be seen in the excerpt, three different solutions were brought up each addressing the documentation problem. This step in the debriefing is one of the most demanding; here the analysis was not only about what had happened previously but concerned creating new practices. The role of the instructor changed to involve helping the team in evaluating different solutions and exploring possible tension that may have been the consequence of the suggested solutions. The instructor used a number of tricks to elaborate such consequences and potential tensions, e.g., he enacted a number of hypothetical scenarios by creating hypothetical situations and interactions between people, including dialogues, in order to illustrate the possible consequences (including tensions) of the suggested solutions.

Excerpt 6	*Debriefing after the first simulation*	
1 Nurse's assistant	I was thinking that after one minute we should take notes of APGAR	Problem identification: the team failed to document the status of the child
2 Instructor	Yes	
3 Nurse's assistant	I asked but noticed that the doctors were so engaged in...	
4 Instructor	Yes. You thought of Apgar but did not say anything?	Tension created by questioning behavior
5 Nurse's assistant	Yes I said it but nobody heard me...so I thought what was going on over there was more important... it was sort sort of left undone... I could have done it better	The nurse's assistant blames herself for it
6 Instructor	OK, Shall we call that "documentation"... and that documentation can get a little better? But what you are saying is a very important matter. They work, but you could have written the Apgar scores...	

7 Nurse's assistant	Exactly	
8 Instructor	How should one do it then? Quiet, silence.	Asking for *solutions*
9 Obstetrician	I think one has to… one can always grab someone, it is always good.	An idea for a *solution*
10 Midwife	If you don't manage to communicate you can always put your hand on a person and say: "what is the Apgar now?" That is, try to look at a person.	The solution is elaborated on
11 Nurse's assistant	But it went better then	
12 Instructor	Did you write Apgar at 5 minutes?	
13	Yes	
14 Instructor	OK, if you stand there and work and an arm grabs you like this (catches his enacts own shoulder) and if I am really focused and (someone says) "What is Apgar!?"	The instructor (verbally and with his body) a hypothetical scenario to illustrate what could happen if the suggested *solution* were followed.
15 Nurse's assistant	It felt uncomfortable	Indicates that she would not be comfortable
16 Instructor	It felt uncomfortable for you to do that? There is always the risk that the person replies "don't disturb me", there is a risk	Points out a potential negative consequence of the solution
17	Mmm	
18 Instructor	Or "I cannot handle all this right now I am ventilating…". You can get that answer.	Enacts another scenario to illustrate other potential consequences of the suggested solution
19 Midwife	Yes absolutely!	
20 Obstetrician	Happens in real life too, you want information and that person….	

21	Instructor	If we pretend now that you do that (looks at the nurse's assistant) and you put your hand on the midwife's shoulder and then you (midwife) say "No, I cannot handle that now!" What should one do in that case?	Continues to explore the suggested solution
22		… mumbling	
23	Pediatrician	But the question is how important…turns to the nurse's assistant. Can you assess Apgar on your own, for instance?	Implies that documentation is not so important (there may be a *tension* between different opinions here) and then brings up another suggestion for a *solution*.
24	Nurse's assistant	Well, sort of, but you want to hear it from … anyway	
25	Pediatrician	I think that in that situation as a team leader… I could also have said let us take it later but if you are very busy with something then maybe I don't know if one should interrupt that because …	Continues to question the priority of the documentation which brings up the *tension*
26	Instructor	Instructor: OK! You (Pediatrician) say to (the nurse's assistant) "Can you say it yourself?". But if you are standing over there (by the whiteboard) then you do not see the child, right?	Enacts a scenario involving the new suggested *solution* to illustrate a problem
27	Pediatrician	No	
28	Instructor	Instructor: how about like this?: if I say like this (very loud) "I WILL FILL IN APGAR, WHAT IS THE HEART RATE?". If I say that, what can you answer in that case? Then perhaps you say – what was it at 1 minute?	Enacts a third scenario with a new *solution*.

29 Obstetrician	Then it was probably about 60	
30 Instructor	OK. And what do you say to her (to the nurse's assistant)	
31 Obstetrician	"One" (an Apgar score)	
32 Instructor	OK. And then you say like this: – BREATHING? COLOR?… What do you think of that? It depends entirely on the situation. But if somebody says "What is the Apgar score?" then it becomes tricky. But if somebody says: – What is the heart rate? – One – What is the breathing? – Zero Then it all goes faster, perhaps. OK, so this thing about documentation can get better.	Continues enacting the hypothetical scenario in order to make his point that asking questions in a more direct and concrete way would be more productive and a *solution* to the overall problem.

In the excerpt above, the cognitive, affective and social aspects of the teamwork are tightly intertwined. One individual had ideas about documentation but was not assertive enough to succeed in communicating them to the team. Different team members had different ideas about the importance of documenting the work, which was a potential tension, but these were not discussed. By enacting hypothetical scenarios to illustrate potential consequences of various ideas, the instructor manages to transform the analysis practice of the team, first by illustrating potential problems and then by helping the team in coming up with alternative ideas. The instructor created tension by questioning suggestions in the hypothetical scenarios. But the scenarios are rather used to illustrate points and consequences – some of which concern potential tension that could be the consequence of the suggestions in real life – rather than to create confrontation.

To summarize, the character of the analysis practice transformed during the course and in the excerpts we have seen how the interactions with the instructor affected the teams' analyzing. This transformation can be described as a trajectory where the practice develops through a number of phases often preceded by a tension, e.g., by instructors questioning the medical team. Initially, the analyses of the simulated cases were characterized by unawareness of serious problems and discussions were frequently about praising each other (excerpt 1). Eventually, questioning on the part of the instructor (excerpt 2) resulted in teams identifying problems (excerpt 3). However, their analyzing often stopped at simply stating a problem or even self-blame (excerpt 4) rather than moving towards a more constructive analysis of how to avoid problems in the future. By prompting for more explanations (excerpt 5) and by pointing out the consequences of suggested solutions (excerpt 6) the instructor shifted the teams' analysis into a more constructive direction. In the last excerpt (6), several suggestions were put forth which in turn led to new tensions caused by competing suggestions that needed to be resolved. Eventually, the practice of analyzing the teams' performance transformed in character from identifying problems to giving explanations, followed by creating and evaluating alternative strategies. This transformation also appeared to modify the teams' expectations of the analysis practice itself, which was first viewed as an individual effort but later as a collaborative task. Initially the goal seemed to be that someone – an individual in the team – should identify the possible problem that took place during the simulation while later the team members collaboratively engaged in putting forth and evaluating different suggestions and their possible consequences for the teamwork (see excerpt 6). Here the focus has been on transforming the analysis practices during simulation training courses and an ultimate goal is that these changes will contribute to improving teamwork during critical care.

Case 2: School–university partnership

This case focuses on describing the nature and scope of transformations in teachers' coaching practices that followed from resolutions of tensions that arose in a school–university partnership. This partnership involved the two-year lasting collaboration at UniC, a secondary school in Utrecht in The Netherlands that was aimed at the redesign of a course module. At UniC, students are coached towards the national school exam, complementing the focus on knowledge acquisition by stressing development of competencies, skills and personal development. By clever organization of compulsory learning materials students are enabled to develop their own talents and interests in a course module in which they plan and perform projects within or outside the school context. This means that every week in the curriculum a half day is reserved for these projects for periods each of which last eight weeks. The school supports the students and offers possibilities to carry out their projects.

Within this pedagogical context, teachers' coaching practices traditionally focus on the development of courses and assignments providing guidance to students' self-directed learning process. UniC expressed the aspiration to challenge their students more towards meaningful learning during these projects. In addition, the teachers' expressed the view that their role during projects was unclear and that they needed more scaffolds to structure their coaching. Consequently, a multi-disciplinary team consisting of educational researchers, teachers, students, dean, process coordinator and pedagogical experts was set up to flesh out the design based on knowledge creation principles, which matched UniC's general pedagogical approach and objectives Paavola & Hakkarainen (2005). The model of knowledge-creation provides a framework to support educators to develop and advance their practices of learning and instruction. A central feature in the knowledge-creation approach is *mediation*; meaning that students collaboratively create knowledge through the development and advancement of shared objects. The knowledge creation view represents a 'trialogical' approach, because the emphasis is not only on individuals or on community, but on the way students collaboratively develop artifacts. The collaborative design, implementation and testing of the new course module implied that high demands were placed on coaching practices of the teachers which provide a platform for tensions to arise.

Empirical findings

Most tensions became manifest as problems identified on the boundary of the intersecting activity systems, showing how team members balanced institutionalized or traditional and newly developed practices. However, the problems that team members identified in current practices were not about the issue at hand, but about the tension it represents (cf. Prins, 2005). This indicated team members' *unawareness* of the underlying structures of belief, perception and appreciation that contributed to the existence of the problem. One particular problem teachers identified involved the specific organization of their coaching practices to be more in line with the new pedagogical approach and at the same time to foster students' knowledge creation processes. As we will show later, however, this problem arises from the underlying conflicting perspectives between researchers and teachers involving divergent taken-for-granted ideas about what their partnership should comprise and how to work together. Excerpt 7 exemplifies this tension during an interview with one of the participating teachers.

Excerpt 7	*Interview Teacher 3; 19 December 2006*	
1 Teacher3	I see that an increasing amount of student groups do not have a clear view of what they are doing, that is what I am afraid of, unfortunately	Identifying the problem
2 Researcher1	How do you coach these students then?	
3 Teacher3	Well, you cannot just leave them, then this would lead to chaos. [...] You can divide tasks in the group and think of who is going to do what, but then I would be too directive and I am not sure whether that should be our intention, so therefore I give them more freedom [...]	
4 Researcher1	[...] Well you mean that you are still in search of what is expected of you as a teacher.	Framing/ explaining
5 Researcher1	What do you need in your coaching?	

6	Teacher3	First I need to know more about knowledge creation, what the idea and what the pillars are, so I can eventually adapt my coaching to that [...] normally I am very clear in my teaching, but in this pilot it seems that I have to discover what the best ways of coaching are [...]	Identifying the problem
7	Teacher3	[...] The question is what should I do now? I would like to hear that from you, how we should tackle this. There has to be an idea behind that	Identifying the problem
8	Researcher1	We want to investigate how knowledge creation takes place in the first place. To which extent is coaching needed and in how far you coach students [...] For us the goal is to see how coaching and knowledge creation happens now	Framing/ explaining

In passage 1, Teacher3 expresses his concern with respect to his observation that students have not been successful in organizing and structuring their work. When prompted for ways to cope with this tension in his coaching, he states that he would like to be more directive, saying "you can divide tasks in the group" (passage 3). At this point, he identifies a problem with what he interprets as the coaching practice which would comply with principles of knowledge creation "but then I would be too directive and I am not sure whether that should be our intention, so therefore I give them more freedom" (passage 3). Eventually, for him to overcome this problem, he proposes that more guidelines for coaching students' knowledge creation processes have to be generated (passage 6). This statement encompasses an indirect comment to researcher1 requesting him for more guidance on coaching students' knowledge creation process. Teacher3's last statement in passage 6: "I have to discover what the best ways of coaching are", adds to this, eventually leading him to directly address researcher1 in passage 7. However, researcher1 does not seem to be aware of the apparent need to reconsider his work practices and instead articulates the epistemological assumption of "researcher as observer", which is characterized by non-intrusive observation (passage 8).

Schön and Rein (1994) contend that between-frame conflicts in small groups are often fundamentally about identity: an attempt to answer the questions who are we and how we do things here. To become aware of the underlying tension with respect to the identity and work practices of team members in the school–university partnership, identification and collective explaining of the factors underlying problems in ongoing work is needed in order to resolve these tensions. Moreover, tensions afford the means for revealing the nature of team members' understanding and the resolution of these tensions by explaining the way things are normally done may uncover a space of alternative actions in these taken-for-granted work practices (cf. Winograd and Flores, 1986).

This tension arose during a meeting with all team members that took place directly after the interview with teacher3. In this excerpt the contribution and roles of the researchers in guiding teachers' coaching practices was explicitly addressed.

Excerpt 8		*Protocol meeting project team; 19 December 2006*	
1	Teacher3	Nevertheless, it is important to get more assistance during work sessions because now we're only with the three of us, that is my first concern	
2	Dean	It should be fixed then, we need teachers for this class […]	
3	Teacher1	Sometimes you [Researchers] are a little blunt It is not criticism but I noticed that you have you own agenda You don't really help us coach, we just have to take care of it. In my opinion that is not really being an actor!	Identifying the problem
4	Researcher1	Well, the idea was that we didn't want to participate as a teacher because we don't have that expertise though we are here to provide you with some advice and answer your questions, if you have any	
5	Teacher1	[…] I am teaching the knowledge creation project on my own which is not an ideal situation, I just want you to think with me. Clearly we don't expect you to teach […]	
6	Researcher1	Well, I believe that is a good thing to hear, I am glad that this came forward	
7	Pedagogical expert	The researchers are used to staying in the background to be able to observe the process as objectively as possible	Framing/ explaining
8	Teacher2	There is a big culture difference because we are used to everyone being involved. You are thinking as observers	

9 Process coordinator	It is a type of participation when you are observing [...]	
10 Teacher2	You could divide one group into two groups so that T1 has to coach his own groups but that T4 and T1 meet each other during class to discuss any problems or to ask each other for advice	Constructing solutions
11 Dean	You can then also ask researchers for feedback [...]	
12 Researcher1	Yes, that would be perfect [teachers nodding]	

This episode shows the *identification* and *framing* of a tension that exists between the work traditions of researchers on the one hand and teachers on the other. The tension that was articulated: "it is important to get more assistance during work sessions because now we're only with the three of us" (passage 1), opened up for explicating the underlying conflict between the perspectives of researchers and teachers regarding their role during the coaching of students' knowledge creation processes. Utterances such as "You don't really help us coach, we just have to take care of it. In my opinion that is not really being an actor!" (passage 3) versus "Well, the idea was that we didn't want to participate as a teacher" (passage 4) illustrate this tension. Subsequently this resulted in a *framing* of these conflicting perspectives from the viewpoint of the traditional work practices of both groups to create common understanding "There is a big culture difference because we are used to everyone being involved. You are thinking as observers" (passage 8). Eventually, partners provided suggestions to overcome this tension by a division of labor "You could divide one group into two groups [...] you can then also ask researchers for feedback during coaching" (passage 10). Moreover, in passage 11 the dean offers a proposal suggesting reconsidering the collaborative practices of teachers and researchers. This eventually leads to both researcher1 and teachers accepting this proposal, which involves providing more direct and proactive feedback (passage 12).

An indication of the effect of the resolution of this tension concerning conflicting identities and roles of the participants is expressed by researcher1 during a meeting of project partners a month later (Excerpt 9).

Excerpt 9	*Protocol meeting project team; 30 January 2007*
Researcher 1	[...] this makes that there is a whole new and more intensive contact between teachers and researchers, agreeing that there is a sort of cross fertilization of ideas now. This means that we provide some information and that you respond and provide feedback on that and vice versa. What can happen in a month right?

In this segment researcher1 articulates achieving to realize the newly developed practices for providing teachers with more proactive feedback on ideas, actions and information. Tension resolution of the aforementioned conflicting perspective eventually resulted in the creation of a joint venture agreement that functioned to materialize the agreed-upon new collaborative work practices between partners.

> *Excerpt 10   Joint venture agreement, first version; April 2007*
> For Utrecht University this agreement involves:
> - To perform research at UniC in collaboration with teachers and students concerning the concept of knowledge creation and support thereof
> - To realize a long-term relationship between research and educational practice, in which knowledge, insights and experiences are exchanged with the aim of learning and capitalizing from each other
>
> For UniC this agreement involves:
> - To obtain more insight and tools to experiment with possible solutions for the challenges and issues which structurally occur in educational practice
> - To realize a long-term relationship between research and educational practice, in which knowledge, insights and experiences are exchanged with the aim of learning and capitalizing from each other

This external artifact served to mediate work practices between researchers and teachers in a second iteration of the school–university partnership, when a new group consisting of six teachers collaborated with researchers to reflect on teachers' coaching practices during the implementation of knowledge creation ideas in the existing curriculum. Two teachers articulated the role of researchers during post-interviews (Excerpts 10 and 11).

> *Excerpt 11   Interview Teacher 6; 15 November 2007*
> Teacher6   I consider you {researchers} to be a huge support for us {teachers}. And if we have questions about how we should coach our students for instance, then we can always ask you […] I think the teachers are more there for the students and the researchers are more for providing us with contents

> *Excerpt 12   Interview Teacher 5; 15 November 2007*
> Teacher5   I think that we {teachers and researchers} complete each other quite well. The teachers have knowledge of our students here and you know more about knowledge creation. We can bundle that nicely together and maybe we can create something together to support our students' knowledge creation processes

In both segments we see indications of changes in the collaborative work practices between researchers in teachers echoing the proposed solutions provided in the meeting of the project team in December 2006 (i.e., line 11), which were offered in response to a collectively identified and framed tension regarding existing practices. Moreover, in these segments teachers materialize the second bullet points in the joint venture agreement by stating that they capitalize on the exchange of knowledge, insights and experiences with researchers.

In this case, it was illustrated that interaction between different knowledge trajectories occurred on both the individual and collective platforms of the design team (Excerpts 7 and 8) and how participants stabilized out of flux by changing their practices accordingly (Excerpts 9–12). During meetings, practical pedagogical enacted knowledge of teachers intersected with social practices of the educational researchers. At this level, developmental tensions surfaced on the nexus of perspectives, agendas and interpretations of the actors involved in the collaborative design in the school–university partnership. The attempts undertaken to overcome the identified tensions involved the creation of artifacts (e.g. the joint venture agreement) that served to objectify and afford this transformation in collaborative work practices between teachers and researchers.

Conclusion

In the present chapter we found similar patterns of how tensions drive practice transformation in two research cases from the fields of respectively medical simulation training and pedagogical design in the context of a school–university partnership. Although the contexts and participants investigated are structurally and functionally different, we found that practice transformations in these different domains can be related back to similar interactional moves between processes involved in resolving tensions between people. However, we do not claim that developmental tensions are the sole impetus of transformations of practices, the investigation of tensions and their resolution helped to identify the constituents of change in practitioners' knowledge practices (cf. Barab, Barnett & Squire, 2002; Engeström, 1987; Koschmann et al., 1998). In the cases reported in this chapter, we have seen similar patterns of managing or resolving tension that can be summarized employing the following labels:

0. *Unawareness*: The level of *unawareness* is a level preceding the other levels of actively taking measures to learn and change practices. This is because the practitioners are not yet aware of their needs for doing so, or not aware of a body of knowledge that exists and which is potentially useful. A typical indication is when course participants are uncritically satisfied with their behavior and appear to miss or neglect challenges, problems or dilemmas;

1. *Identifying a problem:* A tension could arise only as the consequence of one of the practitioners in the knowledge construction work to describe a particular problem at hand. As a result of practitioners knowing what the issue is at hand, the conflicting perspectives, knowledge, attitudes or affects come to the fore, explicating the problematic features of the practices under scrutiny. These tensions are explicated in the voices of the several practitioners;

2. *Framing* or *explaining* the problem: This framing is necessary for creating a shared understanding of the tension and for constructing a representation of

the forces acting in preserving and causing the problematic practices at hand. This will eventually enable practitioners to adapt their practices to be able to overcome the tension;

3. *Constructing solutions:* Finally, practitioners suggest ways of transforming their practices, constructing new tools and implement them in the ongoing knowledge construction work. This involves suggesting alternative ways of behaving which may resolve or avoid a particular kind of problems.

The argument put forward in this chapter is that tensions serve an extremely important function, revealing to practitioners the nature of their knowledge practices. According to this argument, development is accomplished when these tensions lead to a reconceptualization of the object and motive of a particular practice to eventually embrace a more diverse horizon of possibilities. In both cases, we observed that the work around shared objectives and the tensions that emerged from this process served to elaborate and refine existing knowledge practices, and develop new ones in similar ways. We agree with Suchman (2007) and Stahl (1993) in contending that creative externalization was required to overcome tensions, providing practitioners with opportunities to repair understandings and resolve these tensions by reinterpreting meaning structures to arrive at new understandings.

The generic pattern of practitioners' tension resolution may form the basis for generating requirements for fostering productive collaborative work. This means that pedagogical methods designed to overcome tensions in professional groups should aim at acknowledging and identifying the nature of tension in order to enable collaborative reflection as well as opportunities towards learning and development to occur.

Nevertheless, these methods have to consider that tensions in collaborations do not automatically lead to collective reflection and envisioning of new strategies but that their impact is dependent on the interplay between cognitive, social and affective aspects.

Acknowledgements

The present investigation emerged in the context of research and development of the Knowledge-Practices Laboratory (http://www.kp-lab.org, FP6-2004-IST-4, integrated project 27490, 2006–2011) project funded by the Information Society Technologies (IST) programme of the European Community.

References

Argyris, C., and Schön, D. (1978). *Organizational Learning: A Theory of Action Perspective.* Reading, MA: Addison Wesley.

Barab, S. A., Barnett, M., and Squire, K. (2002). Developing an empirical account of a community of practice: Characterizing the essential tensions. *The Journal of the Learning Sciences,* 11(4), pp. 489–542.

Dewey, J. (1968). *Democracy and Education: An Introduction to the Philosophy of Education.* New York: Free Press.

De Dreu, C.K.W., and Van de Vliert, E. (1997). *Using Conflict in Organizations.* London: Sage.

Engeström, Y. (1987). *Learning by Expanding: An Activity-Theoretical Approach to Developmental Research*. Helsinki: Orienta-Konsultit Oy.

Engeström, Y., Engeström, R. and Kärkkäinen, M. (1995). Polycontextuality and boundary crossing in expert cognition: Learning and problem solving in complex work activities. *Learning and Instruction*, 5, pp. 319–36.

Engeström, Y. (1999). Expansive visibilization of work: An activitytheoretical perspective. Computer Supported Cooperative Work, 8, 63–93.

Eraut, M. (2004). Informal learning in the workplace. Studies in Continuing Education, 26, 247–273.

Giddens, A. (1984). *The Constitution of Society: Outline of the Theory of Structuration*. Cambridge: Polity.

Gutiérrez, K., Baquedano-López, P., and Tejeda, C. (1999). Rethinking diversity: Hybridity and hybrid language practices in the Third Space. *Mind, Culture, & Activity*, 6(4), pp. 286–303.

Kaptelinin, V. (2002). Social thinking reaches out to software practice: The challenge of bridging activity systems. In Y. Dittrich, C. Floyd eds., *Social Thinking–Software Practice*, pp. 45–68. Cambridge, MA: The MIT Press.

Koschmann, T., Kuutti, K., and Hickman, L. (1998). The concept of breakdown in Heidegger, Leont'ev, and Dewey and its implications for education. *Mind, Culture, and Activity*, 5, pp. 25–41.

Kuutti, K. (1996). Activity theory as a potential framework for human-computer interaction research. In B.A. Nardi, ed. (1996), *Context and Consciousness: Activity Theory and Human-Computer Interaction*, pp. 17–44. Cambridge, MA: The MIT Press.

Little, J.W. (1990). Teachers as colleagues. In A. Lieberman, ed. 1990, *Schools as Collaborative Cultures: Creating the Future Now*, pp. 165–93. Bristol, PA: Falmer Press.

Nevis, E.C., DiBella, A.J., and Gould, J.M. (1995). Understanding organizations as learning systems. *Sloan Management Review*, 36(2), pp. 75–85.

Paavola, S., Hakkarainen, K.: The Knowledge Creation Metaphor – An Emergent Epistemological Approach to Learning. Science & Education 14(6), 535–557 (2005)

Prins, E. (2005). Framing a conflict in a community-university partnership. *Journal of Planning Education and Research*, 25, pp. 57–74.

Reckwitz, A. (2002). Toward a Theory of Social Practices. *European Journal of Social Theory*, 5(2), pp. 243–63.

Rudolph, J.W., Simon, R., Dufresne, R.L. and Raemer, D. (2006). There's no such thing as "nonjudgmental" debriefing: A theory and method for debriefing with good judgment. *Simulation in Healthcare*, 1(1), pp. 49–55.

Schatzki, T. (2002). *The Site of the Social: A Philosophical Exploration of the Constitution of Social Life and Change*. University Park: Pennsylvania State University Press.

Schön, D.A. and Rein, M. (1994). *Frame Reflection: Toward the Resolution of Intractable Policy Controversies*. New York: Basic Books.

Stahl, G. (1993). *Interpretation in Design: The Problem of Tacit and Explicit Understand-ing in Computer Support of Cooperative Design*. Ph.D. University of Colorado.

Suchman, L. (2007). *Human-Machine Reconfigurations*. New York: Cambridge University Press.

Wenger, E. (1998). *Communities of Practice: Learning, Meaning, and Identity*. New York: Cambridge University Press.

Winograd, T. and Flores, F. (1986). *Understanding Computers and Cognition: A New Foundation for Design*. Norwood, NJ: Ablex Corporation.

Yamagata-Lynch, L.C. and Haudenschild, M.T. (2009). Using activity systems analysis to identify inner contradictions in teacher professional development. *Teaching and Teacher Education*, 25, pp. 507–17.

10

GETTING ON AND GETTING ALONG

Tension in the development of collaborations

Jerry Andriessen, Mirjam Pardijs and Michael Baker

Introduction

When students work together on educational tasks, they have to try to get on with doing the task whilst trying to get on with each other. The way that they learn together will therefore depend on the dynamic interrelations between processes operating on epistemic and socio-relational planes. In this direction, in what follows we present analyses of a series of collaborative group meetings of the same group of three 13-year-old boys who are designing a town area in which students would like to live. Our general approach is qualitative and developmental, focusing on the socio-emotional dimension, within the larger trajectory of task performance.

We understand collaboration as jointly working on a task for a shared purpose, whilst striving to mutually understand that task. Contributions of participants are based on their individual expertise, but are more or less equal in quantity and quality. Participants consider each others' contributions seriously, and also try to interact with each other in a respectful manner. Differences and obstacles give rise to negotiation about how to proceed, as well as to epistemic discussions. We assume that groups collaborating over a longer period of time will get better at this. However, in addition to shared purpose, a mature collaborative working relationship has a shared vision on collaboration itself. Mature collaboration involves awareness on functioning (to a degree as much as possible) at a group level in addition to the individual level: often the group interest precedes individual interests. Below we go further into the implications of this.

In order to better understand collaboration between students, we propose to explicitly introduce the temporal dimension: time, and change (Ludvigsen et al., 2010; Lemke, 2000). It is easy to forget about time, especially in science, which, from a positivist viewpoint is seen as a logical accumulation of results: if the most recent results in some way incorporate previous ones, then only the logic of the present is relevant. It was only in the nineteenth century that Historical Science came to understand history not as a random sequence of events, but as a linked series of events, whereby the previous had some constraining influence on what followed. It was thanks to the philosopher Hegel that historians and philosophers realised there was an order to things (Hegel, 1807). (The fact that this order was interpreted as progress towards a better world is not essential for our discussion). What we want to underline is that collaborative groups can dynamically evolve, sometimes in the positive sense, towards better understanding of each other and the collaboration, towards sharing understanding of various aspects of the task and its complexities, and, most importantly, towards sharing goals and ownership of the shared object that is being elaborated. Of course, due to various tensions arising, group collaboration could also turn out badly, with insensitivity to each other's needs, or become purely formal and schematic, due to a lack of empathy. But there also, collaboration develops. But, how can group development over time be captured?

In this contribution, we present an interpretation of such group development-through examining a number of collaborative sessions by the same group over a period of several weeks. Our unit of analysis is the episode, which is a sequence of actions that belong together, in our case covering between 5 and 10 minutes of collaboration. We have selected six episodes for this analysis, spread out more or less equally over time, because they represent typical activities during a particular week.

We claim that in order to understand how students collaborate, we need to understand (how they understand) their emotions. In the first chapter of this volume, the authors stated its purpose as that of trying to understand how cognitive and socio-relational dimensions interrelate, within some situational perspective. In this contribution, our point of departure is that collaboration between secondary school students can be characterised just as much by the feelings and emotions of the participants as by what they know and have been assigned to do by the teacher. How they feel about the task will be related to their engagement in it, and how they feel towards each other will relate to where they will go in their collaboration. This means that during collaborative learning interactions, epistemic progress is subject to social/emotional dynamics.

We explore these relations by analysing the work of a group of three boys (13–14 years old) during a collaborative project, coached by a teacher. The boys met regularly during a 16-week period for two hours each week to design a town area in which students would like to live. Teachers passed by irregularly.

Our analysis is a sequel of what was reported in Andriessen, Baker and van der Puil (2011), where we analysed socio-relational tensions in an electronic (chat) discussion between two 16-year-old students. A chat means a written discussion, with participants at a distance. In the previous study we looked at the relation between the depth of argumentation (Baker et al., 2007), compared with the tension-raising qualities of the arguments (Muntigl & Turnbull, 1998). This is because argumentation, and the degree of aggression that may or may not be expressed in it, represents a form of interaction that is particularly charged with emotions (Doise & Mugny, 1981; Andriessen, Baker & van der Puil, 2011). Our conjecture was that, the greater the depth of the cognitive conflict, the greater would be the threat to the interpersonal relation, and thus the greater the tension in the interaction. Within the space of one interaction, we did find that the pattern of rising tension and relaxation (derived by interpreting written argumentation) was related to the depth of the argumentation, albeit in an indirect way. Tension-raising contributions by one party resulted in the other party producing new arguments and deepening previous ones, which resulted in the first party raising the tension by rejecting these arguments. Relaxation was produced by (sudden) changes of topic, especially going off-task. Moreover, there seemed to be a kind of remanence of tension, which, once raised, remained for a while, even though the cognitive conflict was manifestly resolved. Thus subsequent cognitive conflicts occurred at a higher baseline of tension. Our conclusion was that there is a relationship between the socio-emotional and the socio-cognitive aspects of collaboration, and in order to understand collaborative working relationships we have to look at the patterns of tension and relaxation during collaborative interaction.

In the current case, we extend this line of research, but now with face-to-face (rather than distant) interactions. We would therefore expect a more versatile interaction and a more profound interactive circulation of affect, including tensions. We have to infer tensions from what people say and how others react in the transcription of the verbal interaction (it was not possible to use video in this study). Collaboration is investigated as a meaning-making trajectory during which various tensions develop and are resolved, concerning the task and concerning personal relationships. What kinds of relations exist between such tensions and the co-elaboration of knowledge through knowledge objects, during a collaborative trajectory of 16 weeks?

Theory

There is a growing interest in learning environments in which learning motivation and self-regulation can best be enhanced. Different authors have proposed instructional models aimed at creating highly motivating learning environments (Assor, Kaplan & Roth, 2002; De Corte, Verschaffel, Entwistle & van Merriënboer, 2003). However, research about the effectiveness of such models is inconclusive, at best (Alonso-Tapia & Pardo, 2006).

In our view, what could be a motivating environment for students is in part an opportunistic and individual matter. Especially in collaborative learning, previous relationships between participants, as well as their first interactions about the learning task, will quickly influence the initial desired level of achievement and effort the students are willing to engage in. We conjecture that their initial achievement goals are probably primarily *socio-relational* rather than epistemic in nature. To some extent, goals and motivations are transient with respect to different situations and participants, but also within the same situation as it develops. Therefore, for any learner, it is more important to understand how to collaborate in any environment than to rely on the motivating effects of some external agency. Learners will conceivably make meaning (e.g. "this guy is useless….") of almost anything they might do; what is at stake is their agency to engage in meaning-making (or elaboration of knowledge) *with others*, for example as in epistemic agency (Damsa, Kirschner, Andriessen, Erkens & Sins, 2010), regulative agency (van der Puil, Andriessen & Kanselaar, 2004), and relational agency (Edwards, 2007).

We need to find a way to more explicitly acknowledge the fact that peers have an important role in the way young learners collaborate, as does the teacher, and the assignment. One way of doing this is by trying to link interaction episodes during task activity to activities and discourse outside the task. Where some people like to define collaborative learning as a process of interactive meaning-making, we view meaning as being made at the level of the "how to", "what to" or "about what" issues, and not only on the level of individual words or utterances.

Our approach here is to try to provide rich interpretations, or "thick descriptions" (Ryle, 1968; Geertz, 1973) of the students' interactions, in order to try to apprehend the complexity of relations between interpersonal relations, affect and task accomplishment, rather than to analyse in terms of pre-established categories. As learning scientists, in order to understand the collaboration of small groups, we have to do an ethnography of group collaboration: "There are three characteristics of ethnographic description: it is interpretive; what it is interpretive of is the flow of social discourse; and the interpreting involved consists in trying to rescue the "said" of such discourse from its perishing occasions and fix it in perusable terms." (Geertz, 1973, p. 20).

It is important to note that we are not interpreting individual utterances here; the unit of analysis is, in a way, collaboration itself: interaction is not about individual utterances, but it is about what participants negotiate as the meaning of an exchange, an episode (Wittgenstein, 1978). The meaning of interaction is a complex process of on-going interpretation, at every level of sense-making in the context of the on-going discourse, and so as much top-down as bottom-up. Therefore, it is necessary to analyse collaboration at least at the level of (collaborative) exchanges between participants (Baker, 2010). Although, in principle, all moves and actions could be potentially relevant, within each episode, we interpret collaboration in terms of what task activities are about, how social interaction is managed, and how the relation between task activity and social relations is handled. Our focus is on tensions arising during interaction, as a consequence of what others say and do, and on how this affects task activity and task progress. What is the role of tensions arising from questions, objections, or counter-argumentation? Is greater task focusing associated with more tensions or more relaxation? It should be noted that we rely on our definition of tension as arising from argumentation and disagreement-in-discourse (Andriessen et al., 2011), not by interpreting visual or physiological symptoms of it.

Then, there is the developmental dimension, of how collaborative groups gradually become better (or worse) collaborators, within the task context. One should realise that many collaborators do not know each other very well, or at least not in the context of working together. In order to interpret the development of collaboration, we need at least some working definition or norm of "good collaboration", that nevertheless largely requires more working out in its full details. Allwood, Traum and Jokinen (2000) discuss the main features of "ideal cooperation" as being cognitive consideration, joint purpose, ethical consideration and trust. Cognitive consideration is needed for shared understanding; joint purpose is required for moving into the same direction. Ethical consideration is about not forcing each other, not preventing the other to pursue something, and making it possible for the other to engage in successful rational action. Trust refers to the certainty of the others sharing the same considerations. While such criteria seem plausible, we know less about their symptoms, and even less about their development within collaborative groups. We may even assume that most collaboration does not meet all criteria, whilst still producing something worthwhile. In other words, the quality of collaboration, as it develops is a matter of degree and combination of multiple aspects. Nevertheless, we will employ the Allwood et al. (2000) criteria, at the episode level, for characterising collaboration during that episode with respect to the "ideal".

What we will try and do is to interpret our episodes in terms of the characteristics of ideal cooperation: cognitive consideration, joint purpose, ethical consideration and trust. We assume that as the collaboration trajectory proceeds over several episodes during several weeks, its nature changes. It is characterising part of this change that we are aiming for. In other words, our "thick description" of collaboration tries to rescue participants' evolving task performance from its transient and evanescent occurrences. This then is combined with our analysis of how participants deal with epistemic and relational tensions.

The context and the task

To come to an interpretation of how the group collaborates, we will start our understanding on a higher level: that of the school in which the group is learning. At the time of the research project, UniC was a secondary school of only four years of age. The school was founded on a specific vision and defined its pedagogical approach in terms of three concepts: uniqueness, autonomy and connectionism. The first stresses that every student is unique in his or her development and interests; this should be acknowledged, encouraged and nurtured in education. The second concept shows the shared responsibility between students and teachers when it comes to motivation and initiative in the learning process. Finally the concept of "connectionism" reveals the importance of collaboration and sharing in the school. Learning to collaborate in and outside the school is important.

UniC practice

At UniC there are no lessons in the traditional sense, which means that there are no small classrooms in which portions of same-level students follow the same lessons, led by one subject-matter expert (the teacher). Instead, students have working sessions of 3.5 hours in the morning and 3 hours in the afternoon. During these sessions they sit together with all students of the same year (around 80 students) in large rooms. Students work individually or together with other students on themes that combine several subjects. They all have their own computer on which assignments and sources are available. The teacher only helps when requested, but tries not to take over the process. While there are no traditional lessons, classes or classrooms at UniC, the role and work of teachers are also somewhat different. A team of teachers is responsible for all education of a given year level. For every working session (morning or afternoon) there are four teachers available for support, but these teachers are not all experts in the subject matter. Themes are assigned to one subject teacher, who then is responsible for the theme as well as for instructing the other teachers, who also support students during the working sessions. UniC teachers themselves are as a result constantly learning.

Free choice

A specific part of the UniC learning practice is made up of a course called "Free Choice". It is a course that is organised in eight-week periods throughout the whole year, in which students are free to choose their own study topic and decide what and how they want to learn. The starting point of the course is therefore the interests of the individual student, which fits perfectly with the pedagogical concepts mentioned above. One teacher (R) explained the basic idea as follows: "During free choice, everything is possible. If a student wants to learn to ride a horse on top of the school building, because he is interested in that, he could do it!" The goal of the course is to enable students to discover who they are, where their interests lie and what they could do with these interests. After the first periods, however, teachers became unhappy with the way the course played out in practice. They remained convinced by the basic idea of the course, but noticed that only a few students were able to use their interests or passions, and to take these to the next level. Most students just had a good time "baking cookies" or "gaming", i.e., doing things they already were good at. According to the teachers the reason for this was that there was too much emphasis on what students wanted to do, and too little attention was paid to the learning process during these activities. That realisation was the start of a process of change in the course, in which focus was shifted to the learning process and not merely the outcomes of learning. These changes brought new issues to light; many students had a difficult time answering questions about learning processes they were aiming at, and teachers were struggling with how to coach students in this process.

This issue of how to organise the course so that students took up challenging tasks was taken up by the school and researchers. Based on theoretical ideas on knowledge creation and the role of knowledge objects in the learning process, three principles were formulated that were taken up in organising and executing the course. These are discussed after a short explanation about knowledge creation.

Knowledge creation

The research described here was part of the KP-Lab project,[1] which aimed at studying and supporting innovative knowledge practices in educational and professional contexts. Within such contexts, the focus is on the "trialogical approach to learning" (Paavola & Hakkarainen, 2005), as opposed to knowledge acquisition and participation in knowledge practices. Learning is seen as a process of knowledge creation concentrating on mediated processes where common objects of activity are developed collaboratively. The approach is termed *trialogical* because the emphasis is not only on individuals (monological) or community (dialogical), but on the way people collaboratively develop mediating artefacts.

During the first phases of the project, researchers and teachers spent time negotiating principles for knowledge creation scenarios at UNIC, within the Free Space time. As we have already said, we arrived at three main principles.

Principle 1: Focus on the (knowledge) artefact

The course will be organised around the development of a shared artefact, the nature of which is decided upon by the students. This artefact should be complex and material. Complex, because the artefact should not be too easy to develop, and should provoke discussions and decision-making. Students have to be challenged by the artefact, and "material", because, in the end, there should be a material thing (or things) that could be shown to and be used by others.

With this principle, we can see a combination of old features of the course and new ideas coming from the theory. The project of the students is focused on design of an artefact, and this (as a consequence of their involvement) should result in the development of new knowledge; but the students were still free to choose the artefact they wanted to create, leaving the basic idea of the free choice course intact. We can also see in this design principle that the concept of the object is still rather vague. No specific features of suitable artefacts were formulated in this principle. This also attributes to the freedom that remains for students to use their own ideas and interests.

Principle 2: Collaboration during the project

As knowledge creation is seen as a collaborative process, students have to work together on developing their artefact. They will work in groups of three or four students. In the old course, students were allowed to work alone; but this changed with this principle. Collaboration is seen as stimulating complexity in the process of working on the object, but at the same time making it possible to take on more challenging projects than when working alone.

Unlike the first design principle, the second principle was a big step away from the initial idea underlying the course. Free choice was founded on the idea that every student could and should follow his or her own (and individual) interest and try to develop this interest further. Collaboratively deciding and working on developing a shared artefact would certainly change this. Groups of students would have to discuss, and come to a consensus about an object everybody agreed on, and in this process probably not every student could follow his or her own ideas completely.

Principle 3: Authenticity: find a stakeholder

Students have to find a stakeholder interested in (using) their artefact; i.e. they make the artefact for genuine use. This principle is a translation of the idea of cross-fertilisation of knowledge as a part of knowledge creation (Paavola & Hakkarainen, 2005). Introducing the stakeholder is thought to have many effects that would contribute to the process of knowledge creation. For instance: by introducing an external stakeholder, students come in contact with the world outside the school and with experts on the terrain of their artefact. They therefore can learn much about expert practices around creating their artefact and use these practices. Besides that, the stakeholder also has a say in the development of the artefact, which complicates development of the artefact. Furthermore, making an artefact for real use and not just for the teacher could motivate and stimulate the students more, which could in turn enhance their learning processes. This design principle was totally new in the course.

The assignment

The students were introduced to the new principles (among other things) in four workshops, moderated by a teacher and a researcher together. The final format of the task, based on the three principles, was negotiated between teachers and researchers.

The task set for the students is: to form a group and decide what their mutual interest is; they should take that as a starting point and try to define a specific (knowledge) artefact they wanted to work on together. For that artefact they have to find a stakeholder that has a need for it. The stakeholder then can support them during the process by being a knowledge expert, but also by defining wishes and constraints. It is important to note is that it is still the (collective) interest of the group of students that is the source of their project. Students have to construct a plan during the first two weeks, which they present to a teacher, who evaluates the proposal and makes a go/no-go decision. Furthermore, no predefined moments for coaching are planned; coaching moments are opportunistic. Every group is assigned one teacher for coaching who is always presented during meetings at school.

Interpretation

In what follows, we present six extracts from five sessions during the students' project and give our interpretations of what happens in these extracts. For each episode, we try first to briefly describe what it is about, in terms of collaboration, task performance, argumentation, and, socio-emotional aspects, such as display of tension, avoidance of conflict, relational aspects. Then, we try and interpret the episode relating these aspects to what happened in the previous episode, and aspects of the learning context as discussed in the previous section. Our main interest is in the relation between socio-emotional and task-related behaviour, and in the development of these within and between sessions. Note that the group was left completely free about the steps to undertake in its project. Even though we were not able to use video recording, one of the authors was present during many of the boys' collaboration sessions; our interpretations thus draw, in part, on this experience of how the students generally got along with each other.

Session 1 (week 3)

The extract from the first session we present (see Table 10.1) took place during week three of the students' project. In the previous weeks, the three students had thought about their collaborative interest and defined for themselves an object to work on, with a possible stakeholder for it. The students were all very interested in urban planning, and decided (inspired by their experiences with the game SimCity) to design a town together. Although their teacher approved their project idea in week two, the concrete form of the object was not clear yet, and a stakeholder was not yet found.

The boys were sitting in a large room with many other students present, all working on their projects, groups sitting behind different long tables, each student with his/her own computer.

In this sequence (Table 10.1), the three boys are searching for what to do, for a way of starting to achieve their task of designing a student area in a town. In the original way in which their task had been defined (see above), they should have had a "client" (stakeholder) for their work (some real person outside the school, whose criteria they had to satisfy), but they had not yet found such a suitable person. Given the attention (as a principle) that this aspect of the assignment was given, it is not surprising that the group was a bit hesitant about how to start. One would expect a group to explicitly consider "what to do". Instead, the group took the bull by the horns immediately: it started to do "something" instead of standing pat.

These three boys had already formed a group outside this session, participating in an online football competition, in which most of the boys of their class participated. This theme appears often in their group work. We interpret their references to football as a sign of, or a need for, confirmation of their interpersonal relationships, and their identities as part of this common domain of reference.

Task-related discourse is in the mode of *"brainstorming"* and accumulation of individuals' ideas. Therefore, – we would say – ideas do not genuinely clash; there is no tension. There is (at least superficially) immediate agreement with almost every proposal, given the high frequency of "yes" and the use of repetitive forms in their language (similar syntax, *I want, wow*). However, this does not imply that the group is in a state of relaxation: they are clearly working, but on what?

TABLE 10.1 First extract

N	Loc	Dialogue
2.	Joseph	We are going to create ideas for the town, come on shall we get paper?
		Someone stays behind and sits there working, two others go for paper. When returning the boys talk about games, specifically an online football game in which they are all participating, about their best player and how much players are worth, against which team they have to play in the next round etc. All behind a computer, surfing online.
3.	Eric	What is a metropolis again?
4.	Joseph	A very large town, ahm, a large city may be called a metropolis
5.	Eric	Sao Paulo, Rio de Janeiro … ah, then she can at least see what we have been doing
		The students talk about football again: which rank they have, how many cups won etc.
6.	Henry	What also may be fun is a student town
7.	Joseph	Yes, I will write that too
8.	Henry	Evening life
9.	Joseph	Yes, a town that is very attractive for students
10.	Eric	Wow, yes, with a complete campus
11.	Joseph	Actually, all teachers have left the group
12.	Henry	Irresponsible, I find that
		Again talking about games, a different one now, a puppet that can perform various actions, they talk about it and do the game
13.	Eric	I want a zoo for economy
14.	Henry	I want a posh quarter for posh people, do we have many of those in Utrecht? Tuindorp, but that is all. In Gouda we do not find that at all.
15.	Joseph	I also want a poor quarter, else we will not get any media
16.	Eric	Ah yes, poor areas
17.	Henry	Utrecht Overvecht and Kanaleneiland, In Gouda there is no rich area, but in Reeuwijk all that happens is rich
18.	Eric	A high school
19.	Henry	And a university
20.	Joseph	City to go out, many sports facilities

From a socio-relational viewpoint, one could say that establishing a team develops as a gradual process: the students confirm the group's identity by expressing common interests, similar manners of speaking and joint agreement about every proposed idea. Idea production is secondary to establishing identity as a working team. Recall, however, that although the boys may know and like each other, and the group was formed on the basis of common interest, they were still working on a school task. The details of this interest and about how to proceed still remain to be established and elaborated. The dominance of socio-relational activity here may either be caused by a lack of complete clarity about the assignment, or by a lack of complete clarity about how this group would function as a team (or by both).

Collaboration can be characterised as having some rudimentary joint purpose ("we are going to design a town"); but we cannot speak here of much cognitive consideration, since ideas are immediately accepted rather than understood or discussed. This, however, does indicate some consideration for the other: to agree and approve, in the interest of the group. Not much can be said about trust either, given that we do not see much expressed, apart from willingness to engage in the interaction. Reliance on established forms of communication (outside the task) may be taken as a sign of trust – in this new situation – that is slowly building up.

In sum, these boys are slowly feeling their way into the task. There is a lot of room for off-task conversation, but this is part of the team formation. There is no manifest interpersonal tension; team formation in terms of agreement, similar behaviour and avoidance of controversy are main characteristics of this episode. The form of idea production is adapted to this main purpose.

Session 2 (week 4)

The second session was a week later. In the meantime, the boys had established contact with a possible stakeholder – a student in urban planning. They sent him an email explaining the task, asking him to be their stakeholder and therefore to tell them what to do. We met up with the students when they discussed his reply. He was not sure that he could participate for the full assignment since he had to go abroad. He gave some suggestions and promised to meet the boys. The first two propositions in the extract (shown in Table 10.2) are quotations from this email.

At the micro-level (the utterance) the boys propose divergent problem definitions and solution elements. Already in the second utterance we see a problem being mentioned, indicating tension (at least according to our definition of it) at that level. The utterances that follow indicate disagreement about whether the problem is there or not. There is ample use of expressions such as *but*, *no but*, *no but really*, *no as he says*, etc. The interpretation of the stakeholder's message takes place by using quotations or concepts, either as evidence in favour (10), or as evidence against (13) some idea. We interpret these as overt manifestations of tension, by the use of argumentation, but without much deepening of the problem. At the end of the fragment, a very powerful form of relaxation is applied (Andriessen, Baker & van der Puil, 2011), by "dissolving" the problem itself, which can be glossed as: "with reference to outside authority, we do not have to solve the problem ourselves".

We can also interpret this discussion as a struggle with the concept of "stakeholder". There is a difference in opinion about the role of the stakeholder. We clearly see one student maintaining his objection: the stakeholder did not give a clear assignment. He holds the opinion that the stakeholder is the one who has this duty. The other two boys are struggling with the idea whether they should or can try to solve this problem themselves, and whether they can in fact make their own decisions about the assignment. This is also revealed by the repeated "but …", "no, but …". The outside appeal at the end can be taken as recognition of the lack of clarity about the stakeholder, accepting the first interpretation of the concept.

TABLE 10.2 Second extract

N	Loc	Dialogue
1.	Henry	OV chip card, public transport, that's a very sexy idea
2.	Eric	But a real assignment has not been given to us yet
3.	Henry	No but
4.	Joseph	Yes, a new area for about 3000 people
5.	Eric	No, but we do not really have an assignment I think
6.	Joseph	Indeed it could be clearer
7.	Eric	But we just do house, road, road, here an enterprise, small school
8.	Henry	No, but really is more than that, because you need public transport
9.	Joseph	Lots
10.	Henry	Yes lots, houses for renting or purchasing, and dealing with locations of existing shopping areas
11.	Eric	But it is an area made up by us
12.	Henry	A made up area
13.	Joseph	No, as he says existing shopping areas
14.	Henry	Yes, but you could imagine an existing area
15.	Eric	Then you have to imagine several areas
16.	Henry	Yes, but for example in a certain town in the neighborhood or something
17.	Joseph	Shall we reply that we are missing a more specific assignment, for example a student quarter or something
18.	Henry	OK

Concerning the relational level, we witness clear threats to the boys' relationship: this is not about establishing a team anymore; this discussion is about the assignment. We can still see some signs of explicit recognition of what the other says, but we also see two points of view circulating between the boys, meaning that disagreement is now an option. Should we expect this so soon from a student group? The relaxation by appeal to the outsider happens before a real solution is found, or a real clash can be observed. This may have been inspired by the need to preserve the relationship.

One week after the previous session, the goal is completely different: it is not mainly about team building; it is about the assignment and getting on with it. Lack of clarity about the assignment causes tension. Not only task aspects but also social aspects dictate the moment and the form when relaxation is needed. We will see this in the next episode.

What can we say at this moment about the collaboration? One way of putting this is by claiming that an externally imposed joint purpose is missing, as there is no assignment, and as a result there is a lack of clarity about what to do. There is improved cognitive consideration, however, as the boys try to come to a shared conclusion, and shared interpretation (consensus building). In a way, this is limited, as the boys also try to go on (collaborate) in the same manner as in the previous fragment by putting forward suggestions. These suggestions are now better taken up and even somewhat discussed. This leads to the consideration that the possible difference of opinion (which is recognised) needs to be resolved by looking outside the group. On the other hand, there is still the same joint purpose as before (design a town), but it is less clear how to achieve it, or better, how the group is required to achieve it by appealing to the outside authority. In a group with more agency (which may be too much to expect here) the boys could have discussed their own preference for what the joint assignment would be like.

Session 3a (week 7)

A few weeks have passed now. The participation of the stakeholder could not be established, so the students defined a more specific assignment with their teacher. Their idea of designing a complete town has been collaboratively specified into designing "a student area in which there is not too much asphalt and a lot of public transport".

The students are now working on drawing several maps (knowledge artefacts) in which they design their student area. In the following extract the students are collaboratively working on one map. The map is lying in the middle of the table and they all sit around it. One of the students is drawing, while the other two are commenting. Issues that are discussed literally arise from the map; the students are deciding what to do next on the basis of what is already drawn. In this extract (Table 10.3), we see the role of the knowledge artefact exemplified.

TABLE 10.3 Third extract

N	Loc	Dialogue
1.	Joseph	Here is the bus stop, how large is a bus stop…a parking space,
2.	Henry	well smaller, I think half of that
3.	Eric	shall I draw Henry?
4.	Henry	No, no somewhat bigger. Good, a nice bus stop, or is that somewhat too small?
5.	Eric	This is the bench,
6.	Joseph	oh, isn't that a bit too small?
7.	Henry	this is the whole parking space, you should not forget the parking this is a full shop parking, so isn't it a bit small I think or not Joseph?
9.	Joseph	How small do you think a bus stop is, more or less, uh, yes, I thought so too
10.	Eric	not at all, you say smaller all the time, smaller, smaller
11.	Joseph	no, that's funny
12.	Eric	not at all, no you idiot
		(discuss soccerplayers)
13.	Henry	I was thinking, we forgot the main road, but we should make asphalt where cars can drive on
14.	Joseph	yes, but maybe one way traffic
15.	Eric	yes, for example so and so

(Continued)

TABLE 10.3 Cont'd

N	Loc	Dialogue
16.	Henry	no, no one way traffic, but there will be few cars anyway
17.	Joseph	You can pass the town here and then you can go there for example
18.	Henry	No but you do not have to make the complete area, if you go, how would you get there then?
19.	Eric	Walk?
20.	Joseph	Yes, only students live there
		(chat about getting angry)
21.	Henry	but that is so, no, but there are parents, visiting their children or friends that do have a car, or ambulances, they have to get here easily
22.	Eric	Yes
23.	Henry	If there is a fire here they cannot take a couple of days for putting it out with a fire engine, maybe you should simply draw a square here
24.	Joseph	then they should come with the fire motorcycle
25.	Henry	He's not very clever that guy, isn't he Eric, then they should come with the fire motorcycle
26.	Joseph	and if you have a large bicycle track here, couldn't an ambulance pass over it?
27.	Henry	Yes, but if you have a large motorway, then cars and bicycles,
28.	Joseph	but we wanted as few cars as possible

The students are now focused on elaborating the knowledge artefact, the architectural plan of the student area. There are detailed discussions of what to draw and how to draw it, with successive detailed refinements. A lot of communication occurs though *deixis* (*there, so and so, here*, with appropriate gestures of fingers), establishing focus and detail.

One of the boys presents at some point (13) a quite complex issue; or, more precisely, by elaborating the issue in the group, it becomes more complex, and the boys turn out to disagree. Then, one of the boys (21, 23) presents an argument with several components, established in two utterances, to make his point. Apparently, this raises tension, since we see concomitant relaxation in the form of a joke, and collective laughter as a follow-up. This is followed by a proposition reconciling the two main issues: not too much asphalt, enough space for ambulances (26).

At the relationship level, we therefore see the group capable of expressing and addressing disagreement. The recognition of the ideas proposed by every member of the group is remarkable. This is not the same as "uptake" (Suthers Dwyer & Vatrapu, 2007), because the team and its progress are characterised not only by task progress as a result of individual contributions, but also by reconciling the person and his contribution within the same utterance. This thereby contributes both to task progress as well as to team building, as two sides of the same coin.

The type of relaxation employed in this episode is not used in order to get rid of the issue, as in the previous episode, but rather as a means of affording collective resolution of the issue after the tension is diminished. Compared with the previous episode, the boys now feel strong enough to proceed with the assignment in their own way. During the past weeks their confidence has grown. The way the group argues (not only the fact that they argue), and the way in which tension is handled shows increased maturity. It may be a special situation in which such maturity is achieved within seven weeks. We return to this point later.

Hence, collaboration has improved. Joint focus indicates joint purpose, at least at a local level. Cognitive consideration is excellent; we see arguing to learn (Andriessen, Baker & Suthers, 2003), which requires a certain level of ethical consideration as well (recognise and try to understand the person and the idea). Trust must have increased as a consequence.

What about the assignment? Are these boys really designing a student area of a town, and is the design worthwhile to be considered seriously? Let us look at what the teacher says in the next episode, which immediately followed the current one.

Session 3b (week 7)

In the following extract (Table 10.4), the discussion of the previous extract is continued (no time-lag), but now in the presence of the teacher. The teacher – whilst

TABLE 10.4 Fourth extract

N	Loc	Dialogue
29.	Teacher	I just wanted to say, I thought the assignment was that it should just be a little bit a car free area
30.	Henry	yes, but it should be reachable, and not isolated, cars, police cars and ambulances must be able to get there
31.	Joseph	we just make a barracks with motorcycles, just motorcycles
32.	Teacher	In Maarssen there is a road, and in principle you could use it with a car, but in fact it is a bicycle track
33.	Henry	We can do that as well, but cars can come there, allowed for parents
34.	Joseph	But cycles always go first
35.	Henry	Yes and you can also come with an ambulance and also a fire car
36.	Eric	1 road is not enough, there should be many more roads
37.	Teacher	But this is one design, who says this is eventually gonna be it, you could make several designs
38.	Henry	yes, could be
39.	Joseph	but this remains, the middle and those three roads
40.	Teacher	yes, because you are in the middle, you are quite limited in what else you can do
41.	Joseph	It is not so bad, we have quite some space left here
42.	Henry	Yes, there as well, if we have houses there or shops, we also need such bicycle tracks
43.	Joseph	I do not see the problem
44.	Teacher	that you may be a bit constrained when you put a park in the middle
45.	Joseph	Each of us could also make our own design and then we could
46.	Henry	That is much harder, because then you have to discuss it afterwards

checking up on all of the groups she was coaching – listened in on their discussion and decided to intervene. Coaching sessions with the teacher did not happen very often, and when they did, they were most of the time focused on an organisational aspect (such as preparing a presentation or how to divide the work). In this discussion, however, the teacher tries to have an epistemic debate with the students.

The teacher starts off with a challenge. The manner in which the students handle this challenge repeats the main ideas from their previous discussion (example 3a). In (31), Joseph even refers to the relaxation joke, without explaining it, however. By doing this, it seems that the students are more focused on confirming the way they handled their previous argument than on elaborating the challenge by the teacher. In other words, at the micro-level we see signs of arguing (as reaction to what the teacher proposes), but on a relational level, the students confirm what they have just achieved.

This also implies that the teacher is not taken in as a member of the group: to the contrary. In the second part of the episode, the teacher tries to challenge the way the students work, and the main goal of the boys seems to be to keep her away (41, 43). They avoid an epistemic discussion with the teacher, operating as a closed front, by making relaxation comments, and by denial of relevance of what the teacher says.

The final comment reveals some awareness of the students' way of doing collaborative work. This not only reveals that the group is conscious about its activities, but also that the students have confidence in themselves as a group that is capable of standing up against external pressure.

The teacher proposes challenges that could potentially be tension raisers. These challenges do not reveal deep insight into what the group has been doing so far, but aim at opening up to the possibility of completely redoing the work. The group presents a closed front aiming at averting this danger, without having to discuss the issues. In sum, the students do not really explain and defend their motives and ideas to the teacher. Hence, nothing about the quality of the work is revealed by this discussion. What is visible is group solidarity, even though the group just went through the trial of a tough debate.

The collaboration now has as a goal the confirmation of joint achievements against the teacher. There is complete agreement and solidarity on this, in other words high ethical consideration, although probably not all ideas are shared.

Sequence 4 (week 9)

In week nine the students present their work to the client, a masters student in Urban Planning. He is considered to be the stakeholder by the students, but is actually more like an expert, since he commented on their work once (by email), and has a meeting with the students in week nine, after which he leaves for a long stay abroad. Because of his absence, he has indicated he cannot be a real stakeholder, but is still willing to meet the students for this session.

As we will see from the next extract (Table 10.5), the "client" is mainly interested in the main structure and purpose of the area, and less so in all the details the students have worked out.

TABLE 10.5 Fifth extract

N	Loc	Dialogue
29	Eric	Well, here we had…because we had to construct so many roads otherwise; we had three main roads, here, here and here. And here are some more small roads. And here are the fields for sports. And here is the police and the fire brigade and here a row of houses.
30	Client	So this area is especially for students?
31	Eric	Yes
32	Client	So it is basically a sort of miniature town?
33	Henry	Yes
34	Client	And did you also, I suppose you know Google Earth, don't you?
35	All	Yes
36	Client	Did you for instance take the real map from Google Earth and put on it all the lines and polygons of your area, you can place your own map over the real map. […]
42	Client	And did you do this?
43	Henry	No, we did not
44	Client	Well, that is a nice idea, because then you can see with all these Lines how your map fits the real map. You did look at the map from Utrecht?
45	Henry	Yes
46	Client	Well, then you can see where all these functionalities, such as police, actually are located and if they are not really close to where you have put them on your map. Or you think, oh, we cannot put this road here, because then we are disrupting the environment. Because you have to check these things. […]
82	Client	So it is OK that you are already thinking of all these little functionalities, but first you have to decide on the structure of your area, that is the most important thing. And I think you can use Google Earth for that and look where everything is already. For instance: there already is a large library at the University Campus. You probably don't know that, but it is there. So you don't have to design such functionality in your area.

We clearly see two different roles acting in this fragment: the expert making his point, repeatedly, and the students taking it in, obediently. The students start out by explaining their map, thereby going into a lot of detail (29). The "client's" reaction is probably based on the expert way of thinking and working, in which there is a certain order to things, in other words, a plan that starts with purpose and structure first, and also with a detailed study of the existing context. One could say that expert and students differ in perceptual ontology (Roth, 2001), that is, in terms of different perceptions of the "same" activities. However, his style is interactive, since he poses challenging questions to the students, who cannot do much more than comply.

Relationally, we can see the students behaving quite differently from the way they did in the previous fragment: they do not object at all, implying that they do not feel threatened. In other words, the authoritarian comments by the client do not seem to raise any tension (cf. those of the teacher). This does not mean that they will do what the client says. With hindsight, we now know that they did not do anything with Google Earth. After this session, there were no changes made in the knowledge object at all. There were other suggestions that were taken up, although these turned out to be too hard for the group to accomplish, e.g. a financial plan for the area.

As for collaboration, we see that there is a difference between the group and the rest of the world. There is a manifest group level, by not showing internal disagreement, which looks like standing up for your own work. This is a standstill for the group. There seems to be no eagerness to learn from the expert.

It is necessary to explain a little more why the expert's interventions were not tension-raising. His role was undoubtedly perceived as that of the expert: to contribute to the quality of the knowledge object. Everything he said could be interpreted as such. Furthermore, the way he proposes his ideas confirms the role difference, and therefore the status of his ideas as not challengeable. With some people such behaviour would raise tension, but not with these students. This could be because they feel they do not have enough knowledge to challenge the expert, or simply because he is in fact external to their group and social world.

The contrast with their reactions to the teacher is obvious. The teacher is not conceived as an authority at all; she is not taken as seriously as the expert. This is not because the students' argumentation (or lack of it) reflects acceptance of what the expert says and contradiction with the teacher, since they could have reacted in the opposite way. Comments by the expert could have been challenged, as lack of expertise could have been ignored. It can be seen that the teacher is taken less seriously because her contributions are reduced by relaxation in a different way: they are not taken up. Instead, with the expert, relaxation is in the form of immediate acceptance of his contributions. Why is the expertise of the expert uncontested? First, because he is announced as such; but this is not the main reason. Second, there is a difference in reasoning style: the teacher takes up the focus of the students, by discussing the details of their work; the expert makes his own point, at a different level of detail, and in a different style. Third, he seems immediately to grasp what the students are doing (wrong), and without explicitly expressing that, he starts making repair suggestions at the appropriate level, without ignoring what is already there. Of course, we should not blame the teacher for not being a knowledge expert. Fourth,[2] there are differences in transience and power: the stakeholder will never be seen again; it's easy to accept what he says and then ignore it. The teacher is going to be around, and evaluating their work for the rest of the course. The expert has no power in relation to them; he is just an outsider. The teacher has considerable power, however benign the design of this school may be.

Finally, we have some more indications about the quality of the work. The students forgot about looking at the existing situation, both in terms of needs and in terms of the existing area. And also, they have no idea about the costs of their plans.

Of course, many more objections could be maintained against the (unfinished) plan. However, what can be said in addition is that they developed their ideas about what should be in the area. This means that they have developed not only ideas, but also a clear frame of reference. The group has created a collective idea of the student area (knowledge creation). This idea does not follow from consulting (external) expertise, or possessing deep knowledge of the topic: it is by discussing the topic, and collaboratively creating the knowledge artefacts, that the ideas in the group have been elaborated. This process has not been one of looking for relevant information, but rather one of interaction and creation.

After this discussion with the client, seven weeks passed without much progress. Incidentally, students worked on small improvements of their maps, or started on other activities, such as the financial plan (as suggested by the client), and finalising a questionnaire. This object came up during a coaching session with the teacher, who suggested inquiring with real university students what kind of living arrangements they would prefer. The students never really adopted this suggestion, partly because they had no idea how to proceed in making, distributing and interpreting the questionnaire. But still they tried to make one and asked for feedback from one of the researchers. He encouraged them to improve the questionnaire by adding an introduction, and that task was still there in week 12.

Final extract (week 12)

In the final extract (see Table 10.6) the discussion centres around finalising the questionnaire for university students.

In the first utterance, we already see how the group deals with external information: it is dismissed. The researcher's suggestion to make an introduction is countered

TABLE 10.6 Sixth extract

N	Loc	Dialogue
1	Eric	Maybe we can put that in the questionnaire we send to…We still have to make an introduction for it, I think we already did that, but well.
2	Joseph	If you adapt the questionnaire. Then Henry should adapt it.
3	Henry	Can't you do it yourself?
4	Eric	Henry already did a lot, more than the two of us together
5	Joseph	Here's the questionnaire Eric (long silence, typing)
6	Joseph	I just thought to set up a company. You have, or the municipality rents houses, or an individual person rents his house, but very often you have large corporations that own a complete area. For example house 500 to house 750, who lets these houses. I could make such a company, such houses are easy to adapt and construct because you ask permission to a company to do the construction work

by the comment "*I think we already did that, but well…*". As a consequence, nothing happens here. The second issue is to improve the questionnaire itself, as the researcher also commented on the content of it. Joseph asks Eric to revise it and Henry to do the introduction. Henry objects, with support from Eric. Joseph simply hands the thing over to Eric, who starts working on it. What strikes us in this fragment is the complete absence of constructive interaction. The long contribution by Joseph shows lack of commitment to the questionnaire issue. Also, this contribution is not comprehensible at all, and shows lack of understanding of the real issues, or looking at things with inside ideas. There seems to be commitment, but to what?

Relationally speaking, there is disagreement about task allocation, but this is handled peacefully, perhaps because none of the students thinks this a very important task. Hence, we do have a team, they are aware of tasks to do, and the need for someone doing it. They are aware of who did what and how much, it seems. That is ethical consideration. There is a lack of epistemic agency, of content, of progress. The group does not want to move on, as if they fear it will be in vain. There is no uptake, only random talk.

The group has come to a full stop, and in the final presentation in week 16 they present almost the same products as they presented in week 9. They do not show the questionnaire, which remained unfinished, and do not elaborate on the financial plan. Their presentation was still convincing enough for them to be given a positive evaluation. During the presentation, the group admitted they got stuck, but not before. Table 10.7 summarises our interpretations of the whole set of sequences.

Concluding discussion

As stated in our introduction, our aim here has been to understand the role of tensions in task progress during collaborative work, and to understand the *development* of a group's work, in terms of the relations between task achievement and a collaborative working relationship, the latter being understood primarily in terms of regulation of emotions and artefact development. Any activity has a social and an epistemic aspect, and which one is more dominant than the other depends on many things, individuals and context. Also, it may be possible to refine these dimensions for particular purposes. Finally, in particular, the analysis of emotions would be enriched by video and other sensory data.

Task achievement by the group studied here can be characterised by production and elaboration of ideas linked to some but not all issues in urban design. The group does not go and look for information; instead, the students work and elaborate a limited number of their own ideas, as far as they possibly can. Because they are not experts, they experience clear limitations and do not employ or learn to employ expert practices. Although they realise their imperfections and admit in the end they got stuck, their approach over the weeks basically has not changed. Of course, knowledge construction activity differs between sessions, and may even have disappeared at the end. However, this seems to depend on the ideas they have on the topic at hand, not on their general approach to the task.

TABLE 10.7 Summary of interpretations of the dialogue sequences

Sequence	Task	Collaboration	Tension-relaxation
1	Brainstorm: what do we think are the elements of a (student) town?	Joint Purpose (**JP**): elementary Cognitive consideration (**Cc**): No elaboration of ideas Ethical consideration (**Ec**): Free to produce ideas, approval Trust (**T**):? (start of the project)	No tension, all free to contribute A lot of off-task conversation (relax)
2	Goal setting, finding joint purpose	**JP:** A clear assignment is missing **Cc:** problem with interpretation of expert message, argumentation **Ec:** We have to resolve a difference of opinion; we have to stop producing different opinions **T:** consensus building	Task related tension: to be resolved by appeal to outside authority; Relational relaxation: joint purpose overrules ethical/cognitive considerations
3a	Discussion around the knowledge artifact	**JP:** Joint focus (deixis) through artifact **Cc:** Good uptake, arguing to learn **Ec:** acknowledgement of different ideas **T:** we can take a conflict, we agree	Argumentation(disagree/counter) creates task related tension, which is well regulated
3b	Teacher intervention	**JP:** confirm achievements **Cc:** disagree with teacher, defending the group **Ec:** group solidarity **T:** the teacher does not know	Group feels strong commitment to relax all tension created by the teacher, thereby avoiding deepening of debate
4	Client	**JP**: survive, he's just passing **Cc**: this is our town as we designed it **Ec**: group solidarity **T**: we agree	Group does not convey anything to the expert, simply agrees to everything he says. High tension is avoided by uniform agreement about the transience and minor importance of the client.
5	Being stuck	**JP**:? **Cc:** peaceful task allocation **Ec:** we know who did what **T:** we are a team	Peaceful handling of tension created through task allocation

We proposed to discuss the development of the collaborative group in terms of the work of Allwood et al. (2000), using the descriptors *joint purpose, cognitive consideration, ethical consideration*, and *trust*, as characterisations of professional collaboration. Already, when discussing joint purpose, we have witnessed complications. Although it would be possible to claim that the main objective for these boys has not changed over time (design a student town), its meaning is not the same in every episode, and there are other objectives, perhaps signifying other trajectories, that are of greater or lesser importance during the task period: *having a joint focus, proposing new ideas, agreeing about what to do, defence against the enemy*, etc. We can neither estimate nor compare the degree to which these objectives play a part throughout the whole task; but some episodes clearly address them more than others. Nor do we feel sufficiently certain to be able to state that the short-term objectives all are instrumental in working towards the main goal. One might even say that the objective *building a student town* was instrumental to the goal *showing we can do it*. As a learning task, we might say this one was successful to the extent that the collaborative work (joint purpose) on the knowledge artefact indeed has interacted with some trajectories that were of some importance to the boys, as individuals and as a group. For example, the boys might have learned that as a group they could stand up against a stronger opponent. Or indeed, they might have learned something about town planning, but that could not have been very much as there was only little external information coming into play. The main idea that any teacher could have conveyed after the task should have been: when confronted with difficult problems, look for external help and information as much as possible.

The working relationship grows to be emotionally stable and very tight. The boys back each other up, and seem to think like one mind, especially when outsiders are approaching. The relationship has grown from being uncertain about each other's ideas and goals, to being very informed about each other's activities, interests and special skills, as well as to possessing shared task ownership and shared responsibility for the object. In other words, as a group, these students display aspects of ethical consideration (Allwood et al., 2000; Andriessen & Schwarz, 2010). However, while they do take care of each other and consider each other's ideas, which of course is a positive thing, they also forget to activate the group in their progress working on the assignment.

In the working relationship of this group, ethical consideration was a constant characteristic, but their task progression fluctuated. This working relationship (which develops towards more sharing of minds) functions optimally in the case of pure within-group activity. Under this condition the students optimally share each other's knowledge. In moments when students have less ideas about how to proceed, and/or there is external pressure present, the working relationship just described is less effective.

This does not mean that the students did not work. They were able to cope with uncertainty about the assignment, internal argumentation (to learn), and comments by the teacher and by a very knowledgeable "client". Also, their task-related discussions, certainly at the beginning, are very rich; the plans that they make for what to include in their town area and why are not superficial. In spite of this hardship, they keep up the level of ethical consideration, that is, they deal with each other's feelings and preferences. Hence, we see a lack of shared epistemic agency (Damsa et al., 2010), resulting in lack of action as a group to solve issues.

As a consequence, the necessary jump to expert knowledge and practice is too high for them to make on their own. The problem is not only in the nature of the knowledge as such (e.g. financial planning, questionnaires) but also in making the jump. Expert knowledge was not acquired, but some sense of it must have resulted from the interaction with the expert. Within the same line of reasoning, one could say that they do not want their relationship to suffer from interventions from outside. In addition, they want the outside world to see a competent team rather than a struggling one.

The students have created "inside group-knowledge", that is in some ways highly resistant to "outside expertise". As long as the group, tied by emotional bonds, does not change in order to assimilate new ideas or plans coming from the outside, nothing will happen on the inside. In other words, maintaining a strong social bonding precludes – in this case – task progress based on external information.

What can we say about the tensions in this group? When discussing their issues, such as a lack of clarity about the assignment, and when disagreeing about smaller and larger roads, for example, we see the tensions that are associated with such interactions. Tensions, however seem relatively mild, and the group does not suffer from them. Relaxing actions are quite strong: agreement, ignoring issues, flattening outside threats, humour, labelling issues as not important, no attacks in the group, passivity towards the end. The group does not display strong emotional tension, either within the group or towards the outside. On the other hand, there is much more relaxation than the overt display of tension might justify. In other words, there may have been tensions, especially related to the assignment, that we were not able to capture.

These findings must be situated in the students' current practice. At some moments we have seen clear frustration about not being able to further deepen the knowledge involved in designing the student area. But this was not a main source of tension, as there was not much at stake for the current task: the evaluation to be expected by their teacher would not be very consequential for them. The teacher was not expert in the area, and was not seen as knowledgeable by the students. Furthermore, the fact that new principles were tried out in the course resulted in a lack of attention for evaluation and assessment of the knowledge object. For example, the role of the client was unclear from the start, and remained problematic during the exercise. Also, teachers were not very clear on how to coach this "new" type of activity. Although teachers and researchers regularly discussed main issues, the setting for teachers, as well as for the students, was one of trying out a different approach. This explains in part why the students did not go deeper into the task than necessary at such moments of frustration.

Educational systems expect *change* that is *positive*; and developmental theory has been influenced by this expectation (Valsiner, 2008), in similarly focusing on development as *change*. But development must also involve something that remains *constant* (this is the "self"); and remaining the same is not necessarily a passive failure, it can be an eminently active process (Hviid, 2008). The "development" of the group analysed here can therefore be characterised as actively remaining the same, or even reinforcing what remains, in terms of their interpersonal relation, in a changing task environment.

In our introduction we claimed that achievement goals during collaborative learning are primarily *socio-relational* rather than epistemic in nature. One could say that our interpretations confirm this statement: the knowledge activities of the student group that we studied were subordinate to the members' consideration of the group work as self-owned, to the importance of everyone's agreement and well-being, and to the outward appearance as being competent, in other words, to social relational goals indeed. Of course, this is a single case study; but we found similar explanations (in which the social dimension dominated) in Andriessen, Baker & van der Puil (2010) and Chiu, Baker, and Andriessen (*in preparation*).

A description of the group's activity in terms of knowledge construction actions only is, of course, possible. But we think that *explaining* the sense-making process and outcomes by referring to epistemic goals only would be too limited.

Acknowledgements

This study was carried out within the EU-financed KP-Lab project. We would like to thank Dave Drossaert, the head of UNIC, the second year teachers from UNIC, Arja Veerman, Crina Damşa and Patrick Sins, our fellow researchers, who all contributed to the processes described in this study. We would like to thank Jay Lemke and Klas Karlgren for their thoughtful comments and suggestions.

Notes

1 KP-Lab stands for Developing Knowledge Practices – laboratory, and was in part funded by the European Union, under FP6, number IST80587, and coordinated by the University of Helsinki, Finland, from 2006 to 2011.
2 This was a suggestion by Jay Lemke.

References

Allwood, J., Traum, D., & Jokinen, K. (2000). Cooperation, dialogue and ethics. *International journal on Human-Computer Studies*, 53, 871–914.

Alonso-Tapia, J. & Pardo, A. (2006). Assessment of learning environment motivational quality from the point of view of secondary and high school learners. *Learning and Instruction*, 16, 295–309.

Andriessen, J., Baker, M., & Suthers, D. (Eds.) (2003). *Arguing to Learn: Confronting Cognitions in Computer-Supported Collaborative Learning environments*. Dordrecht, The Netherlands: Kluwer Academic Publishers.

Andriessen, J., Baker, M., & van der Puil, C. (2011). Socio-cognitive tension in collaborative working relations. In S. Ludvigsen, A. Lund, I. Rasmussen & R. Saljo (Eds.), *Learning across Sites: New Tools, Infrastructures and Practices*, pp. 222–42. London: Routledge.

Andriessen, J. E. B. & Schwarz, B. B. (2009). Argumentative design. In N. Muller-Mirza & A.-N. Perret-Clermont (eds.) Argumentation and Education: Theoretical foundations and practices (pp. 145–176). Dordrecht: Springer.

Assor, A., Kaplan, H., & Roth, G. (2002). Choice is good but relevance is excellent: Autonomy affecting teacher' behaviors that predict students' engagement in learning. *British Journal of Educational Psychology*, 72, 261–78.

Baker, M., Andriessen, J., Lund, K. van Amelsvoort, M., & Quignard, M. (2007). Rainbow: A framework for analysing computer-mediated pedagogical debates. *International Journal of Computer Supported Collaborative Learning*, 2, 315–57.

Baker, M. (2010). Approaches to understanding students' dialogues: articulating multiple modes of interpretation. Keynote speaker lecture, EARLI SIG 17 "Qualitative and Quantitative Approaches to Learning and Instruction"; meeting on "Methodology in Research on Learning", September, Friedrich-Schiller-University of Jena.

Chiu, M. M., Baker, M. J., & Andriessen, J. (*in preparation*). Mutual regulation of tensions in collaborative learning interactions: A methodological exploration.

Damsa, C. I., Kirschner, P. A., Andriessen, J. E. B., Erkens, G., & Sins, P. H. M. (2010). Shared epistemic agency – An empirical study of an emergent construct. *Journal of the Learning Sciences*, 19 (2), 143–86.

De Corte, E., Verschaffel, L., Entwistle, N., & van Merriënboer, J. (2003). *Powerful Learning Environments*. Amsterdam: Pergamon.

Doise, W. & Mugny, G. (1981). *Le développement social de l'intelligence*. [The social development of intelligence]. Paris: InterÉditions.

Edwards, A. (2007). Relational agency in professional practice: A CHAT analysis. *Actio: An International Journal of Human Activity Theory*, 1, 1–17.

Geertz, C. (1973). *The Interpretation of Cultures: Selected Essays*. New York: Basic Books.

Hegel, G. W. F. (1807). *Phänomenologie des Geistes*. [The Phenomenology of Spirit]. Bamberg: Joseph Goebhardt.

Hviid, P. (2008). "Next year we are small, right?" Different times in children's development. *European Journal of Psychology of Education*, 23 (2), 183–98.

Lemke, J. (2000). Across the scales of time: Artifacts, activities, and meanings in ecosocial systems. *Mind, Culture, and Activity*, 7 (4), 273–90.

Leont'ev, A. N. (1981). The problem of activity in psychology. In J. V. Werstch (Ed.), *The Concept of Activity in Soviet Psychology*, pp. 37–71. Armonk, NY: Sharp.

Ludvigsen, S., Rasmussen, I., Ingeborg, K., Moen, A., & Middleton, D. (2011). Intersecting trajectories of participation: Temporality and Learning. In S. Ludvigsen, A. Lund, I. Rasmussen and R. Säljö (Eds.) *Learning across Sites: New Tools, Infrastructures and Practices*, pp. 105–21. London: Routledge.

Muntigl, P. & Turnbull, W. (1998). Conversational structure and facework in arguing. *Journal of Pragmatics*, 29, 225–56.

Paavola, S. & Hakkarainen, K. (2005). The knowledge creation metaphor – An emergent epistemological approach to learning. *Science & Education*, 14, 535–57.

Roth, W.-M. (2001). Situating cognition. *The Journal of the Learning Sciences*, 10 (1–2), 21–61.

Ryle, G. (1968). The thinking of thoughts. What is Le Penseur doing? Reprinted from "University Lectures", no.18, 1968, by permission of the University of Saskatchewan. <http://lucy.ukc.ac.uk/CSACSIA/Vol11/Papers/ryle_1.html>.

Suthers, D. D., Dwyer, N., & Vatrapu, R. (2007). A methodology and formalism for eclectic analysis of collaborative interaction. Paper presented at the International Conference on CSCL, July, New Brunswick, NJ.

Valsiner, J. (2008). Open intransitivity cycles in development and education: Pathways to synthesis. *European Journal of Psychology of Education*, 23 (2), 131–47.

Van der Puil, C., Andriessen, J., & Kanselaar, G. (2004). Exploring relational regulation in computer mediated (collaborative) learning interaction: A developmental perspective. *Cyberpsychology & Behavior*, 7 (2), 183–95.

Wittgenstein, L. (1978). *Philosophical Investigations*. Oxford: Basil Blackwell.

SECTION 5

Argumentation and emotion

11

A SOCIOCULTURAL PERSPECTIVE ON CONFLICT IN ARGUMENTATIVE DESIGN

Nathalie Muller Mirza

Introduction

"We broke you down! You cannot say anything any more!"

This student's account, extracted from a pedagogical activity that aimed at learning by arguing, expresses in a particularly clear way one of the meanings of "arguing"! Such a statement leads researchers in education, convinced by the positive effect of argumentation, to ask questions: are students able to use dialectical argumentation in school, this highly sophisticated way of reasoning that is at the core of democracy and scientific thinking (Rigotti & Greco Morasso, 2009a)? Do students actually argue? To some extent, these questions rely on a very old debate concerning argumentation and its possible relation with reason. Argumentation studies are traditionally divided between dialectical and rhetorical approaches, which are regarded as two incompatible paradigms, each having a different conception of "reasonable" argumentation. Some argumentation theorists observe that "reasonable argumentation", defined as a functional mode of communication developing in a context of disagreement, with parties taking certain commitments and making reference to critical standards of reasonableness (van Eemeren & Houtlosser, 2005), is quite rare. Others consider that argumentation is an everyday practice that, due to its dialogical nature, is a way of thinking about the social world and its "ideological dilemmas" (Billig, 1987). More recently, trying to overcome the "infertile division between dialectic and rhetoric" (van Eemeren & Houtlosser, 2002, p. 137), argumentation scholars focus on the investigation of real argumentation and deal with the analysis of argumentative discourse in contextualized communicative interactions (Muller Mirza, Tartas, Perret-Clermont & Iannaccone, 2009; Rigotti & Greco Morasso, 2009b).

If argumentation is considered as a potential educational means for learning in the eyes of some teachers and researchers, the argumentative situations they set up might take other meanings from the points of view of the students. Adopting a psychosocial and sociocultural perspective on argumentation in this chapter, we shall be interested in participants' concrete argumentative practices and meaning-making processes, in particular in situations in which participants are supposed to engage in argumentation in learning settings. Pedagogical activities that aim at discovering and understanding objects of knowledge through argumentation sometimes lead to results that were not anticipated by the teachers. In order to better understand this kind of "hiatus", I argue that a sociocultural perspective on argumentation is interesting, since it focuses on the participants' interpretative and framing processes. In this chapter, I particularly focus on the way interlocutors in an argumentative discussion interpret the "conflictual" aspect of argumentation. Argumentation is a communicative practice that starts from a kind of rupture, a tension, between two perspectives. How do people – and in particular children – participate and manage situations in which disagreements and conflicts of perspectives occur in everyday activities? What role do disagreements take in cognitive development and learning? I examine the way conflictual dimension of argumentation can be diversely understood, and how they might play a role in fostering or hindering epistemic argumentation in educational contexts. In the last part of the chapter, I shall suggest some hypotheses about elements for what we can call a "thinking space", a space in which disagreement might be integrated into a meaningful activity related to an object of knowledge and in which the identity and affective processes that are embedded in the argumentative practices are taken into account.

Argumentation in a sociocultural perspective: a collective and situated discursive practice

Following a sociocultural framework, individual thinking is developed through social interactions and is mediated by various symbolic and material artefacts (Bruner, 1990; Resnick, Säljö, Pontecorvo, & Burge, 1997; Valsiner, 2007). In this view, it is assumed that thinking cannot be understood independently of the social and cultural context in which it takes place. Moreover, the "context" is not seen only as something that "surrounds" individual actions and thinking, but merely as something that "weaves together" (Cole, 1996), therefore that simultaneously contributes to constituting individual actions and thinking, and is constituted by the participants who interpret it (Grossen, 2010).

The situated dimension of argumentation

Argumentation is "embodied" in actual communicative practices, oriented towards certain goals and towards the other participants and cannot therefore be reduced to a system of formal procedures. Argumentation is framed by the activity in which individuals are involved, their role expectations, and their situation definition. Conceiving argumentation in this perspective means a methodological shift of focus: the unit of analysis is no longer the structure of the discourse, nor the individuals (their competences and skills, their cognitive level of development, etc.), but the "activity" of argumentation involving meaning-making processes.

A cultural practice

Agreement and disagreement are part of our daily life and our cultural practices. Members of a group are not homogeneous. Whilst they are part of a coordinated organization and often are playing complementary roles that fit together, they do not have precisely the same points of view, practices, backgrounds, or goals (Rogoff, 2003). From birth, children participate in a collective culture to which they contribute, through interactions with others and objects, and experience diverse values and meanings and internalize them. In this trajectory, they become members of groups and construct a "personal culture" (Lawrence & Valsiner, 2003).

In the field of communication studies and developmental psychology, scholars study discourses and conversation in everyday contexts as "matrices" of child development. The way agreements and disagreements are managed and resolved in family contexts, for example, stresses the contextual and identity dimensions of argumentation. In this direction, Pontecorvo and her colleagues observe how the participants jointly construct discursive sequences of argumentation, and how the context of production, as a secure and familiar setting for exploration, plays a role in this elaboration (Arcidiacono & Pontecorvo, 2009). Situations of conflict management have significant outcomes. By arguing with others in a familiar context, in personally meaningful situations, children learn not only how to argue, how to use language to communicate and think, but also social rules (how to behave, what are the accepted codes, etc.), and finally what it means to be and become members of a group (Pontecorvo, Fasulo & Sterponi, 2001; Stein & Bernas, 1999). At the level of interactions, it is thus stressed that divergent perspectives, opposition of ideas, can be viewed, not as failed interactions, but rather as specific forms of "intersubjectivity" in which new skills, roles and knowledge are learned and coordinated (Bruner, 1990).

Moreover, if individuals grow up and develop in a heterogeneous environment, individuals themselves can be conceived as "heterogeneous" subjects who draw upon various resources to make sense of their environments (Grossen, 2010; Markova, 2003). In this perspective, discourse – and in particular, argumentative discourse – is a dialogical process, not only because it evolves in a dialogue with others, who are present or not in the situation and whose questions or contradictions create a rupture that has to be elaborated, but also in a more Bakhtinian sense: it takes form and meaning in discourse in which each individual's point of view is a positioning with respect to other possible points of view (Bakhtin, 1981).

A practice embedded in meaning-making processes

Scholars who study argumentation as a form of everyday reasoning point to the fact that the "extra-logical" dimensions cannot be isolated from, but are an integral part of, its nature (Santos & Leitão Santos, 1999). Argumentative skills and strategies will take different forms according to the way the various elements of the situation will be interpreted by the participants. The topic under discussion, for instance, seems to play an influential role in the kind of argumentative strategies that will be prevalent. Voss and Van Dyke (2001) claim that young children have personal experience in conflict situations very early in life. Even though they are not able to verbalize the nature of argument structures, they enter into argumentation. However, the knowledge and the relationship they have towards the topic will differ:

> what could happen if such a child was asked as an individual why people return to prison? (…) the child might say because they committed a crime, or perhaps state some factor, but there would likely be less topic knowledge and experience available to the 3- or 4-year-old than to an adolescent or adult. Whether or not a person is able to perform reasonably in an argumentative situation depends on context, which includes the argument's contents (Voss & Van Dyke, 2001, p. 103).

A growing body of evidence thus supports the idea that children are more skilled arguers than traditionally expected, when the way they experience the context calls for it (Kuhn & Udell, 2007). The specificities of the situation, the topic under discussion, and the purposes the participants display in it play central roles in argumentative production. Everyday argumentation is regulated not only (or rarely) by the intellectual goal of validating the truth and logic of evidence, but also by interpersonal goals. The following section explores the way the relational dimension of argumentation, and in particular the conflictual aspect that it necessarily involves, is an object of interpretation and how it might play a role in the way participants "frame" the argumentative setting.

Argumentation and conflict

Strategies for conflict avoidance

Though disagreement is constitutive to cultural practices and thinking, it seems that in everyday interactions people try to avoid it. Explicitly confronting a point of view that differs from one's own is not a comfortable experience, as many studies in social and developmental psychology have shown. People usually prefer information that confirms their own view rather than facing differences (Asch, 1955). Dissent is seen as a threat for group and individuals, and leads often to rejection.

The preference for agreement

The preference for agreement in the second turns of an adjacency pair is one of the most well-attested patterns, as shown by conversational analysts. This means that when a person makes an assertion or performs another conversational action, a response that is to be taken as agreeing will typically be immediate, while a response to be taken as disagreeing will be prefaced or delayed (Myers, 2004; Sacks, 1987; Schegloff, 1992). The hypothesis of the threat to face of addresses can be useful for understanding this conversational pattern (Brown & Levinson, 1987; Goffman, 1955). In certain cultures, conflict avoidance takes a central role and affects public communication: direct opposition is regarded as impolite. Social harmony instead is valued, as well as discursive forms that tend to be built up in a communal harmonious way with significant efforts from community members to avoid tension in communication (Sekiguchi, 2002; Tran, 2011).

Conflict management behaviours among friends

Children learn early the "skilled art of conversational agreement" (Goodwin & Goodwin, 1983), as if they were aware of the negative effect argumentation and especially its "conflictual potential" may have on the relationship. In studies on child argumentation among friends, it has been shown for instance that young children are able to use sophisticated "conflict management behaviours" in order to de-escalate a conflict and help the dyad move back into friendly interaction. These strategies are among others the reference to a rule, making an offer or a compromise, using a weakened form of the demand that permits face-saving, making a humorous or self-deprecatory remark (Katz, Kramer & Gottman, 1992). However, arguing among friends might also be valued, and function as a form of sociability, not as the breakdown of civility, but only in specific frames, as showed by Deborah Shiffrin: "Speakers repeatedly disagree, remain nonaligned with each other, and compete with each other for interactional goods. Yet they do so in a non-serious way, and in ways which actually display their solidarity and protect their intimacy" (Schiffrin, 1984, p. 311, quoted in Myers, 2004, p. 113).

The psychological cost of doubt

In the eyes of the participants, engaging in argumentation means facing someone else's disagreement and thus having to manage the "relationship" level of the interaction. However, argumentation means also entering into reasoning about a specific content with somebody and thus involves putting one's own beliefs and representations into perspective. This questioning may affect the sense of self and identity. In his analysis of the way students situate themselves relative to scientific thinking, Perry (1970) identifies three main "positions" and stresses the difficult transition from a representation in a "dualistic" structure (world, knowledge and morality are assumed to have a dualistic structure; things are right or wrong, true or false, good or bad) to a "multiplicity" position (world, knowledge and morality are accepted as relativistic in the sense that truth is seen as relative to a frame of reference rather than absolute), to a position in terms of "commitments" (the realisation both that each person partly determines his or her own fate and the recognition that commitments, and hence identity, are constantly evolving). These later stages involve learning to deal with contradictions among various aspects of one's self, and studies show that all students do not reach the third position. Dialectical thinking seems thus costly in identity terms: it might change one's own beliefs about the world and oneself.

The constructive dimension of conflict

Disagreement – and resolution of disagreement – is essential to cultural life, to interaction, as we have seen, but also to cognitive development. This is the claim of authors who, following Piaget and other scholars, have studied the role of the conflict of perspectives in cognitive development and learning. This perspective sheds light on the positive effect that might constitute an "argumentative discussion". The implementation in the classroom of a pedagogy based on argumentation and debate is incidentally often related to Piagetian and socio-cognitive conflict and sociocultural perspective.

In his early work, Piaget claimed that argumentation – and argumentation among "equals" – could develop reflection, objectivity and the construction of knowledge. From his point of view, it is when the child experiences

> the shock [of] our thought coming into contact with that of others, which produces doubt and the desire to prove (…). The social need to share the thought of others and to communicate our own with success is at the root of our need for verification. Proof is the outcome of argument (…). Argument is, therefore, the backbone of verification. Logical reasoning is an argument which we have with ourselves, and which internally reproduces the features of a real argument. (Piaget, 1928/1995, p. 204)

In his work, Piaget insisted on the "symmetrical" relationship between interlocutors. A relationship based on authority mechanisms of social influence (conformism, obedience to authority, etc.) can make any counter-argumentation almost impossible or extremely difficult, and may lead to dramatic consequences (Milgram, 1974).

Research in the field of socio-cognitive conflict has dealt with the role of the confrontation of different perspectives, and especially their resolution on a higher plane: confrontation leads to looking for new information, explanation and coordination of the points of view even before the formal operation stage, under certain conditions (Doise, Mugny & Perret-Clermont, 1975; Perret-Clermont, 1980). What are the reasons why socio-cognitive conflict can promote learning, understanding and cognitive development?

> Facing dissent may lead to the realization that a different point of view than one's own is possible, and therefore produces uncertainty. If more than one answer is possible, one can come to question the validity of one's own answer,

resulting in a "cognitive conflict". Questioning the validity of one's own answer may then lead one to "decentre" from one's point of view and take seriously into account the other's position. To account for the existence of different points of view, one must process and understand the elements that might explain why another person holds another position, which can result in an increase in knowledge (Butera, Darnon & Mugny, 2011).

It is this effect that has been developed in social psychology of intergroup or interpersonal relationships in order to explain the change produced by an active minority: "The diversity which replaces uniformity in the group is a creator of uncertainty and of conflict; doubt is cast upon the hierarchy of responses of each person or of the group and the variability is increased" (Moscovici, Lage & Naffrechoux, 1969, p. 367).

Research has discussed, however, the idea that socio-cognitive would be an "all-purpose remedy" to foster learning and development. Studies rather show that the positive effects of socio-cognitive conflicts depend on the way the partners regulate the conflict: an "epistemic conflict regulation" – focused on the correctness or valid-ity of knowledge – or a "relational conflict regulation", centred on the relative sta-tuses of the partners (Butera et al., 2011). It is interesting to remark that epistemic regulation is favoured when individuals believe in the complementarity of their points of view (Grossen, Liengme & Perret-Clermont, 1997). On the contrary, socio-cognitive conflict is regulated in a relational way when the other person has the potential to be a competitor (Buchs, Butera, Mugny & Darnon, 2004). These results corroborate other observations made in diverse everyday activities. Tannen (1998) for instance notes, in education and family, that to win the argument, par-ticipants in a debate can ignore complexity and nuance; they can refuse to concede a point raised by their opponents, even if they can see that it is valid, because such a concession would weaken their position.

The studies presented above show compelling outcomes of the specificities of socio-cognitive conflict. However, they tend to consider the processes at stake in terms of variables, and do not analyse the dynamic processes within social interac-tions. Adopting a sociocultural perspective, Psaltis & Duveen (2007) examine the communicative processes through which the productive role of social interaction between peers promotes cognitive development by 6.5- to 7.5-year-old children. The authors stress the importance of different types of conversation and how these types have different implications for the progress of the novice. From analysis of verbal interactions between non-conserving and conserving children, in the frame-work of Piagetian tests, they show that "developmental progress was more com-monly a feature of resistance and especially of explicit recognition conversations, which were also notable as the only conversation type strongly linked to the appearance of novel arguments in the post-test" (pp. 82–3). It is interesting to look at the use of the notion of "recognition": it involves not only the importance of taking into consideration the other's point of view, but also of integrating it into one's own perspective – the re-cognition from the other's point of view; it also involves a social and ethical dimension of these processes.

Developing and opening the scope of their own work, Perret-Clermont, Grossen and colleagues (Grossen, 2009; Muller Mirza, Baucal, Perret-Clermont & Marro, 2003; Tartas, Baucal & Perret-Clermont, 2010) pointed out the fact that the situation of socio-cognitive conflict is itself a social situation in which contextual, institutional and identity dimensions are embedded. The way the subjects carry out the task and give responses to their interlocutors is the result of psychosocial processes, which are based upon the characteristics of the task, the way the individuals give meaning to the situation and make reference to other situations in which they have been involved in other contexts. The studies, through analyses of interactive moves, focus on how the participants give meaning to the argumentative activity and how the meaning-making processes transform the activity itself (Muller Mirza & Perret-Clermont, 2008). These studies lead to focusing on the "framing" processes, the way the participants give and negotiate a response to the question "what is it that's going on here?" (Goffman, 1974, p. 8). For research on argumentation at school, this shift points to the importance of understanding how students interpret, "frame" the situation (Berland & Hammer, *in press*). In the next section, I shall discuss some elements of an external framing of argumentation settings.

Exploration of ingredients for a space of thinking

Disagreement is at the core of development and learning, but it is hard to do (in a productive way)! (Myers, 2004). Many educational programmes are dedicated to promoting argumentation and critical thinking by developing settings in which students are invited to test the validity of hypotheses, examine data, understand various positions, and thereby to use argumentation to learn. However, argumentation about scientific knowledge (understood in a broad sense) rarely occurs spontaneously (Schwarz & Glassner, 2003), and even in settings in which students are asked to argue, argumentation is often weak or takes a "relational conflict regulation" form.

Many hypotheses have been developed in order to understand the challenges of argumentation to learn (Andriessen & Schwarz, 2009). Argumentation involves various epistemic and relational abilities: taking a stance towards a content (which is situated in a broader debate), providing reasons (referring not only to the personal goal but also to shared knowledge), using linguistic tools, managing arguments pro and contra, facing and resolving disagreements, etc. Rather than considering argumentation as a set of skills that could be developed through explicit directions and scaffolds, a sociocultural perspective emphasises the importance of context and raises consideration for creating learning environments in which the students' sense of what they are trying to accomplish through argumentation aligns with "epistemic" argumentation (Berland & Hammer, 2011).

The notion of a "thinking space", developed by Perret-Clermont (Perret-Clermont, 2004), may be interesting in the perspective of contributing to the discussion about the dimensions for framing a space that leads the participants to feel authorised to take the risk of (in)validating the observations or claims which are under discussion. This notion is based both on the Vygotskian ideas according to which the structure of the social situation is partially reconstructed on a mental plane, and on the idea developed by Winnicott (1971) that one needs a "good enough" frame to create a space in which freedom of thinking is possible.

In the following sub-section, I shall present and discuss some of the components of argumentative environments to whose design and analysis I contributed, in the frameworks of European Union-funded projects.

Communicative ground rules and sequentiality of the activity

Mercer and his colleagues observed that if students are meant to learn by working and talking with partners whilst carrying out school activities, they usually are expected to work out effective argumentation for themselves (Mercer, 2009). They claim, however, that education should help children gain a greater awareness of how to use language in order to enhance thinking and reasoning. They investigated the role of the teacher in "guiding the development of children's skills in using language as a tool for reasoning" and in particular in using what they term "exploratory talk". In this perspective, the authors showed that when "ground rules for talk" structure the discussion, they lead to a form of dialogical reasoning which not only helps students solving problems but can bring them to improve their generic reasoning skills (Wegerif, Mercer & Dawes, 1999). The conversation rules are defined around the following main principles: all relevant information is shared among the participants; all members of the group contribute to the discussion; opinions and ideas are respected and considered; everyone is asked to make their reasons clear; challenges and alternatives are made explicit and negotiated; the group seeks to reach agreement before taking a decision or acting (Mercer & Sams, 2006).

In the learning environments we tested (see, for example, Muller Mirza, Tartas, Perret-Clermont & de Pietro, 2007), a session before the "debate" itself was set up in order to discuss the communication ground rules. This preliminary discussion, that aimed at making explicit the communicative rules, had a twofold objective in our perspective: it made the students aware of language as a tool for thinking and it created a collaborative frame in which disagreement might be understood as an effective ingredient of the discussion.

The argumentative situation was also constructed such that the debate itself was framed in a broader activity in which several phases were organized a preparatory and introduction phase (which stressed the objectives and the means of the activity) in which the teacher assumed a central role; a second phase focused on looking for relevant information and reading texts found by the students or prepared by the teacher; the "debate" among the participants in which the teacher played the role of animator or provided help when needed; a conclusion phase in which the main points of the debate and the activity were discussed with a reflexive orientation.

Digalo Software

The questions of how to frame and set up argumentative activities in schools have led some researchers to work with ICT tools (Andriessen, Baker & Suthers, 2003). Research shows that external representations can influence the individual's conception of a problem and hence the ease with which a solution can be found.

In the field of argumentation, studies show that visual representations and structured dialogues may facilitate argumentation and the epistemic exploration of a "space of debate" (Baker, Quignard, Lund & Séjourné, 2003). Results point out that they promote more task-focused and reflective interactions. Argumentative maps (such as the ones generated by Digalo), as graphical tools and "representational guidance", can facilitate negotiation and justification practices and the elaboration of a shared understanding through the integration of the points of view of others in the learners' own thinking (Suthers & Hundhause, 2003).

Such maps function as resources for communication and reasoning, as a means for external and internal regulation. They provide the participants with a way to share knowledge and lead them to negotiate meanings; and they can be used as a "reflexive tool" when the participants think together about their own and somebody else's reasoning (Tartas, *forthcoming*).

Digalo software is an electronic environment that has been developed and tested in the framework of the DUNES project.[1] It is an interactive environment that allows visualization of the on-going discussion through an argumentative map (cf. Figure 1).

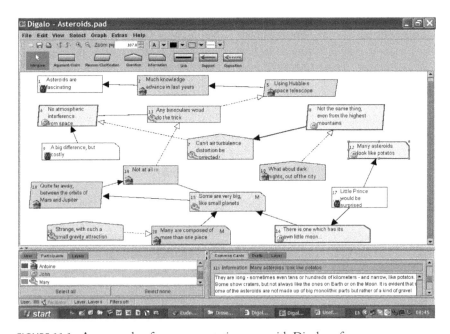

FIGURE 11.1 An example of an argumentative map with Digalo software

The map is progressively elaborated through collaborative discussion and provides a picture of its evolution – who said what, when, to whom, etc. It is then possible to return to the map and analyse argumentative processes, for pedagogical and research purposes. Digalo's various functionalities are meant to sustain argumentation and its main operations, justification and negotiation, for instance with (1) the title window: participants write a title in a "shape", and (as was intended at least by the designers of Digalo) thus formulate, in a few words, their main ideas, their "claims", making them explicit for others and for themselves; (2) the comment window: participants can justify their propositions and points of view; they are thus incited to ground, develop and justify them; (3) arrows: participants are invited to place links (that signal opposition, support or a neutral relationship towards the initial proposition) between the shapes (see Figure 11.1).

In Digalo, the use of arrows is intended to replace some linguistic resources in order to express agreement or disagreement. Rather than saying for instance: "I disagree with you concerning the point x because of y", claims are linked by means of an "opposition arrow" without the linguistic formulation of the disagreement. The disagreement is not expressed but explained: the interactional dynamic is oriented towards the content of the disagreement rather than towards the relationship. Our assumption is thus in continuity with previous results on use of ICT in argumentative settings, and stresses the idea that argumentative maps might also play the roles of "face management mediational tools": participants do not discuss and argue face to face, but can benefit from the distance provided both by the written artefact, its functionalities (the arrows for instance), and the screen. The following example illustrates this point.

In a secondary classroom in the French-speaking part of Switzerland, we invited 16-year-old students to work on a debate about the Valladolid Controversy (a historical event that took place in the year 1550 in Spain during which theologians and philosophers discussed the way the Indians of the New Territories in South America had to be treated, as slaves or free human beings). At the end of an interaction, one of the students said to his partner, who was playing the role of his argumentative opponent: "Let's go on, it does not matter, anyway we are not speaking to each other, this is in writing!" Since they are writing to each other, rather than speaking face to face, their disagreement, "mediated", does not seem to take on the same meaning: the "emotional load" is less important and the interaction can continue.

Role-playing

On the assumption according to which participants tend to avoid a situation of disagreement that may put at risk both the relationship and the self, or tend to engage in a competitive activity searching for imposing respect, influencing or marginalising an opponent (Miller, 1986; Schwarz & Glassner, 2003), some argumentative designers choose to work with role-playing. Role-playing is a methodology derived from socio-drama in the fields of psychology and theatre. Today it is used in education in order to help students understand aspects of literature, social studies, history, science or mathematics and socio-scientific topics or "real world issues" (Albe, 2005; Åberg, Mäkitalo & Säljö, 2010; Duveen & Solomon, 1994; Simonneaux, 2001).

The results of previous studies are encouraging. They show that, in confronting their points of view in role-playing, students are able to clarify their thoughts on a given subject, as observed for instance by Simonneaux in sciences: "the didactic strategy involving class discussions, whether through role play or debate, would seem to be a useful way of helping students to develop their arguments. Although the expressions used by the students sometimes showed a lack of conceptual understanding of the biotechnology examples used, this did not prevent them from taking an active part in discussions and argument" (Simonneaux, 2001, p. 926). Other scholars observed that the presence and frequency of counterarguments in subjects' discourses are improved when role-play instructions are used (Santos, 1996). It seems important, however, to avoid putting participants into two groups (pro/contra a specific question, for instance), since the results of argumentative dynamics analysis show that this tends to polarize responses (Albe, 2005). Participants then develop strategies to win the role-play by displaying even lies, false evidence or fallacies. The finality of the role-play (to win a trial, for example) could be considered to be more important than the social construction of knowledge.

The argumentative activities we designed were based on role-playing. We invited the participants (students from 12 to 16 years old in secondary school classrooms in history and biology lessons, and university students in psychology) to play characters or "instances" which are involved in a complex phenomenon, a scientific controversy or a historical event, and which can help its understanding. For instance we designed an activity called the "Valladolid Controversy" for lessons in History, in which three characters were debating (Bartolomeo de Las Casas, Ginès Sepulveda and the Aztec Indians). Students were assigned or chose the roles that represent the principal figures and their relevant opinions.

From our observations, using role-play instructions involves interesting features at the cognitive, emotional and relational levels:

- it leads participants to understand "from the inside" the issues at stake (and their economical, social and religious dimensions);
- it promotes engagement and imagination thanks to a playful framework;
- it allows the students to explore ideas and (virtual) conflicts: it does not correspond to their own opinions nor to their own ideas or thoughts that are at stake in the play for the participants, but rather to those of the characters whose roles they are playing;
- it allows various and sometimes marginalized "voices" to be expressed in the debate;
- in a broader perspective, it allows students to become familiarized with characteristics of debating in sciences.

It is relevant to recall here the notion of game, as developed by Mead (1934/1967) in his understanding of development as a social process. Mead's claim is that, through her participating in games, the child is led not only to understand the rules that prevail in interpersonal relationships but also to develop her own thinking. It is by playing different roles, and therefore by "taking the perspective of the others", that the child controls progressively the development of her own personality and that thinking may develop: "But only by taking the attitude of the generalized other toward himself, in one or another of these ways, can he think at all; for only thus can thinking – or the internalized conversation of gestures which constitutes thinking – occur" (1934, p. 155). The notion of play is also outlined by Winnicott (1971), who considered play to be of particular importance in the development of authentic selfhood. In his perspective, play can be seen as a "transitional object", having a status between imagination and the real world, helping individuals to be creative. Role-play might therefore facilitate the elaboration of a secure space in which the participants explore diverse perspectives on a given topic, trying out different points of view and co-elaborating new understanding.

Discussion

From the analysis of experiments we conducted in diverse educational settings, several conclusions can be drawn. In spite of some limits of the designs (lack of time, technological difficulties, too short conclusive discussions, etc.), learners were in general able: (1) to play the role they were assigned, (2) to focus on the task, (3) to use and develop a scientific vocabulary that was used on purpose, (4) to articulate concepts (or try to), (5) to make reference in a relevant way to empirical data extracted from textual resources, and (6) to mobilise argumentation skills and construct knowledge in interaction at the same time (Muller Mirza, 2009; Muller Mirza et al., 2007). Some of the usual difficulties of argumentative activities in an educational setting (mainly the difficulty of entering into an argumentative dialogue, and weak argumentation) appear to have been less apparent here.

However, some questions remain open. It would be naïve to think that these dimensions we briefly mentioned here could be an all-purpose answer to the question as to how to foster argumentation and learning. Some studies show, for instance, that ICT tools for argumentation-based collaborative learning can also be used in unexpected ways that favour social group dominance and everyday "primary communicative genres" (Baker, Bernard & Dumez-Féroc, in press; Cole & Derry, 2005). Researchers in this field are aware that electronic tools often involve technical competences and conditions that are not always at the disposal of teachers, and their additional value in pedagogical terms must be well established before being implemented in classroom routines. With respect to role-play pedagogy, this might be understood by the students as an opportunity to express opinions that would not be allowed in another setting at school; and from the teachers' point of view, facilitating a debate oriented towards knowledge construction requires complex skills (Rebière, Schneeberger & Jaubert, 2009).

Conclusion

From the point of view of some teachers and educational researchers, argumentation might be an interesting pedagogical tool that fosters learning. However, they often observe that students are not engaging in epistemic argumentation as they intended them to. In this chapter I tried to contribute to the debate on argumentation in educational settings by focusing on argumentation as a "situated" practice that entails cognitive, social and affective processes, and in particular, disagreement and confrontation of perspectives. These dimensions, as it was claimed, may lead to an interpretation of the setting by the participants as a potential threat to their faces and relationships, or lead them to a competitive interpretation of the task.

Following this perspective, from the analysis of social interactions which developed in the frame of argumentative environments in classrooms, I suggested some "ingredients" which could contribute to a space of thinking, in which the participants can explore new topics and critical questioning: communicative rules that are made explicit at the beginning of the activity, electronic software that provides a representation of the discussion, sustains argumentation and mediates the relationship, and role-play.

The discussion concerning the identity dimensions of argumentation, with a focus on the disagreement and conflict "management", is important in the educational context in order to help teachers to better understand the complexity of argumentation practices and to think of argumentative activities in which students can debate in a productive way. Discussion is important also for a more "ethical" reason. If one of the primary purposes of education is empowering and encouraging critical thinking, and therefore helping students to look at things from more than one point of view, it is important to consider its psychological cost. In our eyes, this discussion lies beyond technical issues about how to frame an argumentative design. The questions that have been raised here rely on what it means to argue, and to argue in a school context, from the participants' points of view.

Acknowledgements

I wish to thank the two anonymous reviewers and the editors for their feedback on an early draft of this chapter.

Notes

1   DUNES (Dialogical argUmentative Negotiation Educational Software) is a European project funded by the 5th Program Frame of the European Commission (IST-2001-34153). It involved nine participants, academic partners and software developers from France, Germany, Greece, Israel, The Netherlands, Sweden, Switzerland and the UK (http://www.dunes.gr/).

References

Albe, V. (2005). Un jeu de rôle sur une controverse socio-scientifique actuelle: Une stratégie pour favoriser la problématisation? [A role-play on a contemporary socio-scientific controversy: a strategy for favouring problem definition?]. ASTER No 40. 2005. *Problème et problématisation*, 67–93.

Åberg, M., Mäkitalo, Å., & Säljö, R. (2010). Knowing and arguing in a panel debate: Speaker roles and responsivity to others. In K. Littleton & C. Howe (Eds.), *Educational Dialogues: Understanding and Promoting Productive Interaction* (pp. 13–31). London: Routledge.

Andriessen, J., Baker, M., & Suthers, D. (Eds.). (2003). *Arguing to Learn: Confronting Cognitions in Computer-Supported Collaborative Learning Environments*. London: Kluwer Academic.

Andriessen, J. & Schwarz, B. (2009). Argumentative design. In N. Muller Mirza & A.-N. Perret-Clermont (Eds.), *Argumentation and Education* (pp. 145–74). New York: Springer.

Arcidiacono, F. & Pontecorvo, C. (2009). Verbal conflict as a cultural practice in Italian family interactions between parents and preadolescents. *European Journal of Psychology of Education*, vol. XXXIV, 1, 97–117.

Asch, S. (1955). Opinions and social pressure. *Scientific American*, 193, 31–5.

Bakhtin, M. (1981). Discourse in the novel (Trans. C. Emerson & M. Holquist,). In M. Holquist (Ed.), *The Dialogical Imagination: Four Essays by M.M. Bakhtin* (pp. 259–422). Austin: University of Texas.

Baker, M. J., Bernard, F.-X. & Dumez-Féroc, I. (in press). Integrating computer-supported collaborative learning into the classroom: the anatomy of a failure. *Journal of Computer Assisted Learning*.

Baker, M. J., Quignard, M., Lund, K., & Séjourné, A. (2003). Computer-supported collaborative learning in the space of debate. In B. Wasson, S. Ludvigsen & U. Hoppe (Eds.), *Designing for Change in Networked Learning Environments. Proceedings of the CSCL 2003* (pp. 11–20). Dordrecht: Kluwer.

Berland, L. K. & Hammer, D. (in press). Framing for scientific argumentation. *Journal of Research in Science Teaching*.

Billig, M. (1987). *Arguing and Thinking*. Cambridge: Cambridge University Press.

Brown, P. & Levinson, S. C. (1987). *Politeness: Some Universals in Language Usage*. Cambridge: Cambridge University Press.

Bruner, J. S. (1990). *Acts of Meaning*. London: Harvard University Press.

Buchs, C., Butera, F., Mugny, G., & Darnon, C. (2004). Conflict elaboration and cognitive outcomes. *Theory into Practice*, 43(1), 24–30.

Butera, F., Darnon, C., & Mugny, G. (2011). Learning from conflict. In J. Jetten & M. J. Hornsey (Eds.), *Rebels in Groups: Dissent, Deviance, Difference and Defiance* (pp. 31–49). Chichester, etc.: Wiley-Blackwel.

Cole, M. (1996). *Cultural Psychology. A Once and Future Discipline*. Cambridge Massachusetts: The Belknap Press.

Cole, M., & Derry, J. (2005). We have met technology and it is us. In R. J. Sternberg & D. Preiss (Eds.), *Intelligence and Technology: The Impact of Tools on the Nature and Development of Human Abilities* (pp. 15–35). New York: Lawrence Erlbaum Associates.

Doise, W., Mugny, G., & Perret-Clermont, A.-N. (1975). Social interaction and the development of cognitive operations. *European Journal of Social Psychology*, 5, 367–83.

Duveen, J. & Solomon, J. (1994). The great evolution trial: Use of role-play in the classroom. *Journal of Research in Science Teaching*, 31(5), 575–82.

Eemeren, F. H. van, & Houtlosser, P. (2002). Strategic maneuvering in argumentative discourse: Maintaining a delicate balance. In F. H. van Eemeren & P. Houtlosser (Eds.), *Dialectic and Rethoric: The Warp and Woof of Argumentation Analysis* (pp. 131–59). Dortrecht: Kluwer.

Goffman, E. (1955). On face-work: An analysis of ritual elements in social interaction. *Psychiatry: Journal for the Studies of Interpersonal Processes*, 18(3), 213–31.

Goffman, E. (1974). *Frame Analysis: An Essay on the Organization of Experience*. New York: Harper & Row.

Goodwin, M. H. & Goodwin, C. (1983). Children's arguing. In S. U. Philips, S. Steele & C. Tanz (Eds.), *Language, Gender, and Sex in Comparative Perspective* (pp. 200–48). Cambridge, London: Cambridge University Press.

Grossen, M. (2009). Social interaction, discourse and learning. Methodological challenges of an emergent transdisciplinary field. In K. Kumpulainen, C. E. Hmelo-Silver & M. César (Eds.), *Investigating Classroom Interaction: Methodologies in Action* (pp. 263–75). Rotterdam: Sense.

Grossen, M. (2010). Interaction analysis and psychology: A dialogical perspective. *Integrative Psychological & Behavioral Science*, 44, 1–22.

Grossen, M., Liengme Bessire, M.-J., & Perret-Clermont, A.-N. (1997). Construction de l'interaction et dynamiques socio-cognitives. In M. Grossen & B. Py (Eds.), *Pratiques sociales et médiations symboliques* (pp. 221–47). Bern: Peter Lang.

Katz, L. F., Kramer, L. & Gottman, J. M. (1992). Conflict and emotions. In C. U. Shantz & W. L. Hartun (Eds.), *Conflict in Child and Adolescent Development* (pp. 122–49). Cambridge: Cambridge University Press.

Kuhn, D., & Udell, W. (2007). Coordinating own and other perspectives in argument. *Thinking and Reasoning*, 13(2), 90–104.

Lawrence, J. A. & Valsiner, J. (2003). Making personal sense: An account of basic internalization and externalization process. *Theory and Psychology*, 13(6), 723–52.

Markova, I. (2003). Constitution of the self: Intersubjectivity and dialogicality. *Culture and Psychology*, 9(3), 249–59.

Matusov, E. (2009). *Journey into Dialogic Pedagogy*. New York: Nova Science.

Mead, G. H. (1934/1967). *Mind, Self and Society*. Chicago: The Chicago University Press.

Mercer, N. (2009). Developing argumentation: Lessons learned in the pramary school. In N. Muller Mirza & A.-N. Perret-Clermont (Eds.), *Argumentation and Education* (pp. 177–94). New York: Springer.

Mercer, N. & Sams, C. (2006) Teaching children how to use language to solve maths problems. *Language and Education*, 20, 6, 507–28.

Milgram, S. (1974). *Obedience to Authority: An Experimental View*. New York: Harper and Row.

Miller, M. (1986). Learning how to contradict and still pursue a common end: The ontogenesis of moral argumentation. In J. Cook-Gumperz, W. Corsaro & J. Streeck (Eds.), *Children's Words and Children's Language* (pp. 425–79). Berlin: Mouton & Gruyter.

Moscovici, S., Lage, E., & Naffrechoux, M. (1969). Influence of a consistent minority on the responses of a majority in a color perception task. *Sociometry*, 32(4), 365–80.

Muller Mirza, N. (2009). Argumentative interactions and learning through a virtual environment: Lessons learned from the implementation of a case in science. In D. Russel (Ed.), *Cases on Collaboration in Virtual Learning Environments: Processes and Interactions* (pp. 95–109). Hershey, NY: IGI Global.

Muller Mirza, N., & Perret-Clermont, A.-N. (2008). Dynamiques interactives, apprentissages et médiations: Analyses de constructions de sens autour d'un outil pour argumenter. In L. Filliettaz & M.-L. Schubauer-Leoni (Eds.), *Processus interactionnels et situations éducatives* (pp. 231–53). Bruxelles: De Boek.

Muller Mirza & A.-N. Perret-Clermont (2009) (Eds.), *Argumentation and Education*. New York: Springer.

Muller Mirza, N., Baucal, A., Perret-Clermont, A.-N., & Marro, P. (2003). Nice designed experiment goes to the local community. *Cahiers de Psychologie*, 38, 17–52.

Muller Mirza, N., Tartas, V., Perret-Clermont, A.-N., & Iannaccone, A. (2009). Towards a psychosocial perspective on argumentation in education. In N. Muller Mirza & A.-N. Perret-Clermont (Eds.), *Argumentation and Education: Theoretical Foundations and Practices* (pp. 67–90). Dordrecht, London, New York: Springer.

Muller Mirza, N., Tartas, V., Perret-Clermont, A.-N., & de Pietro, J.-F. (2007). Using graphical tools in a phased activity for enhancing dialogical skills: An example with Digalo. *Computer-Supported Collaborative Learning*, 2, 24772.

Myers, G. (2004). *Matters of Opinion: Talking about Public Issues*. Cambridge: Cambridge University Press.

Perret-Clermont, A.-N. (1980). *Social Interaction and Cognitive Development in Children*. New York: Academic Press.

Perret-Clermont, A.-N. (2004). The thinking spaces of the young. In A.-N. Perret-Clermont, C. Pontecorvo, L. Resnick, T. Zittoun & B. Burge (Eds.), *Joining Society: Social Interactions and Learning in Adolescence and Youth* (pp. 3–10). New York/Cambridge: Cambridge University Press.

Perry, W. G. (1970). *Forms of Intellectual and Ethical Development in the College Years: A Scheme*. New York: Holt, Rinehart, and Winston.

Piaget, J. (1928/1995). Genetic logic and sociology. In J. Piaget (Ed.), *Sociological Studies* (pp. 184–214). New York: Routledge.

Pontecorvo, C., Fasulo, A., & Sterponi, L. (2001). Mutual apprentice: The making of parenthood and childhood in family dinner conversations. *Human Development*, 44, 340–61.

Psaltis, C., & Duveen, G. (2007). Conservation and conversation types: Forms of recognition and cognitive development. *British Journal of Developmental Psychology,* (25), 79–102.

Rebière, M., Schneeberger, P., & Jaubert, M. (2009). Changer de position énonciative pour construire des objets de savoirs en sciences: le rôle de l'argumentation [Changing enunciative perspective for constructive objects of knowledge in sciences]. In C. Buty & C. Plantin (Eds.), *Argumenter en classe de sciences* [Arguing in science classes] (pp. 281–330). Paris: INRP.

Resnick, L. B., Säljö, R., Pontecorvo, C., & Burge, B. (Eds.). (1997). *Discourse, Tools and Reasoning: Essays on Situated Cognition*. Berlin: Springer.

Rigotti, E., & Greco Morasso, S. (2009a). Argumentation as an object of interest and as a social and cultural resource. In N. Muller Mirza & A.-N. Perret-Clermont (Eds.), *Argumentation and Education: Theoretical Foundations and Practices* (pp. 9–66). New York: Springer.

Rigotti, E. & Greco Morasso, S. (2009b). Editorial & guest editors' introduction: Argumentative processes and communication contexts. *Scoms*, 9(2), 5–18.

Rogoff, B. (2003). *The cultural nature of human development*. Oxford: Oxford University Press.

Sacks, H. (1987). On the preference for agreement and contiguity in sequences in conversation. In G. Button & J. R. Lee (Eds.), *Talk and Social Organization* (pp. 54–69). Clevedon: Multilingual Matter.

Schegloff, E. A. (1992). Repair after next turn. The last structurally provided defense of intersubjectivity in conversation. *American Journal of Sociology*, 97(5), 1295–345.

Santos, C. M., & Leitão Santos, S. (1999). Good argument, content and contextual dimensions. In J. Andriessen & P. Coirier (Eds.), *Foundations of Argumentative Text Processing* (pp. 75–96). Amsterdam: Amsterdam Press.

Schiffrin, D. (1994). Jewish argument as sociability. *Language in Society*, 13(3), 311–35.

Schwarz, B., & Glassner, A. (2003). The blind and the paralytic: Supporting argumentation in everyday and scientifc issues. In J. Andriessen, M. Baker & D. Suthers (Eds.), *Arguing to Learn* (pp. 227–60). Utrecht: Kluwer Academic.

Sekiguchi, Y. (2002). Mathematical proof, argumentation, and classroom communication: From a cultural perspective. *Tsukuba Journal of Educational Study in Mathematics*, 21, 11–20.

Simonneaux, L. (2001). Role-play or debate to promote students' argumentation and justification on an issue in animal transgenesis. *International Journal of Science Education*, 23(9), 903–27.

Stein, N. L., & Bernas, R. (1999). The early emergence of argumentative knowledge and skill. In J. Andriessen & P. Coirier (Eds.), *Studies in Writing: Foundations of Argumentative Text Processing* (pp. 97–116). Amsterdam: Amsterdam University.

Suthers, D. & Hundhause, D. (2003). An experimental study of the effects of representational guidance on collaborative learning processes, *The Journal of the Learning Sciences*, 12(2), 183–218.

Tannen, D. (1998). *The Argument Culture: Moving from Debate to Dialogue*. New York: Random House.

Tartas, V. (*Forthcoming*). Comment les enfants entrent dans la culture scientifique? Interactions sociales, artefacts et construction de concepts en astronomie, [How do children enter into scientific culture? Social interactions, artifacts and construction of concepts in astronomy]. Special Issue (coordinated by Moro, C. & Muller Mirza, N.), *Psicologia culturale*.

Tartas, V., Baucal, A., & Perret-Clermont, A.-N. (2010). Can you think with me? The social and cognitive conditions and the fruits of learning. In C. Howe & K. Littleton (Eds.), *Educational Dialogues: Understanding and Promoting Productive Interaction* (pp. 64–82):?: Elsevier Advances in Learning and Instruction Book. London and New York: Routledge.

Tran, L. T. (2011). Turning the spotlight to international students' internal negotiations: Critical thinking in academic writing. In P. Le Ha & B. Baurain (Eds), *Voices, Identitities, Negotiations, and Conflicts: Writing Academic English across Cultures* (pp. 59–74). Bingley: Emerald Bookstore. Emerald Group Publishing.

Valsiner, J. (2007). *Cultures in Minds and Societies*. New Delhi: Sage.

Van Eemeren, F. H. & Houtlosser, P. (2005). Strategic manoeuvring. *Studies in Communiation Sciences*, 23–34.

Voss, J., & Van Dyke, J. (2001). Argumentation in psychology: Background comments. *Discourse Processes*, 32(2&3), 89–111.

Wegerif, R., Mercer, N., & Dawes, L. (1999). From social interaction to individual reasoning: An empirical investigation of a possible socio-cultural model of cognitive development. *Learning and Instruction*, 9(6), 493–516.

Winnicott, D. W. (1971). *Playing and Reality*. London: Tavistock.

12

EPISTEMIC AND INTERPERSONAL DIMENSIONS OF PEER ARGUMENTATION

Conceptualization and quantitative assessment

Christa S. C. Asterhan

Introduction

The past two decades have witnessed growing interest in argumentation for educational purposes. Based on distinctions made by several theorists (van Eemeren et al, 1996; Walton, 2006), argumentation is defined here as a social activity in which interlocutors attempt to strengthen or weaken the acceptability of one or more ideas, views, or solutions through engagement in reasoning. Researchers in several domains of the psychological and educational literature have recognized that argumentation may serve important functions in learning and development and should therefore receive a more prominent role in classroom activities. For example, science educators have identified argumentation to lie at the basis of scientific inquiry, thinking and practice and have called for a more prominent role of argumentation in science classroom activities (e.g., Driver et al, 2000; Duschl & Osborne, 2002; Erduran & Jimenez-Aleixandre, 2007; Osborne, 2010). Research in developmental and educational psychology has shown that participation in dialogical argumentation can improve students' critical reasoning skills (e.g., Frijters et al, 2008; Kuhn, 1999; Reznitskaya et al, 2001). Finally, there is accumulating evidence that under certain conditions participation in argumentation can also support the learning of complex academic content (e.g., Asterhan & Schwarz, 2007, 2009a; De Vries, Lund & Baker, 2002; Nussbaum & Sinatra, 2003; Schwarz et al, 2000). In the present chapter, I will mainly focus on the latter category, that is: the role of argumentation in knowledge building.

Whereas much attention has been given to the cognitive and epistemic dimensions of argumentation, the socio-relational, socio-emotional and motivational aspects of it have been largely neglected. I will put forward the claim that research on argumentation, learning and education can benefit from considering these dimensions, and that it may uncover some of the reasons behind the difficulty to elicit productive argumentation among students. In the first part, I will describe how 'productive argumentation' is commonly defined as an activity that is co-constructive and critical at the same time. We call it co-constructive, critical argumentation (Asterhan & Schwarz, 2009b). In the second part, I will try to uncover why it is not easy to elicit this particular type of productive discourse among students, and why they often resort to discourse that is void of either criticism or of co-construction, even when specifically instructed to engage in argumentation. In part three, different attitudes towards conflict resolution are described, each resulting in a distinctively different type of discourse, namely consensus seeking and adversarial argumentative discourse. Short protocols will illustrate the difference between them and how they are likely to inhibit learning. Finally, in part four I will present an assessment scheme that attempts to capture key elements of the epistemic as well as the interpersonal dimensions of argumentative discourse. This chapter concludes with outlining several ways in which the presented conceptualizations and the coding scheme may be used to offer new insights into the social and cognitive processes of learning through peer argumentation. The overall goal of the current chapter is to suggest a conceptual framework and a quantitative assessment procedure to capture the differences between different types of argumentative discourse so as to enable empirical research into the antecedents of these different types of argumentative discourse and to further explore their relation with learning.

Argumentative discourse and knowledge building

Even though the study of argumentation and education has strong roots in Vygotskian theory as well, research on the more specific field of learning academic content through argumentation is probably most influenced by the neo-Piagetian notion of socio-cognitive conflict (Doise & Mugny, 1984; Doise et al, 1975). As outlined in detail by Baker, Andriessen and Järvelä in the opening chapter (*this volume*) socio-cognitive conflict theory predicts that students are more likely to experience conflict and therefore more likely to learn, when this conflict has a social origin, that is, when (s)he is interacting with peers that present different views. In a nutshell, the incongruence between solutions or ideas introduces doubt concerning the correctness of one's own knowledge, which is then hoped to cause learners to reconsider and/or reconstruct this knowledge (Doise & Mugny, 1984).

However, as a recent study by Asterhan and Schwarz (2007) has shown, merely being exposed to a different view may not yield learning gains, especially when it concerns complex academic content for which students have robust misconceptions. In argumentative discourse, on the other hand, students actively explore their diverging views and try to settle the conflict through rational reasoning. When doing so they engage in a host of activities that are thought to scaffold knowledge construction: First of all, through articulating and publicly presenting their ideas, students make their own, often erroneous or incomplete understanding of key concepts explicit and open to evaluation. Both the anticipation (Tetlock, 1992) and the actual act of explaining one's own ideas to another human being (e.g., Chi et al, 1994; Coleman,1998; Webb et al, 1995) have been found to improve student learning. In addition, exchanges with a disagreeing peer requires of students to try and understand alternative positions, to answer questions and to address discrepancies in their personal and in their collective understanding (e.g., Baker, 2003; Nussbaum, Sinatra and Poliquin, 2008). Finally, by addressing these differences and to explore their respective and relative validity, students have to consider which view, idea or explanation is more acceptable than another and why. Among others, they have to consider whether a certain idea is or is not warranted by the right data, or whether a proposed counterargument does or does not successfully challenge a certain idea. Through the combination of these processes, engagement in argumentative discourse is believed to result in better cognitive processing and to more meaningful and elaborated knowledge structures (see Schwarz & Asterhan, 2010 for a more complete review).

Indeed, a growing body of empirical evidence has now accumulated that supports the claim that peer-to-peer argumentation can improve students' understanding of complex scientific concepts (e.g., Asterhan & Schwarz, 2007, 2009a; Chin & Osborne, 2010; deVries et al, 2001; Nussbaum & Sinatra, 2003; Nussbaum et al, 2008; Schwarz et al, 2000). Moreover, recent findings show that individual conceptual gains on particularly complex content are primarily predicted by the presence of critical-dialectical aspects of argumentative discourse (i.e., contradiction, challenges, rebuttals, opposition), and less so by consensual reasoning moves (such as providing supporting reasons, explanation and elaborations) (Asterhan, 2007, 2009a; Howe, 2009).

Most researchers agree, however, that in order to be conducive to learning, argumentation should not only be characterized by criticism and dialecticism. Students should not only try to break down erroneous ideas, but should also try to collaboratively construct better ones. They should not only try to find the flaws in each others' reasoning, but also be able to identify, accept and integrate successful ideas into their own reasoning. In other words, they should be critical and constructive at the same time. This type of ideal argumentative discourse, one that balances between critical reasoning and collaborative construction, is described by a number of researchers and surfaces under different names in the literature, i.e., 'collaborative argumentation' (Nussbaum et al, 2008), 'exploratory talk' (Mercer, 1996; Wegerif et al, 1999), 'critical discussion' (Keefer et al, 2000), deliberation (Kroll, 2005), and 'co-constructive, critical argumentation' (Asterhan & Schwarz, 2009b). In this chapter, I will use the latter term, co-constructive, critical argumentation (CCA hereafter). In spite of the different labels, the descriptions of these idealized types of dialogue are strikingly similar and can be characterized by the following common features:

(1) A general willingness to listen to and critically examine all the different ideas that are proposed in the course of a discussion and to search for alternative perspectives that have not been considered yet.
(2) A willingness to make concessions in response to persuasive arguments.
(3) An atmosphere that is characterized by collaboration and mutual respect.

(4) The activity is perceived as a competition between ideas and not between the individuals that proposed them. As Keefer and colleagues (2000) put it, the discussion is *issue-driven* and not *position-driven*.

Unfortunately, however, this ideal type of argumentative discourse is not easily elicited among students. Even task designs that maximize differences in perspectives or opinions and provide explicit instructions to engage in critical argumentation cannot assure that students actually will (Asterhan & Schwarz, 2007). In the next section, some of the reasons behind this difficulty are explored.

The self, the other and the social in argumentative discourse

Early research on individual differences in argumentative performance focused on cognitive skills, age and schooling (e.g., Kuhn, 1991; Means & Voss, 1996). Whereas cognitive ability and development may indeed be part of such differences, it cannot be the entire story. In group learning settings, students are concerned not only with mastering the academic content, but also with issues such as social belongingness, interpersonal relations, self- and other-perceptions and how their performance reflects on competence, to name a few (Hijzen et al, 2007). These concerns often coexist simultaneously and may lead to conflicts between different goals. In line with these distinctions, I propose that the request to engage in a critical discussion with a disagreeing peer may be perceived by many students as conflicting or even incommensurate with the desire to maintain pleasant, harmonious relationships with co-actors and the desire to be perceived as competent and knowledgeable, leading to different (less productive) discourse types.

First of all, students need to feel comfortable in articulating and sharing their own, incomplete solutions to complex problems with others in the group. An increasing body of evidence underlines the importance of students' independent grappling with complex materials and proposing their own, often faulty and incorrect, solutions before receiving information on the correct procedures and answers (e.g., Kapur, 2008; Schwartz & Martin, 2004). However, to do so in a public, social context requires of students to (temporarily) put their egos aside and propose explanations and answers that are likely to be proven wrong later on and about which one has little confidence to begin with. In addition, the expectation of others critiquing these ideas may enhance subjective uncertainty (McGarty et al, 1993) and threaten self-competence (Butera & Mugny, 1995; Pool et al, 1998). Then there is the actual confrontation with an alternative, competing solution and/or having to deal with critique on one's own solution. Darnon et al (2007) proposed that interacting with a disagreeing peer introduces a 'double uncertainty': an uncertainty about the validity of an answer and an uncertainty about (relative) personal competence. This uncertainty about relative competence may be further enhanced in a competitive context (Butera & Mugny, 1995). Darnon et al (2007) showed that when a disagreeing peer expressed his/her disagreement in a way that emphasizes competition and superiority, students reported more frequently that their partner threatened their self-competence than when this disagreement was phrased in neutral terms.

In order to protect themselves from such uncertainties and threats to perceived competence, some students may then choose to avoid the conflict altogether and seek a quick consensus without much cognitive engagement and without further exploring the differences between the different solutions and conceptions (Smith et al, 1981). This discourse type, which is in fact void of critical-dialectical argumentation, may be further encouraged by a third uncertainty: uncertainty with regard to inclusion and acceptance by the group. The prospect of having to disagree with one's partners and critique their ideas may raise concerns about being able to maintain a positive relationship with them and be accepted by them.

Others may choose to address perceived or expected threats to self-competence by trying to hold on to and defend their initial position to 'win' the argument. They may address the situation as some sort of debating contest, characterized by competitive, verbal sparring between two (or more) opponents. Such adversarial, competitive argumentative discourse is not likely to be as beneficial to learning as its critical, co-constructive counterpart (Johnsson & Johnsson, 2008; Keefer et al, 2000; Nussbaum, 2008). When focused on 'winning the argument', students tend to ignore or discount potentially useful ideas proposed by others without further consideration (Butera & Mugny, 1995; Tjosvold & Johnsson, 1978). A study by Carnevale and Probst (1998) shows that anticipating a competitive interaction causes an unintentional alteration in underlying cognitive organization. They found that expecting conflict instead of cooperation in a negotiation task negatively impacted individuals' cognitive flexibility and their performance on individual problem-solving tasks that were unrelated to the negotiation task or topic. Therefore, students are likely to miss crucial opportunities for learning in adversarial argumentation, since they are not open to considering alternative views or to revising their own reasoning in response to critique.

In sum, concerns about self-competence, self-presentation and interpersonal relations may divert students' attention away from the epistemic dimension of the conflict (a conflict between ideas) and heavily focus on the interpersonal dimension of the conflict (a conflict between persons) and all its implications, often resulting in argumentative discourse that is either void of critical discourse (*consensual discourse*) or void of collaborative construction of knowledge (*adversarial argumentative discourse*).

I do not mean to claim that it is *impossible* to reconcile the social and the epistemic-cognitive dimension of socio-cognitive conflict, and that they are by definition incommensurate. In our 2007 data set (Asterhan & Schwarz, 2007), we found several dyads that managed particularly well to preserve the delicate balance between critically examining each others' ideas while maintaining a collaborative atmosphere and avoiding face threats (Brown & Levinson, 1987) with a variety of self-invented techniques. In some instances, they engaged in spontaneous role-playing and agreed that each was only a role representing a certain side in the discussion. The technique of role-playing provides an excellent opportunity to introduce critique, alternative positions and even unpopular ideas, without risking the social consequences of such actions. In other instances, dialogue partners articulated hypothetical 'What if…' questions that explored the boundaries of another person's explanation with an inquiry, instead of directly opposing or refuting them (see Asterhan & Schwarz, 2009b for detailed descriptions). I do propose however that without further support, explicit instructions or guidelines, many students may *conceive* them as incommensurate and find it therefore difficult to be both critical and co-constructive.

In the next section, I will provide examples from consensual and adversarial argumentative discourse and present anecdotal evidence of how they are less likely to lead to learning gains.

Argumentative discourse that is void of criticism or of co-construction

All protocol excerpts presented here are taken from studies in which undergraduate students with no formal background in Biology and Earth sciences were shown a short educational movie that presented the Darwinian account of animal and plant evolution, after which they were paired in dyads and asked to collaboratively solve a set of novel items through engagement in argumentation. Students' individual understanding of natural selection was assessed with the help of pre-tests and delayed post-test. The communication formats were either, face-to-face and oral (Asterhan & Schwarz, 2007) or computer-mediated and textual (Asterhan et al, submitted). Natural selection has been extensively documented as a topic in which intuitive misconceptions are abundant and extremely robust to instruction (e.g., Bishop & Anderson, 1990; Jimenez-Aleixandre, 1992; Ohlsson, 1992; Shtulman, 2006).

Consensual dialogue and quick consensus seeking

As aforementioned, the willingness to make concessions in the face of convincing arguments is an important feature of productive argumentation. A general aim to reach consensus at the end of the discussion is also valued, provided this is achieved through reasoned argument. However, empirical research has shown that whether students actually reach an agreement or not does not predict whether they actually learn from the interaction (Asterhan & Schwarz, 2007; Howe, 2009). Moreover, too strong an emphasis on consensus seeking may be counterproductive and undermines the main goal of argumentation, especially when students are willing to accept the first solution that is proposed without any critical exploration of the different viewpoints (Keefer et al, 2000). The latter has also been referred to as *quick consensus seeking* (Weinberger & Fisher, 2006).

The following short excerpt shows how two students, who proposed two very different accounts for the evolution of ducks' webbed feet, failed to explore the differences and therefore missed important learning opportunities.

Excerpt 1.

Alicia: Okay. Do you have an idea?

Ella: Ah, yes. Because the area was flooded with water and those with legs that suited the water actually survived.

Alicia: Humhum.

Ella: And then those that survived, developed and continued themselves.

Alicia: That is, that ducks developed webbed feet especially to survive/

Ella: /Yes/

Alicia: /in areas that once were dry and became flooded with water?

Alicia: Yes, that sounds reasonable.

First, Ella proposes a Darwinian account of the evolution of the webbed feet of ducks, based on principles of intra-species variability and differential survival rates. Alicia then apparently paraphrases Ella's account, but actually proposes a very different account, based on the idea that ducks intentionally developed these traits *in order* to survive. Neither Alicia nor Ella capitalizes on this difference and further explores it. They quickly settle on an agreement and move on.

The next excerpt from a computer-mediated dialogue between two male students shows similar results, this time on a question relating to the white fur of polar bears:

Excerpt 2.

Guy: What do you think?

Yoni: I think that the bear needed to assimilate into his living environment for a variety of reasons, for hunting needs as well as because of the weather, and therefore his fur changed [from brown] to white.

Guy: Yes, maybe it prevented him from being hunted.

Guy: Even though I cannot imagine who eats polar bears.

Yoni: He is the primary hunter in his area… I meant hunting in the sense that he needs to hunt other animals, and therefore needs to disguise himself.

Yoni: *primary

Guy: Yes that sounds reasonable.

Guy: Shall we write?

Yoni: Yes.

The pre-test data of these four participants showed that in both cases each dyadic partner used distinctively different explanatory schemas to explain evolutionary change. In the first excerpt, this difference is represented in the dialogue, but not further explored. In the second excerpt it is not even expressed: Even though Guy's written explanations were distinctively different from his partner's, he quickly agrees with Yoni's explanation and does not even attempt to propose his own explanation, let alone explores the differences between them. In both cases, important learning opportunities were missed.

Even though these two protocol excerpts show examples of students who quickly reached a consensus without further conversation, consensual dialogue does not necessarily have to be as short as in these excerpts. Other examples show students engage in long conversation, where they transact on each other's reasoning with elaborations, justifications in favor of their collectively accepted solution, explaining parts of the solution to each other, and so forth (Asterhan & Schwarz, 2009a). What is characteristic of consensual dialogue, however, is that they do this in a consensual manner, that they do not critically explore these solutions and do not consider alternative solutions. Mercer (1996) terms this type of dialogue 'cumulative dialogue' and describes it as dialogue '(…) in which speakers build positively but uncritically on what the other has said. Partners use talk to construct a 'common knowledge' by accumulation. Cumulative talk is characterized by repetitions, confirmations and elaborations' (p. 369). In some ways the concept of consensual dialogue is somewhat similar to Mercer's cumulative talk, with the important addition that it does not always stop with simple repetitions and elaborations; students may also engage in one-sided reasoning (providing justifications and citing supporting evidence in favor of the explanation proposed) and collaborative constructions of explanations, without actually juxtaposing them and exploring their differences.

Adversarial argumentation

In our data, several dialogues were found that were clearly dialectical in nature and had a high frequency of critical argumentation moves (i.e., reasoned challenges, reasoned rebuttals, oppositions), but lacked the collaborative, shared thinking effort and the openness to alternative viewpoints characteristic of co-constructive, critical argumentation (CCA). In these dialogues, students seemed to perceive the activity as an interpersonal competition and their dialogue partner as their adversarial. We therefore termed this type of dialogue *adversarial argumentation*. It is illustrated in the following excerpt, in which two male students, Avi and David, discuss the evolution of webbed feet in a face-to-face discussion format. The pre-test data of these two students showed that the explanatory schemas they used to explain evolutionary change were distinctively different from each other, which also clearly surfaced in their dialogue. The short excerpt presented here is a representative sample of the entire dialogue, which lasted for a total of about 10 minutes.

> *Excerpt 3.*
> Avi: It's like we saw in the movie, that they change according to the… environment. To the weather. So they probably stayed in the water more and then developed…ehm…webbed feet.
> David: I think that…those who had webbed feet survived, and they produced more offspring that also had webbed feet.
>   [short silence]
> Avi: No, but it seems to me that before they did not have webbed feet at all.

David: But I think that they say that evolution it…it is not that an animal develops anything, but that…that those that are well adapted to the environment survive. So, let's say that there were mutations of ducks with webbed feet…and…so those that had survived and produced more offspring, because they had an advantage.

Avi: No, but they also changed. It is not that-…The change was because of the environment.

David: I don't think that an animal adapts himself to the environment. I think that it…I mean, those that are fit survive. Say, it is not like the giraffe…did a lot to make his neck longer, but that those giraffes that had a long neck survived and produced offspring.

[short silence]

David: Cause I think that an animal cannot develop webbed feet

Avi: I dunno, but let's say that…an animal…a certain animal is immune to a certain substance. It develops immunity to a certain substance.

David: I think that that…I mean, think about human beings. Imagine that we start to live in water. I don't think that…that we would develop webbed feet. I think that maybe there were mutations that had webbed feet and then these mutations…like, were more adapted and they produced more offspring.

[short silence]

David: I think that this is also what they said about the finches in the movie. Like, it is not that the finch developed a larger beak, but that those that had larger beaks produced more offspring that year.

Avi: Yeah, but…but the…the weather conditions affected the food. And that also affected, like, its change.

[…]

This dialogue opens with the presentation of two different explanations for the evolution of webbed feet: Avi presents a typological account, whereas David proposes a Darwinian-inspired explanation. This perfectly complies with the instructions according to which each participants was asked to first present his/her own explanation to the phenomenon. It is followed by a silence. Avi challenges David's explanation to argue that *before they did not have webbed feet at all*. By arguing so, he challenges the idea of survival of adapted specimens to replace it by the idea of typological development of a specimen in response to needs. David, in turn challenges Avi's claim that animals can change themselves and elaborates his Darwinian explanation in an attempt to persuade Avi (*So, let's say that there were mutations of ducks with webbed feet…so those that had survived and produced more offspring, because they had an advantage*). Avi does not really cope with David's elaboration, but simply opposes with a counterclaim that specimens also change and repeats that this occurs as a result of reactions to the environment. David reacts with an opposition of his own (*I don't think that an animal adapts himself to the environment*) and appeals to the example of the giraffe's neck to illustrate his initial claim. The silence that follows this turn is instructive. The two interlocutors stick to their initial claims and fail to integrate the arguments of their peers in their own to elaborate better arguments. In particular, they do not try to deal with the different challenges that each poses to the other. Instead, they respond to them by returning simple unreasoned oppositions and by presenting yet more analogies and information that are intended to support their own viewpoint. In addition, at no point in this entire dialogue did the two come to some sort of agreement or did they engage in some form of consensual, collaborative construction of ideas. In spite of the fact that Avi was exposed to some rather convincing arguments in favor of the Darwinian explanation for evolution, his post-test nevertheless consistently showed typological answers.

Keefer et al (2000) and Mercer (1996) refer to this type of dialogue as, respectively, *eristic* and *disputational* talk, which is characterized by a lack of concessions and lack of serious consideration of how others' challenges and arguments bear on their own viewpoints. In contrast to Mercer's descriptions, however, the dialogue exchanges do not necessarily have to be short. The dialogue in excerpt 3 shows that these two students are not simply re-stating and re-asserting their own standpoints through repetition and without further reasoning. They are in fact offering justifications, explanations and analogies to support their own views. The crucial difference is that they are not dealing with each other's challenges and seem to be talking in parallel. An additional distinction between Mercer's and our conceptualization of adversarial argumentation and CCA is that a prevalence of disagreement and critical reasoning (e.g., counterarguments, challenges, oppositions) is not only characteristic of the former, but also a defining feature of CCA. According to our distinctions, the difference between the two lies in the way that this disagreement is regulated: In a way that focuses on the epistemic conflict (Doise & Mugny, 1984) or in a way that emphasizes conflict and competition between the persons that personify these positions.

The importance of this distinction became even more evident in several other dialogue protocols, in which students were observed to react to and build on each others' reasoning, but were doing it in a way that conveyed a competitive – and sometimes even antagonistic interpersonal intent. Excerpt 4 illustrates this point. It presents a computer-mediated CHAT exchange between two male students, again on the evolution of webbed feet. At the beginning of the discussion, Oren proposed an explanation based on crossbreeding. He also specifically claimed that the changes in ducks' feet were not contingent on environmental changes and that they happened long before that. Eyal, on the other hand, argues that there must be a link between the two. The excerpt starts at turn 19 into the dialogue:

Excerpt 4.
[...]
Oren: I think that the duck changed a long time before global warming, which has only really accelerated in the last centuries.
Eyal: After every ice age there is period of warming up.

Oren: These are not facts, but hypotheses. If that were true than we should have witnessed similar changes in the last two centuries of science.

Eyal: But it is a specific given in the question [i.e., the test item they received] that the living grounds of these proto-ducks were flooded, a very substantive change. I am not ruling out that as a result of the flooding, they met up with other species and there was a hybrid development of some sort.

Oren: Okay, but that does not answer the question why only ducks changed and why there are also other creatures that have webs.

Eyal: But webs are mainly used for swimming, that's a pretty solid fact. These webs make it hard to walk. There is clearly a direct influence of an environmental change here.

Oren: How would I know, I haven't tried.

[…]

This excerpt shows two students that are building and transacting on each others' reasoning, integrating aspects of each other's arguments into their own reasoning and even making concessions (*I am not ruling out that…*). However, even in this short excerpt there are still subtle indications in their choice of language that seem to convey a competitive, rather than a collaborative intent. For example, they use specific rhetoric to strengthen their own standpoint (e.g., *that's a pretty solid fact; these are not facts but hypotheses; clearly*) or resort to sarcasm to dismiss their partner's arguments (*How would I know, I haven't tried…*). Also, their challenges and counterarguments are posed straightforward, without any attempt to soften the conflict and in a way that leaves no doubt about the fact that their viewpoints are directly opposed to one another. The dialogue continued for another 41 conversational turns, and by the end of the dialogue they even came very close to a Darwinian account of evolution. However, neither showed any learning gains on their individual post-tests.

Thus, the difference between CCA and adversarial argumentation is not always only a matter of different epistemic moves (i.e., more disagreements, less consensual construction), but also a matter of *how* the interpersonal interaction is regulated: Are students perceiving and treating the interaction as a collaborative activity in which they work together to achieve superior understanding through critical reasoning, or are they viewing it as a situation in which two antagonists compete to win an argument and only one of them can prevail?

Summary

The previous examples illustrate how consensual discourse and adversarial argumentation each lack some of the defining features of co-constructive, critical argumentation, or CCA: Consensual discourse is constructive and collaborative, yet even though conversational partners often engage in one-sided reasoning and provide elaborate explanations, they do not critically examine their own and each others' ideas. Adversarial argumentation on the other hand is critical, but not constructive, both in the sense that they do not collaboratively construct new explanations, and that their verbal interaction is characterized by interpersonal competition. The anecdotal evidence presented here show how these types of dialogue do not fully exploit the learning opportunities that socio-cognitive conflict has to offer: In consensual reasoning, students fail to consider alternative perspectives to their own and to explore possible flaws in their reasoning. In adversarial argumentation, on the other hand, students rigidly defend their own positions without genuinely trying to incorporate the other's ideas or critique in their own reasoning or to collaboratively work towards a more satisfying solution. In both cases, students are then likely to miss important opportunities for improving their understanding of complex concepts.

More tightly controlled empirical research is needed to (1) further investigate the relation between these different types of argumentative discourse and learning gains; and (2) to study the conditions, instructions and settings that will elicit these different types of discourse. Before such studies can be undertaken, however, the issue of assessment should be addressed: How can these different types of argumentative discourse be reliably distinguished in a systematic manner? In order to quantitatively link dialogue characteristics with learning gains, a coding scheme should be developed that is capable of capturing the critical features of these different dialogue types.

In the remainder of this chapter, I will describe some of our current efforts to develop a coding scheme that is capable of capturing the key features of the epistemic as well as the social-interpersonal dimension of argumentative discourse.

The epistemic and the interpersonal dimensions of argumentative discourse in situ: an assessment tool

The previous review and examples show that the difference between consensual dialogue, adversarial argumentation and CCA is defined by *what* students are saying about the concepts and solutions (i.e., the epistemic dimension), as well as by *how* they communicate with each other (the interpersonal dimension). In order to quantitatively distinguish between these three types of dialogue, we developed a coding scheme that aims to identify and quantify aspects of both the epistemic as well as the interpersonal dimensions of the dialogue.

The data on which this coding scheme was developed consisted of 19 CHAT-mediated, dyadic dialogue protocols (Asterhan et al, submitted). The protocol transcripts included only verbal, written dialogue, without any additional discourse and interaction properties. Turns were automatically parsed by the software interface, that is: each time a discussant posted a new written entry by hitting the "enter" button. As a first step, a distinction was made between turns that directly related to the topic of discussion (on-task) and those in which participants engaged in off-task dialogue or task-regulation efforts (such as, for example, regulating turn-taking, courtesy exchanges, social talk). Then, two complementary, independent coding schemes were applied: The first, which focused on the epistemic dimension of the dialogue, was developed in a previous study (Asterhan & Schwarz, 2009a). The second was developed with a bottom-up verbal analysis approach similar to that described by Chi (1997) and assesses selected aspects of interpersonal regulation. Both schemes use turns as the unit of analysis and both are non-exhaustive. Two independent, trained coders coded 16% of the dialogue transcripts. Measures for inter-rater reliability are $\kappa = 0.87$ (for on/off task), $\kappa = 0.80$ (for epistemic dialogue), and $\kappa = 0.79$ (for interpersonal regulation).

The epistemic dimension

This coding scheme assesses the prevalence of different types of epistemic dialogue moves (De Vries et al, 2002, Ohlsson, 1995) in a conversation. Epistemic dialogue moves are moves in a conversation that are 'concerned with the knowledge and the concepts underlying problem solving rather than the execution of problem solving actions' (De Vries et al, 2002, p. 64; see also Ohlsson, 1995). Asterhan and Schwarz (2009a) distinguished between two different categories of epistemic dialogue moves:

(1) Dialogue moves that reflect *critical reasoning* (hereafter referred to as CR) in which the validity and strength of a thesis or an attack on that thesis is disputed, or any other act of reasoning that is embedded in a dialectical constellation (i.e., challenges, raising doubt, counterarguments, rebuttals, simple oppositions);
(2) Dialogue moves that reflect *consensual construction and validation of explanations* (hereafter referred to as CCVE): These include verbal acts in which ideas are developed, explained and constructed, or in which students provide reasons that are intended to strengthen and validate the epistemic status of a certain explanation in a non-dialectical constellation (i.e., elaborations, explanation construction, justifications, agreements).

This coding scheme does not consider whether the dialogue move is posted in response to a posting by the other or the self. In other words, it only codes the epistemic nature of on-task content: For example, a move of CR could be a challenge to an idea proposed by either the partner or the self. Other dialogue moves, such as for example, simple claims, requests for information or clarification, and repetitions, are not by themselves classified as either CCVE or CR (see Asterhan & Schwarz, 2009a, for more details).

Interpersonal regulation

The aim of the second coding scheme was to assess the different interpersonal-relational goals that students were pursuing during the verbal interaction, and in particular to distinguish between *competitive* versus *collaborative* motives during interaction with a same-status peer. There are many different information sources that could be used to capture these two different motives, such as facial expressions, gesture, body posture, pitch and other auditory features. Partly because many of these information sources are not present in computer-mediated textual communication, we chose to focus on the rhetorical and expressive features of verbal dialogue content and the way these convey information with regard to the interpersonal goal of the speaker and the way that (s)he appears to perceive the situation at that point in the dialogue. The scheme was inspired by existing distinctions from communication theory (Brown & Levinson, 1987; Muntigl & Turnbull, 1998) and previous empirical works (Chiu & Khoo, 2003).

(1) *Competitive interpersonal goal.* This was scored when expressive and rhetorical indicators within a turn reflected a competitive focus on winning at the expense of the other. Examples include verbal content that overtly increased face threat during disagreements, linguistic markers that emphasize interpersonal rather than epistemic conflict, and ego-enhancing moves that promote the self or devalue the partner's contributions or competence.

(2) *Collaborative interpersonal goal.* This was scored when expressive and rhetorical indicators within a turn reflected a constructive, collaborative intent and a focus on joint problem solving and learning. Examples include the use of verbal content to reduce face threat in case of disagreement, self-deprecating statements, linguistic expressions of a shared goal, and expressions aimed at maintaining a pleasant atmosphere and a positive relationship with the partner.

Examples from protocols are presented in Table 12.1. Whereas the epistemic dialogue scheme considered only turns coded as on-task, this scheme coded all turns.

Combining epistemic and interpersonal features of verbal dialogue content

The fine-grained distinctions offered by this dual coding scheme can be useful for research in a number of different ways: First of all, the schemes provide fine-grained information on the turn level and can therefore be employed to study fluctuations in dialogue and social regulation during the interaction phase (e.g., Chiu & Khoo, 2003). Secondly, the detailed information enables empirical investigations into the contingencies between quantitative features of the dialogue and individual measures, such as student learning gains or individual perceptions, or specific task settings, such as different instructions. For example, in a recent study (Asterhan, Butler & Schwarz, submitted) we examined whether different goal instructions affect student discourse when asked to engage in a computer-mediated, argumentative dialogue on the topic of natural selection. All students were instructed to engage in a critical discussion with a same-sex peer, but the goals of this activity were framed differently: In the competitive condition, a critical discussion was presented as a means to win and prevail, whereas in the constructive condition it was framed as a means to promote learning and understanding. The results showed an overall effect

TABLE 12.1 Collaborative and competitive interpersonal regulation: categories and examples

Description	Examples
Collaborative behavior	
Actions that reduce face threats during disagreements	Using hypothetical propositions ("Let's say that …", "What if…"), presenting the opposing view as a third person's ("Darwin would say that…"), presenting opposing view as an additional option ("It is also possible that…"), partial agreement and accrediting ("Yes, that makes sense, but…"), using first-person plural pronouns ("We do not have any evidence to back this up though").
Ego-reducing moves	Hedging own propositions ("I am not sure, but it might be a matter of selection"), accrediting and acknowledging other's contributions ("That's an excellent point", "Your answer is better") and competence ("You know a lot about this stuff"), self-humoring ("Don't give up on me yet, I'll get there")
Linguistic markers of shared responsibility and collaborative intent	Using first-person plural pronouns ("We should try to come up with the most plausible explanation possible"), and overt expressions of collaborative goal.
Attempts at maintaining a pleasant atmosphere and a positive relationship	Using positive emoticons (such as, smileys), encouragements and compliments, courtesies at the beginning ("Hi, how are you, my name is…) and end of conversation ("It was a pleasure talking to you"), using funny wording.
Competitive behavior	
Increase of face threat during disagreements	Using linguistic markers that emphasize the disagreement, such as explicit reference ("No, that is not true") and expressive language ("No, no, no!", "That does not make any sense!!!!!!")
Ego-enhancing moves	Devaluating other's knowledge or competences, either directly ("Your assumptions are all wrong"), by using sarcasm ("And you really believe that brains can evolve…!", "You should have your head checked") or by emphasizing a difference in status and competences ("You just think about that for a while"); or emphasizing the importance of own contributions and attributing progress to self ("That is what I have been saying all along!")
Linguistic markers that emphasize the interpersonal repartition of ideas and conflict	Using first- and second-person singular pronouns (e.g., "*I* think that…., whereas *you* say that…", "Do *you* agree with *my* explanation now?", "No, you don't understand, …"), or overt references (e.g., "Give me a convincing explanation that will cause me to believe you").

TABLE 12.2 Defining different discourse types

	Epistemic dimension		Interpersonal dimension	
	Cons. Constr. & Valid. of Expl.	Critical reasoning	Collaborative markers	Competitive markers
Consensual discourse	High	Low	High	Low
Adversarial argumentation	Low	High	Low	High
Co-constructive critical argumentation	High	High	High	Low

on the dialogue characteristics: When instructions for argumentation were framed in terms of a competitive debate, dialogues were characterized by higher rates of critical reasoning and more competitive markers than when it was framed in terms of an opportunity for learning. Moreover, and in line with the expectation that CCA supports learning in socio-cognitive conflict settings, students whose dialogue was high on both critical as well as constructive discourse features showed substantive cognitive gains and significantly more so than the other groups.

Finally, a coding scheme such as the one presented here can be used to define more detailed profiles for the different types of discourse discussed in this chapter (see Table 12.2): According to the distinctions proposed in this chapter, consensual discourse is characterized by high frequencies of CCVE and collaborative markers and low frequencies of CR and competitive markers. The exact opposite would be true for adversarial argumentation. Co-constructive critical argumentation, on the other hand, is high in CCVE, CR and collaborative markers, and has few competitive markers. The distinctions could also be used to define other dialogue types that were not discussed in this chapter. For example, low frequencies of both CR and CCVE would be characteristic of dialogues that have almost no epistemic engagement with a dialogue partner. Examples of such types of dialogue are, among others, quick consensus seeking (as seen in excerpts 1 and 2) or dialogues in which one student dominates and imposes his/her solution on the other(s) without much further discussion. Further distinctions between different types of epistemic dialogue moves could be used to distinguish between what we termed adversarial argumentation and Mercer's descriptions of *disputational talk* (many repetitions, simple claims and unreasoned oppositions, few reasoned critical moves).

Conclusions

The study of peer collaborative learning has been a central theme in psychological and educational research and considerable progress has been made in the identification of the cognitive mechanisms that enable learning in and from collaborative settings (e.g., Asterhan & Schwarz, 2009a; Coleman, 1998; Gillies, 2004; Howe et al, 2005; Okita & Schwartz, 2006; Shirouzu et al, 2002; Webb et al, 1995). In spite of these advances, a considerable amount of the variance in both group productivity as well as individual learning gains remains unaccounted for. Furthermore, whereas much attention has been given to the underlying socio-cognitive mechanisms, the study of collaborative learning has often neglected the socio-emotional, interpersonal and motivational aspects of these inherently social settings (Salonen et al, 2005). In the present chapter, I have addressed this caveat in one specific subfield of collaborative learning, namely: learning through peer argumentation.

It was proposed that productive argumentation that supports learning of complex content is characterized by both critical inspection of ideas and collaborative knowledge construction, (i.e., critical, co-constructive argumentation). It was furthermore proposed that the reasons behind the difficulty to elicit this ideal type of discourse among students should not only be sought in the cognitive realm, and that researchers of argumentation may benefit greatly from incorporating theoretical concepts and empirical findings from social psychology. In particular, concerns about self-presentation, self-competence and social relations are likely to cause students to disproportionally focus on the social dimension of the conflict instead of its epistemic dimension, leading to two types of discourse that are less productive for learning complex content: consensual discourse (which is void of criticism) and adversarial argumentative discourse (which is void of collaborative knowledge construction). Based on these conceptual differences, a dual coding scheme was proposed to quantitatively assess defining features of the epistemic dimension and the interpersonal regulation of argumentative discourse.

Hopefully, the conceptual distinction and the dialogue analysis tool that were presented here will enable more systematic research into the role of socio-relational and socio-motivational antecedents, outcomes and processes of argumentative discourse. A set of studies that was very recently completed in our lab shows that this is not only feasible but also a very promising line of research: Thus far, we found that students' achievement goals are associated with self-reported differences in argumentative discourse goals (Asterhan et al, 2009), that different argumentative discourse goal instructions significantly alter the type of discourse students engage in (Asterhan et al, submitted) and that controlled differences in argumentative discourse are indeed associated with differences in learning gains (Asterhan & Babichenko, 2012).

These first findings show that the study of argumentation and learning has much to gain from considering these and other 'hot constructs' (Sinatra, 2005) in future empirical research. Findings from such investigations will not only benefit theories of learning, but also have implications for the design of argumentative activities in educational practice. Over the course of twelve school years, most students are rarely exposed to − let alone asked *to engage* in − constructive, yet critical discussions. Standard instructions for group work in classrooms emphasize the consensual, collaborative dimension of interaction and do not encourage critique, or even exploration of different perspectives. Argumentative activities in classrooms, on the other hand, are often times framed as debating contests, instead of deliberation (Kuhn & Crowell, 2011). Students' expectations, goals and norms for argumentative discourse are shaped through participation in such activities. It may therefore be not surprising that many students do not succeed in conducting a constructive, critical discussion, even when directly instructed to do so (Asterhan et al, submitted). The design of argumentative tasks should then be meticulous and take into account the 'hot aspects' of these inherent social situations, in addition to their "cold" cognitive counterparts. A mapping of the different motivational, interpersonal and cognitive factors that affect student argumentation will enable practitioners to make informed design decisions about how to elicit the type of discourse that they are aiming for. We hope to have contributed to this end by conceptually and operationally differentiating between different goals for argumentative discourse and how these may affect learning from argumentation.

References

Asterhan, C. S. C., & Babichenko, M. (2012) 'The effect of discourse style and human presence on conceptual change learning through argumentation', Paper presented at the biannual meeting of the EARLI Special Interest Group (SIG3) on Conceptual Change, September, Trier, Germany.

Asterhan, C. S. C., & Schwarz, B. B. (2007) 'The effects of monological and dialogical argumentation on concept learning in evolutionary theory', *Journal of Educational Psychology*, 99: 626–39.

Asterhan, C. S. C., & Schwarz, B. B. (2009a) 'The role of argumentation and explanation in conceptual change: Indications from protocol analyses of peer-to-peer dialogue', *Cognitive Science*, 3: 373–99.

Asterhan, C. S. C., & Schwarz, B. B. (2009b) 'Transformation of robust misconceptions through peer argumentation', in B. B. Schwarz, T. Dreyfus, & R. Hershkowitz (eds.), *Transformation of Knowledge through Classroom Interaction*, New York, NY: Routledge, Advances in Learning & Instruction series.

Asterhan, C. S. C., Schwarz, B. B., & Butler, R. (2009) 'Inhibitors and facilitators of peer interaction that supports conceptual learning: The role of achievement goal orientations', in N. A. Taatgen & H. van Rijn (eds), *Proceedings of the 31st Annual Conference of the Cognitive Science Society*, Mawah, NJ: Erlbaum.

Asterhan, C. S. C., Schwarz, B. B., & Butler, R. (submitted) 'Adversarial debate or collaborative deliberation? The effect of gender and discourse goal instructions in argumentation for learning', paper submitted for publication.

Baker, M. (2003) 'Computer-mediated interactions for the co-elaboration of scientific notions', in J. Andriessen, M. Baker, & D. Suthers (eds.), *Arguing to Learn: Confronting Cognitions in Computer-Supported Collaborative Learning Environments*, Utrecht: Kluwer Academic Publishers.

Bishop, B. A. & Anderson, C. W. (1990) 'Student conceptions of natural selection and its role in evolution', *Journal of Research in Science Teaching*, 27: 415–27.

Brown, P. & Levinson, S. C. (1987) *Politeness: Some Universals in Language Usage*, Cambridge: Cambridge University Press.

Butera, F. & Mugny, G. (1995) 'Conflict between incompetences and influence of a low-expertise source in hypothesis testing', *European Journal of Social Psychology*, 25: 457–62.

Carnevale, P. J. & Probst, T. M. (1998) 'Social values and social conflict in creative problem solving and categorization', *Journal of Personality and Social Psychology*, 74: 1300–09.

Chi, M.T. H. (1997) 'Quantifying qualitative analyses of verbal data: A practical guide', *Journal of the Learning Sciences*, 6: 271–315.

Chi, M. T. H., DeLeeuw, N., Chiu, M., & Lavancher, C. (1994) 'Eliciting self-explanations improves understanding', *Cognitive Science*, 18: 439–77.

Chin, C. & Osborne, J. (2010) 'Supporting argumentation through students' questions: Case studies in science classrooms', *Journal of the Learning Sciences*, 19: 230–84.

Chiu, M. M., & Khoo, L. (2003) 'Rudeness and status effects during group problem solving', *Journal of Educational Psychology*, 95: 506–23.

Coleman, E. B. (1998) 'Using explanatory knowledge during problem solving in science', *Journal of the Learning Sciences*, 7: 387–427.

Darnon, C., Doll, S., & Butera, F. (2007) 'Dealing with a disagreeing partner: Relational and epistemic conflict elaboration', *European Journal of Psychology of Education*, 22: 227–42.

Darnon, C., Harackiewicz, Butera, F., Mugny, G. & Quiamzade, A. (2007) 'Performance-approach and performance-avoidance goals: When uncertainty makes a difference', *Personality and Social Psychology Bulletin*, 33: 813–27. DOI: 10.1177/0146167207301022.

De Vries, E., Lund, K., & Baker, M. (2002) 'Computer-mediated epistemic dialogue: Explanation and argumentation as vehicles for understanding scientific notions, *Journal of the Learning Sciences,* 11: 63–103.

Doise, W., & Mugny, G. (1984) *The Social Development of the Intellect*, Oxford: Pergamon Press.

Doise, W., Mugny, G. & Perret-Clermont, A.-N. (1975) 'Social interaction and the development of cognitive operations', *European Journal of Social Psychology*, 5: 376–83.

Driver, R., Newton, P., & Osborne, J. (2000) 'Establishing the norms of scientific argumentation in classrooms', *Science Education*, 84: 287–312.

Duschl, R. A., & Osborne, J. (2002) 'Supporting and promoting argumentation discourse in science education', *Studies in Science Education*, 38: 39–72.

Erduran, S., & Jimenez-Aleixandre, M. P. (eds) (2008) *Argumentation in Science Education: Perspectives from Classroom-Based Research*, Dordrecht: Springer.

Frijters, S., ten Dam, G. & Rijlaarsdam, G. (2008) 'Effects of dialogic learning on value-loaded critical thinking', *Learning and Instruction*, 18: 66–82.

Gillies, R. M. (2004) 'The effects of communication training on teachers'and students' verbal behaviours during cooperative learning', *International Journal of Educational Research*, 41: 257–79.

Hijzen, D., Boekaerts, M. & Vedder, P. (2007) 'Exploring the links between students' engagement in cooperative learning, their goal preferences and appraisals of instructional conditions in the classroom', *Learning and Instruction*, 17: 673–87.

Howe, C. (2009) 'Collaborative group work in middle childhood: Joint construction, unresolved contradiction and the growth of knowledge', *Human Development*, 39: 71–94.

Howe, C., McWilliam, D. & Cross, G. (2005) 'Chance favours only the prepared mind: Incubation and the delayed effects of peer collaboration', *British Journal of Psychology*, 96: 67–93.

Jimenez-Aleixandre, M. P. (1992) 'Thinking about theories or thinking with theories?: A classroom study with natural selection', *International Journal of Science Education*, 14: 51–61.

Johnsson, D. W. & Johnsson, R. T. (2009) 'Energizing learning: The instructional power of conflict', *Educational Researcher*, 38: 37–51.

Kapur, M. (2008) 'Productive failure', *Cognition & Instruction*, 26: 379–424. DOI: 10.1080/07370000802212669.

Keefer, M. W., Zeitz, C. M. & Resnick, L. B. (2000) 'Judging the quality of peer-led student dialogues', *Cognition and Instruction*, 18: 53–81.

Kroll, B. M. (2005) 'Arguing differently', *Pedagogy*, 5: 37–60.

Kuhn, D. (1999) *The Skills of Argument*, Cambridge, MA: Cambridge University Press.

Kuhn, D., & Crowell, A. (2011) 'Dialogic argumentation as a vehicle for developing young adolescents? thinking', *Psychological Science*, 22: 545–552

McGarty, C., Turner, J. C., Oakes, P. J. & Haslam, S. A. (1993) 'The creation of uncertainty in the influence process: The roles of stimulus information and disagreement with similar others', *European Journal of Social Psychology*, 23: 17–38.

Means, M. L. & Voss, J. F. (1996) 'Who reasons well? Two studies of informal reasoning among children of different grade, ability, and knowledge levels', *Cognition & Instruction*, 14: 139–79.

Mercer, N. (1996) 'The quality of talk in children's collaborative activity in the classroom', *Learning and Instruction*, 6: 359–75.

Muntigl, P. & Turnbull, W. (1998) 'Conversational structure and facework in arguing', *Journal of Pragmatics*, 29: 225–56.

Nussbaum, E. M. (2008) 'Collaborative Discourse, Argumentation, and Learning: Preface and Literature Review', *Contemporary Educational Psychology*, 33: 345–359.

Nussbaum, E. M., Sinatra, G. M. & Poliquin, A. (2008) 'Role of epistemic beliefs and scientific argumentation in science learning', *International Journal of Science Education*, 30: 1977–99.

Nussbaum, E. M., & Sinatra, G. M. (2003) 'Argument and conceptual engagement', *Contemporary Educational Psychology*: 28, 384–395.

Ohlsson, S. (1995) 'Learning to do and learning to understand: A lesson and a challenge for cognitive modeling,' in P. Reimann and H. Spada, (eds.), *Learning in Humans and Machines: Towards an Interdisciplinary Learning Science*, Oxford, UK: Elsevier.

Okita, S. Y., Schwartz, D. L. (2006) When observation beats doing: Learning by teaching. Proceedings of the 7th International Conference of the Learning Sciences (ICLS), Bloomington, IN.

Osborne, J. (2010) 'Arguing to learn: The role of collaborative, critical discourse', *Science*, 328: 463–66. DOI: 10.1126/science.1183944.

Pool, G. J., Wood, W., & Leck, K. (1998) 'The self-esteem motive in social influence: Agreement with valued majorities and disagreement with derogated minorities', *Journal of Personality and Social Psychology*, 75: 967–75.

Reznitskaya, A., Anderson, R. C., McNurlen, B., Nguyen-Jahiel, K., Archodidou, A. & Kim, S. (2001) 'Influence of oral discussion on written argument', *Discourse Processes*, 32: 155–7.

Salonen, P., Vauras, M. & Efklides, A. (2005) 'Social interaction – What can it tell us about metacognition and coregulation in learning?', *European Psychologist*, 10: 199–208.

Schwartz, D. L. & Martin, T. (2004) 'Inventing to prepare for future learning: The hidden efficiency of encouraging original student production in statistical instruction', *Cognition & Instruction*, 22: 129–84.

Schwarz, B. B., & Asterhan, C. S. C. (2010) 'Argumentation and Reasoning', in K. Littleton, C. Wood, & J. Kleine Staarman (eds), *International Handbook of Psychology in Education*, Bingley, UK: Emerald Group Publishing.

Schwarz, B. B., Neuman, Y., & Biezuner, S. (2000) 'Two wrongs may make a right...if they argue together!', *Cognition & Instruction*, 18: 461–94.

Shirouzu, H., Miyake, N., & Masukawa, H. (2002) 'Cognitively active externalization for situated reflection', *Cognitive Science*, 26: 469–501.

Shtulman, A. (2006) 'Qualitative differences between naive and scientific theories of evolution', *Cognitive Psychology*, 52: 170–94.

Sinatra, G. M. (2005) The "warming trend" in conceptual change research: The legacy of Paul Pintrich, *Educational Psychologist*, 40: 107–15.

Smith, K., Johnsson, D.W. & Johnsson, R.T. (1981) 'Can conflict be constructive? Controversy versus concurrence seeking in learning groups', *Journal of Educational Psychology*, 73: 651–63.

Tetlock, P. (1992) 'The impact of accountability on judgment and choice: Toward a social contingency model', in M. Zanna (ed.), *Advances in Experimental Social Psychology*, Vol. 25, San Diego, CA: Academic Press.

Tjosvold, D. & Johnsson, D.W. (1978) 'Controversy within a cooperative or competitive context and cognitive perspective-taking', *Contemporary Educational Psychology*, 3: 376–86.

Van Eemeren, F. H., Grootendorst, R., Henkenmans, F. S., Blair, J. A., Johnson, R. H, Krabb, E. C., Plantin, C., Walton, D. N., Willard, C. A., Woods, J. & Zarefsky, D. (1996) *Fundamentals of Argumentation Theory: A Handbook of Historical Background and Contemporary Developments*, Hillsdale, NJ: Erlbaum.

Walton, D. (2006) *Fundamentals of Critical Argumentation: Critical Reasoning and Argumentation*, New York, NY: Cambridge University Press.

Webb, N. M., Troper, J. D., & Fall, R. (1995) 'Constructive activity and learning in collaborative small groups', *Journal of Educational Psychology*, 87: 406–23.

Wegerif, N., Mercer, N. & Dawes, L. (1999) 'From social interaction to individual reasoning: an empirical investigation of a possible socio-cultural model of cognitive development', *Learning & Instruction*: 9, 493–516.

Weinberger, A., & Fischer, F. (2006) 'A framework to analyze argumentative knowledge construction in computer-supported collaborative learning', *Computers & Education*, 46: 71–95.

13

"LOOK WHO'S TALKING"

Identity and emotions as resources to historical peer reasoning

Baruch B. Schwarz and Tsafrir Goldberg

Introduction

In the following chapter we present a discussion of the place of identity and emotion in argumentative learning. We support it with a case analysis tracking the impact of students' identity in the framing of goals, arguments and cognitive moves during peer learning of an identity-relevant historical controversy. While discussing this case, we stress the importance of relating the "talking" or learning in discussion to the issue of "who is" the discussant-learner and how his identity and emotions impact on interaction. The call to "look" at who it is that talks is both an analytic suggestion and an educational didactic advice. In the specific case study presented, which is derived from historical thinking, research awareness of speaker identity carries parallel significance for the content and process of learning.

Global warming has recently spread over the Learning Sciences community. This community has progressively moved from the study of the "cold" solipsist logical learner, to that of the specialist learner, the situated learner, and finally to the "warmer" image of the learner as an intentional agent. The intentional learner intends, wills to learn, self-regulates his learning, sets his goals, self-monitors and self-regulates his own goals, even his own motivation and the contextual features of his learning, including social engagement. A good example of this warming trend concerns conceptual change. The study of this process has been borne out of Swiss Piagetian glaciers, as cognitive conflict has primarily been unanimously recognized as the central mechanism for triggering change. However, several scientists (Pintrich, 1999; Pintrich, Marx & Boyle, 1993; Sinatra, 2005; Sinatra & Pintrich, 2003) have considered self-efficacy, epistemological beliefs, interest in a specific topic, goal orientation, or control beliefs as possibly affecting conceptual change in socio-cognitive conflict settings. The warming literature of conceptual change begins to consider the above list as constituents of conceptual change rather than factors affecting it: the need to overcome a conflict does not originate only from a cognitive discomfort (as Piaget thought), but from, say, the belief that knowledge can be constructed by the self through rules of inquiry, the interest that one has for a certain topic, the willingness to collaborate with disagreeing peers, to engage in an activity in which one should be ready to modify initial views, etc. More generally, conceptual change has been recognized as of a multifaceted interactive nature (Sinatra & Mason, 2008).

But there is more. The warming trend not only encompasses intentions and wills but also currently heads towards the emotional states of the agent. A famous early bird in this trend is of course Csíkszentmihályi's book, *Flow: The Psychology of Optimal Experience* (1990). Csíkszentmihályi identifies emotional states that explain (lack of) learning gains when students engage in tasks: arousal, anxiety, worry, apathy, boredom, relaxation, control and flow are, according to Csíksentmihály as many emotional states as learners can feel when engaging in tasks, which depend on a match between the level of their skills and the challenge that the task offers them. People are most happy when they are in the emotional state of flow – a state of concentration or absorption with the activity at hand and the situation. The flow state is an optimal state of intrinsic motivation, where one is fully immersed in what he or she is doing (see <http://en.wikipedia.org/wiki/Mihaly_Csikszentmihalyi>). This is a feeling everyone has at times, characterized by a feeling of great absorption, engagement, fulfillment, and skill — and during which temporal concerns (time, food, ego-self, etc.) are typically ignored. Csíkszentmihályi described flow as "being completely involved in an activity for its own sake. The ego falls away. Time flies. Every action, movement, and thought follows inevitably from the previous one, the whole being is involved, and the using of skills to the utmost." To achieve a flow state, a balance must be struck between the challenge of the task and the skills of the performer.

This global warming trend in learning towards positive psychology, towards a quest for flow, hides a subliminal message, the fact that the recognition of the importance of emotional states in learning situations is, except perhaps for the flow state, somehow a threat, the opposite of rationality and clear perception, an obstacle to professional and disciplinary practice, while the notion of the discipline itself connotes a harnessing of emotion and impulse. And indeed, researchers in the Learning Sciences that have capitalized on principles of positive psychology have focused on well-designed tasks in which instants of flow could be detected. However, especially in social interactions, the threat of emotional warming up is ubiquitous: According to social cognition theory (Fiske, 2002), emotions such as belonging and esteem seem to override clairvoyance. The need to identify with a group and to protect group esteem is associated with perceptual flaws in evidence evaluation, selective sampling and attributional bias (Pettigrew, 1998).

There is hardly a discipline in which emotional states are more pronounced than history. Of course, domains such as mathematics often involve strong feelings of failure, frustration, low self-efficacy (Bandalos, Yates & Thorndike-Christ, 1993, Fennema, 1989) and subsequent disengagement in individual and collective tasks.

The case of history constitutes an even richer ground in which cognitively challenging tasks such as elaborating historical interpretations on the basis of multiple texts are dealt with in socially loaded issues and in a social context that arouses strong emotions. However, in spite of the centrality of emotion in history learning, this issue has been hardly studied. Researchers have recognized the impact of collective memories on individuals to show that students' attribution of significance to past events is mediated by family and ethnic collective memories (Seixas, 1994), by students' racial and social background (Epstein, 2000), or by media conveying a collective memory (Wineburg, Mosborg & Porat, 2001). Also, educational research has paid growing attention to two practices that are quite prone to social and emotional influences: (1) the ways students evaluate and interpret historical evidence (Lee & Ashby, 2000; Wineburg & Schneider, 2010); (2) the use and intgeration of multiple historical sources. (Hynd, 1999; Perfetti, Britt, Rouet, Georgi & Mason, 1994). However, research did not focus on whether, or how, collective memory functions as a socio-cultural tool that guides and facilitates individuals' historical thinking. Current research on history education tackled a wide scope of practices such as causal explanation, narrative construction, and evaluation and use of multiple sources (Stearns, Seixas & Wineburg, 2000), in detachment from group identity and collective memory, and as such in detachment from emotion. The interplay between historical memory, collectives and the individuals learning which is at the heart of historical education has been neglected.

We argue in this chapter that this detachment mutilates the study of history reasoning, especially in adolescents in quest of their identity. For them, their group identity and their collective memory are crucial resources that are brought to the surface in historical issues: when adolescent interpreting identity-relevant situations, they adopt three approaches. The first describes a primary concern with the adaptive development of private self-attributes in the relevant social environment. This growth-oriented approach is characterized by the status of moratorium and by the evolutive or the informational oriented styles of identity formation. The action that this frame calls for includes internal and external exploration such as self-reflection, information-gathering, and in-depth processing that aim to advance informed identity-relevant decisions concerning values, beliefs and goals (Leary, 2007).

The second approach describes a primary concern with validation and enhancement of the self along normative standards that the person adopted uncritically. This validation-oriented approach is based primarily in the motive for self-enhancement and characterized by the status of foreclosure, or by the normative-oriented identity style, and is based in a self that comprises commitments to values, beliefs, and goals that were adopted from significant others' expectations. The action called for by this approach involves conforming and attempting to excel according to normative standards. It also involves avoiding and rejecting experiences and information that seem to threaten perceptions of one's self as measuring-up to or as excelling along these standards.

The third category describes a general lack of a stable coherent core of personal beliefs and values and the reliance on situated indicators by significant others as standards for self-perceptions and for action. Characterized in the literature as the diffusion status, or as the diffuse/avoidant-oriented identity style, this avoidant-oriented approach to identity is based in a self that is fragmented and that is staked on the peer group's perceptions and ascription of roles. It calls for the avoidance of meaningful engagement in identity-relevant tasks and deference to the situated norms of the significant peer group for decisions and action.

Although the first approach is more valuable than the second and the second considered as superior to the third, adolescents can and do have in their repertoire all three approaches to identity. However, adolescents differ from each other with regard to the primary approach they would employ in identity-relevant situations. Situations might be able to override the adolescent's primary identity-processing strategy by strongly highlighting self-worth or by providing a very secure environment in which making mistakes has little consequence. Our claim is that history education can provide opportunities for overriding primary-processing strategies. Historical situations can confront adolescents with other adolescents from outgroup identities with different collective memories, but also with the historical discipline, the critical reading of texts. These confrontations, we argue, invite the exploration and the self-enhancement approach at the same time in a burst of emotions and biases, for the sake, as we will also argue, of the adolescents' identity development.

In spite of the absence of systematic research on the interplay between historical reasoning, collective memory and identity formation, there are several pioneering studies suggesting interesting historical reasoning biases may be related to issues of identity and the collective past. As social psychological research reveals, the implications of an historical issue may lead to group and ego protective biases in the individual's recollection or evaluation of information about the collective past (Doosje & Branscombe, 2003; Roccas, Klar & Liviatan, 2006). Gottlieb, Wineburg, and Zakai (2005) have shown how experts' national and denominational identity influenced their inquiry stance towards historical issues they had studied. The significance they attributed to the issue influenced in turn the epistemic strategies they chose in confronting evidence about it.

While such epistemic inconsistence may be judged as flawed learning, Gottlieb and his colleagues (Gottlieb et al., 2005) viewed it quite differently. They interpreted such "epistemic switches" as expressions of sophisticated maintenance of balance between cultural and academic commitments. In line with this interpretation we would like to further explore the impact of identity and identity-related emotions on learning. We also rely on our findings about argumentative progress being accompanied by strong identity influences (Goldberg, Schwarz & Porat, 2011) whose biases do not necessarily hinder disciplinary practices.

Such findings differ from critical thinking expectations for "open-minded thinking independent of prior beliefs" (Stanovich & West, 1997). What motivated individuals to protect their group's cherished narratives of collective memory from contradicting evidence were their very prior beliefs. Research shows such strongly held views may also lead to strong "confirmation biases" that guide evidence evaluation and accumulation (Nickerson, 1998). Initial "story models" about past events tend to make individuals filter and downgrade evidence contradicting them (Kuhn, Weinstock & Flaton, 1994). This may even lead to enhancing confidence in own version when encountering counter-evidence (McKenzie, Lee & Chen, 2002). However, taken from a wider cultural and activity perspective, these "diversions" from objectivity norms represent a use of cultural tools. Identity and commitment are not just biases but furnish the essential motivation and goal without which no active use of cultural tools takes place.

The potential of argumentative activities for learning to reason in history

The various biases that may arise in historical reasoning do not augur, a priori, occasions for learning gains in rich social interactions involving students with different views since the social interactions risk exacerbating these biases. However, researchers and educators have advocated learning history through interaction and group discussion for a long time (Lee & Asby, 2000). But this very general advice is not precise enough. A growing literature in the Learning Sciences indicates that social interaction is productive when students are presented with multiple texts that convey contradicting "facts" or views, and are acculturated to dialogic talk/argumentation (Schwarz, 2003; see a review in Schwarz, 2009).

Indeed, some research was conducted on actual instances of discussion and collaborative learning in history (Fassulo, Girardet & Pontecorvo, 1998; Epstein, 2000) or of learning of historical debates and controversies (Rouet et al., 1998). In those studies rational discourse seems to dominate and implicitly serves as a model of good talk for learning history in classroom interaction. In light of the numerous biases that may srise in historical reasoning, these studies may be surprising. However, a close scrutiny of the issues discussed in these studies indicates that the researchers created conditions for a "clean" cognitive conflict without "messing it up" with identity and emotional side effects. Issues such as the depiction of the Huns by a late Roman historian (in Fassulo et al., 1998) or the causes of Panamanian independence (in Rouet et al., 1998) are quite removed from students' historical memory. Even when facilitating acknowledgement of conflicting views, these topics didn't have group identity implications. When such issues did come up they were referred to as a diversion from normative reasoning (as in Perfetti et al.'s, (1994) mocking reference to participant which consistently identified with official US stand as "the ideologist"). With such "cold" topics, it is not surprising that biases did not play a central role...

In a series of studies we conducted, and of which the present study is a part, we deliberately "heated the atmosphere" with socially charged historical issues. Students engaged in historical learning practices such as prolonged evaluation of sources. In addition they participated in ethnically mixed-group discussions of a controversial interethnic relations issue on the basis of these sources. Social identity implications of the issue intervened and enlivened argumentation, motivating and promoting flow in learning. Students progressed from initial states of mutual threat and low-level use of cognitive tools to higher efficacy and more developed argumentation. The task of interpreting the past in light of evidence at hand came to be closer to their capacities. Participants managed to keep themselves aroused, overcoming anxieties which stemmed from encounter with historical uncertainty. However, contrary to the idealized notion of flow as harmonious learning for its own sake, high motivation for discussion and argument elaboration was fuelled by social identity needs, conflict and competition.

As we shall see, students' engagement with the learning task was also an engagement in the enactment of identity and the defense of group esteem. Therefore we see the search for a better explanation of the past coming with, and initially driven by the quest for a better representation of in-group. But gradually, as peers challenge each other's interpretations they master the tools of historical discourse. Participants in discussion elaborate their argumentative and disciplinary moves and, in turn, sometimes even adopt more impartial, normative practices. Learners use various stratagems to attune to social identity needs, sometimes elaborating these to a point of turning against themselves.

In our first study (Goldberg, Schwarz & Porat, 2008), we investigated the effect of the vitality of historical issues in collective memory on students' history learning processes and products. Twelfth-grade students of different ethnic background participated in two historical problem-solving learning tasks based on argumentative design. The historical issues were found to differ in their vitality in collective memory as signified by students' consensus, certainty, and connections to the present. Additional analyses showed effects of issue vitality on narrative and argumentative change, and on the relation of historical source evaluation with narrative change. An interaction was found between issue vitality and ethnicity in the source evaluation: more vital collective memory narratives were more resistant to change and more prone to ethnic identity bias.

This first study, as well as the research findings in social psychology succinctly referred to above, suggests that collective memory and collective identity bias learning.[1] However, a closer analysis of learning in the context of a vital collective memory issue (Israel's "Melting Pot" policy of immigration absorption) revealed effects for design and identity (Goldberg, Schwarz & Porat, 2011). Even against the backdrop of a consensual collective memory narrative, argumentative condition produced improvement in the argumentative level of writing and promoted narrative change. Surprisingly, in the context of strongly held collective memory narratives, no evidence of confirmation bias was found in students' evaluation of sources and in final narratives. However, identity did seem to have strong impact, as the narratives of students from different ethnicities differed in the frequency, direction and degree of changes. Narrative change apparently bolstered in-group image. Argumentative design seemed to facilitate adoption of new perspectives, while social identity needs seemed to motivate it. In other words, emotional factors which could be thought as detrimental to historical learning seemed to boost it.

The above effects were traced on the basis of pre-post learning outcomes comparisons. They may attest to the formative influence of identity but not to the ways it is enacted during the process of learning and arguing. Since we view both argumentation and identity as interpersonal, time has come to delve into interactions instead of relying solely on interpretations based on inferential statistics. In the present chapter, we scrutinize students' interactions and confrontations in collaborative learning of a charged historical issue in ethnically mixed groups. We explore how emotions were intertwined in the learning of an ethnicity-relevant historical issue, heating up, but also promoting reasoning processes.

A case study to inquire the role of emotions in learning a charged historical issue in argumentative activities

The case we analyze is part of a quasi-experimental study on historical thinking, identity and collective memory among high-school students. Twelfth-graders of diverse ethnicities from a nonselective Israeli state public school studied a historical controversy with high relevance to their ethnic identity (elaborated below). The study was based on a "pre-post" design with students writing their narratives and arguments about a historical controversy, prior to and following a learning intervention. The intervention was a complex learning task designed to promote use of historical disciplinary practices. Students received coaching in evidence evaluation and contextualization, performed an individual evaluation of a series of conflicting sources, and engaged in small group discussion of a historical controversy on the basis of the sources. Discussions were peer led and audio-taped by discussants.

The historical disciplinary practices and stances to which we shall refer in our analysis are (1) *historical empathy*, (2) *the use of evidence in argumentation*, and (3) *evaluation of reliability*. In our definition and implementation of these concepts we adopt a loosely developmental approach. However, since we refer to practices or strategies, the levels of development do not necessarily refer to inner capacities or intelligence. Higher levels mainly reflect a practice enabling the learner to solve or interpret more complex problems.

Historical empathy refers to the ability to put oneself in "the other's shoes", and to reconstruct historical agency in terms of mentality, context and intentionality. *Historical empathy* ranges from inability to view historical figures as intentional agents, to the ability to explain historical agents' actions in reference to their inherent intellectually deficiency in comparison with the present. At a less stereotypical (though not much more disciplinary) level, one may perform a presentist reconstruction of historical agents' motives and mentality according to one's current consciousness. At the more proficient end of the continuum, a picture of the historical agents' mind and motives is developed taking into account their context, their inherent otherness and uniqueness of their "zeitgeist", the knowledge and alternatives accessible to them (Lee, Ashby & Dickinson, 1995). It is reasonable to assume that the development of historical empathy accompanies moral and cognitive development from egocentricity to acknowledgement of others' values as in

Kohlberg's "sixth stage" (Colby et al., 1983). Empathy, or perspective taking, is one of the highly advocated and operationally under-defined concepts in history education (Barton & Levstik, 2004). We shall attempt in our analysis to exemplify its expression in students' interpretation of historical agents' actions.

Evidence use and *evidence reliability evaluation* are two potentially, though not inherently related skills. *Evidence use* refers to reasoning on the basis of evidence. At its lowest level, evidence use is not deemed necessary to back historical claims. Higher up is the reference to generalized collective memory images. A more proficient use of evidence would be citation of a historical source relevant to the claim made. In the full disciplinary level a learner combines sources on the basis of relevance to claim and of evidence reliability. However, a learner may ignore the reliability of evidence, unintentionally or for a deliberate rhetorical reason (Rouet et al., 1998).

Evidence reliability evaluation is a dialectical process in which the learner determines in what way and to what degree the information contained in a source may be biased or flawed. At its lowest level all evidence is taken as true with no reference to reliability or bias. At higher levels, evidence reliability is evaluated through content and style cues, corroboration and contextualization (Lee, Ashby & Dickinson, 1995; Wineburg & Fournier, 1994).

These disciplinary practices of rational inquiry in history seem trivially prone to social and emotional influences. Evidence evaluation is one of the preliminary practices of the historian, prior to narrative synthesis, and one for which impartial and rational reasoning is expected. The sampling of the sources is expected to be performed according to relevance and to refer the widest variety of accounts and views avoiding possible selection biases. However, both evaluation of evidence and sampling have been shown to reveal strong in-group preferences (Doosje, Spears & Koomen, 1995). Perspective taking, historical empathy and the discourse of intentionality and agency, all cherished goals of social studies, may be seen as especially prone to attributional biases. It should be noted that the process of reconstructing the historical agents' consciousness inherently consists of attributing them intentions and constructing mini- or meta-"theories of mind". Biases, such as the tendency to attribute inner foci of control to out-group actions with negative effects while exempting in-group from responsibility to similar deeds, may therefore easily distort these disciplinary practices (Doosje & Branscombe, 2003). Thus we may rightly suspect emotion to have detrimental effects on the acquisition of disciplinary norms and practices in history. Such caution may all the more be justified in the case of historical issues related to intergroup contact and conflict. Indeed, there is evidence that history teachers tend to evade such charged and many times controversial issues to avoid emotional excesses. Our first study (Goldberg et al., 2008) indicates that learners perform differently in the different contexts of charged and more neutral historical issues. We would like to claim, however, that socially charged issues, and the "hot" cognition accompanying them, while fueled by biases, may actually foster such cherished practices as evidence evaluation and perspective taking. We shall try to exemplify and elaborate this claim through one in-depth analysis of an unguided small group discussion on a "hot" issue.

The following protocol is taken from a discussion on Israel's cultural policy of immigrant absorption in it first decade – the "Melting Pot" policy. This policy was initiated by the Zionist leadership of Israel which at the time constituted mainly of the "Ashkenazi" – European Jews. The policy sought to educate immigrants in the image of the "New-Jew" (secular, productive citizen capable of armed defense of the country). Accordingly educators sought to eradicate the "corrupting influences of exile" such as Diaspora Jewish traditions and religiosity.

The diffusion of modernist pioneering culture and erasure of traditions aroused tension between veterans and new immigrants. Antagonism to absorption policies, most notable among the more traditional "Mizrahi" ("oriental") Jews, led to a series of conflicts, the earliest of which was a controversy about the "uniform education" institutions in the Yemenite immigrants' camps to which many of the documents that the students read referred. Conflicting accounts of the methods and impact reflect both the historical and the current historiographic debates on the policy. This historical issue carried relevance to the identity and family history of our research participants in general and particularly to the two discussants presented below.

Research was performed in an integrative school situated in a low socio-economic status neighborhood of an Israeli city. The school manages to attract also students from outside the neighborhood due to its vision of integration and social commitment and its comparatively high academic standards. Most of the students from the school neighborhood come from low-income, politically and denominationally conservative Mizrahi families. Their parents or grandparents immigrated to Israel from Muslim countries during the mass immigration of the 1950s, the era of the Melting Pot policy. Many of the students from outside the neighborhood come from middle-class, liberal left secular Ashkenazi families. In many cases their origins can be traced to the labor movement-affiliated founding elites who emigrated from Europe in the pre-state era and were involved in the initiation of the Melting Pot policy.

Yakov is a descendant of immigrants from Yemen and Kurdistan, whose grandparents lived in the transfer camps of the great immigration period. Prior to the discussion he reported their loss of a baby due to the harsh conditions. He also participated in an academic program aimed at empowering students from the school neighborhood. Gadi is the son of a wealthy entrepreneur, ex-brigadier in the Israeli army, whose family came from Poland and Germany in the 1930s. The family participated in the creation of the pioneering Socialist-Zionist collective settlements and in the war of independence of 1948, and lost one of its sons in the battles.

As we can understand, the two students could be seen in some way as embodying the sides of the interethnic relations and controversy arising from the "Melting Pot" policy. Thus there was reason to expect that discussing the historical topics would prompt identity issues governing not just cognition but also emotions. The students reached the discussion phase following a learning intervention which consisted of a coaching exercise in critical historical thinking. Following it students read and evaluated conflicting sources about the "Melting Pot" policy, which they had at their disposal during discussion. The students were instructed to discuss and try to convince each other towards a joint answer to two discussion questions: "Did uniform education institutes promote equality or was it an expression of discrimination?" and "was uniform education an essential measure for the state or a destructive political takeover?". Capital lettered words indicate rising of voice. Three dots mark hesitation or short pause.

> G: [reading the discussion question aloud] Did uniform education institutes promote equality or was it an expression of discrimination?
> Y: in my opinion it was an expression of discrimination and it hurt the immigrants because they came to make a kind of western approach, more than oriental. They tried to harm all of oriental culture this way.
> G: why do you think that they tried to hurt? Don't you think they tried to help them integrate?

As we may see, Gadi assumed the facilitator's role right at the start, along with the neutral inquisitive tone fitting it. Yakov immediately takes a more emotional, one-sided stance, attributing the initiators a destructive intention (in a classical example of attribution bias). Gadi as yet does not oppose. Instead, he keeps on taking the role of facilitator, inquires and suggests weighing an alternative. Such an instance of the discussant from the more privileged ethnicity taking the role of the "protocol and process" keeper is known from other inter-group encounter studies (Ben-David Kolikant, 2011). In some ways it seems to replicate power relations and to curb emotional overflow.

It should be noted that both students do not find it necessary to back their claims with data from the sources. Neither student refers to the historical agents' perceptions. At the same time they do not really differentiate between actions, outcomes and intentions. Such a differentiation as well as reference to agents' mentalities is assumed necessary for historical understanding, empathy and narrative construction (Shemilt, 2000). This superficiality at first dominates the scene:

> Y: they could have helped them integrate with an approach conserving tradition. But they didn't. They drew them apart from their families
> G: but there was no problem of tradition. After all they let people…people suddenly…it's not that people…they simply put them in a certain framework which already existed.

Thus Yakov assumes that if a policy is ethnocentric its initiators *intended* to harm others, not differentiating between acts and intentions. At the same time Gadi argues the educational framework "simply…already existed", ignoring the importance of how immigrants may have perceived it. It is worth noting that as Yakov continually attacks the founders of the state and their policy, Gadi gradually leaves his neutral stance, falling into a defensive apologetic. However, and somewhat unexpectedly, the discussion did not simply regress into an exchange of unsupported assaults and defenses. As emotion and group esteem came to dominate the discussion, students elaborated their claims. In the following exchange of turns, Yakov makes his first specific reference to information from the sources to back his argument. Moreover, he refers specifically to the immigrants' consciousness and perceptions which Gadi ignored:

> Y: They certainly hurt their religion in dancing with girls. They did many things which hurt their religion which is …their tradition, with songs and folkdance which aren't oriental dances and they didn't let them do what they want.
>
> G: In my opinion it was in order for them to integrate. What's this thing about folkdance, what…think you were coming. They're putting you in school with all kinds of people and then everybody goes dancing and only you stand aside.

As we can see in his response, Gadi himself tries to reconstruct the Melting Pot policy initiators' intentions. He does this through assuming how the initiators perceived the immigrant children's feelings. Historical empathy is here less than fully elaborated since it is based on a presentist or universal generalization rather than on sources and context. In other words, Gadi's view of children's aversion to being exceptional and marginal is a universal phenomenon which existed at all times, making reference to evidence redundant. However, it is clearly a significant elaboration of his former simplistic apologetics. This argumentative move puts up in fact two "nested" mental models or theories of mind. The prominent one is the reconstruction of the Mizrahi immigrant children's presumed feeling of rejection due to lack of acquaintance with folkdance. This insight into out-group members' mind is used to explain what took place in the minds of the Ashkenazi initiators of the policy. This move lightens these members of the discussant's in-group more positively.

As noted in many cognitive performance and development studies progression to higher phases isn't linear or irreversible. As Yakov criticizes the veteran Israeli educators' choice of folkdance he makes use of counterfactual arguments. In these moves (usually considered far from disciplinary norms) he more clearly relates to his ethnic identity as a descendant of Yemenite and Kurd immigrants. This is also where Gadi's use of analogy denotes a more specific and closer relationship with Yakov. When Gadi entices Yakov to compare the immigrant students' emotions with what Yakov would feel coming to a new school, he also in some way relates to Yakov as a representative of the Mizrahi group in school.

Along with the surfacing of identity comes the heating of emotions. This growing oppositional tone of conversation is notable as we shall see for it signifies a departure from norms of consensus; norms to which apparently students would have liked to stick, as we will later point out in the closing lines of the conversation. Under Yakov's continuing "assaults", Gadi, whose confusion and frustration are quite evident, reverts at first to short "excuses" that are not exactly convincing:

Y: Why don't they dance Yemenite step, why don't they dance the Kurdish
    Zorna? Why don't they do all these things?
G: Dunno….cause it wasn't usual?
Y: Unusual? It was usual to dance folkdance in the transfer camp?
G: I don't think it was. I'm also not sure they knew how to dance

Eventually the dance skirmish drives Gadi over the edge. But just as he is about to
explode he makes his yet most elaborate expression of contextual data-based historical thinking:

G: Folkda-dance. Listen, there's some one here saying that at the times when
    they didn't have food and were dying of starvation and all that, all that
    united them was folkdance. The spirit of Israeli Zionist existence.

Gadi manages to recreate the initiators mentality in relation to their formative experiences and beliefs, based on his first relevant and accurate reference to the sources.
Not surprisingly, he employs this empathy towards, and in defense of, his in-group.
The discussion goes further to relate to the possibility of adapting the Israeli culture
to the immigrants' values, again, in quite a heated tone. Yakov proposes another
counterfactual suggestion, which is clearly based on current pluralistic norms:

Y: right. But you can always change the culture according to their people.

In contrast to Yakov's presentist claim, here it is Gadi who makes a reference to historical context, even trying to base it on evidence (quite inaccurately, as our scrutiny
of the sources taught us, as both historians cited in the source leaflet didn't refer to
Arab military threat):

G: You can. But the question is whether it was the right time to change the
    culture when you've got all the Arab states sitting on your head… like
    that historian here at the end says…
Y: THAT ONE'S DUMB![2]

Yakov's dismissal of "that historian at the end" as "dumb" definitely doesn't stand up
to disciplinary norms. This goes even beyond the lapse into vulgar language, which
may characterize adolescent speech style. The last source in the booklet was an
excerpt from an historian featuring a favorable assessment of the melting pot policy.
Its rejection, without a word of explanation or backing, seems like a clear social
identity bias in evidence rating. A source which may lighten the moral burden of
the Ashkenazi group and denote that Mizrahi immigrants could gain from Western
culture may reduce the comparative esteem of the Mizrahi group. Its rejection in
extreme terms may denote threat felt by Yakov.

Yakov's emotional personal derogation of the cited historian would lead us to
expect a deterioration of the discussion. The derogative term used may implicitly be

also turned against his peer who believes the "Dumb2 historian". Offense taking is more than expected as Yakov repeatedly rejects his peer's explanations of the historian's interpretations (dropped for economy of space). However, Gadi, though clearly stressed and unsure, responds with an elaborated differentiation based on the sources:

> G: Don't know...like you have here...these kids talking with their teacher... she was like... there are two excerpts...there's one where they're saying it wasn't good for their parents actually; [while on the other] the kids say they themselves did progress.

Differentiation between parents and children shows an "unpacking" of the historical agent. It acknowledges the possibility of contrasting outcomes and perceptions of the same events or actions. The contextualized specification is also evidence based. Yakov responds quite emotionally, to the degree that the language he uses merges him with the historical agent:

> Y: The victims were their parents who were traditional and their kids were going dancing with girls who exposed their body. That's what people are now coming to...say I don't want my son to see naked girls

We see here that in spite of the "unprofessional" fusion of subject and object, or perhaps even due to it, Yakov seems to make quite a profound perspective taking move: He merges his perspective with what he sees as victims then (That's what people are *now* coming to...say *I* don't want *my* son to see naked girls). Although still a teenager quite attuned to contemporary liberal fashion norms, he manages to see it through traditional parents' eyes. To some degree this could be seen as the "merging of horizons" advocated by Gadamer (1989) of Hans Gadamer. This "merging of horizons" may be seen as an acceptance of Gadi's invitation to Yakov to put himself in the place of the immigrants. Thus we may see discussants adopt each other's ways of historical understanding and empathy.

Two opposite directions of historical thinking appear here, those of differentiating and of merging. Both seem to serve the goal of presenting historical members of a speaker's in-group more favorably. Gadi's emphasis that the policy was beneficial to children, if not to parents, presents Ashkenazi initiators of it as benevolent. Yakov's explanation of traditional oriental Jewish immigrants' rejection of folkdance makes them sound more reasonable. However, it is noteworthy that on the way to achieving this social-emotional goal, both discussants strive to achieve a more elaborate understanding of the historical agent. Of special concern is the fact that here both students construct the agency or "give voice" to members of the subordinate group. As Penuel and Wertsch (1998) remark, members of such groups are usually underrepresented and hardly referred to using verbs describing their actions or thoughts.

As the discussion goes on, the argument starts to repeat itself, with the same overtones, returning to the dance issue. Here Gadi strongly reacts to Yakov's description of the dance as promiscuous, by referring to it again as driven by ideals. The repetition of the idealistic representation of the Israeli founding fathers arouses a cynical critical stance from his peer. Yakov's suggestion that idealism is a post hoc rationalization or cover could be perceived as an insult. Interestingly, instead of the expected higher adherence to one's stand in a conflict, Gadi expresses uncertainty about the possibility of achieving historical truth. To use Kuhn's (2001) typology, Gadi progressed from an *absolutist* epistemological predisposition to a *relativist* stance. Again, this could be considered as an elaboration of historical understanding, reflecting awareness of the limits of historical knowing and again, seems to protect the initiators of the policy.

> G: THEY BELIEVED IN IT! It was a sort of Zionist belief
> Y: everything has an excuse, you know
> G: you can't know what happened there

Indeed, resort to uncertainty may have been perceived by Yakov as a protective move; as we can see below, he quickly claims that certain knowledge can be acquired through reference to evidence. This time he refers not to folkdance but to a second allegation against the Melting Pot educators – that of cutting the ritual side locks of students. He cites the source considered by all students as most objective, the immigrant education inquiry committee's report. In what seems to be a continuation of the merging of horizons, the historical agents become natural "participants" in the conversation:

> Y: Listen. You can ask the children. The children say: [quotes the source] "the teacher said everybody who wishes to go on the trip must cut his side locks…"

The notion that historical evidence can help us "know what happened there" is an elaboration of historical understanding. However, Yakov's use of evidence is somewhat misleading and doesn't express a further development of epistemological stance. His first direct citation is presented in a "facts speak for themselves" manner which is more typical of the *absolutist* epistemological predisposition (Kuhn, 2001). In fact, this citation doesn't contribute decisively on the critical question it was brought to bear on – the "real" motivation of the policy initiators.

The chosen piece of evidence is a descriptive account. It is factual, therefore perhaps conforming to a notion of "true" knowledge. Still, factuality by itself without interpretation cannot support perspective taking. It seems as though Yakov's emphasis on the power of evidence leads him to neglect the interpretative moves needed for historical empathy, which he has shown himself capable of before. We are reminded by this relapse that development of understanding and practice is not linear, but emphasizing the strength of evidence does contribute to a general development of reasoning. The further turns in the conversation are intensively backed by relevant citations:

G: Sure. It's because of the louse. On the other hand, Itsik [a former student in an immigrant camp school] says…just a second [quotes] "there was no alternative…you can't pass this process of turning into Israeli without the process of "total-Israelization".

And as we can see, Gadi uses evidence to refer to the historical agents' perspective on the issue of immigrants' cultural transformation. This move will lead his peer to a more elaborate interpretation of the educators' choice making, based both on evidence and on contextual argument construction:

G: At the time they had no time for it [for religious observance]. There was a war.
Y: What's that got to do with it? Why did they cut their side locks? Because of the louse? Right? Because of the trip, right? Whoever doesn't cut his side locks won't go to the trip. THERE WAS TIME FOR A TRIP, RIGHT? AND NO TIME FOR BIBLE?

As we shall see below, the punch line of this argument is tackled by Gadi through a new combination of evidence-based reasoning and empathy. He cares to use evidence relevant to the question directed to him. However, again we see that the development of ideas is not linear. The new attempt to reconstruct a motive actually means leaving the more contextualized evidence-based empathy, and coming back to Gadi's primary argument. Impairment of immigrants' tradition is interpreted as arising from the veterans' generous attempt to save immigrant children from embarrassment:

G: Well, they got this thing with the louse. But If you look here. It's… I'm… here it's written about Judaism, it's written here that generally they did learn bible… here [quotes] "bible will be explained and emphasized from the aspect of…well, maybe they didn't fully stick to it. But it [the cutting of side locks] was a technical thing. This was just a part of…like think they're bringing you in, right?! Study with 30 guys in shorts and khaki and crew cut and you suddenly show up with side locks?"

As we see, during most of their debate, neither of the students changed their standpoint significantly. Bearing in mind their preconceptions and social identity, this is not quite surprising. Lack of stand change may be explained by both cognitive and social identity theories. Cognitive psychology would note the comparatively well-framed stands students seemed to harbor in advance, leading do a strong confirmation bias. Social identity theory would explain students' entrenchment as resulting from the negative implications each discussant's narrative would have on the other's group esteem. However, what may be seen as surprising is that despite entrenchment, and in the process of conflict, both of the discussants use more developed evidence-based argumentation, refer more to context and elaborate their historical empathy.

It is worth comparing the rich heated argument discussed above to a sequence towards the end of the conversation when the two adversaries (surprisingly) express agreement. Looking at this excerpt one can't escape noticing the lower level of argumentation and historical understanding. This may also be due to exhaustion, but it seems that agreement and lack of emotional drive have to do with the shallowness of discussion. Here, slogans and assertion of solidarity take the place of mental reconstruction reference to context and to evidence.

G: Was uniform education an essential measure for the state or a destructive political takeover?

Y: Very essential measure

G: I think so too

Y: They had to....

G: implement the state's values

Y: right

G: the fathers…for the next generation to see…what they should work on

Y: [laughs]

G: you had to educate them uniformly

Y: both those from Yemen and from Poland for the goal they immigrated to Israel.

G: right

Y: they all immigrated for the same purpose

G: everyone's Jewish, we're all Jews, that's democracy

The reference to a shared overarching identity is one of the classical cohesive strategies noted in inter-group contact studies (Pettigrew, 1998). It accompanies the students' reassertion of consensus as a basis for maintenance of relations. It seems students' notion of a shared space such as the school serves to maintain, motivates them to achieve a consensual closure. Interestingly this abandoning of debate for the sake of uniformity seems to the students as consonant with democracy. This may arise because of association of democracy with the notion of the rule by majority (in Israel the Jews are the majority ethnicity, dominating the Arab minority).

The uniformity of conclusion students strive for seems to carry an interesting content-process parallel with the topic discussed – the unifying policy of the melting pot. The motivation for a consensual ending may also stem from the school's inclusive-integrative credo (also highly related to the ideals of the Melting Pot). While discussing disharmonies and contradictions of integration, students also reasserted it. The interplay between the emotional need for inter-group cohesion and the need for in-group esteem drove forward the discussion. However, the solving of this tension may have also stagnated argumentation. Both strive for cohesion and reference to majority rule seem to be related to lower-level argumentation. Cohesion, built upon taken-for-granted-truth primal identity may be related to absolutist thinking. Decision by majority rule fits nicely with a multiplist-relativist epistemological predisposition (Kuhn, 2001) since, when there is no criteria for truth, it leaves "Vox populi vox dei" to rely on.

Looking at the above discussion we arrive at an insight arising from the intersections of identity, identification and higher-order thinking in history. Identity issues were at the core of the "hot" cognition and expressions described above. It was students' identification with historical agents from their identity group that led to their emotional responses. These emotional responses also made their way into the students' (sometimes quite heated or biased) cognitive and argumentative moves. However, emotion did not only bias thinking, but also enhanced it. Identification with the historical figures served as a motive to find new arguments to protect their image and reconstruct their intentions. Furthermore, identification sometimes served as means for that reconstruction of consciousness. Indeed, students tended more to use historical empathy and reconstruct mental images of in-group historical figures, turning them into agents. Their identification with historical figures from their identity group served to bridge the chronological and mental abyss which actually exists between them.

Initially mental reconstruction and argumentation were based on presentist or universal assumptions. This level of empathy can be seen as based on the assumption of similarity between discussant and the historical agent, perhaps resting on straightforward identification. Gradually the reciprocal challenges discussants posed to each other drove them to search for more contextual evidence-based reasoning and mental reconstruction. Still, identification seems to be the ongoing mechanism at hand as hinted by the "merging of horizons" mentioned above. But identification with in-group and esteem defense were not the only forces at work here. We should also note the impact of encounter with the other.

Encounter with a peer who was also an out-group member aroused identity loyalty but also awareness of the other. On the interpersonal or interlocutionary level, challenge posed by the other demanded acknowledgement of a different perspective and a stronger backing for one's own. Along with their growing awareness of identity issues, students also heightened awareness of context and bias in sources. In the intrapersonal cognitive level, awareness of the other as member of the historical figures' identity group facilitated attempts at taking their perspective. Such an attempt in reconstructing the intentions or perceptions of out-group historical members was still aimed at maintaining in-group esteem. However, in the process students gave voice and agency to figures they were less likely to identify with – the "other" or the subordinate. Such an attempt may be seen as more mature or decentered practice.

Conclusions

It is tempting to conclude that in the process of negotiating a charged historical issue, students' "hot cognition" led them from an egocentric to an "other oriented" or universal approach. Such a development could be seen as somewhat parallel to the courses of development outlined by Piaget, Erikson and Kohlberg, in the cognitive and moral realms. As Piaget exemplifies, the transformation of the concept of liquid quantity goes from contextual dependence on vessel to universal assumption of quantity conservation. Analogically we can see Kohlberg's theory of moral development as moving from self-centered interest to contextual conventional morality to universal principles. Similarly our discussants progressed from solipsistic unsupported claims to reasoned argument addressing peers' challenge. They progressed from ignoring historical agents' consciousness to explaining it on the basis of historical context and human feelings' universality. However, the picture may be more complex both practically and theoretically.

The change during interaction described above is characteristic of micro-genetic studies, and cannot be assumed to represent achievement of stable new cognitive stages. Progression described is definitely not linear and unidirectional as the developmental theories hint. Discussants' argumentative moves were fueled by ego and social belonging needs, not just by universal principles. They moved from universal to contextual explanations to individualized personal testimony-based reasoning. But furthermore, it could be that the understanding of progression in human action has to be conceptualized in a somewhat different direction. In most cognitive developmental theories the direction is from the individualized egocentric, to contextual and then to the universal reasoning. In understanding actions of human agents in distant time or culture it seems that learners should abandon universalistic assumptions in favor of more contextual and even more individualized mental reconstruction.

Our assumptions about hierarchies of cognitive and moral development as moving from egocentric to universal, from emotional to objective may be questioned. It may be that it stands on a natural sciences-oriented paradigm which slowly conquers other sciences. Sam Wineburg lately claimed that when referring to historical thinking, Bloom's hierarchy of cognitive tasks (learning objectives scaled from piecemeal information to synthesis) may have to be inverted (Wineburg & Schneider, 2010). It may be that on a parallel line we should reassess the hierarchy between emotion and "neutrality" in fostering higher-order thinking in the humanities and social sciences.

Our position concerning this hierarchy is more nuanced. Gadi and Yakov are adolescents. Their struggle with conflict and dilemma alternates between stereotypic conventional reasoning, and post-conventional acknowledgement of the historical agent and context (Colby et al., 1983). Their learning of the Melting Pot, important as it may be, occurs in the background of the development of their identity formation – the combined operation of ego and social-cognitive processes (Erikson, 1968; Marcia, 1980). The educational context in which the Melting Pot task has been administered indeed overrides the adolescents' primary identity-processing strategies. On the one hand, the school deliberately integrates students from different socio-cultural horizons by acculturating them to collaborate in various tasks and to confront and respect their opinions. On the other hand, the teacher instilled norms of critical reasoning and dialogical thinking. This context naturally invites a goal orientation of mastery which encourages students to adopt an exploration identity-formation style.

Design of the Melting Pot task, which confronts students from different ethnicities on a hot issue, invites a self-enhancement approach style. The strong emotional states that we could detect in Gadi and Yakov's argumentation express, we believe, the adoption of a mixed approach, between self-exploration and self-enhancement. In this unique argumentative context, emotions are intense, and draw students to personal and specific resources, but argumentative norms are critical and dialogical. This context maintains a fruitful tension between the specific and the universal. This deliberate kind of appeal to emotion in educational tasks is, we believe, an important venue to deep learning as well as to development of identity.

The educational implications of this approach vary. We believe it calls upon educators to overcome their hesitation to tackle "hot issues" and mine the resources such issues hold for fostering argumentation. This means controversy and use of controversy in learning design should be welcomed. We also believe our findings invite a reference to identity in learning, both in the choice of topics and in the creation of collaborative learning groups. However, reasoned use of heterogeneous groups should be accompanied by induction into reasoning (for example through argumentative design) as a way to channel emotion into learning.

Notes

1　These effects were observed immediately after social interaction. In a case study, Porat (2004) already observed a similar phenomenon as he compared interpretations by students of two identity groups who analyzed the *same* historical texts.

2　In all the protocols, capital letters refer to loud voice production.

References

Bandalos, D. L., Yates, K., & Thorndike-Christ, T. (1993) "Effects of math self-concept, perceived self-efficacy, and attributions for failure and success on test anxiety", *Journal of Educational Psychology*, 87: 611–23.

Barton, K. C., & Levstik, L. S. (2004) *Teaching History for the Common Good*, Mahwah, NJ: Lawrence Erlbaum.

Ben-David Kolikant, Y. (2011) "Nurturing dialogical capacity among tomorrow's adults", *Journal of Russian and East European Psychology*, 49: 90–6.

Colby, A., Kohlberg, L., Gibbs, J., & Lieberman, M. (1983) *A Longitudinal Study of Moral Judgment: A Monograph for the Society of Research in Child Development*, Chicago, IL: The University of Chicago Press.

Csíkszentmihályi, M. (1990) *Flow: The Psychology of Optimal Experience*, New York: Harper and Row.

Doosje, B., & Branscombe, N. R. (2003) "Attributions for the negative historical actions of a group", *European Journal of Social Psychology*, 33: 235–48.

Doosje, B., Spears, R., & Koomen, W. (1995) "When bad isn't all bad: The strategic use of sample information in generalization and stereotyping", *Journal of Personality and Social Psychology*, 69: 642–55.

Epstein, T. (2000) "Adolescents' perspectives on racial diversity in U. S. history: Case studies from an urban classroom", *American Educational Research Journal*, 37: 185–214.

Erikson, E. H. (1968) *Identity, Youth, and Crisis*, New York: Norton.

Fassulo, A., Girardet, H., & Pontecorvo, C. (1998) "Seeing the past: Learning history through group discussion of iconographic sources", *International Review of History Education*, 2: 132–53.

Fennema, E. (1989) "The study of affect and mathematics: A proposed generic model for research", in D. B. McLeod & V. M. Adams (eds.), *Affect and Mathematical Problem Solving: A New Perspective*, London: Springer-Verlag.

Fiske, S. T. (2002) "What we know now about bias and intergroup conflict, the problem of the century", *Current Directions in Psychological Science*, 11: 123–8.

Gadamer, H.G. (1989) *Truth and Method*. London: Sheed and Ward.

Goldberg, T., Schwarz, B. B., & Porat, D. (2008) "Living and dormant collective memories as contexts of history learning", *Learning and Instruction*, 18: 223–37.

Goldberg, T., Schwarz, B. B., & Porat, D. (2011) "Changes in narrative and argumentative writing by students discussing 'hot' historical issues", *Cognition and Instruction*, 29: 185–217.

Gottlieb, E., Wineburg, S. S., & Zakai, S. (2005) "When history matters: Epistemic switching in the interpretation of culturally charged texts". Paper presented at the 11th EARLI conference, Nicosia, Cyprus.

Hynd, C. R. (1999) "Teaching students to think critically using multiple texts in history", *Journal of Adolescent & Adult Literacy*, 42: 428–36.

Kuhn, D. (2001a). How do people know? *Psychological Science*, 12(1), 1–8.

Kuhn, D., Weinstock, M., & Flaton, R. (1994) "Historical reasoning as theory-evidence coordination", in M. Carretero & J. F. Voss (eds.), *Cognitive and Instructional Processes in History and the Social Sciences*, Mahwah, NJ: Lawrence Erlbaum Associates.

Leary, M. R. (2007) "Motivational and emotional aspects of the self", *Annual Review of Psychology*, 58: 317–44.

Lee, P., & Ashby, R. (2000) "Progression in historical understanding among students ages 7–14", in P. N. Stearns, P. Seixas & S. Wineburg (eds.), *Knowing, Teaching, and Learning History: National and International Perspectives*, New York: New York University Press.

Lee, P., Ashby, R., & Dickinson, A. (1995) "Progression in children's ideas about history", in M. Hughes (ed.), *Progression in Learning*, Clevedon: Multilingual Matters.

McKenzie, C. R. M., Lee, S. M., & Chen, K. K. (2002) "When negative evidence increases confidence: Change in belief after hearing two sides of a dispute", *Journal of Behavioral Decision Making*, 15: 1–18.

Marcia, J. E. (1980) "Identity in adolescence", in J. Abelson (ed.), *Handbook of Adolescent Psychology*, New York: John Wiley.

Nickerson, R. S. (1998) "Confirmation bias: A ubiquitous phenomenon in many guises", *Review of General Psychology*, 2: 175–220.

Penuel, W. R., & Wertsch, J. V. (1998) "Historical representation as mediated action: Official history as a tool", *International Review of History Education*, 2: 23–39.

Perfetti, C. A., Britt, M. A., Rouet, J.-F., Georgi M. C., & Mason, R. A. (1994) "How students use texts to learn and reason about historical uncertainty", in M. Carretero, and J. F. Voss (eds.), *Cognitive and Instructional Processes in History and the Social Sciences*, Mahwah, NJ: Lawrence Erlbaum.

Pettigrew, T. F. (1998) "Intergroup contact theory", *Annual Review of Psychology*, 49: 65–85.

Pintrich, P. R. (1999) "Motivational beliefs as resources for and constraints on conceptual change", in W. Schnotz, S. Vosniadou, & M. Carretero (eds.), *New Perspectives on Conceptual Change*, Oxford, UK: Elsevier Science.

Pintrich, P. R., Marx, R. W., & Boyle, R. A. (1993) "Beyond cold conceptual change: The role of motivational beliefs and classroom contextual factors in the process of conceptual change", *Review of Educational Research*, 63: 167–99.

Porat, D. A. (2004) "It's not written here, but this is what happened: Students' cultural comprehension of textbook narratives on the Arab-Israeli conflict", *American Educational Research Journal*, 41: 963–96.

Roccas, S., Klar, Y., & Liviatan, I. (2006) "The paradox of group-based guilt: Modes of national identification, conflict vehemence, and reactions to the ingroup's moral violations", *Journal of Personality and Social Psychology*, 91: 698–11.

Rouet, J.-F., Marron, M. A., Perfetti, C. A., & Favart, M. (1998) "Understanding historical controversies: Students' evaluation and use of documentary evidence", *International Review of History Education*, 2: 95–116.

Schwarz, B. B. (2003) "Collective reading of multiple texts in argumentative activities", *The International Journal of Educational Research*, 39: 133–51.

Schwarz, B. B. (2009) "Argumentation and learning", in Muller Mirza & A.-N. Perret-Clermont (eds.), *Argumentation and Education – Theoretical Foundations and Practices*, New York: Springer Verlag.

Seixas, P. (1994). Students' understanding of historical significance. *Theory and Research in Social Education*, 22(3), 281–304

Shemilt, D. J. (2000) "The Caliph's coin: The currency of narrative frameworks in history teaching", in P. N. Stearns, P. Seixas & S. Wineburg (eds.), *Knowing, Teaching and Learning History*, New York: New York University Press.

Sinatra, G. M., (2005) "The warming trend in conceptual change research: The legacy of Paul R. Pintrich", Educational Psychologist, 40: 107–15.

Sinatra, G. M., & Mason, L. (2008) "Beyond knowledge: Learner characteristics influencing conceptual change", in S. Vosniadou (ed.), *International Handbook of Research on Conceptual Change*, Netherlands: Springer.

Sinatra, G. M. & Pintrich, P. (2003) "The role of intentions in conceptual change learning", in G. M. Sinatra & P. R. Pintrich (eds.), *Intentional Conceptual Change*, Mahwah, NJ: Lawrence Erlbaum.

Stanovich, K., & West, R. (1997) "Reasoning independently of prior belief and individual differences in actively open-minded thinking", *Journal of Educational Psychology*, 89: 342–57.

Stearns, P. N., Seixas, P., & Wineburg S. (2000) *Knowing, Teaching, and Learning History: National and International Perspectives* , New York: New York University Press.

Wineburg, S. S., & Fournier, J. E. (1994) "Contextualized thinking in History", in M. Carretero & J. Voss (eds.), *Cognitive and Instructional Processes in History and the Social Sciences*, Hillsdale, N.J.: Erlbaum.

Wineburg, S. S., Mosborg, S., & Porat, D. (2001) "What Can 'Forrest Gump' tell us about students' historical understanding?", *Social Education*, 65: 55–8.

Wineburg, S. & Schneider, J. (2010) "Was Bloom's taxonomy pointed in the wrong direction?", *Phi Delta Kappan*, 91: 56–61

AUTHOR INDEX

SUBJECT INDEX

Introductory note

References such as "178–9" indicate (not necessarily continuous) discussion of a topic across a range of pages. Wherever possible in the case of topics with many references, these have either been divided into sub-topics or only the most significant discussions of the topic are listed. Because the entire work is about 'affective learning', the use of this term (and certain others which occur constantly throughout the book) as an entry point has been minimized. Information will be found under the corresponding detailed topics.